If we do not want to be immortally unhappy we must fill every moment of this life to the full with the wine of happiness.

Andrei Bely

(Photograph taken 1912)

OTHER BOOKS BY DANIEL H. SHUBIN:

History of Russian Christianity in 4 volumes:
From the Earliest Years through Tsar Ivan IV
The Patriarchal Era through Tsar Peter the Great: 1586 to 1725
The Synodal Era and the Sectarians: 1725 to 1894
The Orthodox Church of the 20th Century: 1894 to 1990

Daniel and Alla Andreev

Leo Tolstoy and the Kingdom of God within You

Skovoroda: The World Tried to Catch Me but Could Not

Helena Roerich: Living Ethics and the Teaching for a New Epoch

Russia's Wisdom

Tsiolkovski: The Cosmic Scientist and His Cosmic Philosophy

Concordia Antarova

Tsars and Pseudo-Tsars: Russia's Era of Upheavals

Monastery Prisons

The Gospel of the Prince of Peace

Kingdoms and Covenants

Attributes of Heaven and Earth

Rose of the World (Tr.)

The Grey Man, Menace Eastern-Light (Tr.)

The Third Testament (Tr.)

# ANDREI BELY

## LIFE, LITERATURE, SYMBOLISM, ANTHROPOSOPHY

DANIEL H. SHUBIN

Cover Photograph taken 1929.



ISBN 978-1-387-02223-6

Email: danhshubin at yahoo dot com

# TABLE OF CONTENTS

PORTRAIT PAINTED 1905, BY LEON C. BASKST

PHOTOGRAPH TAKEN 1906

# IMPORTANT DATES IN THE LIFE OF ANDREI BELY

| | |
|---|---|
| October 14, 1880 | Son Boris is born to Professor Nikolai Vasilyevich Bugaev and his wife Aleksandra Dmitrievna (Egorova). He is their only child |
| September 1891 | Boris attends the private school of L.I. Polivanov. |
| 1896 | Bely begins his intense studies of the philosophers of western Europe, also studying the Bible and the Upanishads, and books on theosophy. |
| Autumn 1898 | The Bugaev family purchases a family summer home at Serebryanni Kolodez, Tule Province. |
| September 1899 | Boris enters Moscow University as a student of Physics and Mathematics. |
| Early 1900 | Boris Bugaev begins using Andrei Bely as his pseudonym in literature. So he is known for the balance of his life, apart from family and legal areas. |
| 1900-1902 | Bely writes his 3 of the 4 volumes of poetry, the *Symphony* series. |
| 1902 | Bely attends some theosophist meetings. |
| May 29, 1903 | Nikolai Vasilyevich Bugaev passes away. |
| Summer 1903 | Bely writes *Symbolism as Ideology*, *About Theurgy*, *Criticism and Symbolism*, and his book of poetry *Gold in Azure*. |
| Summer 1904 | After graduating in physics and mathematics, Bely returns to Moscow University as a student in language and history. He writes his 4th volume of poetry in the *Symphony* series. |

| | |
|---|---|
| February 1905 | Bely writes *The Book of Revelation in Russian Poetry.* |
| April 1905 | Bely joins the Religious Philosophical Society at the Morozov home. |
| November 1905 | Bely meets Asya Turgeneva. |
| Summer 1906 | Bely composes *Green Meadow.* |
| September 1906 | Bely quits the university and leaves to travel in Europe by himself. |
| January 1907 | Bely has a serious medical operation in a Paris hospital. He returns to Russia. |
| Summer 1908 | Bely publishes his next 2 volumes of poetry: *Ashes* and *Urn.* |
| Summer 1908 | Bely attends regular theosophical meetings and study groups. |
| Autumn 1909 | Bely completes his first novel: *Silver Dove.* He writes *Emblematic of Meaning, Problems of Culture, the Magic of Words.* |
| June 1910 | Bely and Asya Turgeneva marry. |
| November 1910 to March 1913 | Bely and Asya travel Europe, north Africa and the Middle East. |
| May 1912 | While in Germany, the couple meet Rudolf Steiner and attend his lectures, and they become disciples of anthroposophy. Bely will be under Steiner's influence the next 15 years. |
| August through December 1913 | Bely leaves Russia with Asya. They travel through Europe listening to Steiner's lectures. Eventually they settle in Dornach, Switzerland, to help build Steiner's Goetheanum. |
| October 1913 | Bely's novel *Petersburg* begins a serial publication. |
| August 1916 | Bely returns to Russia to fulfill his military obligation. Asya remains in Dornach. |
| October 1916 | Bely completes his novel *Kotik Letaev.* |

| | |
|---|---|
| 1916-1918 | Bely lives between Moscow, Petersburg and Serebryanni Kolodez, writing and lecturing. He works at the Government Archival Office, then the Proletariat Cultural office, and then at the Preservation of Monuments. |
| December 1917 | Claudia Nikolaievna attends a lecture delivered by Bely and meets him. |
| January 1919 | Bely becomes part of the Liberal Philosophical Association, elected as president. |
| December 1920 | Bely falls in the bathtub, has a concussion, and is hospitalized for 3 months. |
| 1920-1921 | Bely continues to write his *Letaev* series, *First Meeting*, and other volumes of poetry. Lecturing at various halls and societies on symbolism and anthroposophy. |
| October 1921 | Bely leaves for Europe to find Asya. |
| November 1921 | Bely meets with Asya in passing. In April they meet again and their relationship terminates, Asya leaving Bely for another man. Bely meets with Steiner and their relationship also terminates. Bely is devastated. |
| 1922-1923 | Bely lives in Germany, travels Europe, continues to write poetry and his recollections. |
| September 1922 | Bely's mother Aleksandra Dmitrievna dies. |
| October 1923 | Bely returns to Russia. He and Claudia Nikolaievna live together as common-law husband and wife. |
| 1924-1928 | Bely continues to write and lecture in Moscow and Petersburg. He publishes his next novel *Moscow*.<br>Bely writes his recollections of Rudolf Steiner in 2 volumes. |
| September 1925 | Bely is admitted to the Moscow Union of Writers. |

| | |
|---|---|
| August 1926 | Bely is struck by a streetcar. He has a minor brain concussion and shoulder dislocation. |
| Summers of 1927, 1928, 1929 and 1930 | Bely and Claudia vacation in various spots in southern Russia: Crimea, Armenia, Georgia, and Abkhazia. |
| 1929-1932 | Bely writes his 3 volumes of recollections: *On the Frontier of Two Centuries*; *Beginning of the Century*, and *Between the Two Revolutions.* He finishes the 2 volumes of his recollections of Rudolf Steiner. Bely completes his next volume of poetry, *Masks.* |
| March 1928 | Bely writes his *Why I became a Symbolist.* |
| May 1931 | Claudia is arrested and spends 6 weeks in prison with other anthroposophists. |
| July 18, 1931 | Bely and Claudia are legally married. |
| December 1931 | Bely completes his book, *The Mastery of Gogol.* |
| October 1932 | Bely becomes a member of the Organizing Committee of Soviet Writers |
| Summer 1933 | Bely and Claudia vacation in the Crimea. On July 15, Bely has a stroke and they return to Moscow. |
| December 8, 1933 | Bely is admitted to a hospital in Moscow for a cranial aneurysm. |
| January 8, 1934 | Andrei Bely dies from internal bleeding in his cranium. He is 53 years of age. |

SILHOUETTE OF ANDREI BELY AT THE PODIUM

By E. Kruglikova

ANDREI BELY AND ASYA TURGENEVA

1912

CLAUDIA NIKOLAIEVNA BUGAEVA

(Andrei Bely's second wife)

# INTRODUCTION

## Regarding Andrei Bely

Andrei Bely was the literary pseudonym of Boris Nikolaievich Bugaev, a name he assumed at the turn of the $20^{th}$ century. His choice for Andrei, Russian for Andrew, was based on he being the first of the disciples summoned by Jesus Christ, and due to Boris' profound religious faith. Bely, the Russian word for the color white, was suggested by his friend Vladimir Sergeevich Solovyov, as white light being the radiance of Divine Wisdom or Sophia. Andrei also based his choice on the concept of white light as the culmination of all colors, and that true love has no color, but is always white. Another friend, Aleksandr Blok stated that white light is the sign of Divine Humanity. Even then, the name Andrei Bely was used primarily in his published writings, while in most communication and personal matters he was still referred to as Boris Bugaev, and the 2 appellations are interchangeably used in this text based on the original Russian source of information.

Andrei Bely was a person beyond the imagination in terms of intellectualism. At the age of 16, he was consuming the compositions of European philosophers in Russian translation and some of them in their original French and German. He had a fluent knowledge of the entire Bible, and likewise studied the Upanishads and other Hindu writings. In later years he would read theosophical literature and which convictions he accepted and incorporated into his life. As a teenager his mother took him traveling in Europe, southern and central Russia, and Ukraine. Being an only child Bely's parents provided him the best education with tutors at home, and then the best private school in Moscow. Next was Moscow University, where he excelled in physics and mathematics, and then returned to continue in language and history. In terms of music Bely played piano fluently and was able to compose music. As an artist he created many sketches that presented his symbolism in graphic terms and so be more understandable by his audience. Bely had a mastery of French and German.

After his death friends wanted to printed his collected works, and they estimated 47 volumes of decent size would be required to contain it all. Bely composed poetry, prose, articles and commentaries at lightning speed. His articles encompassed every aspect of Russian society: polity, religion, philosophy, socialism, and interweaving science and art and music into it all. At the same time, he did not fear criticism and was not intimidated by Soviet officials, always speaking his mind.

In regard to public speaking, Bely would mesmerize and entertain audiences for 2 to 3 hours at a time, auditoriums filled to capacity, never losing their attention, and on a regular basis between Moscow, Petersburg and Kiev, and later in Armenia and Georgia. He was a genius in every aspect of the word. His mastery of the Russian language, and especially his vocabulary, excelled above any other author of his era and most of the previous century, in addition to his fluency in several European languages. He also took the time to travel, first with wife Asya all over Europe, northern Africa and the Middle East, and then later with Claudia, several times in the Crimea and Caucasus regions and southern Russia.

However as a result of his sheltered life and domineering mother, Bely could not develop a close friendship with anyone, until Claudia entered his life, and she was it, she became his life. He could not succeed in personal relationships as he seemed to tower over every person to whom he attempted to draw close. In addition few of his associates did not have some personal altercation with him, and those who would associate with him were at a distance for the most part. Bely had no children through either marriage, and there is no indication as to why. He seemed to live in a fantasy world when in the presence of others, a superficial and socially tolerable environment, and no doubt because he was so advanced beyond them, as though living in another galaxy. Half the time people felt he was aloof and naive the other half of the time.

Many of his personal letters to people, and especially to women whom he imagined as allegorically representing some divine female essence, reflected his imagination. His use of symbols, allegories, metaphors, examples, pervade every stroke of his pen. Perhaps it was the bad impact his mother had on Bely that he lived in an imaginary world when dealing with women, and especially with Asya Alekseevna, his first wife, and the others he pursued.

Living in a fantasy world also had its benefit for Bely, as it gave him motivation to never abandon his convictions, to persevere, to ignore what was occurring around him, the criticism and malign. He seemed to always think the best of other people, regardless of the number of times and amount they would cause difficulties for him. He could not understand why, and so he got above the matter and went to his next novel or volume of poems or next set of recollections of people or some human interest article, or some philosophical tract or lecture. Anthroposophy did well for Bely, as it kept his mind on a higher plain than the balance of all those with whom he associated. He was in a space shuttle on its way to some distant galaxy, while others just had their heads raised and their feet on the ground, and so watched him and could not understand what they were seeing, and as a result what they did had no effect on Bely.

Not having much for a father in terms of a personal relationship Bely sought for it elsewhere, chasing after other Russian writers at their various meetings, until finding a substitute in Rudolf Steiner. Bely chased Steiner all over Europe listening to his lectures and dedicated himself to constructing Steiner's monument to himself, the Goetheanum. Although claiming it to be the materialization of anthroposophical thought, it was actually a promotion of Rudolf Steiner's ability to create a new philosophic trend. Not until later in Bely's life did he realize this and it devastated him and made a fool out of him, until he returned to Russia to get his life together, and only with Claudia's help, the only person who understood him and cared for him.

Being a genius caused Bely an inability to deal with mundane issues, and primarily his inability to handle money. As much as he wrote and lectured he seemed to earn little. Unscrupulous book publishers, magazine editors, associations that arranged his lectures, took advantage of his talent for their own financial advancement. Working at Soviet sectors paid him little relative to his worth and contribution. For the most part of his life Bely lived either hand to mouth, or in destitution and malnutrition, although his series of lectures and books were non-stop. It was not until Claudia took over his financial affairs after his return from Europe in late 1923, that Bely became financially solvent.

What also made life difficult for Bely is that after his return from Europe in 1923, and after the death of his mother, he was essentially homeless and transient. Bely was dependent on the kindness of others for a shelter. A repercussion of his financial insolvency was his inability to afford a permanent residence, and this was exacerbated by the Soviet government not accepting his vocation as a symbolist writer and philosopher as an acceptable vocation making Bely qualified for state-assigned housing.

What caused Bely's premature death at the age of 53 years and 3 months? He did have a couple of minor head injuries a few years earlier, so the effects could have lingered somewhat dormant. Stress was the major factor in causing a brain aneurysm. It was all the worries and the pressure, the demands on his life, his busy schedule, dealing with book publishers, lectures, survival during the years of First World War and the Russian Revolution and subsequent Civil War, physical labor and the tedious effort in building Steiner's monument to himself, the failure of his first marriage, his discard by the person he admired the most, not to mention subtle persecution by Soviet administration. The terminal blows to Bely's head were the following 2 issues. Bely was an symbolist and this was inherent in his writings, and he was never going to capitulate to their demands and become a Soviet writer, and he was an anthroposophist and he was never going to compromise his convictions and become a Soviet socialist. This killed him in the end. This also killed other writers of the Silver Age, except for those who migrated to Europe, which Bely refused to do, since he considered himself Russian and had hope in the future of Russia.

## COMMENTARY ON ANDREI BELY'S PUBLICATIONS

I have offered a minimum of commentary and opinion regarding Andrei Bely's compositions. What is included is some of the opinions of the era, as reflected in newspaper reviews and the such. The reason is that I want the reader to provide their own opinion of his books by purchasing a copy and reading it.

## ANTHROPOSOPHY

I have not described or explained either theosophy or anthroposophy to any depth. This book is not about these religious philosophies – as I like to call them. This book is about Andrei Bely. Only enough information about these matters are included to provide to the reader their relationship to Bely, meaning, to his activities, writing, membership in groups, reactions to people and their reactions to him.

There are several good books available on these topics for the reader to purchase and study.[1]

---

[1] A couple of these are the following: Carlson, Maria. *No Religion Higher than Truth, A History of the Theosophical Movement in Russia, 1875-1922*; Seddon, Richard, *Rudolf Steiner*.

## SELECTIONS FOR TRANSLATION AND THE TRANSLATIONS

Only original Russian sources have been used in the compilation of the biography, researched and translated by myself, and oriented such to create a good cross-section and understandable life and purpose of Andrei Bely. (I have not used any sources in the English language.) Information on his associates is included to the extent necessary to understand their impact on his life, and well as historical information on Russia of the era and Bely's part of it. I have included as many selections of Bely's letters, memoirs, articles, books and lectures for the reader to know Bely as a person, to know his thinking, his philosophy, his convictions and beliefs and his polity, also translated by myself. As much as feasible is provided so not to overburden the reader with Bely's verbosity, but enough to especially follow him in his search for divine truth and a purpose in life, and his desire to utilize his talents for the benefit of society. Many of his letters are very symbolic or allegorical, especially the early correspondence with many of the women with whom he associated. These are included not because of Bely's infantile infatuation with them, but because of their literary structure and content. They reflect Bely as a symbolist poet. So with the balance of his letters, they open Bely for us to look inside of him, inside of his heart and brain.

Some of Bely's articles of a symbolist nature, and the final is autobiographical, are included in English translation, also translated by myself, in the Appendix. It is a small selection but enough to provide the reader Bely's symbolist thinking and compositional talent and personal reflections on his life.

If you do not understand what Bely wrote, or if it is beyond your intellectual faculty to fathom or comprehend what you are reading, or if you have no clue about what Bely is relating or saying or what his concepts or ideas are, or if what he wrote is totally alien to you, that is all right, it is not you. It is Andrei Bely. It is not the translation from Russian into English. What I have translated is exactly what he says. It is Andrei Bely. And you are not alone. Most people who read Bely, apart from his novels, arrive at the same perplexity. So it is not you if you do not understand it. It is Andrei Bely. This is his literary symbolization, it is how he writes.

Daniel H. Shubin
July 16, 2017

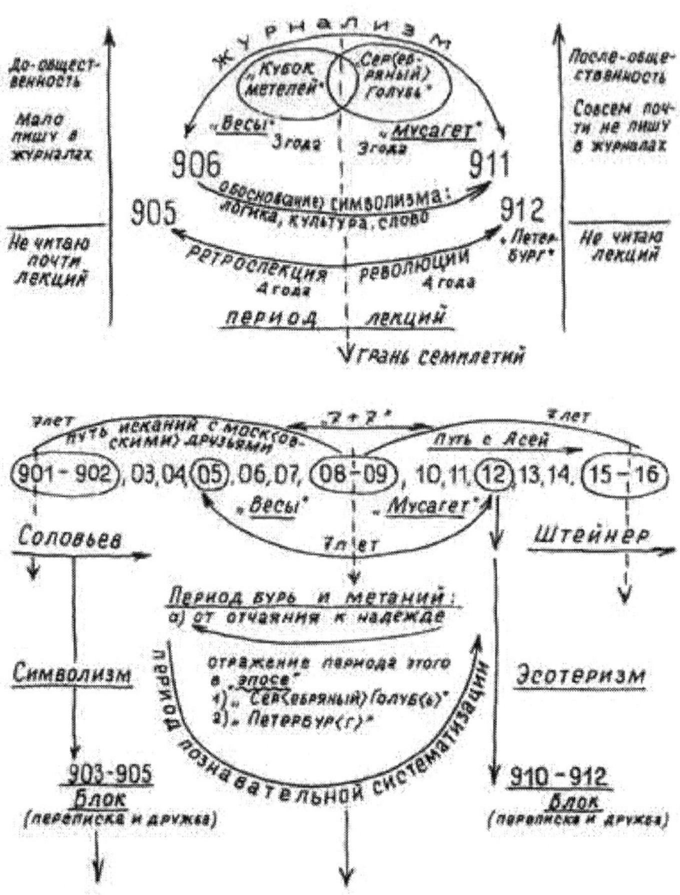


SCHEME OF THE STAGES OF ANDREI BELY'S LIFE
FROM 1901 TO 1916.

(drawn by Andrei Bely about 1918)

# The Life of Andrei Bely

## Early Years

The father of our subject was Nikolai Vasilyevich Bugaev (1837–1903), a popular mathematician and a professor at Moscow University. The year of the birth of his only child, he was dean of the Physics and Mathematics Department, and president of the Moscow Mathematical Society. All the children of Russia were taught arithmetic in elementary schools using his textbooks. An extremely kind and talented person, he was loved by his colleagues and students, but often he was ridiculed for being absent-minded and for having a child-like mind and attitude. He was never boring and enjoyed reading fiction, but only selected works. He seemed to avoid new trends in poetry and prose.

Nikolai Vasilyevich was also interested in philosophy and even wrote a series of serious articles on the theme, *Mathematics and the Scientific-Philosophic Universal Aspect.* As far as philosophical thought was concerned, he placed Leibnitz as the greatest of thinkers and no less a great mathematician. Bugaev in 1893, composed a philosophical volume titled *Basic Principles of Evolutionary Monadology*, due to his influence of Leibnitz's concepts of monads – the elementary spiritual-material particles of existence. The volume consisted of 184 treatises of his.

The father's scientific convictions undoubtedly had an effect on the cosmic ideology of his son. Bely recognized this and in 2 poetic compositions dedicated to the memory of his father, he recollected philosophical conversations he had while strolling together with him in the meadows outside Moscow:

You say, "Flying monads
On splashing waves through eons of time
Is why we exist." And we are immense,
Here in the world flickering lights are ignited.

In us are the depths of the world.
Around us are worlds dug.
We become the world.
Over the world will we arise.
We gaze at immeasurable universes,
Unseen sensations of warring darknesses.

Unseen sensations of damaged gods.
We arise in the worldwide hall.
And I was silent,
And someone along the road
In the gloom was swinging a lamp.

The mother of our subject was Aleksandra Dmitrievna Yegorova (1858–1922). She was a genuine beauty and evolved from a family of salespeople. She was so pretty as a child that she would be taken to people's homes just to beautify the dining table. She was spoiled rotten from birth, mentally imbalanced, and a hysteric woman. Aleksandra was over 20 years younger than her husband Nikolai and married him because she felt she was hopeless in finding anybody younger as a mate. Once married she could not accept the life of a professor's wife, or as a dedicated and domesticated spouse. Eventually she turned the life of both of them into a living hell. Nonetheless her home was almost always filled with famous guests, other instructors, and students of Professor Bugaev. She conducted herself appropriately in the presence of others and they had no suspicion of her true nature in the privacy of her home.

The 2 of them only had the one child: Boris Nikolaievich Bugaev, born October 14, 1880, in Moscow.

Bely described the situation in his family and home in his memoirs:

> It is difficult to find 2 people who were so opposite to each other as my parents were. A father who was physically strong and with a clear mind and mother suffering from a mental disorder with some neurological disease and who was often totally bedridden. A husband as trustful and honest as a child and a hypochondriac mother who was almost still a child, never having reached any level of maturity. A rationalist matched with a total irrational female. It was the strength of mind against the hurricane of an opposing attitude subjected to the worst and oddest displays of upheavals. The man of science, with no will of his own, would run from his home to the university, to his social club. Mother would then saturate the home with her presence consisting of laughing, crying, loud music, pranks and her capriciousness. She was a beautiful person who was the ugliest. He was almost elderly and she was still adolescent. The first year of their marriage she still played with dolls and later together with her new son. He was an entity that could not harm anybody, not even a fly, and never hindering freedom of activity or thought, and she was an arbitrary entity who felt no guilt in any of her actions, causing us in the house to walk on tiptoes and act like angels.
>
> What could evolve from the life of such characters, mutually pecking each other, and forced to cohabitate in a small apartment over the course of some 23 years? And what would their child turn into, forced into seeing all of this drama, day to day, hour to hour, over 20 years of his cognizant life?

The child was raised in an environment of a permanent scandal, overwhelmed by a mother who regularly traumatized his soul. Recognizing the tragedy of the situation she created, he suffered grievously. As Bely further recorded:

> In their lives I carried a cross of torturous horror and I felt the horror of their lives. They could have divorced, but yet they still recognized the need for each other. Mother valued the moral beauty of father, but nothing more. But her value for what he had and she did not would drive her into hysteria and became an excuse for torment.

In later years Bely would express this concealed and suppressed anxiety toward both parents in his autobiographical articles and novels. The events continued to harbor in Bely's memory and haunt him. In 1921, at the age of about 41 years, Bely communicated to the young poet Irina Odoyevtseva:[2]

> My parents fought a struggle over me. Each pulled me in their direction and they tore me completely in half. Yes, yes. They shredded my infantile cognizance and my childlike heart. So from childhood I was halved and so sensing sin and which tormented me for 4 straight years. It was sin to love my mother, it was sin to love my father. So what was I, a sinner? What could I do to cover my sin? I was forced into this domestic drama. I loved and I hated. I would talk to myself and almost with terror. From adolescence I was a potential patricide. Yes, yes. I harbored tendencies of patricide. Somehow merging with a Oedipus complex that was distorted by love. My mother beat me for loving my father. She cried at me, "You love him more than you love me."
>
> My mother was a genuine beauty. But no. Dostoyevsky was not right when he said that beauty will save the world.[3] How will it save it? Mother was very unhappy. You know, beautiful women are always unhappy and so transmit this unhappiness to others. And especially to their sole son. But she was a beauty, but not so inwardly. So sorrowful. For her and for me.

---

[2] Irina Vladimirovna Odoyevtseva, 1895-1990, Russian Soviet poet and novelist. In 1922, she and husband poet Georgy Ivanov immigrated to Paris.

[3] Feodor Dostoyevsky, from *The Idiot*, stated by Lev Mishkin.

This constant oscillation between father and mother was the cause for his duplicity or a dual personality: one superficial in his regular social and business intercourse, and one internally suppressed and occasionally surfacing in private and in his compositions. Nonetheless, Bely acknowledged the following:

> Father influenced my thinking toward life; mother had an effect on my will due to her pressure. In my personal feelings, I was torn between them. My father had a nice smile and plainly captivating. He had a glorious face, not quite like Socrates and not quite like a Pecheng[4] or Scythian.[5]

These experiences with his mother would have been the reason for his difficulty in creating a stable environment and relationship with a wife and perhaps the reason why Bely never had a child with either wife. His involvement with theosophy and a development of deep religious faith may also have been a means of distancing himself from the trauma of his adolescent years.

Bely still loved his mother unconditionally, regardless of her fanatical tyranny. In another respect, Aleksandra did provide for her only son what some mothers only dream of providing, and which she was able to do because of first, the finances available and second, due to her own cultural upbringing. She did possess exceptional musical talents and hoped to pass them on to her son. It was obvious she possessed a hypertrophied maternal instinct. Aleksandr demonstratively refused to allow her husband any educational influence on Bely during his childhood. She feared that due to Nikolai's influence, another mathematician would arise in the family, and this would just ruin her son's life. So the mother deliberately attempted to feminize her son. During his childhood his mother would dress him in girl's dresses and have him wear long hair and curls.

During Bely's childhood, Aleksandra taught her son to play the piano, but as with all else, it turned into a nightmare for Bely,

---

[4] A semi-nomadic tribe of central Asia.

[5] Predecessors of the Ukrainians who lived along the northern shore of the Black Sea.

as she controlled every lesson and would ruthlessly and painfully beat his fingers with a stick if he should play the wrong note. He was hardly able to go to sleep without his mother playing for him on the piano melodies from Ludwig van Beethoven, Robert Schumann and Frederic Chopin. Eventually Bely became an accomplished pianist and would even compose some original music. Mother Aleksandra also impressed all of the literary classics upon her son. She started to read to him beginning when he was able to start talking, and then later they read together many books. Bely's favorite of them all was a translation into Russian of Charles Dickens *David Copperfield.* This book remained in Bely's possession the balance of his life. At the age of 10 years, Aleksandra read Nikolai Gogol's novels to him, and he became Bely's favorite Russian author. He was impressed with the symbolism and clear metaphors in his stories, and it was *Taras Bulba* that had the most effect on Bely, and which style he incorporated in his own novels in later years.

Whatever Bely had for a family, even though not very much, played an important role in the formulation of his ideology, and his concept of ecumenical and individual existence. But it was not based on the home, but based on activities that distracted him from his home, that offered him an escape from the domestic turmoil. So did Bely describe it in his memoirs:

> In song, in tales, in the sound of music was the exit provided for me from this mirthless life. The world became for me an aesthetic phenomenon. No harm, no fear in the residency of our empirical life. Life is joy and this joy was located in tales. My game of life began with tales, and this game is the truest form of symbolism.

Most of Bely's exposure to the outside world was provided by governesses and private tutors hired by mother Aleksandra. But none of them lasted very long in the Bugaev household due to inevitable conflicts with Aleksandra. Bely did retain for his entire life warm feelings toward some of them. One German governess familiarized him with the stories of Hans Christian Anderson and the Brothers Grimm. Another caused him convulsions and fright by reading Johann Goethe's ballad *Der Erlkonig* (*The Forest King*) to him.

It was Ms Bella Raden who had a special influence on the development of the future author. Her father was French and her mother was German. Ms Raden served in the Bugaev household as a governess for over 3 years, longer than any other. She became for Bely not only a beloved housemother, but also a genuine older friend and she was the sole pleasure in his life at home as an youngster, from late 7 to almost 11 years of age. Ms Raden had the ability to turn every lesson into some type of game or entertainment. Her specialty was geography and so he was able to quickly learn the names and locations of the world's countries, as well as their capitals, populations, economy, polity, military, and the geography of each. A cultured and educated person, Ms Raden taught Bely the biography of many important historical personages: scholars, artists, composers, authors and poets, along with their compositions. It was an education in culture in the widest sense of the word. She brought happiness into his life and especially because of his inquisitive nature. Bely learned the German and French languages as well, and which helped him in later years when living in Germany and Switzerland and traveling through Europe, and reading their books in the original languages. As Bely recorded in his memoirs:

> While Ms [Raden] was present, I started to run a lot and climb into trees. I seemed to have become a great tree climber and suddenly I developed a genuine gymnastic agility and to my own amazement as a child. She helped me in this area by taking me to the local German Gymnastic Club on Sundays and where she was also allowed. So for the 2 years before I entered high school I would skip and jump and exercise. Later on as a teenager I would swing in different ways on the trapeze, run races, do the high jump. I trained myself to walk with a lit candle on my head. I even climbed to the top of 4 chairs standing on top of each other. It was Ms [Raden] who was the motivation to do all of this.

At the end of April 1890, the family left Moscow and traveled together to the Horodyshche region near Kiev, to visit his father's relatives. They spent May 4 through July 19, there. On the return trip they stopped at Boyarka, to visit Lev Kupernik,[6] a family friend. The family returned to Moscow on July 24.

A month before his 11th birthday, in September 1891, Bely's private home education concluded successfully and he entered the prestigious private high school of L.I. Polivanov, considered one of the best in Moscow. Bely at this early age was already dividing his life into periods using a graphic and numeral scheme and which he titled the *Line of Life*. He would divide his life into stages, each called by some inflated appellation of an epoch.[7] So the initial stages of his development were a movement from fairy tale to consciousness, and migration from the role of a governess in his life to that of the epoch of high school and then to the creative genius.

Bely recollected his years at the private school:

> Lev Ivanovich Polivanov was a finished artistic masterpiece. A style to which nothing needed to be added and from which no typical trait of his needed to be removed, as the sum of these traits composed his personage. In one respect he was not a person, but some type of two-legged incarnation of the concept of the ideal pedagogue.
>
> The lightning of Polivanov's lessons excited me.

He taught Bely and the other students the compositions of Homer, Sophocles, Shakespeare, Pushkin, and other Russian classics and including ancient Russia tales. It was here that Bely acquired a mastery of the Russian language, and especially composition. It was during the years spent here that Bely first became interested

[6] Lev Abramovich Kupernik, 1845-1905, Russian lawyer and journalist.
[7] A sample of a life scheme is included in this volume.

in philosophy, and beginning at his 5th year – he would have been 16 years of age – he read all the issues of the magazine, *Questions of Philosophy and Psychology*. Like his father, Bely also delved into the study of mathematics, and especially numerology. So it was about the age of 16 that what was expected did occur to Bely: he internally flared with a consuming passion toward the study of Russian and world literature.

Bely read as much as he could of Feodor Dostoyevsky, Ivan Turgenev, Ivan Goncharov, Nikolai Nekrasov, Afanasy Fet, and Semyon Nadson. He enjoyed the poetry of Yakov Polonsky, Feodor Sologub, Zinaida Gippius, and Ivan Bunin. Henrick Ibsen's works in Russian translation overwhelmed Bely and became, as he mentions, his canon of life and within a hour after reading Ibsen's books they turned him into a symbolist at the age of 16. Bely likewise delved into the available *Faust* by Johann Goethe and *Aesthetics* by Georg Hegel. (For some reason Bely was not attracted to Leo Tolstoy until later in life.) His personal library at home also consisted of much mathematical literature, while little fantasy, dime novels or pulp fiction. As a young man, Bely was attracted to the social circle and personal association with those Russians above who were still alive.

The later success of Bely as a writer is heavily due to the positive and intensive instruction provided by Polivanov's high school. Apart from his school studies, Bely at home devoured his mother's library of European classics, including the French authors Emile Zola and Guy de Maupassant, and reading them in their original French. It was not unusual for Bely to spend evenings at local Moscow libraries until closing time. Bely studied the Bible thoroughly, and had an excellent and almost photographic memory of the Old Testament prophets, the Gospels, the letters of Apostle Paul, and the Book of Revelation.

Bely records having mystical experiences at the Trinity-Arbat Church and then on Voronyukhinaya Hill in Moscow, when he was 16 years of age.

It was also during the years of Bely's attendance at the Polivanov school that he met Mikhail Tolstoy, the son of the famous writer, who was also attending the same school.[8] Mikhail was initially a year ahead of Bely, but then failed a grade and ended up in the same class as Bely later on. They became friends.

According to oral tradition, when Bely was just a child Leo Tolstoy would visit the Bugaev home along with his wife Sophia Andreevna and bring Mikhail with them. In return, the Bugaevs would visit the Tolstoys. Supposedly the great Tolstoy held the young Bely on his lap and this left a lasting impression on Bely. But as mentioned above, Tolstoy was not one of Bely's favorite writers and no evidence is available in his writings to authenticate the oral tradition. In later years, in his late teens however, the Tolstoy daughters – Tatyana, Aleksandra and Maria – were friends with Bely, and he did visit the Tolstoy home at this time along with his schoolmate Mikhail.[9] Bely's reaction to the presence of father Tolstoy, and which he did record, was that he was cold and impersonal.

About this time Bely had the opportunity to visit an exhibit of French impressionist paintings in Moscow and especially the paintings of Claude Monet and Edgar Degas. Of course, the exhibition had a positive impression on the young writer.

During June and July 1894, mother and son did some traveling together, to Spasski county, Tambov province, to the estate of Aleksandria Butlerov, a family friend, and then to the nearby city of Lupiga. From there to Liebpaja, in western Latvia on the Baltic sea coast, and then back to Moscow in August. Also in May through June 1895, mother and son vacationed in Kislovodsk, near Stavropol, in southern Russian. Then to Bobrovka in Tambov province from July to August. Then they spent the balance of the summer again at the Butlerov estate.

Bely's governess when he was 14 years of age was Afima Ivanovna Lavrova. Bely's describes her as being very simple and almost illiterate, and that they spent a lot of time playing games together. Lavrova also noticed that there was something different about Bely, that he had a special cognizance or acute perception into items that he read and saw and studied.

---

[8] Mikhail Lvovich Tolstoy, 1879-1944, the same age as Bely within a year.

[9] Tatyanna and Maria were considerably older, while Aleksandra was younger.

A new family now moved into the same apartment building as the Bugaevs and who would become close to them. This was Mikhail Sergeevich Solovyov and his wife Olga Mikhailovna with their son Sergei, who was about 5 years younger than Bely. Mikhail was a teacher and book publisher, the son of the famous Russian historian Sergei Mikhailovich and brother of the no less famous philosopher Vladimir Sergeevich and popular Rosicrucian and historical fiction author Vsevolod Sergeevich. Olga had gained her own reputation as an artist and translator. The 2 boys became friends regardless of the difference in age.

Bely became a frequenter at the Solovyov home and primarily because the latest Russian and European literature, and foreign magazines, were always available there, and the latest issue of the Russian magazine *World of Art*. It was at their home that Bely for the first time heard the names of European and Russian symbolists and became familiar with the poetry of the young Aleksandr Blok, which were yet unpublished and still in manuscript form. Bely was drawn to each member of the Solovyov family as each had something to offer him. Young Sergei was a personal friend. Olga was scholarly and intellectual with a dedicated interest in art and was also able to discuss religion and philosophy in a profound and objective manner. Mikhail was unobtrusive and unpretentious and yet impressed Bely with a sense of morality and logical thinking. His time was mostly spent in gathering the writings of his philosopher brother Vladimir and preparing them for publication. Tables and chairs in Mikhail's study were piled with Vladimir's letters and notes and manuscripts, and all of which were available to the young Bely to read. He would spent hours leafing through the hand-written pages as through they were sacred.

In his later memoirs, Bely described Mikhail Solovyov:

> Mikhail Sergeevich Solovyov was truly an exceptional figure: contrite, concentrated. He was very contemplative and thoughtful and maintained perspicuity and wisdom. He united the boldness of those searching for new paths with a

> monumental conservatism of good taste. It seems he was alone of all the Solovyovs who was not deceived by literary or social credit. Vladimir Sergeevich Solovyov ran solely to him for help during times of crisis in his life or thought. M.S. was a genuine inspiration for Vladimir Solovyov. Somehow he could understand to the end the level of importance the aspiration of theosophy was for the deceased.[10] But M.S. was twice as exceptional [as his brother] since he was quiet, tranquil, balanced, not seeking fame with superficial displays of his life, he was never argumentative or seeking recognition, as was his brother. He was short with blue eyes, blond hair with a small and puffy mouth, wore a bright and white moustache and the same type of beard although wavy, although his face had a pale shade. Outwardly he was strikingly distinguishable from the full-figured and dark-haired and deep-set grey-eyed Vladimir Solovyov.
>
> It was worth gazing at the 2 brothers when they sat next to each other to play checkers and drink tea. After watching them at the table the immense difference was obvious, and along with it, each maintained his resolute and uncompromising, personal religious concepts.

Association with the Solovyov family had an immense influence on the formulation of Bely's ideology and worldview. With the resources available at their home, he became familiar with the masters of Eastern and Western philosophy, with selections from the *Upanishads*, and the treatises of Lao-Tse, Confucius, Immanuel Kant and Georg Hegel. He read the theosophical books of Helena Blavatsky, and consumed Arthur Schopenhauer's *The World as Will and Representation*, writing an abstract of each chapter each day for his personal record as he read it. Along with all the above, by the time Bely reached 16 years of age he was also mature enough to sufficiently absorb Vladimir Solovyov's philosophy. He mentions studying the poetry of Lugwig Uhland,[11]

---

[10] Vladimir Solovyov died July 31, 1900. This passage was composed by Andrei Bely after his death.

[11] Johann Ludwig Uhland, 1787-1862, German poet.

and Heinrich Heine.[12] He also studied ancient Russian legends and fables and tales.

Bely mentions in his memoirs some serious illness at the age of 3 years. Later as a teenager he was stricken with scarlet fever. He was in a state of unconsciousness and delirium for 60 days, as he records. During this state Bely had several dreams that he still remembers. After this crisis and recovering his health, his attitude toward the world became that of an adult, and not as an adolescent, and he had a tendency to notice instances and aspects of matters that were either unknown or inaccessible to regular people, whether adolescent or adult. At this time in his life, after recovering from scarlet fever, and due to its effects on him, Bely became a symbolist.

So Bely started writing poetry about the age of 15 or 16. The quality was poor and he would imitate the compositions and style of other poets. Realizing this he discarded all of his early work. Now the introverted and unsociable Bely became very verbose, and this occurred parallel with his intense studies mentioned above. A sudden interest in music also flared within Bely. His father had 2 memberships in the Moscow Conservatory of Music, but he never attended, preferring to spend his extra time away from Aleksandra and with his friends or at the club. Now Bely had access to music of the highest cultural level and he took advantage of it and attended as often as he could. His favorites were Richard Wagner, Edvard Grieg, and Nikolai Rimsky-Korsakov.

During May and June 1896, mother and son again went on a vacation and this time abroad. Together they visited Berlin, Germany, Paris, France, then Berne, Thun and Zurich, Switzerland. While at Thun they spent some time with professor N.A. Yumov, who would later have an influence on Bely.[13]

After 8 years at Polivanov's private school Bely was 19 and his term of education there successfully ended and he needed to

[12] Christian Johann Heinrich Heine, 1797-1856, German poet and essayist.

[13] Nikolai Alekseevich Yumov, 1846-1915. Russian physicist and mathematician.

decide on his further education pertaining to a vocation. It was a decision between science and art. His father made the decision for him and in September 1899, Bely became a student at the Physics-Mathematical Department of Moscow University, the best education that could be provided. Bely still had his personal agenda and his intent was to quickly conclude the courses for physics and mathematics, and then transfer to philology. He would become, as he expressed it, an aesthetic-naturalist. In the meanwhile he would dedicate himself wholly to physics and mathematics, and the related biology and chemistry, to successfully complete the curriculum as his father wanted for him.

While attending Moscow University, Bely was especially influenced by Kliment Arkadyevich Timiryazev, a physiology professor. It was Timiryazev's method and style of delivery and teaching that impressed Bely, his ability to control the audience, his vocal variations and selection of vocabulary to convey the subject matter, and his body movements and the rhythmic gestures of his hands. He was able to make the simplest detail of the physical nature of the human body something enticing and worth learning about. Recognizing Timiryazev's effectiveness, Bely adopted some of his style in his own manner of public speaking when later delivering lectures on anthroposophy. This helped Bely to become a very effective communicator in front of an audience.

During autumn 1898, father Nikolai Bugaev purchased a summer estate at Serebryanni Kolodez (Silver Well), in Efremovsky county, Tule province. Now both the Bugaev family and Timiryazev family had dachas – summer homes – in the same area outside of Moscow, and Bely often met with the professor in informal conversation. He spends his first summer at the estate in June through August 1899.

Another professor at Moscow University who influenced Bely was Nikolai Alekseevich Yumov. He taught physics but was also a cosmic thinker. Bely was so impressed with the scientific concepts provided by Yumov that he even wrote a poem regarding the atmosphere of the class and dedicated to Yumov (it rhymes in Russian):

> And there was much, much thinking,
> And metaphysics, and noise.
> And my austere physic's mind
> Was raised by professor Yumov.
>
> He sang of the cosmic darkness,
> Combing through his hair and stretching his neck,
> That Maxwell's Paradox
> Destroys entropy.
>
> That outbursts full of sparks,
> Melt Thomson's Scattering,
> And that immense worlds
> Did not succumb to atomic powers.
> That thoughts fly like dynamite.

Bely recorded that there were 4 main principles that Yumov formulated to establish his rank as a natural scientist. First was to confirm the power of humans over energy, time and space; second was the ability to limit the cause of humanity's sufferings; third was to democratize the capabilities of people in their service to humanity and to cooperate in ethical progress; and fourth was to acknowledge the architect of the universe and utilize it to build a foundation of creative and useful knowledge. The universe, according to Yumov, was always rational and always accessible to discovery. It was eternal with no past and no future: it was eternally present and had no limits either in space or in time. Energy is continuing to assemble and dissemble matter, its great role in the universe, to continue to recycle matter in the creation and reduction of worlds. Deep in the recesses of space existed invisible fabric interweaving matter and life. Yumov came to the conclusion of the necessity to include in the scientific picture of the universe the existence of a supreme knowledgeable intellect. All of this had its influence on Bely's thinking.

Bely in his memoirs acknowledges something striking, that during his first year at the university he started to contemplate the space-time continuum and the concept of relativity as he learned it from Yumov while listening to his physics' lectures (and this was several years before its popular dissemination by Albert Einstein).

While at the university and apart from science Bely became a dedicated devotee of Friedrich Nietzsche, studying him in what spare time he had. In his memoirs Bely explained his inclinations toward Nietzsche:

> Beginning with autumn of 1899, I lived Nietzsche. He was my rest, my intimate minutes when I, after setting aside my textbooks, wholly devote myself to his intimate views, his phrases, his style, his composition. In his aphorisms I saw areas that possessed a symbolist composition. It was impressionable music on me, music in my soul, captivating me with nothing remaining of me. And the fact that Nietzsche was a musician in the literal sense, and to the point of being a composer, this was not just incidental during this period of my life. As a result during these years I clandestinely snuck to the piano when my parents were not home and for hours I abandoned myself to improvising my own musical tunes. The philosopher-musician seemed to me to be the symbolist type. Nietzsche become for me such a symbolist through every motion of his life and to his tragic fate.
>
> Nietzsche was never a theorist to me, who would just answer my questions in a scientific sense. He was also not an aesthete regurgitating phrase after phrase. He was to me a creator of the most life-providing forms, whose theoretical or aesthetic meanings blazed a trail for creativity and not just contemplation. Finally, Nietzsche was the anarchist; Nietzsche was the fighter dealing with his degeneracy, aware of what was deep inside of him; he was the frontier between the end of the old period and the beginning of the new; and all of this vivaciously drew him to me. I saw in him first, a new man;

> second, a practical culture; third, a rejecter of obsolete existence (all of which attraction I experienced within myself); and forth, an ingenious artist whose rhythm proceeded to sustain all artistic culture. For the most part, it was Nietzsche who decorated the period of my life from autumn 1899, to 1901: reading his compositions and returning to them again and again. *Thus Spoke Zarathustra* became my altar Bible.

The 19th century concluded with Bely at the age of 20 years. It was at this time that Boris Bugaev became a new person under the new appellation of Andrei Bely (or Andrew White in proper English).

Studying the natural sciences, Bely all the more felt the need to express in words those thoughts and forms that entered his mind from some abyss somewhere. They had nothing in common with contemporary axioms that were impressed on him by most of his university professors, which Bely would call baggage. He felt a gift of clairvoyance residing within himself and simultaneously realized that he was capable of comprehending more than any of the persons that surrounded him. He sensed literary ingenuity and these chaotic concepts floating through him demanded organization. But for them not to be forgotten, not sink into oblivion, it was necessary to codify them, relegate them to paper, explain them in prose and poetry. So began the development of the new person heretofore unknown to the world – Andrei Bely.

It seemed that the cosmos opened to him the door accessing the holy of holies, directing to him the route to decipher all of these hidden secrets. So then a thinker-symbolist materialized, a writer, poet, philosopher, aesthete, and chronicler. Bely became their incarnation and now had the responsibility to accept this and disclose it to the general public. Symbolism was the means of achieving this revelation, a new direction in literature and art in Russia.

Symbolists did exist in earlier ages, such as the American William James,[14] the English William Blake,[15] the French Charles

Baudelaire,[16] and the Spanish Francisco Goya.[17] Except that most of the symbolists either past or present did not have the religious depth or mystic penetration, or this spirit-identity with the intangible and ethereal realm, that Bely had. He was beyond a poet or novelist or philosopher in his symbolist thought and due to his profound religious devotion and belief in the ecumenical architect, the supreme Deity. Bely's selection of the first of the disciples – Andrew – as his name bears testimony to this: he was to be the first of the Russians to preach a native adaptation of anthroposophy, which was easier for Russians to assimilate than theosophy. Here were new disciples of a new means of acknowledging the Deity within us and Who resided in the universe of which we are part and parcel, and are a definite part and important role in the life of every Russian. Bely's label of symbolism was a means of extracting these concepts and transmitting them to his audience to easier understand and assimilate them.

Bely described symbolism as follows:

> Symbolism underscores the primacy of creativity over knowledge, the possibility in artistic creativity to depict forms of reality. In this sense symbolism underscores the significance of forms or artistic compositions where on its own the fervor of creativity is reflected. As a result symbolism underscores cultural thought in learning style, rhythm, the literal monuments of poets and novelists; it recognizes the principle significance in resolving questions of technique in music and art. A symbol is an image derived from nature and transformed through composition. A symbol is an image uniting in itself the experiences of the artist and traits captured from nature. In this sense every artistic product is symbolic in essence.

---

[14] William James, 1842-1910, American physician who was also a philosopher.

[15] William Blake, 1757-1827, English poet, painter, and printer.

[16] Charles Pierre Baudelaire, 1821-1867. French poet, essayist and translator of American classics into French.

[17] Francisco Jose de Goya y Lucientes, 1746-1828, Spanish painter.

Bely essentially disclosed and substantiated one more diversity of symbolism: the profound rhythm of nature and life. With all the vibrations of his soul he sensed this time-derived rhythm of the universe. Of course he attempted to express his intimate sensations, his experiences, in word form through poetic and prosaic texts and in lectures one after another. His lectures delivered in university and academic auditoriums were accompanied by rhythmic gestures remindful of some type of slow mystic dance. For many attending he seemed perplexing and esoteric. To Bely the symbol was more important than mundane reality. Secularism, monotony, boredom and uniformity, was terminal. But the symbol was a fiery sign, a lamp capable of lighting the heart, illuminating the gloomy dusk of mundane existence, helping a person to penetrate into the depths beyond the frontiers.

Without any doubt Bely shared the thesis that was common with him and both Arthur Schopenhauer and Nietzsche, that beyond the visible world a second genuine reality is hidden. So our orientation to gain a perspective of this unseen realm does not depend on scientific methods or the laws of logic, but on intuition, mystic experience and inspiration, and perhaps even a good imagination.

Bely considered language the primary means of transmitting notional symbolism:

> Language is the greatest, most potent tool for creativity. When I refer to an object by its appellation, I confirm its existence. Every acknowledgement evolves from the name of the object. Comprehension is impossible without words. The process of comprehension is establishing the relation between words that eventually transmit into objects that coincide with the words. Grammatical forms providing the conditions for the possibility of the subject matter are possible only when words exist for the purpose. When I confirm that creativity needs to proceed before comprehension, I confirm creative primacy.

> Descriptive speech consists in words logically expressing my inexpressible impression of the objects surrounding me. Living speech is always inexpressible music. The word is the expression of the hidden essence of my nature; and to the extent that my nature is nature in general, the word is the expression of the most hidden of the secrets of nature. Every word has a sound. Spatial and causative attitudes that emanate from outside of me become understandable to me by means of the word. If language did not exist, then neither would the universe.

Some of the early Russians who were labeled as symbolists were also labeled as decadents. These writers included Dmitri Sergeevich Merezhkovsky, his wife Zinaida Nikolaievna Gippius, Feodor Sologub, Valeri Brusov, Vyacheslav Ivanov, and Konstantin Balmont. The label was applied to them by the early 20th century literary critics of Russia who felt that their compositions were a decay of the traditional type of writers of 19th century Russia, which was labeled as the Golden Era of Russian Literature. This new age of contemporary writers was labeled as the Silver Age, and included the above writers along with Alexsei Tolstoy,[18] Anton Chekhov, Aleksandr Blok, Leonid Andreev, Nikolai Gumilyov, and Osip Mandelstam. Bely associated with most all of these writers at one time or another during his own writing career.

Although not a secular writer, but a religious philosopher and dedicated Russian Orthodox Christian, Vladimir Solovyov was also included to a certain extent in the symbolist circle. Bely claims to have had some mystical experiences during discussions with religious-philosophy with Vladimir Solovyov. Bely had the opportunity to meet Solovyov at the end of April and beginning of May 1900, shortly before his unexpected death in August of that year at the age of 47, and he had extensive conversations with

[18] Aleksei Nikolaievich Tolstoy, 1883-1945, Russian Soviet science fiction and historical fiction and children's writer.

him. At the time Bely also read Solovyov's *Short Treatise on the Antichrist.*

Bely was 20 years of age by then and wrote of him in his memoirs:

> Solovyov always seemed to reside under the radiance of a bright dawn. The secret muse of his mystic philosophy – he would refer to her as *she* – evolved out of the dawn. She appeared to him as though he was a child. She appeared to him in a British museum and whispered to him, "Be in Egypt." So the young lecturer threw himself to Egypt and almost perished in the desert there. The vision visited him there also, penetrated with a golden azure. It was here in the Egyptian desert that his Gnostic theosophy was born: the teaching of the eternal female principle of the Deity. His muse became the norm of his theory, the norm of his life. We can say that this aspiration toward the dawn caused Solovyov to go into debt, and the 8 volumes of his compositions were dedicated to the disclosure of this debt.
>
> When he was reading *Narrative on the Antichrist*, when he reached the passage, "John ascended as white light," he likewise ascended as though stretched out over a cross. It seemed that the dawn's light was sparkling through the windows. Solovyov's face agitated in the inspiration of the distant sparkles.

Vladimir Solovyov's writings on Sophia the Divine Wisdom, the feminine aspect of the Supreme Deity, was also absorbed by many of the later symbolists after Solovyov's death.

Once Bely devoted himself to the composition of poetry, it was a flood of volumes one after the other.

The first publication of Bely's poetry was his *Second Dramatic Symphony,* released in September 1901, but not published until March 1902, and it was published under his pseudonym of Andrei Bely. Subsequent to this was his next volume, the *First Heroic or Northern Symphony,* released in July 1903, but not published until early 1904. The next volume was the *Third Symphony, Return* (Vozvrat), released in September 1904, but not published until 1905. Then it was the *Fourth Symphony, Goblet of Blizzards*, published in 1908. In between the above Symphonies was Bely's most popular collection of poetry *Gold in Azure*, published late 1904. Apart from *Return*, the balance were published by Scorpion Book Publisher, Moscow. Subsequent volumes of poetry were *Ashes* in early 1909, and *Urn* in late 1909. Likewise in between were several articles on the concept of symbolist composition.

Bely's' *Symphonies* unveiled a new genre in Russian and world literature. His intent was to create a verse that would be read as words but heard as music. They were composed in various beats with various moods expressing a concealed rhythm of the universe, as Bely described them. For the unseasoned reader, the *Symphonies* seemed to be a series of disconnected statements of independent topics unrelated to one another and without any noticeable goal or plot or conclusion intended. Deeper concentration unveils a sequence connecting various aspects of the universe connected with the process of earthly life. Often Solovyov's concepts of Sophia the Divine Wisdom will pervade the text. The *Symphonies* enjoyed tremendous popularity among the Russian literary population as it was different than the basic story and plot or rhyme of general literature, and with the use of many metaphors, symbols and interesting language.

Meanwhile studies continued in their proper order at the university for Bely. He attended lectures and seminars, wrote his abstracts and course papers, he worked at the laboratory, and spent time in physical exercise. After about 3 years at the university, his educational plans were moved to the back burner as they interfered with his true calling – literary creativity and new tendencies in philosophy, theosophy, aesthetics and art. His time was overwhelmingly consumed now with writing: poetry, prose, theoretical and critical essays, mysterials, and letters. Apart from the university professors whose help he appreciated and company he enjoyed, Bely attached himself to a new circle of associates who were likewise dedicated to the new direction of

Russian literature, some of whom were mentioned above: Merezhkovsky, Gippius, Brusov, Alexandre Benois,[19] Sergei Diaghilev,[20] Pavel Batushkov, and Konstantine Balmont, all of whom were already established in Russian literature and art.

But there were also several younger individuals, Bely's new friends, exceptionally talented and active and likewise whose careers were just beginning. Bely especially became close to the poet Lev Kobilinsky, later known under the pseudonym of Ellis,[21] and the journalist Emilie Metner.[22] His previous associate Sergei Solovyov also joined their circle. What brought all of them together was an attachment to the philosophy of Fredrick Nietzsche and Vladimir Solovyov, as well as their similar literary and artistic pursuits.

The group selected a name for themselves – the Argonauts, in consideration of the ancient mythology of Jason and the Argonauts (their ship named the Argo), in search of the golden fleece in the land of Colchis.[23] The group could identify with the ancient myth, with themselves likewise seeking for a golden future on an astral ship on a journey toward the sun. Eventually Bely would become the inspiration for the group and organizer and honorary leader. He described them in the following manner in his memoirs:

> The Argonaut concept was not an ideology, not a codex of rules or laws. It was only an impulse of distraction from the obsolete existence, sailing in the sea of discovery whose goal was visible through the fog of the future. As a result we did not turn our attention on dogmatic influences residing within any of us,

---

[19] 1870-1960. Founding member of the magazine World of Art, influential on the Soviet ballet and stage.

[20] 1872-1929, founder and director of the Soviet ballet theater.

[21] Lev Lvovich Kobilinsky or Kobylinsky, 1879-1947, poet, historian and Christian philosopher. He would later migrate to Europe and become a Catholic Jesuit.

[22] Emilie Karlovich Metner or Medtner, a journalist and musical critic, He was also the symbolist publisher of *Musaget,* and older brother of the famous music composer Nikolai Medtner.

[23] Georgia along the Black Sea coast, an important place in Greek mythology, as well as the destination of the Argonauts and home to the Golden Fleece.

instead hoping to clear the sclerosis of dogma using the fire of enthusiasm in the search of a new style of existence and a new ideology.

Kobilinsky praised life erected on parallelisms. Vladimirov[24] dreamed of new styles of art, of the rise of a national myth; he yearned for a commune of symbolists. Malafeev[25] fantasized in his unique fashion of a new peasant community.

Personally, no one held tight to the nickname and actually, many had a difficult time exactly defining the notorious concept of being an Argonaut. Ellis would often rise to a state of excitement for one reason or another and announce that he was an Argonaut, whatever that was.

Imagine a handful of adolescents, halfway annoyed by their mundane existence, traumatized by smashing heavy Arbat[26] rocks for the cause of building a worldwide cultural revolution, having this hope of wanting to rebuild Moscow in three years, and after it the entire world. And so you can see that the composition of the circle could only contain eccentrics or freaks.

Nonetheless the Argonauts left some traces in the culture of artistic Moscow during the first decade of this century. They [artistic Moscow] blended with the symbolists and counted themselves symbolists, published their writings in symbolist magazines (as I did and Ellis and [Sergei] Solovyov), but we were distinguishable from them due to the style of our public display. We derived nothing [financially] from our literary pursuits, and gained nothing from any fame we might have achieved. We were just a series of the most interesting of personages, original not due to something superficial, but their essence, having traversed the Argonaut concept.

In our circle there was no deeply impressed ideology, no dogmas. From the time we started and to the present we

---

[24] Vasili Vasilyevich Vladimirov, one of Bely's closest friends as a teenager, they also attended Moscow University together.

[25] N.M. Malafeev, early friend of Bely's, a serious Christian, he debated the effectiveness of symbolism, and was more traditional. He eventually became a medical doctor.

[26] Bely and others lived on or in the vicinity of Arbat St in central Moscow.

> united in our searches, and not in our achievements. And so many among us seemed to be involved in a crisis of our yesterday, and in a crisis of our ideology, which always seemed to be obsolete. We greeted it in attempts of a birth of new thoughts and new situations.

Bely also described in his memoirs the sacred structure of the symbols surrounding the golden fleece and its identification with the sun:

> My desire [to attain] the sun increases all the more. I want to plunge through the dark emptiness, swim through the ocean of timelessness, but how can I plough through emptiness?
>
> Stenka Razin[27] drew a sketch of a boat on the wall of his prison, all the while laughing at his executioners, saying all the while that he will sit in it and float away. I know it was this way. I will act myself pretty much the same way: I will build for myself a sun-ship – the Argo. I want to become an Argonaut. And not just me, but many want to. But they just do not know it, but it is this way.
>
> Right now in the bay of expectation a flotilla of solarized battleships are harbored. The Argonauts are shooting for the sun. It will take a lot of despair to break their small idols, but this despair only turns them even more toward the sun. They request directions to arrive there. They have dreamed the unimaginable. They are guarding themselves against the gilded fabric of solar rays stretching toward them through the million chaoses of emptiness, yet all are a summons to them. They have cut leaves of gilded fabric and utilized them on the surface of their winged desires. The many sun-ships they have assembled emanate beams as brilliant as lightning. Flotillas of such ships now float in our calm bay so that with the first gust of wind they will sail through the terror after the golden fleece. On their own they have secured gold armor to their dark

[27] Stepan Timofeevich Razin, 1630-1671. Cossack leader who led a revolt against Russian domination of Ukraine.

figures. The shining armor-clad sailors now walk among people, arousing in them either ridicule or fear or respect. These are the Knights of the Golden Fleece. Their shield is the sun. They lowered their blinding visors, and when they raise them a gentle and austere face filled with courage smiles at those who see them.

All of these are the Argonauts. They soar to the sun. Here they walk aboard their ships. The solar gust has ignited the lake. Outstretched gilded tongues lick the rocks penetrating from the water. At the helm of the Argo stands a sailor in shining full body armor and he blows a trumpet as it is the time to return.

Something pushed the ship. The stretched wings of the ship displayed a shining zigzag and they rose high above the curious spectators. Now a silent thunder is heard from the distant expanses. What the Argonauts leave behind is like the burning smoke from a cannon. They route is distant. Let us pray for them, since we are gathering to follow right behind them.

We will gather sunshine to build our own ships! Emilie Karlovich. The outstretched gilded tongues lick the rocks penetrating from the water. The beams of sunshine beat the windows of our homes. Here they struck the ceiling and walls. All around us is illuminated.

Gather, gather this radiance! Scoop the spilling brilliance using buckets! Every drop of it is capable of birthing a sea of light. The Argonauts, let them pray for us!

The many and diverse depictions of the ship Argo and the golden fleece – the coveted goal of the Greek Argonauts – will quickly become symbols in Bely's first complete poetic compilation, *Gold in Azure*. Cosmic symbols pervade the text: gold = sun, azure = sky and particularly outer space. In one of his letters to Margarita Kirillovna, Bely wrote:

I love. I rejoice. Through the gusts of snows, the excitement of the snowstorms, I hear the azure music of your eyes. Azure

> prevails everywhere. Heaven is with me. You are the azure flight to the sky so radiant to me. What happiness that you exist.

According to the memoirs of Nina Petrovskaya,[28] the Argonaut club members were drawn to Bely as sunflowers do toward the sun. He was inarguably recognized as their leader and he compiled their inspiration in prosaic form. They considered his literary and artistic talent incomparable to other representatives of this genre.

Ellis wrote in this regard:

> In all of contemporary Europe perhaps, there are only 2 names stigmatically sealed with our *I*. Our shredded, our insane – due to the rays of the dawn that has never yet glowed – *I*, only 2 names that stand as living slogans, banners consisting of the flesh and blood of that central aspiration of the best souls of contemporary humanity, a coveted goal who appears at the thirst at the terminating point of recovery, a summons to the great miracle of the transformation of the entire inner person toward new routes and new distances of contemplation through the reevaluation of all values, to other forms of existence through a reevaluation of the concept of contemplation. To say this in brief, for the generation and development of a new entity, or the new spiritual nature of an entity, a new impending race, these two names are Nietzsche in Western Europe, and A.Bely among us in Russia.

Members of the Argonaut circle managed to mythologize all and everything around them. They loved to be conniving, imagining themselves as centaurs, unicorns, fauns. They played games and tricks right in Moscow environs, they turned their acquaintances into mystical characters. Imagination in pranks was the goal and as much fantasy as their adolescence permitted. There is no actual

---

[28] Nina Ivanovna Petrovskaya, 1879-1928. Russian poet. She migrated to Europe in 1911, and eventually lost all she had and lived in destitution. She committed suicide in a Paris hotel room.

timeline for the effective activity of the Argonaut circle, but probably from about 1901 to 1904, seems reasonable and based on the statement made above about rebuilding Moscow in 3 years, and Bely would be 24 at this time and preparing to leave the university.

The novice poet was able to win popularity and a place under the sun, meeting and associating with famous writers of the Silver Age. M.S. and O.M. Solovyov provided conditions for his advancement. Fated encounters occurred in their apartment: with Valeri Brusov, with Merezhkovsky and his wife Gippius.

There was some contact in the past between Bely and Brusov: they both attended the Polivanov private school, except that Brusov was 7 years ahead of Bely and he took no note of Bely at the time, as well as being 13 years his senior. Brusov was already an established poet by the time Bely was just starting to be published, but they became acquainted and were lifetime friends as a result.

Bely describes in detail in his memoirs the beginning of their association:

> On December 5, 1901, I met Brusov. Petrovsky was in my apartment when I received a note from O.M. Solovyova, "Brusov is here. We await you." We rang and entered and I see at the table sitting a strong appearing person with high cheek bones and a thick brunet beard with a large forehead. He did not look like a Chechen or a Tatar, his skin was a moldy shade with black and white spots. He stared at us from under his chin with a restrained frown, and he was reading something. He raised himself, stood erect, and quickly rose his hand, and then shook mine, and quickly sat again.

In return, Brusov also in his diary recorded his impression of this first meeting with Bely, his new symbolist companion:

> Bely visited me. He read his verses. Talked about chemistry. He is not the most interesting person in Russia. His lack of

> maturity and a mental dishevelment is due to his strange adolescence.

At Solovyov's apartment Bely also met the spouses Dmitri Sergeevich Merezhkovsky and Zinaida Nikolaievna Gippius, this occurred on December 6, 1901. Bely retained impressions from that encounter likewise his entire life.

Bely spent the summer of 1902, at Serebryanni Kolodez. Bely would travel here occasionally and would write his poetry and prose, and read Kant's and Nietzsche's philosophies in the original German. Thirty years later one person asked Bely whom his 3 favorite authors were and he immediately responded:

> The Gospels, Gogol, and Nietzsche, meaning *Zarathustra.*

On his return to Moscow from the family estate, the young symbolist defended his genre of writing. In the middle of November 1902, he got acquainted with Sergei Pavlovich Diaghilev and Alexandre Nikolaievich Benois. In the December issue of *World of Art*, 2 of Bely's articles were published, *Female Singer*, and *Forms of Art*. About 6 months later a passionate manifesto having the title, *A Few Words from a Decadent to Liberals and Conservatives*, was published to answer questions that were bothering Bely internally in regard to the symbolist movement in literature. He speaks on behalf of the young creators of art and literature who have seemed to lost connection with the older generation. The argument of the young symbolist is immediately presented as a paradox:

> They criticize us for having no principles. But this is an illusion. Visible unscrupulousness is incomparably better than limited scrupulousness. A limited principle leads to a active reaction to those positive principles that are not included in this principle in the light of its limitedness. But such principles can be incomparable greater than the one included

in a popular principle. Visible unscrupulousness is a lesser evil in comparison to principles that are limited.

Yes, we are severe toward the past. We are a bridge upon which our more happier children will pass. Our children will pass over our bodies. They will scramble toward even greater slopes. They have attentive ears and will catch the first breeze before the daybreak, so that with a clean heart they can announce the sun. Perhaps such will evolve from among us, to whom such happiness will also be given.

Our pride, our fearlessness, our strength, our contempt, and our summons of death, resides in this greedless assignment. It would be a joke to suppose that there are many of us, that the young people are composed particularly of us. We are decadents, we have a pretension to suppose that we are the kernel of contemporary adolescents, we are the praetorians proceeding at the head of its army.

The magazine *World of Art* was published in Petersburg. Its symbolist counterpart in Moscow became the magazine *Scales*, a new branch of the book publisher *Scorpion*. The founder of both of them was Sergei Polyakov.[29] As a person he was contrite, shy and reserved, but was not stingy when it came to publishing quality editions and paying royalties to native Russian authors, poets and artists. He entrusted Brusov with the role of being primary ideologist of the direction, and organizer of the editing and publishing activity, of the 2 magazines and book publishing.

Apart from Brusov as a published *Scorpion* author, among the many other authors who were especially sustained by the generosity of Polyakov were Konstantin Balmont and Vyacheslav Ivanov, both becoming famous poets of the Silver Age.

In February 1903, a burst of fresh air rushed into Moscow among the symbolists, the young poet and artist, Maximillian Voloshin. Like Bely and about the same age, he was a devotee of Nietzsche

[29] Sergei Aleksandrovich Polyakov, 1874-1942, a successful textile fabricator, patron of the arts, benefactor of Moscow symbolists, an expert in the art world and translator from Norwegian into Russian.

and Vl. Solovyov, so how could the 2 of them not become the best of friends. Born in Kiev, Voloshin was raised in Sebastopol and Taganrog in the Crimea, and attended high school in Fedosia, but moved to Moscow in 1893 for his higher education. Beginning 1899, Voloshin crisscrossed Russia, and traveled all over Europe, the middle East, and central Asia. In Paris, he studied painting and sculpturing and European modernist culture. Then back to Moscow in 1903, but returning to Paris in 1904, and in 1905, he there became a Mason. It was back to Russia in 1906, and then he married Margarita Sabashnikova and settled in Petersburg, but the marriage did not last long, only a year and then it dissolved, although they remained friends. Margarita would often visit the family estate in the Crimea.[30] Voloshin was friends with Balmont from early times together in Europe. Voloshin brought with him much poetry he composed while in Paris, and which was very favorably accepted by his new fellow symbolists.

The one stain on the reputation of Voloshin is his duel with Nikolai Gumilyov[31] over Elizaveta Dmitrieva,[32] another poet, on November 22, 1909. Neither party was injured, however this terminated all association between them until just before Gumilyov's death in 1921. As with Bely in later years, both Voloshin and his wife Margarita and Elizaveta Dmitrieva became Anthroposophists.

Voloshin recorded the following about Bely:

> Within Andrei Bely a certain menagerie is maintained, but it is covered with only a thin radiance of insanity. His eyes are inscribed hot coals, unnaturally and insanely located close to the nose bridge. His lower eyelids seem to blink, while the

---

[30] Margarita Vasilyevna Sabashnikova, 1882-1973. In 1922, she permanently settled in Germany.

[31] Nikolai Stepanovich Gumilyov, 1886-1921, a popular poet the Silver Age. He was arrested on August 3, 1921, on fabricated charges of an anti-Soviet conspiracy and executed August 25, with 61 other innocent victims. He was married to the famous Russian poetess Anna Akhmatova.

[32] Elisaveta Ivanovna Dmitrieva, also Cherubina de Gabriak, 1887-1928, poet with a nebulous and scandalous history.

upper are wide open and stationary. On his narrow and high forehead are 3 upright, thick clumps of long hair.

The above short biography is provided because Bely and Voloshin will become closely connected in life due to their literature and philosophy, and Bely would vacation at the Voloshin estate in the Crimea in later years.

The year of 1903 was tragic in Bely's life. On January 16, his neighbor Mikhail Solovyov unexpectedly died of pneumonia. On the same day, his wife Olga Solovyova, deeply affected by his death and unable to deal with the loss, killed herself with a shot from a revolver. They were buried alongside each other at the Novo-Devichi Convent.

Bely wrote and dedicated a poem to their memory, likewise in the symbolic tradition:

They decorated their graves with wreaths.
Without our hats we stood melancholy.
The agitation of the snow swilling about us,
The circling winds banish them to grey eternity.

For a long while Bely had thoughts of building something of the sort of a literary salon in his apartment. A pilot project was attempted at the end of April 1903. At the literary evening festivity, accompanied by a light meal and tea, Brusov, Balmont, Jurgis Baltrusaitis,[33] and Ellis, from among the poets, and Polyakov and Sergei Sokolov, from the publishers, and a few friends, attended. More than all else Bely feared that his conservatively oriented father, who did not accept the concepts of symbolism would initiate a aggressive and unnecessary rant and lead the conversation into some fruitless course. But fortunately this did not occur. Nikolai Vasilyevich contained himself

[33] Jurgis Baltrusaitis, 1873-1944, Lithuanian symbolist poet. President of the Union of Soviet Writers in 1919.

dignifiedly and as a considerate host made all the guests feel welcome.

Bely still had to complete his classes at the university that semester to gratify his father, who had invested so much into his education, even though they were distant from Bely's true loves of writing, aesthetics and philosophy. This final semester of final examinations consisted of botany, zoology, anatomy and physiology, and some additional general education classes. Due to Bely's mental acuity and almost photographic memory, and delving into all the texts for a week straight and solid prior to the examinations, he was able to successfully pass them.

Bely recorded in his memoirs:

> To my amazement I was able to pass the test on anatomy, and by pedantically following a method of memorization that I devised and taught myself: the evening before each examination, before dark, I would undress as though it is evening, and mentally visualize the entire course in front of me, viewing it as though a movie, scene after scene, noting the formulas. If there was a spot in the program that appeared to be foggy, I noted it with a pencil. So in five or six hours I reviewed the entire course. What I did not understand I compiled in notes. I slept until about 3 in the morning and then jumped out of bed to review my missing areas until 10, when I would go for the examination. My nerves would be shattered until I answered the questions, and then answering them, I would devolve into abulia. Leaving, a fog covered the entire course.
>
> My anatomy professor, Peter Petrovich Sushkin, hissed at me before the examination, "I cannot tolerate these decadent youngsters." But he gave me a grade of 3. My triumph.

On May 28, 1903, Boris Nikolaievich Bugaev received a diploma with the highest grade on the completion of the Physics-Mathematics requirements at Moscow State University. It was that night after returning home, that his father had a fatal heart attack. Bely's mother was not at home, since she earlier left for the family estate at Serebryanni Kolodez, and so a telegram was sent for her to immediately return. Nikolai Vasilyevich was 66 years of age at his death.

Just as Bely consoled his friend Sergei Solovyov over the death of his parents, Sergei then consoled his friend over the loss of his father.

A few months after the death of his father, Bely relocated to Serebryanni Kolodez for an entire year. He was there able to have some breathing space and ability to work hard on his writings, postponed due to completing his university studies. For the initial 2 months he worked on his first complete volume of a collection of poems: he rewrote old verses, wrote new ones, and gave the volume the title *Gold in Azure*. In mid-August, Bely sent the package with the manuscript by parcel post to Brusov for publication by *Scorpion*. The balance of time spent at Serebryanni Kolodez was on writing what he considered principally important articles, among them *Symbolism as an Ideology*, as well as further in depth study of Kant in the original German, and catching up with correspondence, a great favorite of Bely's.

He grew a beard at this time, but felt it appeared so barbaric on him that he shaved it and never grew a beard again.

Bely returned to Moscow in September 1904, and it was necessary for him to seriously consider his daily bread. His father had no excess capital in the bank remaining, all that he accumulated went to the purchase and maintaining of the Tule estate. His mother had never worked and so had nothing saved or any dowry. The family however did have another parcel of property in Adler, near Sochi, on the Black Sea coast, that was undeveloped. The property was given to father Nikolai as a bonus by the government due to his excellent work as a professor at the Imperial Moscow University, president of the Moscow Mathematical Society, and member of the Petersburg Academy of Sciences. Bely thought about selling this parcel and so would allow him some immediate means for his individual survival and some income for his mother, and who was now dependant on him.

As far as royalties were concerned for his published works, they were little and irregular. The Adler property eventually sold in later years, but since it was distant and undeveloped, little profit was made.

Bely then turned to his father's friends with a request to help him organize a series of lectures at the university regarding new trends in literature. However the reputation of the decadents had a bad effect on the classical and conservative administration. Bely now had to find an auditorium somewhere else. From this time forward, lecturing became Bely's regular occupation. After the release into public of *Gold in Azure* and the publication by critics of reviews of the book and its author that were somewhat scandalous and radical, the people rushed to listen to the lectures of this extravagant if not eccentric poet and he became popular just in days. A crowd of excited devotees likewise appeared surrounding him, but of course not as many as with Brusov or Balmont, but for Bely, it helped pay the bills.

The collection of verses *Gold in Azure* immediately made Bely one of the leading and most brilliant representatives of Russian symbolism. Readers divined a new scale of previously unknown meanings in Bely's symbolic language and new feelings that would penetrate the reader's senses. The excitement of Ellis, for example, had no limits, as he wrote in his review of the volume of verses:

> There exists a special, distinctively intimate connection between the *Dramatic Symphony* and this recent publication of *Gold in Azure*, with the subtitle of *Scarlet in Thorns*.[34] A hidden expectation resides in them, the boldest and most insane ecstatic outburst. The multifaceted prism of symbolism is clearly clairvoyant through them. The initial movements of the most profound disappointments, a feeling of the end, and the despair of unrealistic expectations, reside in them. The most bitter and painful noise of transcendence is located there.

[34] The title based on Jesus' crown of thorns and scarlet robe.

> The most brilliant new form of prose and lyric is here to be found!
>
> *Scarlet in Thorns* as a lyric even more lyrically, more subjectively and more penetratingly announces what the *Second Symphony* contains. It even more fervently and turbulently aspires to turn contemplation into a magic act, prose into a prayer of conjuration, subjective premonition into prophecy, creativity into service. It is not knowledge of essence, not joy of accomplishment, but the thirst for perfection, the ecstasy of sacred love and the terror of fate that has inspired this holy book.

Another published commentary was the following:

> Everything is symbolic in the collection *Gold in Azure*. Even the book itself, each image in it, each verse, each line and each word in this poetic composition. The outstanding symbol is the Golden Fleece, the travel of the poet and his friends to find it, the young Argonauts. It is portrayed as sailing for the Great Truth hidden in the depths of the distant universe. The essence is ciphered or encoded in a multitude of sacred symbols and it is particularly that the Golden Fleece surfaces as the key and with its utilization the slammed shut doors can be opened and the hidden secrets can be penetrated. The only ones that are capable of understanding the mysteries of the world and its laws through these symbols are those who attain the decisive role in the cognizance of the indivisible unity of the macrocosm (the universe) and the microcosm (the human). So aesthetic cosmic imagery and cosmic ideology were born through means of contemplation, as a transformation of reality through its spiritual development and mystic illumination allowing an attainment of the mysterial meaning.
>
> The illustration of the heroes of Greek myth of the sailing Argonauts is reinterpreted as the symbolic sailing of the children of the sun to their cosmic father Helios and even further, to the unfathomable recesses of the universe.

Ellis commented on the general capacity of Bely to write poetry:

> Using flowers can we characterize the most complex psychological states. One moon can be represented by azure with a pinkish-gold tint, another with the color grey with a lilac-green reflection, a third as black colored with yellow and scarlet spots. The dark lilac and black colors reflect a world of catastrophe, psychological fractures, poisonous plants, collapse into the abyss, self-immolation, Satanism, insanity, suffocation. With the help of colors, their unification, their shades, indescribable and ineffable become visible. We the symbolists, through colors have the capacity to speak of eternity, timelessness, the sunset of the soul, the summons of the dawn, the impact of epochs, spiritual shades, fear of the night, the world of elusive and imperceptible whispers, inaudible footsteps.
>
> So who among the experts of world poetry wrote at any time about the bronze eternity? And who in general, other than Bely, called eternity his beloved? Not in vain did the young Marina Tsvetaeva, who met the young Bely at a circle of the Argonauts, told him right to his eyes, "This is the one who is eternity."

The future religious philosopher Pavel Florensky, regardless of his conservative Orthodox tendencies, saw a creative benefit in Bely's poetry, as he stated in a review, defending Bely from criticisms:

> For them, these are just fragmented phrases of this category of poets, and they are inclined to discard Bely since he is not aligned with their point of view.
>
> It is necessary to find a center of perspective, so as a result the private and plain will provide something public and infinite. This approach is indispensable in order to see through Bely's concrete images translucently, and so through them to see the allegorical representation.
>
> People do evolve from sound and light.

Others on the other hand criticized Bely particularly for his distracting use of "coloration effects," as they called it. He had no center of perspective, no unity, no concreteness, no consistency, and he had a tendency to apply depth and infinity to shallow and temporal items. That Bely seemed to see what other people were unable to see was an insult to their intelligence. Yet such criticism had no impact on people's interest in the new wave of symbolist poetry.

Eternity, as with the infinite universe, is portrayed in Bely's poetic cognizance as a fusion of all the colors of the rainbow. Bely wrote the following passage in a letter to Aleksandr Blok in February 1905:

> My dear, my dear. The world must hate us, because we must not be derived from the world, but from gold, pink, azure, snow-white and the color purple. The azure-golden and snow-white purple roses of Eternity.

Returning to Moscow in the middle of September 1904, Bely ventured into having regular Sunday discussions at his apartment. Beginning that autumn all seemed receptive to start and continue with the potential participants not rejecting the invitation. The hardest part was just to start on a day of the week where all were free and not committed to something else. Balmont and Brusov were occupied with the publishers *Grif* and *Scorpion* along with other symbolists.

At the first Sunday meeting Bely presented an abstract prepared based on his personal defining article, *Symbolism as an Ideology*, written that summer. As he wrote in this treatise: The primary task was the definition of the philosophical roots of contemporary symbolism. First it was Kant who, according to Bely, awakened the European intellect from sleep and struck the bell of cognitive criticism. Subsequent to him was Schopenhauer and Nietzsche, for whom it was easy to route philosophy to the side of symbolism. Symbolist ideology and creativity was the frontier of geniuses, while the essential goal was cognizance of eternity through the route of the transformation of the individual. The best examples for imitation are Lermontov and Blok.

As far as a fixed definition of symbolism was concerned, it only applied to Bely conditionally. He was never attached to prepared text, but preferred to extemporize and improvise, speaking freely, as though inspired. While presenting his ideas he would walk about the room or hall or back and forth on the stage, or even run, jump a bit and dance. Many of Bely's memoirists turned their attention to this manner of his communication with the audience.

Feodor Stepun,[35] himself an experienced lecturer and profound thinker, remembered the following about Bely at one of his lectures:

> He spoke innovatively. With his broad-winged concepts, in an whirlwind flight of speech, in lightning speed, he would tie together all of his new paradoxes, those which seemed to have meanings that had absolutely nothing in common with one another. The more inspirational he spoke, the more often the logic of his speech was implied by nothing more than the phonetics of his words. Intellect was converted into inarticulate speech. Philosophic terminology was defined in symbolic signals. Within a few minutes comprehensive meaning almost vanished from his speech, but bearing with the indistinctions, Bely not for a minute lost his amazing gift of verbal composition.

Nina Gagen-Torn[36] supplements the above impression with her opinion of Bely's conduct at the podium:

> The lecturer walked over to the podium. Everybody's preconceived impression vanished. How to explain to you Andrei Bely's appearance? He has a bulbous nose, slanting

---

[35] Feodor Avgustovich Stepun, 1884-1965, a Prussian writer, philosopher, historian and sociologist who lived in Russia until migrating to Europe in 1922.

[36] Nina Ivanovna Gagen-Torn, 1900-1986, Russian and Soviet poet, writer and historian. She spent a good part of her life either in prison or in exile, the years 1936 to 1942, for contra-revolutionary activities.

eyes, somewhat thin. I guess what a professor should look like. Then his eyes would grow large and it seemed that nothing remained except for his eyes. His hands were agile but strong, and with just a gesture they could raise everything up. They almost danced as they provided motion to his concepts. The impression he gave was a movement of a very well-built body in a dark suit. His movements spoke just as expressively as words. They were full of rhythm.

The audience, forgetting about its purpose there, listens to him telling them their fortune. The world is encased as though in a crystal ball. Bely gestures as though having one in his hands and pretends to twirl it and the crystal ball effect radiates flames of diverse colors. Everything seemed to circulate in this light blue light.

Try to see what we saw there. Right in front of us a geyser suddenly erupted from the ground with a spray of hot fog and foam. Try to grasp how high its flight will be. What wind in its face. The spray then showering upwards, downwards. The sun-shining rays tangled in them and turned into a rainbow. They were now translucent, now white from the force of the steaming. Perhaps the geyser will uplift all that surrounds us? Then what? We don't know. But joyfully, the brilliance and force subside. Can you believe, it is as though I heal myself. Right now I will catch it, I will right now grab the geyser. I know, I know. What I always knew sparkles in the showers, I cannot describe it. This is how it is! And we did not know that meanings can be unveiled and new revelations are promised, those I was aware of from somewhere from the beginning of time, at sometime in some deep unknown place. I cannot tear myself away from the geyser.

Even Bely's ideological antagonists were impressed and paid attention to his unique and inimitable oratory abilities. One of whom was the poet Vadim Shershenevich,[37] who recorded the following in his memoirs:

---

[37] Vadim Gabrielevich Shershenevich, 1893-1942.

> Andrei Bely spoke impressively. A person could listen to him for hours, and not understand all he was saying. I am not convinced that even he understood the phraseology he was reciting to us. He spoke using either a series of syllogisms based on his personal conclusions or just disconnected propositions. If he flatteringly said about himself, "I write like a shoemaker," he could just as well have said, "I speak like Pythia."[38]
>
> His blue eyes sparkled with eternity, with such an infinite light blue color such as does not exist even in the skies of Gagra, while the sky of Abkhazia is bluer than any other blue color.[39] His hair beginning at the forehead flowed to his nape.
>
> He had the capacity to speak about anything on his mind, and always appearing inspired. He spoke the way typesetters use different fonts. The tone of his voice would underscore his mass of statements.

Others who listened to Bely's lectures concluded that he was not so much speaking on his own, as much as outside his volition. As Bely described it, he was transmitting what he was being prompted to say, what the noosphere was relating to him. Bely knew this, but he could not explain it rationally otherwise.

Women of all ages, and especially the young, fluttered continually around the symbolists like moths around a light bulb. Konstantine Vasilyevich Mochulsky[40] recollects the following:

> As if from underground a swarm of modernist girls appeared: skinny, pale, fragile, enigmatic, some were indiscreet, like the heroines of Maeterlinck's stories.[41] They overfilled the hall of the artistic and literary circles and symbolist salons.

---

[38] The Oracle of Delphi.

[39] At the foot of the western end of the Caucasus Mts, along the coast of the Black Sea. Gagra is a popular health resort and vacation spot.

[40] Lived 1892-1948, a Russian literary critic and professor of theology. He migrated to Paris in 1922 to escape communism, and later became a Russian Orthodox priest.

It is completely natural than many beauties of the female gender condescended to taking decisive steps to gain Bely's attention, attempting to become close to him by doing whatever they felt they had to. However Bely relied on dependable tactics he developed in addressing the forward attitude of such devotees. With eyes of angelic purity he would speak with each of the importunate girls in one and the same manner, "Please read Kant's *Critique of Pure Reasoning*, and then I will be very pleased to further talk with you." This response would overwhelm the devotee and she would never return.

As some other contemporaries recorded, Bely would use his gift of supra-intellectual verbosity to whirl the heads of these women who attempted to impose their attention on him or who flattered him, and it was not without great satisfaction that he would do this. The shallowness of such women did annoy Bely overall, often feeling it was a insult to his intelligence that they actually thought he would expend his valuable time catering to their base needs. One Russian poet, Vladislav Khodasevich, who knew Bely well for almost 2 decades, was open about this matter in his memoirs:

> Women agitated Andrei Bely considerable worse than people are inclined to think. However it is in this sphere with especial retrospection that his dual character surfaces. He always had one and the same tactic: he would mesmerize the women with his charm, almost enchantingly, displaying himself in some mystic aura, always excluding any thoughts of any type of sensual attraction from his side. Then he immediately abandoned himself to an attraction toward her, and if the woman, struck by this unexpected behavior, and often even insulted, did not reply to him in mutual manner, he would go insane.

---

[41] Maurice Polydore Bernard Maeterlinck, 1862-1949. A Belgian author, awarded the Nobel Prize in Literature in 1911.

> Conversely, every time he was able to succeed in gaining his desired result, he sensed himself defiled and degraded by the incident and so become upset with himself. Often times he would reach a point of having to somehow bail himself out, and so he would flee the situation mentally, just as the handsome Joseph did.[42]

The opinion of women who surrounded Bely at the time is sufficiently expressed by Brusov's sister-in-law, Bronislava Pogorelova. She was employed at Brusov's magazine *Scales* and at the symbolist publisher *Scorpion.*

> From one perspective he possessed a rare beauty, a direct angelic beauty. He had large eyes, as smooth as a still lake, but they were unusually closer together, although shined with a constant ecstasy. The color of his face was beautiful, dark eyelashes and eyebrows beneath ash-blond curly hair, which with its unkempt flare caused an impression of a special golden aura over his beautiful forehead. B.N.[43] was extraordinarily polite and well tutored. By the way, this good breeding did not interfere with him being unrestrainedly talkative. He could talk without stopping for entire hours, and whether what he had to say to his converser was interesting was not important to him.

It was not only women who took notice of his unusual eyes, but men likewise. As Mikhail Pantyukhov recollected:

> His eyes were of an interesting sort. They were a bright grey that seemed to beam several yellow golden rays, lightly misty.

Anton Chekhov was buried in Moscow on July 9, 1904. Some 4,000 were in the funeral procession. Although Bely was not able to

[42] As Joseph fled from Pharaoh's wife due to her enticement, Gen 39.
[43] Boris Nikolaievich

participate in the funeral, he did visit the grave of his favorite writer shortly after.

Bely was in Moscow during the Russo-Japanese War of 1905, and he felt its repercussions, recording it in just a few lines in his memoirs, *Beginning of the Century*.

> War is broken out. The fumes of the immense faraway fires seem to stretch even this far over Moscow. The defeated advance-guard at the front has made this known to us. Port Arthur rumbles. In the illustrations I see Stessel[44] and his regiment in formation on the field. The stately Moscow is become a pit. Tsushima[45] hangs in the air.

Before beginning the next set of courses in the history-philology department of Moscow University, Bely was able to travel with his mother during the second half of August 1904, on a pilgrimage to the Diveyevsky Monastery near Arzamas, also known as Sarov, 250 miles east of Moscow in Nizhni-Novgorod province. In earlier years Seraphim of Sarov was always a guiding star for Bely, his favorite saint, heavenly protector and representative of Orthodox culture. His friend Emilie Metner was living there at the time and they were able to spent one day together.

Upon returning to Moscow, he registered at the university and immediately attended philosophy seminars taught by the leading professors of the era, Lev Mikhailovich Lopatin (teaching Leibnitz) and Sergei Nikolaievich Trubetzky (teaching Plato). At the same time and with great enthusiasm, Bely started listening to a series of lectures on the history of philosophy from ancient times to the present. Among those also taking the same classes were his fellow symbolist and friend Ellis and Pavel Aleksandrovich Florensky, the future religious contemplator. Together with Bely Florensky

---

[44] Anatoly Mikhailovich Stessel, military general responsible for the loss of Port Arthur to the Japanese on January 2, 1905.

[45] Tsushima Island in the Korea Straight. Location of the defeat of the Russian naval fleet by Japan, May 27-28, 1905.

was a member of the Student's Historical-Philosophical Society, and he later became a professor at Moscow Religious Academy.

Prior to the university Florensky occasionally visited Bely at the Arbat apartment, and at the beginning of 1905, he corresponded with Bely on philosophical debates. Florensky even attended a few of the Sunday symbolist circles held at Bely's apartment, but due to his conservative Orthodox nature, Florensky was not comfortable there, and for the most part sat somewhere off to the side silent but listening closely, contemplating every spoken word. He had much respect for Bely, and to the extent that in April 1904, Florensky dedicated to Bely a poem of 8 lines he wrote.

It is incomprehensible as to where Bely acquired all the energy and time to do all of this: attending lectures and seminars at the university, composing his literature, his daily work as an editor at the magazine *Scales*, uninterrupted encounters with fellow activists and poets, personal public appearances, attending musical shows and concerts in the evenings and different types of social gatherings, reading philosophic classes in the original languages, spending Sundays with neo-Kantians and his fellows symbolists and poets, and continual correspondence with his many friends and acquaintances. Not every person can handle the ordeal of such an insane schedule, but Bely did and even promoted himself as an example and set the format for others.

Bely incidentally was in Petersburg on the day known as Bloody Sunday, January 9, 1905. He was at the Blok residence that day and heard about the events. Blok was incensed to no end.

From there Bely went to the Merezhkovsky residence, where people from all over the city arrived with more and more news of the number who were killed and injured. The 14 year-old daughter of Russian poet Feodor Sologub died in the shooting and she just went to watch the demonstration.

Petersburg society boiled from contempt. There was not one of the intelligentsia who did not condemn the conduct of the Imperial army. Those gathered at Merezhkovsky's decided to contribute by instituting their own demonstration. Zinaida Gippius,

Merezhkovsky's wife, took the initiative and proposed they all go to the Aleksandrinsky Imperial Theater and there protest by interrupting the spectacle and voicing their concerns.

Gippius and Bely went first, and a group of empathetic students accompanied them into the theater. They distributed themselves in various sections of theater, wherever there were vacant seats. When the first scene began they interrupted it with loud cries condemning the unwarranted execution of peaceful citizens. The majority in the theater supported their protest, the curtain then fell and the crowd entered the street. Gippius and Bely directed the crowd to the Free Economic Society, where another protest was being organized. Maxim Gorki was one of the many accompanying them. Father Gapon was the speaker there now agitating the crowd to utilize violent means against the government, since peaceful means had failed.

Bely was ready to join them, but Gippius, knowing better, was able to restrain him. Violence was not part of the symbolist's agenda or tenets. Bely would later write in his memoirs:

> The revolution had a tendency to dampen all else.

Bely did not have and could not afford a residence in Petersburg so the Merezhkovsky's magnanimously offered him a place in their home. Now the night-long vigils started, Bely and Gippius ascertaining and resolving thousands of problems, those dealing with polity, literature, philosophy, and mysticism, and even the most intimate details of their personal life. Gippius seemed to have this capacity to extract such information from Bely without any problem, but Gippius did not disclose much in this area. Merezhkovsky participated in the discourses occasionally, but only until midnight when he would isolate himself in his library. Attempting to go to bed he would terminate their conversation.

Eventually the Merezhkovskys left Russia for Europe in February 1906. Gippius had contracted tuberculosis and by now it was already serious and she needed constant care as well as better medical treatment that was not available in Russia. Merezhkovsky also had heart disease. The couple traveled back and forth between Russia and Europe until 1916, until World War I, now remaining in Russia for the interim. In 1919, the Merezhkovskys left Russia never to return, spending most of the balance of their years in Europe.

In Petersburg Bely saw Blok irregularly. They would walk together along the streets and shores, silent more than speaking. Bely and Lubov attended Richard Wagner's opera *Siegfried.* They also watched the brilliant dancer Isadora Duncan when she performed in Petersburg.

Returning to Moscow, Bely was overflowing with new feelings and plans.

During the Moscow uprising between December 7 and 17, 1905, Bely carried a gun with him as a means of self-defense. Although pacifist by nature of his theosophical convictions, the dangerous environment and events of the era seemed to put the fragile and physically weak Bely at a disadvantage, so he armed himself during this short interval.

# MARGARITA MOROZOVA, NINA PETROVSKAYA, LUBOV BLOK, AND ANNA SCHMIDT

Vladimir Solovyov had considerably influence on much of Bely's ideology and writing as well as his interaction with women. It seems that every woman that Bely met on his life's route, whether it be platonic or romantic or friendship, she would be an incarnation of one or another of the infinite figures of Divine Womanhood.

The first of such women was Margarita Kirillovna Morozova, a beautiful woman and wife of the businessman, industrial magnate, philanthropist, and patron of the arts, Mikhail Abramovich Morozov. They subsidized the publication of several Russian authors, and some of those who were identified as symbolists, as well as being the primary financier of the Moscow Artistic Theater. On one occasion at a symphony concert held at the Theater, Bely saw Margarita for the first time and she left an indelible impression of her beauty on Bely. Of course, he was not indifferent about this representative of the female gender and so here a mysterial passion literally consumed him. In Margarita Kirillovna Bely saw not an object of the gratification of lust, but a transcendent, celestial display of Eternal Womanhood. That evening he wrote her his first letter and in the morning anonymously sent it via the postal service. Initially she did not know her secret admirer, but ascertained it later. Bely always signed the letters as her knight. This letter and all those that followed it, and there were several, Margarita Kirillovna preserved her entire life. Here it is:

> Very respected Margarita Kirillovna! To a person who has long ago fallen asleep to life while alive; inexcusable is some of your destiny due to your boldness. For whom the world remains an illusion, he possesses greater right. Who in reality opened a second reality, he is outside of conditions. If my letter is not understandable to you, view it as not applying to you specifically, but to your ideas. All of us live through the twilight zone, whether dusk or dawn. Do you know nothing about the great grief beyond the dawn? The illuminated dawn turns everything around; it places people as if outside the world. The dawn's grief, this is solely what summoned this letter. What is nearby becomes distant; the distant – close. Not believing what you do not understand, you accept a repulsion toward such. You drown in an indolent sympathy. Do you know nothing about the great grief beyond the dawn? It is so difficult to remain without a prayer. Do not judge me. Do not judge prayer! We are exhausted due to the eternal dawn. We have accomplished all that was necessary, but the sun is not yet risen, the twilight is not ended. We have hung a peaceful flower on the past, turned our gaze to the distant Benares,[46] awaiting new eras. New eras did not bring news. New eras are shadowed by the past. The sun is not yet risen, the twilight is not ended. And we were the only ones to feel this with the dawn as earlier. We drank our glasses of tea to the bottom and at the bottom saw our personal refection, a funny one. We became extreme terrified, returned, turned back, as children. But all changed.
>
> I found a living symbol, an individual sign, all that I sought, but why has the time not arrived to accomplish this? You are my future dawn. In you are the impending events.

[46] The city Varanasi, India, the spiritual capital of Hinduism and Jainism.

You are the philosophy of the new era. For you I have denied love. You are the sealed one! Do you know this? When I walked to the edge of the abyss, I reached the end. "A great apparition appeared in the sky: A woman clothed in the son. Under her feet was the moon and on her head was a crown of twelve stars."[47] The mystery is unveiled. You are the sealed one! Are you aware of this? Beginning here it all seems to me that as though you are my comrade. Due to my yearning [for you] it is as though I have torn off an imperishable rose, I have moved the sky, I have drowned the past. You are the sealed one! Are you aware of this? I dared to write to you only when all that was burning and bitter became blindingly clear.

If you will ask about yourself, "Do I love you?" I will answer, "Insanely." But out of fear, in case you understand my love in a distorted manner, I declare that I do not love you at all. Here is insanity, having traversed all the stages of health, children's rhetoric, meekness, and an approach to the Kingdom of Heaven. Do not forget that my words are only a prayer that I confirm day to day, but only when on my knees. Prayer and prostration! Every person maintains his reason to live. This is on its own a symbol and prefigure. I do not need to know you as a person, because I comprehended you as a symbol and so announce this as a great prefigure. You are the concept of future philosophy.

Your knight.

No doubt Morozova felt the infantile infatuation of the anonymous author toward a married woman interesting if not humorous, not necessarily able to grasp its innocuous intent or symbolism. She soon received another letter from Bely. It contained a selection from one of the poems of Vladimir Solovyov dedicated to the concept of Eternal Womanhood. The following is part of the letter:

If in you resides the incarnation of the soul of the world, Sophia Divine Wisdom; if you are the symbol of a brilliant

---

[47] Rev 12:1

> female friend, a female friend of bright paths; if you are finally the radiant dawn, then illuminate the horizon of my expectations. My tale, my happiness! And not just mine. My incarnation of the revelation, my good news, my secret banner. The banner will unfurl. This will occur on the day of Ascension. I throw my cry into the star-filled sky. It is not you I look upon, but I look on that what is greater than you. It is approaching near as the time is near. I am inspired.
>
> Your knight.

The subsequent letter contained a repetition of some of the text of the initial 2, but also added the additional:

> Somewhere they love you to insanity. No, they do not love you, but it is something more, something greater. There you appear as a profound, profound symbol, something similar to a gilded cloud at sunset. There you are a nebulous tale, and not a reality.

Although his correspondence continued for several years he never disclosed his identity. It was not until the publication of Bely's *Second Symphony*, and until Margarita Kirillovna read it, that she noticed the resemblance and similarities between the letters she received and the text of the volume of poetry, and concluded that her Knight was Andrei Bely. In 1904, Margarita moved to Switzerland until returning to Russian a year later. She and Bely corresponded during the interval.

Margarita Morozova returned to Moscow in April 1905. Still having some religious inclinations, Morozova with a few others started the Moscow Religious and Philosophical Society and her home became a place of regular literary and philosophical gatherings, as well as having discussions dealing with social problems of the era. It was initially organized by the Merezhkovskys and Dmitri Filosofov.[48] Bely likewise attended and

[48] Dmitri Vladimirovich Filosofov, 1872-1940, Russian writer, religious thinker, newspaper editor and political activists. He fled Russia in 1919, and settled in Poland.

their friendship again materialized and the 2 frequently met. During her years in Moscow, Morozova became closely associated with Pavel Miluikov,[49] a professor at Moscow University and later a powerful figure in the interim government, and he likewise became friends with Bely.

Miluikov inserted a passage about Bely in his memoirs about Morozova:

> In the center of M.K.'s[50] festive accumulation was Andrei Bely. He bore an element of ostentatious ceremonialism that was rather interesting. Bely did not just plainly walk, but soared through the air as a supraterrestrial creation, hardly touching the floor. With his hands he would create these serpentine movements, as though he had wings and which M.K. would dearly reproduce. He did not just plainly speak. He announced and his words were enigmatic like the statements of the Sibyls. Some secret was hidden in them and inaccessible to laymen.

Bely recorded his relationship with Morozova during this period.

> Margarita Kirillovna supported me with her soft epic pathos during my difficult years. She sense the despair deep inside of me and summoned me to be open about it in order to ameliorate my pain. We did this on a cordial basis. Her eyes, so majestic, sparkling, blue, poured into my soul. Our conversation migrated from religious or moral deliberations, to the subject of the day, to concrete experiences of my personal life. Yes, I will say this directly. We would attend Morozova's residence for moral support.
>
> I loaded upon her all and more: regarding myself, of my attitudes toward people. I told her of my associations with A.A. and L.D.[51] Margarita Kirillovna would silently listen. I

---

[49] Pavil Nikolaievich Miluikov, 1859-1943, Russian secular and religious historian. He immigrated to France in 1921.

[50] Margarita Kirillovna's

[51] Aleksandr and Lubov Blok.

> recollect how she would tuck herself into a soft comfortable talma. The fiery brilliance of her diamond eyes would play with the experiences of your personal life.

Bely spent several days in July 1905, at the Morozov estate in Morkino Gorodische, near Popovka in Tver Province, and which solidified the relationship between the Morozovs and Bely. They picnicked together in the villa, went on boat rides, watched bonfires at night, and slept outside under the stars. Bely would regularly read his poetry, and Morozova recollected one occasion he did this:

> It seemed to be out of the ordinary, like a cute refrain on a song. The rhythm and even the tune was almost reminiscent of a gypsy song. It caused many of us to laugh out loud.

But Bely, as he mentioned in his memoirs, was not embarrassed by such a reaction from his listeners, he just modified his manner of addressing his audience.

Bely took his friend Emilie Metner, a musical critic, with him to the Morozov residence for their gatherings. He was also the symbolist publisher of *Musaget,* and older brother of the famous composer Nikolai Metner. As a result Morozova became friends with both brothers.

Morozova would regularly listen to conversations between Bely and Emilie Metner, and which drew her into them with fascination, yet she could not always decipher Bely's responses. Morozova recorded this in her memoirs:

> In some places he attracted me and had my interest, but I could not ascertain the entirety of what he was saying. And it always seemed to me that he did not yet find the total and detailed expression of all that was generated in his ingenious imagination.

According to Emilie Metner, Bely enjoyed an audience and especially the company of females, and he was always very relaxed in their presence. He would entertain them with his theatrics of reciting poems as though in a trance, or lying flat on the floor, or even while sitting under a table. Then Morozova, the hostess, would insist on Bely having some elegance in his behavior or polite manners at her residence. His extravagance irritated some of Morozova's academic friends, such as Pavel Miluikov and E.N. Trubetzky, who would often feel Bely's conduct to be an insult to their intelligence, and they would criticize Morozova for involving herself with the symbolist group.

As far as the Morozov philosophical gatherings were concerned, Bely wrote:

> She was completely helpless in her ability to decipher the currents of thinking, art, science, and society, yet Morozova possessed an immense capacity to get people who outside of her salon were irreconcilable and uncontrollable to reconcile and accustomed themselves to one another. This special character of the hostess consisted in her instituting in her residence a correct manner of discourse and a toleration of one another's concepts or antagonisms incurred during any of their discussions. As a result the guests conducted themselves such in order to provide the opportunity for the representatives of the most diverse ideological, political, philosophical and cultural currents and aspirations to explain their views.

Morozova in her memoirs emphasizes the issue that there was no romantic relationship between herself and Bely, and that she never experienced any passion toward him. Any adolescent infatuation on the part of Bely was quickly and early replaced by a simple friendship of people having similar traits. One item worth mentioning is that Morozova did not approve of Bely becoming closely associated with Asya (Anna Alekseevna) Turgeneva, the future Mrs Boris Bugaev, and she shared this opinion with Bely's mother. Morozova also refused to become captivated by the anthroposophy of Rudolf Steiner, to which both Bely and Turgeneva adhered. They eventually stopped attending the gatherings at the Morozov residence, however Bely and Morozova continued to value their friendship. Bely's poetic compositions of earlier years were solely allegorical as he felt Morozova to be another incarnation of the perfection of femininity, the Beautiful Dame, and this deeply occupied Bely's mind as he continued his poetry in that vein.

Many of the poems in the *Fourth Symphony*, published 1908, are dedicated to Morozova. Over 15 years later, Bely composed his best series of poetry yet, having the title, *First Meeting*. The heroine of the poem, Nadezhda Lvovna Zarina, is a portrayal of Morozova.

Bely continued with his letters of mysterial love toward Morozova, as he wrote to her in an anonymous letter in late September 1905, although she well knew it was him.

> Your knight.
>
> I want to sit quietly alongside you, maintain an infantile happiness and laugh and weep. To look in each other's eyes and think of nothing. Let my soul smile at your soul. So much about you has manifested in quiet dreams of my youth.
>
> I want to insanely tell you, to cry through the expanses, that you are a light to me. I do not know why I am so happy, why I do smile, when I gaze at you. But I still laugh, smile, rejoice. My soul radiates.
>
> You are the dawn. Your soul dawns. The days fall in the cup of eternity. And this cup, which is the soul, is filled with the past: day after day, drop after drop. Do you know I hear from a distance; perhaps the music of your soul is accessible to me. You are the bright ray of my life.
>
> Something again sings in my heart, clearly and pleasant to my soul. And this is the result of seeing you today. You are such a fairy tale to me. I need you so much, as a person and as a tale. Truly you are a symbol to me.

That summer of 1906, Morozova took her children to their estate in Tver Province, and in August invited Bely to join them. Quickly they became an indivisible pair. Every day for long periods they would stroll together, often to late into the night, and even the entire night to daybreak.

Morozova recorded her memories of these days:

> To listen to Boris Nikolaievich was a complete novelty for me, it was a pleasure that I had never experienced before. I have never met, not before, not after, a person with such – can I say this without exaggeration? – genuine poetic imagination. I sat and listened to him narrate the most marvelous, enchanting fables, his stories about what he was composing, or telling me of his intentions of writing. This was definitely genuine improvisation. I remember that his especially favorite subjects were snowstorms and twilight, especially the sunsets, which appeared to him as a leopard's skin, that is, gilded, scarlet, with scattered small dark clouds in the sky. He loved them so much, but was suspicious of them as though a premonition of something bad to occur. His vital poetic language which penetrated us with its unexpected astonishing figures, comparisons, unusual combinations of words, new words he devised that had implications of subtle connotations and disclosed deep matters where, it seems, a person would want to look.
>
> In front of us opened certain kinds of wide spaces, portrayals of nature were illuminated, and just with 2 or 3 tossed words. So with people, often our common acquaintances, friends, received something of his imagination in these improvisations, while occasionally the caricature of some form.
>
> In general, listening to Boris Nikolaievich, it always reminded me of Gogol, whom I especially loved from childhood, but of course Gogol was now modernized.
>
> Boris Nikolaievich was alone in his class in conversation, not to be compared to anyone. All of course were drawn to what he was saying, while his conversers listened to him as though mesmerized.

As in the recent past Bely again experienced an immense flood of creative inspiration. He isolated himself from associations and city and stayed at the family estate in Serebryanni Kolodez for almost a month, where he was able to concentrate on composition. Here without distraction he in almost one breath wrote one of his best arranged series of stanzas, *Green Meadow*. In allegorical poetic form he greeted the expected revolutionary renewal of the homeland. Inspirationally does Bely equate Russia with the *Green Meadow*, and also Sleeping Beauty, and with the Cossack Katerina, the tragic heroine of Gogol's *A Terrible Vengeance*.

Bely described the poem in a letter to Blok:

> In recent eras Russia slept. The route to life, as with the route to death, were equally distant from it. Russian is similar in a symbolic sense to the sleeping princess Katerina, whose soul was stolen by the terrible sorcerer in order to torture and torment her is some foreign castle.[52] Princess Katerina must consciously decide to whom she will give her soul: to her beloved husband, the Cossack Danilo who is fighting against the foreign attackers in order to preserve the native aroma of the greed meadow, or the sorcerer from the foreign country who is clothed in a fiery overcoat.
>
> This is why among the fruitless debates and visible severance from life, life itself, the life of the green meadow, beats the same in the hearts of the simple and the wise of the Russian population.

Later, Bely reflected on the symbolism of the composition in his memoirs:

> There in the birch tree silence, as in the sky, our souls meet. And when from these birch forest expanses we gaze at each other through the eyes of the birch forest expanses, a whirlwind unwittingly circulates around our souls. And the birch sky over us becomes our common single soul – the soul of

[52] Reference to Gogol's story, *A Terrible Vengeance*.

> the world. The sound of swallows, insanely stinging our ears, breaks the expanses and wounds the heart with silent closeness.
>
> Over us the blue bird of eternity sings, and the blue silent love overflows in our hearts, the love in the whiteness shining through the abyss. And we see one thing, hear one thing in the form of what cannot be formed. The instituted forms become the means by which to notice what still must be formed. Here begins a special category of symbolism, something indigenous to our epoch.
>
> I know we are together. We migrate in the same direction. We are eternal, unimpeded. Our souls are woven in an unimpeded dance of the great wind. This is the wind of liberation.
>
> Russia, awaken! You are not Princess Katerina to play this game. Know that your soul is worldwide. Return your soul to you. Awaken and you will be given wings of a great eagle in order to be delivered from the terrible prince who calls himself your father. But he is not your father, but a Cossack in a red overcoat, while the contender is the Fire breathing dragon gathering to steal you and to consume your child.[53]

Morozova who knew Bely well was not about to ignore her impression of him and likewise consigned it to her memoirs:

> Boris Nikolaievich's features, and especially his manner of speaking and his gestures, were very uniform. Regarding his superficial appearance, at first sight, what first struck your eyes was his high and projecting forehead, and his eyes, large, bright grey-blue, with black eyelashes curled upward, and which for the most part were widely opened and watchful, not blinking but focused. His eyes were very impressionable and constantly changing. His forehead was framed by a few rare hairs. His face was oval and possessed a very soft trait. He

[53] Bely here combines the dragon of Rev 12 wanting to devour the child of the woman clothed in the sun and the heroine and other portions of Gogol's story mentioned above.

> was not very tall and was rather thin. He walked in a funny manner, as though stealthily, often looking around, oscillating as though on tiptoes and rocking as he motioned forward.
>
> Over his entire entity was an impression of great nervousness and some kind of special receptivity, it seems that the entire time he was listening to something. When he spoke with agitation about something, then he would immediately stand, straighten, throw his head back, his eyes would become dark and almost close, his eyelids somehow quiver and his voice – which in general was rather vocal – would drop in pitch, and his entire figure became somewhat stately or triumphant.
>
> And sometimes the opposite occurs. His eyes expand all the more, not moving, as though he is not solely listening to something within himself, but something that is coming from somewhere else, some kinds of voices, and he leans his head to one side, silent and not moving he looks around and is soundlessly muttering something, only his lips are moving saying, "Yes, yes."
>
> When he listens to someone, then as an indication of agreement he widely opens his eyes, he opens his mouth in an astonishing manner, and silently whispers, "Yes, yes," and nods his head several times.

Morozova was the object of Bely's poetry of love and solely allegorical. Of course this did not annoy her husband, knowing it was innocuous and an adolescent infatuation if anything. He knew that it could not last forever.

One of Bely's first sensual loves was Nina Petrovskaya, who later herself became a writer. She was one of the most popular and tragic figures of the Silver Age. Her husband was Sergei Sokolov, who published verses under the pseudonym Krechetov, but more popular as the owner of the book publishing house *Grif,* and later the editor of the magazine *Pass (Pereval).*

As soon as the Argonauts materialized Sokolov joined them. Nina would accompany her husband to the meetings. She was incredibly beautiful, distinguished by her independent views and liberated conduct. During this period she carried on a turbulent although fatal romance with Balmont, and her husband Sergei knew about it. For Bely, Petrovskaya initially, visibly and tangibly, incarnated the duality of the Womanhood Principle – divine and sinful. It was at this time that Bely wrote:

> In the atmosphere the Eternal Womanhood is sensed: the Woman clothed in the sun. But the great whore is not slumbering.

Associations at the literary assemblies were initially normal but eventually and speedily they grew into intimate relations, Petrovskaya was 19 years old and Bely was 23 at this time in 1903. Initially Bely attempted to route the nascent sensation along the same trail of mysterial love that he blazed in the past with other voluptuous women. Bely at the time composed a series of romantic poems in a ballad titled *Tradition*, and dedicated it to Sergei Sokolov. Bely depicted himself as a prophet, while his immortal beloved Nina was depicted as the prophetess or oracle Sibyl.

> He was a prophet.
> She was Sibyl in the temple.
> Their love like a flower
> Burned red in the evening incense.
>
> Under the rays of his eyebrows
> Shine gazes of fiery lights.
> Hanging curls of hair
> As wine cascading like golden foam.
>
> He said to her, "Through love, death
> Is defeated, and through death,
> Passion is defeated.

I will sail away and again will descend
To dry ground, as a deity,
Displaying my face."

And the waves of time beat.
The years passed. Under the shade
Of the temple she aged lonely,
Among the pillars an azure incense.

And the heavens were again intoxicated
With the smile of marital sunset.
And it glowed as though gilded,
And in deep purple.

However the abundantly loving Nina attributed little to an abstract mutual association between them. Quickly she was successful in drawing out of Bely corresponding and totally sensual sensations. The passionate romance did not last long, less than 6 months. It terminated just as fast as it originated.

When Bely was totally immersed in this entangled romance with Nina Petrovskaya, his correspondence with Blok acquired a rotating character, but it was Bely's sole outlet, allowing him to hope for the best. In the middle of April 1904, Bely wrote to Blok:

> Dear, dear Aleksandr Aleksandrovich. Thank you for the letter. It made me warm and comfortable, and comfortable in a state of discomfort. I remember the fiery sunsets, the green grasses and many lilac flowers. The aroma of the fields and indescribable bliss has now departed from me. It is spring, and soon to be autumn, but even in November somehow spring returned to me and sang. But how do I know that when I am broken and weakened, fleeing from insanity, I will arrive at a green forest and in my exhaustion I will die forever in the flowers. You will understand me and not start to inquire about anything. I kindly love you for his, as though all of this has already occurred. I am in no position to speak of intelligent

> items pertaining to God and people. I am tired and want only to think about flowers and about nothing else.
>
> Flowers, flowers, the landscape! We will wander in the forests. Silver streams ripple through the sedge.

Blok's response to Bely's dilemma was in just as allegorical terms as his complaint.

On his return to Moscow at the end of summer 1904, Bely finally and immutably realized that there was a fated inversion entering into his life. He decisively explained the situation to Nina Petrovskaya, but she mistakenly understood the situation in a sensual application, that another woman, Lubov Dmitrievna, Blok's wife, was taking her place in Bely's heart.

Although the abandoned Nina was hurt, feelings previously unknown to Bely overfilled him. Life now acquired for him a new tint of exuberating joy. At the end of summer 1904, Bely wrote to Blok:

> Life is so beautiful, so life-providing, airy. I want to sing, rejoice, shed tears of joy, because I conquered life in suffering. This suffering rang bells of joy in me. Suffering smiles on this white, blindingly bright day and the blinding teeth of a sparkling face that I just saw on the street is happily laughing! O, I am so grateful for the day of my birth. My life is so beautiful.

On the eve of the romance's termination Bely wrote a letter to Nina indicating reconciliation and forgiveness, and likewise in symbolist terms:

> I entrust the spirits of the wind to deliver to you my many kisses. Dear one, dear one, all of this is unessential. I love, I pray, I rejoice for you. I kiss your little image. O, what joy it is for me to see you, my dear, my dear. To stare into your eyes and smiling without words. My dear one, may Christ be with you, He is with you and I am consoled.

Bely's letter to Petrovskaya is interesting as a reflection of long lost love and testifies to his poetic talent and even in a dear John letter from the opposite gender. Yet Bely felt he lost some of his innocence with this affair with a married woman. His view of the opposite gender was supposed to be representative of higher truths, meaning, a symbol of spiritual beauty and divine love. The occasion of defiled adulterous love soiled Bely's immaculate vision of the purpose of the female, and especially outside of a legitimate marriage.

Bely recorded his intimate reaction to the event in his private diary:

> What occurred is what brewed over the course of a few months – my fall from Nina Ivanovna. Instead of daydreams of mysterial brotherhood and sisterhood, what occurred was plainly a romance. I was perplexed. In addition to this I was stunned. I cannot say that Nina Ivanovna was not attracted to me. I loved her in a brotherly manner, but I did not feel any deep true love toward her. It was clear to me that all that occurred between us from my side was an impulse of sensuality.
>
> This is why I consider the romance with Nina Ivanovna as a fall. I saw that she had deep feelings toward me, but with me a brotherly attitude prevailed, but then my sensation changed under the circumstances. I did not quickly ascertain this. This is why I could not immediately put all of this for Nina Ivanovna to see. I sensed bewilderment, questioning, and primarily I felt severance. I tried to explain this to Nina Ivanovna, that it needs to be Christ between us. She agreed and then suddenly it happened, the rupture. The mysterial and the theurgic suffered defeat.

Three decades pass and then in Bely's second volume of memoirs does he, and not without some upheaval of feelings, evaluate his early romance with Nina Petrovskaya:

Having a dual attitude toward everything, sick, tortured by an unfortunate life, with a distinct infection of psychopathy, she was melancholy, gentle, well-meaning, and capable of active discussion and social association, almost to the point of insanity. She lived and experienced all that was inserted into her ears and with such a radiant force. Her life was always exclusively whatever were the words coming out of others, turning life into a delirium and into abracadabra. Always some strange impression would grasp me whenever I crossed the threshold of her home.

Unconsciously she enticed me into her bundled role: teaching me life. And she would strengthen within me the illusion that I am indispensable to her, that without me she would perish. So my worries over her started to unconsciously fill my days, and filled it in the following manner: my visits to her residence became as frequent as almost a daily occurrence. Conversations between the 2 of us prolonged. It seemed that of all living entities she alone correctly understood me. She was kind and acute and considerate and she was excessively sympathetic and adaptable to the point of any violation of mine.

Getting upset with something said she did not understand, she would somehow make do, independent of what would flare inside of her. She experienced attacks of depression to the extent of having psychological spasms, to obsessive deliriums. At one time she was prepared to grab a revolver and shoot at herself, at others, to take vengeance on an insult supposedly imposed on her. In attacks of the most horrifying hysteria she would talk to herself endlessly, and babble nonsense at others. She was a congenital liar as with every hysteric and had a tendency to believe lies and any slander of others or herself. Anything said to her in confidence she would distort and tell others. I learned Balmont's secrets from her, and in turn Balmont learned my secrets from her.

She destroyed relationships, manipulated people against one another people to the point of one wanting a duel with the other. She got friends to quarrel with one another and so become enemies. She attempted suicide due to the effect of the heavy pressure on her conscience. An atmosphere of danger and ruin and fatalism seemed to surround her.

However Petrovskaya felt matters still needed to be concluded with Bely, especially with Bely being drawn to a new representation of spiritual feminism: Lubov Dmitrievna, the wife of Aleksander Blok and daughter of the famous chemist, Dmitri Mendeleev. As the situation seemed to Petrovskaya, Bely's spiritual or symbolic concept of the female gender was corrupted by her sensuality and so he found another that seemed to be the allegorical image of divine yet corporeal perfection that Bely sought.

Petrovskaya's marriage to Sergei Sokolov failed at about this time.

Feeling she was dumped, as opposed to realizing that Bely needed to escape for his own mental stability, Petrovskaya took a fatalist approach. She started to carry in her purse a loaded revolver, not having yet decided whom she will shoot: the lover who abandoned her or herself; who will be the unfortunate sacrifice. Later Bely related that Petrovskaya attempted to shoot him, but the gun misfired. He was somehow able to calm the desperate woman, getting his friend Valeri Brusov involved. Subsequent to Bely, Petrovskaya's next victim and romance was Valeri Brusov, who likewise wrote and dedicated some of his verses to her. Brusov was 11 years older than Petrovskaya and she was 20 at this time. Matters went well between Petrovskaya and Brusov for some 7 years and then soured.

Brusov wrote his novel *The Fiery Angel*, published 1908 by *Scorpion*, having the undertones or plot based on the romance of Petrovskaya with both Bely and himself. Petrovskaya was the part of Renata, a young and beautiful but demon-possessed woman, while the knight-contenders Ruprecht and Heinrich were Brusov and Bely respectively.

It was not as if Petrovskaya would let Bely off the hook. She manipulated him against Brusov as though Brusov was an interloper, telling Bely she still loved him and he still loved her.

Bely fell for the intrigue and as a result he became jealous of Brusov and this caused a rupture in the relationship between the 2 poets. Bely recorded in his memoirs:

> Brusov mesmerizes me with all of his conversations, he turns my life into gloom. I have no doubt of Brusov's genuine reasons for such a strange attention he has toward me. The reason is simple: Brusov is in love with N.I. Petrovskaya and is working at making this mutual. N.I. loves me and tells him so. In addition to this, she forces him to listen to her hysterical exaggerations of my bright demons. Brusov maintains toward me a sharp feeling of hatred and curiosity. He would destroy me if he could, and so take vengeance on me for humiliating him, although this was never my intent.
>
> He cannot be satisfied with conversations with me on topics that interest me. He strives with his powerful hypnosis to influence me, to corrupt me, to depress me.
>
> A corridor has formed between hell and I. Along the corridor someone is running, catching up with me. I feel this person running is the enemy. His shadow is already on me. The enemy is Brusov.

As time progressed and Petrovskaya drew close to Brusov and became an inspiration to his writings, Bely slowly severed relationships with the both of them.

Bely and Blok were the same age, within a month difference. Blok made his home in Petersburg, but visiting Moscow on a regular basis and especially his relatives, Mikhail and Olga Solovyov, who lived in the same apartment complex as Bely's family. Bely's association with Blok initially started indirectly with the opportunity for Bely to read some of Blok's yet unpublished poetry that he left with Solovyov's after a recent visit. Bely was ecstatic over it due to its quality.

Sometime in 1902, Bely requested that Olga put him in contact with Blok, with an address for them to correspond. Interesting that simultaneously, Blok read Bely's article published in *World of Art*, titled *Forms of Art*, in the final issue of 1902. Bely wrote on the connection between prose and music, and this motivated Blok to contact Bely and further the development of this concept. Olga passed the mailing addresses of each to the other. In the beginning of 1903, the 2 wrote letters to each other, mailing them a day apart and the other not knowing, so the letters crossed paths in transit between Moscow and Petersburg. One of the concepts close to Bely that the 2 discussed in correspondence was "eternal return," a concept that Bely learned from his studies of Nietzsche and which he adapted into his own philosophy. Bely's respect of Nietzsche extended further because of Nietzsche's musical talent, including composition, and his ability to apply it to philosophy. Bely as a result felt music had the ability to cause eternal return within a person. Bely wrote the following regarding it:

> Music internally echoes and so has its external expression in allowing meaning to be understood, and this closest of all pertains to envisioning what is beyond our frontiers. Here we find a clear reflection of what is beyond the corporeal. Goodness is ever extending, but evil is likewise ever extending. These contradictory reflections echo and struggle in music. It is the art of movement. It is not without good reason that in the *Symphonies*[54] there are always two contending themes: the musical theme in diverse variations, but also the redemption through the fire of dissonance. Rhythm as the repetition of a regular pulse is tied with the concept of Eternal Return, and is musical based on its fundamental essence
>
> Nietzsche, a majestic stylist and author of the understanding of *The Spirit of Music*,[55] was likewise a beautiful musician and even a composer. He was the first to exemplify this in the environment of the Return.

[54] Bely refers to his 4 volumes of poetry with the title of Symphony.
[55] Perhaps referring to Nietzsche's *On Music and Words*.

Soon however they migrated to the subject that was both their favorite – Eternal Womanhood. Bely took the role of being the greater advocate and promoter as well as being the more impatient and so Bely wrote to Blok on the topic:

> First of all I write to you regarding one point that is important to me. Here we write to one another regarding her – the Radiant Female Friend, and between us is this a distinct tune as through we already know what pertains to Her. We know who She is, and from where we speak regarding Her, although earlier this did not exist, referring to the situation that we have not yet looked at one another right in the eyes.
>
> The methods of symbols are good; they are best of all. What is logically indefinable is defined psychologically. It is on this basis that I love the speech of imagery more than all else. This is the shortest route into profound comprehension, but often it is also necessary for the surface to provide its mirror reflection of the depths. It is important for us to walk the same route logically as we walk it intuitively. This is why I turn to you with a direct question and without any preconceived thoughts. Define what you think of Her. It is very, very important to me, and more important than you think.

Blok responded vaguely and abstractly, not wanting to share something of allegorical depth with a person he had not personally met. Yet Blok did invite Bely, sight unseen, to his wedding to Lubov Dmitrievna Mendeleeva, and even to be his best man, planned for the middle of August, 1903. Bely had to cordially refuse as he had to accompany his father that summer for a vacation to the Caucasus Mts, where he could be treated for an illness. Blok's invitation arrived at the end of April, but within a month Nikolai Bugaev died unexpectedly, and which overturned Bely's life and his future was now unpredictable. However correspondence with Blok in the vein of the topic continued.

In March 1903, in the third issue of the almanac, *Northern Flowers*, a series of poems composed by Blok was published, titled, *Verses about the Beautiful Dame.* Of the 23 compositions that

Blok submitted to Brusov the editor for publication, he only selected 10 of them. It was something still a novelty for the general Russian public, and even though Brusov aligned himself with the symbolists he still had apprehensions about the success of Blok's verses. Lubov Dmitrievna, Blok's bride, was the embodiment of the Beautiful Dame.

Blok spent the period from the middle of June to the middle of July, 1903, in Germany. Beginning at about this time, Bely began correspondence with Blok's bride, Lubov Dmitrievna. The relationship between the 2 was purely spiritual imagery, she being the personification of Eternal Womanhood, depicting divine femininity in her conduct and display. So did Bely write to her:

> You are a bright Angel, you are a majestic Angel. You are the goddess of my corporeal desires. I will be infatuated without end, I will be passionate, I will be your devotee and slave. You will be and I will be – One. Regarding this whirlwind, regarding these sweet and insane moments that we will never forget our entire lives, I relate this to you for you to impress it on your memory. In your eyes, in your movements, in your features, in your shivering hands, I saw and recognized this, that you are what will be. I am infatuated. Do you know this? I am infatuated to the deepest of depths, completely penetrated by love.
>
> You know that I love all that is in you, all that I know and when I even do not know. Even with all else alive in the world, your gilded shade covers me always. All that is valuable to me is connected one way or another with you. Never forget your eternal superiority, your majestic right over my life. It is gracious and destined for me.
>
> Dear, dear, my sole entity, my beloved, holy, incomparable, favorite, my sun, my light, my treasure, my life, and more. There is no way for me to enunciate all. Believe me. I am with you. My entire life will be spent at your feet. I am tormented with love, I triumphantly love, it is astral love, loving you with a worldwide love, You, you alone, the single one, my pearl, my sole holy, great and omnipotent entire. You are all, all, all.

> Never, never has something like this occurred to me, nothing like this has even been. It is terrifying for me to love in this manner. To love this way and not realize it is better. These words, what type of words are these: pitiful, stony, powerless? Do you believe? Do you believe? Repeat to me if you believe all of this? Repeat, my divine spark. Repeat, Virgin, Theotokos, Mother of light! Repeat, my little love.
>
> Thank you so much for showing me the light.
>
> I kiss your burning trail. I passionately await you, my fiery queen. The glow of the sunrise. I love you, the little girl with golden curls. I love you with more strength than I can possibly possess.
>
> My God, how I want to see you soon and forget all of this from its start. When I see you, I want to think of nothing else, or even to speak, but only to stare into your eyes. My dear one, my beauty, my beloved, my happiness.

So did Lubov Dmitrievna present herself to Bely the first time, in this manner did she display herself in his inspired dreams. Lubov as a woman was far from a beauty in the classical sense, and even in her younger years. When she was in the company of other women there was nothing physically attractive about her. Lubov was full-figured with wide hips but not obese, and she had a nicely shaped head, although setting on a torso that was disproportionately larger. So did her contemporaries describe her from their fault-finding point of view.

But if a person was able to catch the inner essence of Lubov, they would definitely agree and state that there was no woman more beautiful than she that they ever met. So did other women say about her. The first one to conclude this was Blok himself; the second was Sergei Sokolov, and the third, of course, Bely. They all came to the same conclusion and independent of one another that Lubov Dmitrievna was no one other than the contemporary corporeal incarnation of the concept of Sophia the Divine Wisdom.

Nonetheless, Bely still did not attend Blok's wedding to Lubov Dmitrievna that was held in Shakhmatovo, a suburb of Moscow. Exhausted due to the graduation examinations at the university, and the impact of his father's death, this had a bad effect on Bely's health. That autumn Blok did compose a couple of verses and which he dedicated to Bely. One of them was accompanied by some quotes from Bely's own poetry dedicated to the concept of the Beloved of Eternity. In poetic and partially allegorical form Blok responded to the questions posed by Bely back in April.

Blok referred to the incarnation of the concept of Eternal Womanhood as the Maiden of the Rainbow Gates, who for a long while already illuminated the furthest corners of Bely's enthusiastic soul with its unfading radiance. She was a continuation of the imagery provided earlier of Blok's Beautiful Dame. During the short interval of his family happiness Blok also realized that no one else other than his spouse Lubov Dmitrievna could even get near to contending to be the corporeal incarnation of the Woman clothed in the sun.

So it was not until the following year, in January 1904, that Bely finally personally met both Blok, with whom he corresponded much already, and his newly-wedded wife Lubov Dmitrievna, of whom he wrote about so much. Blok was 23 years of age and his wife was a year younger. Bely was so excited about the encounter that he recorded the event for his friend Irina Odoyevskaya, and several times in his memoirs and with interesting details:

> January 10, 1904, during a frosty and clear bright day, the doorbell rings. They ask for me. I walk out and see a nicely dressed woman wearing furs. A tall student, removing his coat, hangs it, tightens the gloves to keep his hands warm, he wears a warm hat.
>
> The Bloks!
>
> He had wide shoulders, a nice suit that fit him well, with a thin belt around his waist, a high collar that seemed to be choking his neck. The poet's wife was dressed pronouncedly conservative. In the air was the smell of perfume. She was young and joyful, and they seemed to be an elegant couple. No, no. Is this Aleksandr Blok? This young man, whose face glows a bright red as though it was wind burned? Looking closer he was not so young. And not standing like a stately soldier. He

restrained his actions, but gently moved appearing to be shy, his head was slightly bent to one side, and he smiled at me. He walked toward me with his wide only blue eyes, almost on tip toes, and staring at me to get as good a look at me as possible in just a few moments.

"Boris Nikolaievich?"

We embraced.

So with great emotionalism and even nervousness did Bely narrate his first encounter with Blok. The couple could not stay long, but promised to return the next evening for dinner and they left. After this fateful meeting Bely did not sleep the entire night and did not even retire for the evening. He just laid around his apartment.

Bely continued in his memoirs:

I feared not living to see the next day. I guess I was in love with him too much. I feared that his train might run off the tracks, that he would die in some railway catastrophe, and not be able to spend time with me.

But at the specified time – and right to the minute – the doorbell rang. I went into the porch, but the maid already let them in. I looked at him and shook. Never in my life, not before, not after, did I experience such burning clumsiness.

I shook hands with him and for some reason grabbed Lubov Dmitrievna's muffs, and then realizing what I did, I gave them back to her and apologized. I noticed that Blok was no less uncomfortable than I was, but he had good control of himself. She was completely calm and casually looked at herself in a mirror, adjusting her bright curls under her large hat with ostrich feathers. She seemed like a very sociable person.

My mother dominated the conversation and how boring and heavy it was for me. Once my conversation started with Sasha,[56] from that very minute, unconsciously I started to love

[56] Russian diminutive for Aleksandr.

him and in a new manner. I immediately felt that our encounter will not pass into oblivion or be futile.

Nothing especial occurred that evening at dinner as they just became acquainted with one another, or the time together in the subsequent days. No such "love triangle" occurred, as many gossiped in later years and some actually included in their biographies of the Bloks and Bely. All was social and literary oriented and since there was much in common with both Blok and Bely in the symbolist world.

Over the next 2 weeks the Bloks spent time in Moscow reacquainting themselves with old friends and the literary circles. Blok however was disappointed with both Brusov and Balmont, but he was infatuated and sincerely excited with the young group of symbolists, all of whom in unison recognized Blok as Russia's supreme poet. All were fascinated with Blok's enchanting verses and especially the manner that he recited some of them to them. Blok seemed to be organically connected with the poems as he read them.

Prior to the Bloks leaving Moscow, he and Bely and Sergei Sokolov got together and created their special tripartite union or secret club, calling themselves the Brotherhood of the Knights of the Beautiful Dame. Lubov became their Wife clothed in the Sun, Sophia the Divine Wisdom, the Maiden of the Rainbow Gates, and the Beautiful Dame, all embodied in one person. Apparently they also had a streak of humor deep inside of them, apart from the seriousness of their writings and their religious and philosophical devotion.

All of a sudden in Bely's life a new impulse materialized. He informed Moscow University of his intention to receive a second diploma, this one in both history and philology.

During the summer of 1905, Bely decided to visit Blok, in Shakhmatovo at the time, and took a friend with him, one his close Argonauts, Aleksei Petrovsky, employed at the library at the Rumyantsev Museum in Moscow. Just before leaving, Sergei Sokolov decided to join them, now finishing college. Meeting again the Blok couple, Bely composed a poem pertaining to the 2 of them, title *Prince and Princess*. At this time, Bely still considered Lubov to be the incarnation of the concept of the Woman clothed in the sun.

Everything seemed to go well with this vacation, returning to nature, with their group and Bely recorded the event in his memoirs.

> Never will I forget such quiet paths in all my working and maturing days. I will not forget this beautiful period of my life, as monotone as it was, although inwardly it was so turbulent. A.A. and L.D.[57] did not live in the main house, but in a more comfortable small cottage with 2 rooms, cover with flowers. If my memory is correct, the cottage was something out of a fairy tale. I could almost hear the footsteps of fairies on the steps of the terrace, but it was the happy and quiet A.A. and L.D. entering. A.A. wearing his traditional Russian shirt. L.D. wearing a rose colored loosely-fitting dress.
>
> Our conversation was simple and the topics of the conversation intermittently changed.
>
> Our sitting together in the mornings truly migrated aimlessly into a golden amble along the shores of some kind of sea, across which suddenly a ship will arrive – for me it was the Argo – and sail us across the sea to some New Light.
>
> Very often we would move to the adjoining room, expansive and bright, with comfortable and soft furniture nice arranged. L.D. seated herself with her feet on the sofa, while we settled into the cushioned chairs. Quite often, standing in front of them, I would begin to develop some sort of theory, and while building an improvised lectern. Essentially, the vein of my words, theory and lecture was not to try and convince those present, but as a litmus test paper of my own sort, watching their reaction whether it would turn purple or bright purple or dark blue.

[57] Aleksandr and Lubov Blok.

> A.A. was able to splatter the fabric of my thoughts with different shades of his thoughts: humor, silence, curiosity, trust. "You know, Boris, I nonetheless think that is it not this way." So did A.A. in one phrase embellish his attitude to one or another of my philosophical, religious or aesthetic questions, while I unconsciously provided him the means to embellish them, shoving at him various fabrics based on my theories, utopias and conclusions.
>
> From here it became clear that he was for me at this time his own sort of embellishment of my aspirations, providing me value and impulse.

In his memoirs, Bely recollects how in the morning prior to their departure from Shakhmatovo, they all gathered together and it was impossible for them not to feel sorrowful that the short communal residence was ending. Bely recorded in his memoirs:

> When they brought the horses, it felt like we were returning to an old world from this special world where we felt ourselves as though in new expanses, as though in a new era of time. Here we experienced a genuine illumination.

Beginning early October 1905, Bely's attraction toward with Morozova began its decline, and was replaced with an increase toward Lubov Blok. But with Lubov, the infatuation became an obsession and as a result caused upheaval in the marriage of Aleksandr and Lubov. Bely seemed to want concessions from Blok regarding access to his wife, which Blok was not about to concede. Bely now crossed the line of decency and wrote a demanding and tactless letter to Blok. In return Blok responded in a letter dated October 2, but with some criteria to ameliorate the situation, but the terms were not acceptable to Bely, as Blok accused Bely of treason, replacing his previous concept of Lubov being the personification of the Beautiful Dame with mundane motives.

This likewise agitated Lubov and she responded with a castigating letter on October 27, to somehow terminate the matter.

Boris Nikolaievich:

I no longer want to received your letters until such a time that you redeem the lies in your letter to Sasha. You have forgotten that I am with him. If he perishes, so will I. And if I am saved it will only be because of him and only him. Remember that the tone of your superiority with which you approached him is intolerable for me. Until you redeem him I will not change my disposition. It is not right for you to recognize me while discarding him. Even then, I do not believe in this attitude of yours toward me. Now you are very alien to me.

L. Blok

Bely would not concede. He more and more contended for his indisputable right to Lubov. So rather than possessing an objective attitude, a torrent of emotion enveloped Bely and to nobody's benefit, and he could not realize that he was the cause of it.

After the revolutionary unrest and demonstrations of October 1905, Bely realized how infinitesimal the disagreement was between himself and the Bloks, and especially when compared to infinity, and they were professional people. Yet Bely's love for Lubov did not leave him, but seemed to be reinforced every day. Bely decided to travel to Petersburg and meet with him.

The encounter occurred at some neutral restaurant, and each felt themselves to blame, as torturous each had to endure the event. Bely was in Petersburg 3 weeks this occasion, living with his friends the Merezhkovskys. However the intentions of the encounter backfired and Lubov sensed a personal attraction toward Bely, although she had an obligation toward her husband.

Time for Bely to return to Moscow so the Bloks accompanied him to the train station, this was November 1905.

Shortly after his return, Blok received a letter from Lubov:

All that you write to me is so close, so close to me. And I am so happy and smile over all of it. I very much want for to you to return to Petersburg, to again visit us. Then you will personally see my attitude toward you, and even if I should not say anything. Can you arrange your affairs to come here at the end of February? You know how much we want this.

Loving you, L. Blok

Lubov's internal tug-of-war of continued about a year, inclining toward her husband, then to Bely, then back again, yet living with her husband.

Bely returned to Petersburg, arriving about January 15, 1906. The first thing he did was to send a bouquet of flowers – hydrangeas – to Lubov by courier. That evening he went to their apartment. Between the Bloks and Merezhkovskys, Bely's days were saturated with happy visits and associations, and which continued until the Merezhkovskys left for Paris on February 25. Before leaving Gippius recorded a note in her diary regarding the relationship between Lubov and Bely:

> Lubov Dmitrievna cannot but love him. They are plainly created for one another.

In a private conversation Bely was able to convince Lubov to finally tie the knot of the future solely with him. The rupture occurred the evening of February 26, after the 3 of them watched Wagner's *Parcifal.* Lubov recollected the event in her memoirs some 30 years later.

> Sasha was in a sled with his mother, while I was with Boris. For a long while I knew his love, I accepted it flirtatiously and supported it, but not allowing it to cause discord in my feelings. I easily arranged his interest in me within the frame of a sibling relationship. But here – and I remember where, on the shore near the home of Peter the Great – he said something to me and I turned my face to him and became petrified. Our encountering glances were so close, and this was it, this was it. Poison is so sweet. My world, my poetry, where

> Sasha did not want to return. The entire time I sensed foolishness, nonsense, impossibility.

So after long doubts and oscillations Lubov Dmitrievna Blok finally decided to divorce her husband Aleksandr under the conditions that Bely take her to Italy. Now what remained was the most difficult for both of them: to explain this to her husband. Of course he was able to guess it all anyway, but they had to discuss the conditions of separation in a personal conversation.

Bely described the conversation in his memoirs as though it was a cheap novel:

> The monstrous tragic spring of 1906. I could not depart from Lubov Dmitrievna. She demanded, herself demanded, that I give her an oath to deliver her, even against her will. While Sasha was silent, abysmally quiet, or maybe he attempted to be funny, or maybe walked away to drink some red wine. And then we went into the living room where Sasha was now. So I gave her my oath. Her eyes spoke, "Not necessary." But I was ruthless and said, "We need to talk." And he, his lips vibrating from the pain, smiled through the pain, quietly, "So am I to be happy about this?" And he smiled at me in some infantile manner.
>
> I told him about the situation as through defending myself. He did not respond and the two of us silently left the room and quietly closed the door behind us. She started to weep, and I started to weep with her. I felt ashamed for what I just did, and also for her. But he was so valiant, so courageous.

So did Blok indirectly agree with the decision of Lubov and Bely, as psychologically devastating it was for him. She subsequently provided Bely several reasons for her final decision, yet she was reluctant to finalize it. As Bely recorded:

> She asked me to temporarily go to Moscow and to leave her alone, to give her time to reorganize her thoughts. At the same time she says she loves me more than she does Alex. Alex., and

> that I should fight on her behalf for her to select the path of the two of us together. I gave her something of a promise that from this time forward I consider us united in spirit and that I will not permit her to remain with Alex. Alex.

In order to go abroad, to where the couple decided, demanded money and much of it. Bely left for Moscow to somewhere acquire some. Lubov wrote to Bely in Moscow supporting their decision, how difficult it was for her. But the subsequent letter indicated some despair in her decision. The next letter confirmed her love for Bely. Lubov in the lettering following adamantly states that her love for husband Blok had returned, and the additional letters alternated between the 2 positions. It was obvious Lubov was confused in her thinking and was unsure of herself and doubt whether her selected choice was the right one. The letters continued until March 20.

What finally terminated the indecision was Lubov becoming seriously ill, either bronchitis or influenza, or perhaps pneumonia, based on the symptoms noted in the memoirs. Blok wrote to Bely for him to remain in Moscow until her health recovers, but by the time that Lubov recovered from the illness, so did her disposition change. Due to her husband's and in-laws' influence, Lubov decided to postpone her departure with Bely to Italy at least to autumn. The primary reason was Blok's state examinations were approaching at the university and he needed his wife's support and help to pass as well as restfulness and a clear frame of mind.

Lubov's next letter was April 10, 1906. She tells him not to visit her should he be in Petersburg until her husband passes all his examinations. Then their family will spend the summer at their estate in Shakhmatovo, and then in the autumn she will travel with Bely to Europe. This most recent letter overwhelmingly irritates Bely in addition to the content of Lubov's previous letters. So regardless of the warning Bely departs for Petersburg, realizing that all of this was to his disadvantage. When Bely did meet with Lubov, Blok was at the university taking his exams. All Lubov told him was the same as she wrote in her most recent letter: to wait until autumn. Bely left Petersburg back to Moscow with a heavy heart.

What did not help matters is that Blok started to drink and heavily due to the depression the impact his unstable marital situation was causing him.

After Bely left Petersburg, leaving the Blok residence, he decided to spend part of the summer at their family estate at Serebryanni Kolodez, and part of it with Sergei Solovyov at their summer estate in Dedova. But once the Bloks left Petersburg for their summer estate in Shakhmatovo, Bely wrote to Lubov almost every day, but she did not answer the letters. Later he discovered that she burnt each letter without reading it and as soon as she received it.

In the middle of June 1906, Bely and Sergei Sokolov stayed with the Bloks in Shakhmatovo. This new occasion did not have the same vitality or excitement as the previous, and it seemed to be a drama and burden rather than an enjoyment and relaxed. The hospitality aspect of the Bloks seemed to have changed, although Bely and Sokolov did their best to have an enjoyable time.

Prior to leaving Shakhmatovo, Bely gave Lubov a letter consisting of his explanation of love. The letter of course was long contemplated and earlier composed, however the letter has not survived to the present and its existence is based on the response that Lubov wrote to Bely regarding its contents:

> Dear Boris Nikolaievich.
>
> I am happy that you love me. When I read your letter it was so warm and serious. To love me is very good. This only can I tell you, this I know. But to help you live, help you to depart from torment, this I cannot do. I cannot do this even for Sasha. When you want to see me again, please come. We can and need to see each other. I will always be happy for you and this will not be difficult or wearisome, not to you, not to me. I will never discard you. I will often think about you and I will summon with all my strength, and on your behalf, quiet dusks.
>
> Loving you, L. Blok.

If we were to imagine the contents of the original letter, it would be from the perspective of some adolescent infatuation toward the personification of the ideal woman in every aspect. The passion or sensual aspect is absent, and replaced by Bely's capacity of allegory and emotion in his prose composition. If course, if there was any genuine physical attraction, no doubt Blok would have terminated it, but himself being a poet of the symbolist category, all that Bely wrote in the past and would continue to write in the future was innocuous verbosity.

However on August 6, 1906, she did respond in a letter, to take the next step in somehow terminating Bely's preoccupation with her and having him to face reality: she was Blok's wife and she was not going to leave him and run away with Bely to Europe. So she wrote:

> Since spring all has changed so much, to the point that for us to see each other or for you to visit us is completely impossible. Even incidental encounters, wherever you or I might be, will also be uncomfortable and unpleasant for me. You must deliver me from [your association], so please do not travel to Petersburg. And it would also be better to stop this correspondence. It is not necessary and especially since so little truth is there contained. So much has changed and now we know each other so little.

The second step she took together with Aleksandr. On August 8, they left Shakhmatovo and arrived in Moscow. Arrangements were made to meet with Bely at a restaurant. The conversation hardly lasted 5 minutes with Lubov doing all the talking, the Bloks restraining themselves from showing emotion. It was an ultimatum to Bely: leave Lubov alone, do not write any more letters, do not go to Petersburg with intentions of seeing them, discard out of your head any thoughts of them running away together to Italy. Bely attempted for a concession, to still see her as friends when he is in Petersburg. Lubov flatly refused any concessions.

After listening to Lubov, fright enveloped Bely and he jumped up and ran out of the restaurant. The Bloks finally felt they were relieved of his interference in their marriage and hopefully Bely would understand. The Bloks returned to Shakhmatovo.

Bely returned home and found a black mask he would were at masquerade balls, and wore it when guests would arrive, so was he reacting in this infantile manner. He then convinced his friend Ellis to go to Shakhmatovo and on Bely's behalf demand that Aleksandr Blok agree to a duel. Ellis complied with his friend's request, but when he informed Blok of Bely wanting a duel, he just laughed, not taking it seriously at all. He told Ellis to pass on to Bely that he needs rest to recover his senses. The Bloks hurried to Petersburg.

Bely in Moscow with his mother moved into a new apartment, a small one, leaving the large and expensive one on the Arbat behind. He felt betrayed, as though experiencing a tragic drama comparable to death, and that Blok had no right to deprive him of seeing his wife. So Bely continued to write his letters hoping for some condescension on the part of Blok, understanding that Bely was a human and a fellow poet, and requested a social meeting with Lubov in Petersburg. The following is an excerpt from one letter and now Bely's hysterical obsession and infatuation with Lubov reaches its desperate pinnacle:

> I swear that she is the sanctuary of my soul. I swear that I have nothing other than the sanctuary of my soul. I swear that only through her can I gain control of myself and return to God. I swear that I will perish without Luba. I swear that my hysteria and my gloom is due to not seeing her. I swear that the strength of my holy love is about seeking God. I swear that in Him there is only one, one, one route and this is Luba. I swear that the storm clouds that hang over me are due to Luba's decision, for me to remain at a distance, never to return. I swear to you, Luba and Aleksandr Aleksandrovich, that I will reside where Luba resides all my entire life, and this should not be terrifying to Luba, but a necessity and inevitable. I swear that if I agree to be distant from Luba, I

> would not longer be myself, not Andrei Bely, but a nothing, a no one, and this is why my soul needs to migrate toward you, for our closeness to remain.
>
> Since it is impossible for a person to breath without air, so Luba is the indispensable air of my soul. I swear that my hysteria is due to a lack of air. I swear that if I remain in Moscow, I will perish for this and for the coming world. To travel to you is not just a trip, but a pilgrimage. Even if I can see Luba on rare occasions, but I must, must, must see her.
>
> I am preparing to meet Luba in Petersburg, or wherever she might me, just like for a sacrament.

Blok responded negatively and that the letter does not bother him one bit. He stated the need for some considerable length of time to pass, and then maybe in the future a social relationship can again be formed, but the Bloks would determine when and how. Bely refused the response and on August 23, he traveled to Petersburg. There he wrote a letter of apology. After a week, Lubov met privately with Bely, again the meeting lasted 5 minutes and she did all the talking. Lubov again repeated her husbands conditions: not to meet or correspond with them until they set the time and conditions. Bely finally acquiesced and he decided to travel through Europe to distance himself from the matter.

While in Paris Bely wrote three letters to Blok, hoping to salvage the relationship, now with time passed to heal and some distance between them. One of them contained a poem filled with nostalgia dedicated to Blok:

To A.A. Blok

I remember I was in a cold meadow
Your bright lamp of an aura
When you freely along the road
Walked unrestrained along the road.

We extinguished like candles,
As at night the sun sets.

Did you forget our previous conversations,
My strange mysterious brother?

You see in the colorless expanses,
The coveted goal is hidden.
But in torment, but in secret horrors,
Brother, will you really forget?

Do I mean nothing to you?
Am I your foe and enemy?
You see me call and weep,
You see I am destitute and naked.

But dear one, I do not believe I have lost;
The summit's edge is not declining its light.
Silence I do not believe, do not believe.
I do not believe, and I await: respond.

Boris

There is no evidence of any correspondence with Lubov, and Blok only responded once to Bely's letters.

Bely's return to Russia from Europe did not terminate his preoccupation with Luba, but instead it renewed in him. He felt an alleged insult and humiliation as a result of one of Blok's articles in *Golden Fleece.* Bely wrote to Blok, who in turn wrote back to Bely, and this time Blok was the one who requested a duel. Additional correspondence led to a meeting between then, Blok traveling to Moscow from Shakhmatovo, early October 1907. They met at Bely's apartment at 7 in the evening and talked until 11 than night. Blok invited Bely to Petersburg to again meet with Lubov to somehow rectify the issue. The next morning Bely gave a lecture and the 2 of them together left the following day to Petersburg, Blok taking Bely to a local hotel.

Bely met with a different Lubov than he knew earlier. She was turbulent and aggressive, and he realized that the husband and wife now led their separate lives. The events they endured over the time that Bely spent in Europe psychologically devastated them, in addition to their illnesses. But no way could she return to Bely, not at all, even with Blok's affair with Natalia Volokhova, Lubov decided to stick it out. All of this agitated Bely, yet he was now glad to have put it all behind him and move forward with his own goals and purpose.

Bely did not stay long in Petersburg and returned alone to Moscow, although with intentions of returning to Petersburg in about 2 weeks. So again he was in Petersburg November 1 through 17, 1907, met with Lubov Blok, had a horrible argument with her, and Bely returned home to his mother. His next opportunity to meet Lubov was 8 years later. It took this long and this much aggravation caused to the Bloks for Bely to terminate his fantasy of a mystic relationship with Lubov, and allow her to live and stabilize her own life with her husband. Blok also wrote a letter again to state concretely the termination of their association, and Bely did the same and with the words:

> In view of the complexity of our attitudes I am liquidating this complex issue, severing all communication with you, except for accidental encounters and indirectly at gatherings with common associates. Do not rely. All the best.

Lubov's negative attitude had its own detrimental effect on husband Blok and he found other women to fill the fantasy role of the Beautiful Dame: first the actress Natalia Nikolaievna Volokhova[58] and later the opera and concert singer Lubovi Aleksandrovna Delmas.[59] They were both very popular with the general public in their vocations in the entertainment field. However neither of these women had nearly the qualities to identify themselves with Lubov's character, and so they were short lived. About this time the affair of Lubov with the poet

[58] Lived 1878-1966. Later in her life she wrote memoirs of her association with Blok.
[59] Lived 1884-1969.

Georgy Chulkov became public. But this was quickly terminated and became part of history.

While Blok was having an affair with Volokhina, and it lasted 2 years, his wife Lubov divorced him in February 1908, and left on a tour with the Meyerhold (Moscow Art) Theater Group. She returned within 6 months and pregnant due to a casual affair. In the meanwhile Blok and Volokhina permanently separated in June 1908. With Lubov's return in August 1908, Blok agreed to reunite with his wife and adopt the child as his own, Lubov felt relief and the couple returned to Petersburg, but the child died about a year later and which devastated the couple. All of this had a deleterious affect on Blok's health and which just worsened in the future.

They traveled to Germany and Italy later in 1909, returned to Russia, and then again traveled to France, Belgium and Netherlands in 1911, but not returning to Russian until 1916.

As much as Bely wanted to patch his relationship with Blok, it was not working very well. When Bely was in Petersburg to deliver lectures in January 1909, he met Blok at their favorite restaurant. They were friendly on personal terms, but animosity prevailed on literary issues. Bely's next volume of poetry, his *Fourth Symphony, Goblet of Blizzards*, was published in April that year by Scorpion Book Publisher, Moscow, and Bely dedicated considerable effort toward his final volume of the *Symphony* series, working long hours on it. After receiving his copy Blok responded to critics:

> This is not only alien, but its mood is deeply hostile. I have never met anybody so internally confused and whose association is so difficult.

There was no more correspondence between Bely and Blok for the next 2 years. Bely recorded later in his memoirs about the conclusion of this matter:

> I and A.A. continued with friendly correspondence, but we felt that to speak to or see each other was not worth it. Rarely did we even write to each other, and finally we just stopped dialogue. We understood that it was without bad will that we decided to dissociate. Our dialogue slowly died, but only for it to renew after several years. It was the strangest lifeless course with which I had to deal: no light and no darkness, no concrete communication, no clear departure.

Later however Bely and Chulkov were also at odds with each other, although at a distance, the reason being Lubov Blok. As noted above, she and Chulkov were exposed as having an affair, making him the victor for her heart as opposed to the defeated Bely, whose involvement with her was purely mystical. So did Bely surmise the situation in his unrelenting pursuit for Lubov, although she was still Blok's wife. Bely could not abandon the matter, now resurrecting the issue with his return to Russia. Zinaida Gippius wrote of the matter in a letter from Paris, interested in his love life. This irritated Bely and he responded with a letter in return, and very symbolic as with all others:

> Dear and kind and very kind Zina:
>
> You ask me about Luba. I have a serious inclination toward Luba, as life and death. But I am no longer in a position to justify her, and in no position to even find a path to her. Let her wait on her own. And I do not know if I will even forgive her. My most recent letter I sent her was a nice one. In response I receive an unsigned one with accusations against me, but these were lies. In response I told her how I am resolving matters with Sasha – an idiot, scoundrel, or infant to say the least. So did everything unravel.
>
> After reading his recent article in the *Golden Fleece* magazine, and which was directed at myself, although indirectly, I concluded it would be best not to meet with him again, since I see no reason to stretch my hand to him to shake his, it will result in nothing. I am unable to write of all of what occurred, and even then, she probably forgot all there was

> between us, and this is what always occurs with stupid people. And if Luba wants to figure a means of meeting me, even after all of this, I will eternally wait for her. However I will not make the first move to meet with her ever, never.
>
> I have cut 9/10 of my soul from me due to its infection with gangrene, and only 1/10 of my previous soul remains, but it is still soul. I can still live and survive without Luba with the little remaining. This is all. After returning to Moscow I did not take any effort to visit her, even residing nearby, this was May 20 to June 25. About 20 times I thought to go and meet her, but I took control of myself and I did not. And she did not either. I know that I can wait for years and for years I will not see her. So no need from my part to exert the effort any more.

But exactly how did Lubov Dmitrievna feel about all of this symbolism imposed on her as the embodiment of these men's imagery? Did she really want to be the Beautiful Dame and the other allegories? Once on the scene she was adored as though she was the reincarnation of the Theotokos and due religious devotion by the young generation of Russian symbolists and readers who were attracted to this new genre of writing, much different than the classic style of the 19th century novelists and poets. From another facet, and much evidence of the record of her contemporaries testifies to this, her instinct rejected all of this fantasy. Lubov Dmitrievna as a young, interesting, healthy woman just wanted normal human love and compassion and the simplicity of a husband and family and domestic happiness. She did not draw herself toward being a symbolic Madonna or Joan of Arc of the symbolist movement. She disclosed her honest attitude and feelings not long before her death in 1939, in private memoirs. Here Lubov Dmitrievna in detail and candidly related how tragically her intimate life was disoriented and how distant she actually was from the Beautiful Dame depicted in their poetry.

While Bely was enveloped with other men's wives as being the materialization of the female world soul, the Woman Clothed in the Sun, the Beautiful Dame, Sophia Divine Wisdom, and etc, one woman did enter his life that did fit all that Bely sought, except that Bely could not allow the spiritual to overcome the physical.

Anna Nikoliaevna Schmidt was a newspaper reporter in Nizhni-Novgorod. Residing in Astrakhan while her father was in exile, she received revelations in the years 1885-1886, that she was the corporeal incarnation of the Holy Spirit, which she understood as the feminine aspect of God, meaning, Sophia the Divine Wisdom. Anna considered herself the earthly representative of the Woman Clothed in the Sun and the spirit wife of Jesus Christ of the contemporary era. All of her revelations she codified in a book titled, *The Third Testament.* Anna was looking for a publisher for her book, and she was also looking for the second incarnation of the male aspect of God, and which she felt she found in Vl. Solovyov.

Through letters written in 1899 and 1900, Schmidt informed Vladimir Solovyov that on the 3 occasions that he experienced the apparition of Sophia the Divine Wisdom as a female figure, he was actually encountering her. So according to Schmidt, it was she that Solovyov encountered, the soul of the world and the young female friend of whom he wrote about in his poetry. Although he did not know it at the time, however now Schmidt was disclosing this to him. It was divine providence that he was to meet her at these locations in visions, but now she was waiting for him to meet her in person, and she was residing in Nizhni-Novgorod. The two did have an opportunity to meet, and just a few months before his death, but Solovyov could not grasp the possibility that of what he wrote could actually materialize in a corporeal person, so he rejected her claims. He died a few months later.

Schmidt now started to contact people in Moscow and Petersburg whom she felt would support her, and especially the young poets of the new genre of symbolist literature as well as Mikhail Solovyov.

Bely met Schmidt on October 1, 1901, at the home of Mikhail Solovyov, brother of Vl. Solovyov. She was 50 years old, but according to Bely her physique gave the appearance that she was decades older. He describes her as short and old with dry lips, grey eyes, grey and dingy unkempt hair, her dress was disheveled and tattered, her face had the consistency of a baked apple. All she had to her benefit was an expression of playful enthusiasm in her encounter that exposed the happy child deep within her.

At the meeting she attempted to convince them of the reality of her revelations and her personal status. Schmidt still felt they might understand her concepts and so proceed to take the initiative to publish *The Third Testament.* But neither of them took her seriously. Bely recorded the following in his memoirs:

> My concept of the woman clothed in the sun is a young, beautiful girl, not an old woman having a very unattractive appearance.

Bely includes a reference to Anna Schmidt and her group in his book *Petersburg,* at the end of chapter 2, calling them, "The female sectarians of Nizhni-Novgorod." Bely identified the group as a materialization of Vl. Solovyov's cult of Sophia, and mentions that some felt Russia will be the cradle of the Church of Philadelphia.

In 1903 and 1904, Schmidt corresponded with Aleksandr Blok and further with Andrei Bely.

Schmidt traveled to Moscow again in 1904. She again met with Bely that year on April 6, and as to why he would not approve of the publication of her article in *Novi Putz.* She also met with Aleksandr Blok at his family estate in Shakhmatovo on May 12 and 13. After meeting Schmidt, Blok wrote to Andrei Bely regarding her:

> A.N. Schmidt arrived here. She left a muddled impression, but in any case a good one. She is extremely sincere and has a clear mind, and deprived of any infernalities. She spoke of

> many subtle things, but which were hardly understandable to me.

As with Bely, Blok was seeking the physical to complement the spiritual. Their disappointment of identifying Schmidt with the Divine Sophia was only obvious, although her features and physique were entirely superficial and their determination should have been spiritual. However they could not defeat the physical. (Anna Schmidt died in 1905. Eventually Professor Sergei Bulgakov published her manuscript.)

# ANDREI BELY – THE SYMBOLIST

With events occurring in Moscow over October 1905, Bely was attending meetings non-stop at the university. He was one of the active and vocal orators. Together with the radical Mensheviks, he voiced his opinion, calling for an immediate cessation of all activities dealing with turning the university into a revolutionary tribunal. But his resolution was rejected. Bely as an theosophist was against violent overthrow of government. For a while however Bely did listen to Nikolai Volsky (later Valentinov),[60] a member of the Socialist-Democratic Party, although nothing resulted from it.

Protests enveloped Moscow all of October. One Bolshevik revolutionary, Nikolai Bauman, was killed October 18, by a member of the radical Black Hundreds. Bely was witness to his funeral on October 20, which turned into a massive demonstration and a spectacle to commemorate the first Bolshevik martyr. Supposedly 100,000 mourners attended the funeral procession.

Vyacheslav Ivanov and his wife returned to Petersburg in early 1906, also part of the symbolist group, and their apartment become a gathering place for Bely during his visits and other symbolists. The Ivanov home was in a tower, and so was nicknamed the Tower, and had a Bohemian atmosphere. Here

[60] Nikolai Vladislavovich Volsky, who wrote under the pen name of N. Valentinov, 1879-1964, Russian philosopher and economist. He also authored a book titled, *Two Years with the Symbolists*. He lived in Paris from 1928, and died there.

eroticism in their writings was permitted and the sexual relationships of those attending was very unrestricted. Their topics included culture, social realism, mystic symbolism, occultism, neo-christianity, contemporary secular literature, and related progressive trends, as opposed to the Merezhkovsky home where a conservative religious attitude pervaded the atmosphere. Another regular patron of the Ivanov home was the newly popular poet Nikolai Gumilyov.

It was at one of these Ivanov gatherings that Bely read his philosophic-mythological essay *Phoenix*, dealing with the legend of the eagle-like bird that every 500 years dies in Heliopolis, ancient Egypt and then resurrects. The Phoenix is the sun-bird dedicated to Osirus, and the Phoenix is likewise the soul of the sun god.[61] The Phoenix is the symbol of uninterrupted rebirth, which signifies immortality. So in this mythological form Bely's classic and favorite concept of eternal rebirth manifests, and which connects with the Christian concept of the general resurrection. In this regard the Phoenix personifies the grand cosmic cycle with everything returning to its original state and then the cycle beginning again. Bely includes the Egyptian Sphinx in his allegory as being contradistinctive to the Phoenix.

As Bely wrote:

> Egypt is the cradle of the lightning myth of the bright bird that dies and resurrects on the third day according to Scripture. The religious tragedy of the suffering resurrection is already provided in this symbol, and it is the ray of the future that will illuminate all cultures. Phoenix is the eternal resurrection through the fire of the light-bearing feathers, definitely the radiant dawn, burning and singeing the difficult past. The Sphinxes disperse, from the primal eras flying into the sacred land together with the yellow clouds of sand.
>
> Sphinx and Phoenix individually form a single progressive struggle. That which these images portray is some kind of

[61] This is how Bely comprehended the concept of the Phoenix in his writings, similar to the Egyptian Bennu with a 500 year regeneration. This is somewhat based on the history of Herodotus.

completeness. The difference in understanding the subject completeness is displayed as defeating the past – the Sphinx – or as defeating the future – the Phoenix.

The Sphinx, personally speaking, is a misunderstood Phoenix. This is an aspiration to life without a valuable attitude to life. Existence that is true and valuable is replaced by existence that is mundane. True life becomes corporeal life. Sphinx and Phoenix are essentially the single symbol. But in the cognizance of the contemplator they possess a duality like day and night, morning and evening, future and past, fleeting and stationary, light and heavy. Sphinx and Phoenix then appear as contradistinctive to each other. This is the start of their fight.

The Sphinx and Phoenix fight in our souls. And upon all, whatever the spirit of humanity has produced, lies the seal of the Phoenix and the Sphinx. This is why out of the formations of our thoughts, and in the creations of art and science, and in societal creativity, the objects of the images of Egypt resurrect – the Phoenix and Sphinx. They oppose each other in one direction, but in another [direction] they appear indivisible. The secret consists in that the Phoenix cannot be retained in the Sphinx. But the Sphinx is half of the complete Phoenix. Consumed by fire the Phoenix dies. The Phoenix is scattered into ashes. The death of the Phoenix does exist. But the Sphinx is the victory of the bestial past over the future. But the Sphinx is particularly death. And the Sphinx and Phoenix arrived here by flying in the same manner for this purpose. The Sphinx is the one confronting. Both fight against fate. One possesses an obvious enmity, the other defeats destiny through love. And the Phoenix arises alive and complete. This is why the struggle between the Sphinx and Phoenix is not a struggle of principles that are equally right, but a struggle of parts against the whole. This struggle is between life in general and life of creativity. But life in general flows out of creativity. Life is a portion of creativity.

Fly, Phoenix, to the sun on flapping wings, but do not attempt to weary! If you are afraid, Phoenix, what will happen to you when you understand that no matter how many times you may resurrect, you will fly out of the ashes again and again? You will arrive flying an infinite number of times at your bonfire to endure the torment of cremation. But the Phoenix through love conquers death. And as soon as it says, "Let death occur," the eyeless traveling companion of the days – the Sphinx – will become scared and scatter. And as soon as it is clothed with a scarlet robe of fire, a cool breeze will whisper to it, "Return, again return," and immortality floating on the wings of the world will descend to it, and it will arise on the third day according to Scripture, and it will say, "My immortality returned to me. It and only it watches over me through life and death."

You, sages, established as Phoenixes! You travel along the Milky Way. The Milky Way is a handful of valuables thrown into the world. The Milky Way is a bridge cutting across heaven. It is under your feet that terror is unleashed and to traverse further you create a new valuable object. And once creating it you gain the conquest. You manufacture a new valuable object, and once creating it you conquer. So does it continue without end, without end. Without end do you create and then conquer.

You are comets, insanely happy, insanely tearing through the fabric of the black gloom from primordial times. Your existence behind your shoulders, history cast in concrete, is the sparkling, light and feather-like tail of the comet, the translucent robe of a flying sage. And the darkness of the long night will infinitely show colors due to its infinite robe.

The sage is wrapped in his robe, spread across the sky with his wings of air-filled sails. He will recognize the Milky Way and nebulas and planetary systems. He will comprehend them all watching through the layers of his robe. He will comprehend the universal life of planets. He will comprehend the generation of nations. He will see himself, cast into the rotation of existence and he will laugh at himself. He lovingly looks at himself. He announces, "Come to me." And his distant summons like the dawn penetrates the dream that he is dreaming. And to him and to another who is captive in his dream, who is dreaming the dawn and hearing someone's gentle and familiar voice, calling in a tender tranquil manner, "Come to me, come, you who labor. I will give you rest. Come, come."

So the sage contemplates the inscription patterned on his robes. So the sage forgets himself, immersed in his personal dream. And he daydreams of infinite existence. But it is worth it for him to turn his veiled face, just as the picture of galaxies unfolds before his view. He is thrown among them in his accelerating and flexible flight.

The Phoenix and Sphinx are allegories with a contrast of one opposed to the other. Essentially there are 3 contrasts that Bely is providing here that applies to his era. The first is political and economic. The Sphinx is socialism. Cold, impersonal, visionless (or eyeless), and dominated by the state, yet forever existing and enduring the wind blown sands of time and will continue so and never terminate. The Phoenix is free market enterprise, soaring through the sky, building the state. Even though the economy may fall it will rise again. Both are traveling the same direction, but contradistinctive to each other.

A second contrast is art. The Sphinx is the conservative forms of literature, painting, sculpture, architecture, and it also endures time and its eroding effects. The Phoenix is symbolism, where the artist is the god of his own artistic world, he is the spark of deity, just as God is the creator of the universe. So the symbolist must soar above the mundane, not existing within the frame of the old tradition. Mortality and immortality are only ideas of our intellect.

The final contrast pertains to Bely personally and so can extend to others in a individual application. Bely is the Phoenix, the symbolist poet aspiring to spiritual and mystic heights, and no matter what disaster may occur to him, he will resurrect and again soar. Blok is the Sphinx: enduring but lifeless and impersonal. So this applies to each individual, whether to be a Phoenix and a comet and so soar into the skies and galaxies and nebulas, or be a Sphinx, heavy and stationary. Yet both will endure in the long run.

Bely then returned to Moscow and isolated himself from any social activity. On September 10, he gave notice at the university for his resignation as a student. His excuse was his intent to travel abroad. The request was granted on September 19, and on September 20, 1906, Bely left Moscow to go abroad. The three people closest to him accompanied him to the train station to bid farewell: his mother, Sergei Solovyov and Ellis.

His new temporary home was Munich, Germany, arriving there October 4. As a result of the distance from Russia, his preoccupation with women, such as Margarita Morozova, Lubov Blok and Nina Petrovskaya eventually subsided. His physical health as well as his psychological improved and his mind was now on a steady course. Every morning with great enthusiasm he would patronize the Munich art gallery, where in its quiet halls he would familiarize himself with the works of the old German masters. In the book section he slowly fingered and studied pages of the pictures painted by great painters, from Albrecht Durer to Lukas Cranach the Elder. He would pass the evenings, as with most Munich denizens, in some tavern or smoking lounge, associating with the local residents or other Russian tourists. Of course, he was back to writing again with his mind freed from so many self-imposed and unnecessary anxieties.

The sudden severance from his home, his homeland, friends and symbolist circle was difficult for Bely. He still felt the pain from the emotional wound he felt he received from the Blok scenario and it was healing very slowly. The following is a selection from one of Bely's letters to his mother written shortly after his arrival in Munich.

> I did not write any letters these past days because I am working hard on my next *Symphony*. If I do not write to you, this does not mean that I forgot. Here it is quiet with wide surroundings. I heal myself through silence, concentration and

solitude. Every extra month that I pass here adds that much more health to me, I can feel this. I am regaining control of myself after the stupid turmoils of the recent years.

Most of the people with whom I am now familiar seem to me to be nothing more than useless marionettes who only interfere with some person wanting to find himself in life. I find myself immersed into their boisterous words spoken in a quiet atmosphere. When I return to Russia I will take all measures to preserve myself from any further impact of unnecessary influences. Now in plain view a plan of future and greater literary works is ripening, they will create a new form of literature. I feel within myself a supply of immense literary strength. If only the conditions of my life will permit me to dedicate myself to this work.

While in Moscow I squandered so much strength and words on worthless people, I was some kind of pack mule and the result was a nervous breakdown and physical exhaustion. It took me the past several months to recover from this.

I am grateful to fate and to you, for making the decision to travel to Munich.

So my essential goal is to save myself, to preserve my belief in Light, God and a purpose in life. Recently all I did was experience these superficial burdens that caused me inner and emotional upsets, so I just made a mess of everything. The more that I now can resolve these complexities, to the same extent I can proceed on the tangible route conforming to that Ideal that is instilled in me. And it is not external events that directly created this painful hysteria in me and this feeling of a crevice opening right under my feet, but an entire series of inner events in my soul prepared me for these ahead of time, so I succumbed to them.

This inner, ideal facet of my essence and the questions tied with it I sometimes ignored due to completely natural reasons, but without them, that is, without this Holy of Holies in my soul and belief in truth, it was absolutely impossible for me to pick myself up from these external factors of my life. When I left to go abroad, I left first to regather my corporeal strengths,

> and second to utilize these strengths, those so necessary to me, to resolve issues in my life, the goal of my route, how I can be of useful service to humanity and how to consciously manifest benevolence. So my relocation flows out of hidden inner plans, and they are not accidental. Because I am at a distance, it is difficult to provide you a picture of my experiences tied with my actions. So just believe that I relocated for the sake of my salvation.
>
> When I felt the need to escape and proceed toward light and clarity, the entirety of Munich seemed to me the nourishment my hysteria needed to heal from these memories. It was difficult for me to remain in this one room where I relived the pain, but along with it I felt that the basic kernel of truth residing within me was moving and growing and strengthening. There was this need to not further recollect the pain and fear by having new surroundings. As soon as I changed my location I immediately calmed.

Bely likewise wrote to Brusov from Munich, now with their relationship healed and proceeding on a normal vein. Brusov's latest volume of poetry was dedicated to Bely as a sign of their renewed relationship. So Bely wrote:

> I live quietly and focused. The sky here is very blue and the weather is warm. In the evenings I sit at an opened window with my pipe and I picture the stupidity of the recent years of my life. Now I know this was not the way to life. Right now these shadows of the past are cast on my solitude.
>
> I hear a sweet breeze. I believe, believe that it even may be voices, the distant past of my childhood returning to me, or perhaps premonitions of my old age. I know that this immense and dreadful period of my life is vanishing from me like a mirage. "I see the sun of the covenant, I see sky in the distance. I await the universal light from the resurrected land."[62]

[62] A quotation from one of Blok's poems.

Although painful and grievous being along, but it is tranquil. If I have caused pain to someone, I ask for forgiveness. I so much want to be repentant to everybody, in order to depart from them all, to go there, where the voices summon me.

There was a period here in Munich when I became familiar with all of them, and then just as fast I severed all the acquaintances. Interesting.

In the mornings I troll through an immense golden-yellow park or sit at a collection of engravings at the art gallery. I work from 2 to 6 o'clock. The evenings I spend with Vladimir[63] at my apartment and we have tea with snacks. Then we sit for a long while with our pipes. We sit in silence and the quiet consoles our souls. Sometimes we go to the café and sit silent over glasses of tea, listening to a waltz. So do I pass day after day.

Loving you, B. Bugaev

Unexpectedly a letter arrived from Paris from the Merezhkovskys. Dmitri and Zinaida Gippius invited Bely there. The relationship Bely had with the Merezhkovskys was always friendly and close. The literary-religious circle of the Merezhkovskys in Paris was no different than what they had in Petersburg, and they had almost the entirety of Parisian Russians in their home every Thursday. Bely left Munich November 30, and arrived in Paris the next day.

In Paris Bely rented an inexpensive room with a kitchen in a boarding house near Bois de Boulogne, a large public park. Nearby lived Jean Jaures, the popular political activist, leader of the French Socialist Party, and founder of the newspaper the *Humanist*. Bely had the opportunity to speak with Jaures considerably during Bely's stay in Paris and Jaures would often dine with Bely at his room. Bely of course spoke fluent French as well as German. His favorite topics with Jaures was neo-Kantian philosophy and French socialism, as Jaures in earlier years taught philosophy at the Lycee and Paris University. These were areas of

---

[63] An artist Bely befriended in Munich.

study than Bely knew little since he was enveloped with his symbolist poetry and circle while in Russia. Bely attended several seminars taught by Jaures acquiring as much as possible from the socialist and philosophic mentor.

Paris imparted an indelible impression on Bely, as he wrote to Brusov:

> I have vehemently come to love Paris, even as little as I have seen of it. You will discredit it and claim it to be uncultured. But I enjoy ambling about the street and sitting in a café drinking beer and smoking my pipe.

Just before the new year of 1907, Bely experienced excruciating internal pain. It started at the theater where he was attending with Zinaida Gippius, and they quickly left and she took him to his room. The Russian biographers only call it a painful tumor or swelling that would not allow him to stand or walk or sit or lie, and it caused a high temperature. He needed emergency surgery. Based on the available information, Bely had acute appendicitis. His poor diet, chain smoking, coffee, alcohol, all would have provoked the inflammation. Bely waited in his room for a doctor, but instead his friend Nikolai Gumilyov arrived, visiting Paris at the time. By now Bely was in a state of delirium and exceedingly high temperature. On January 2, 1907, between Gumilyov and the Merezhkovskys, they were able to get Bely to a hospital for immediate surgery. By the next day the danger was behind them.

Zinaida Gippius attended to Bely daily at the hospital, and she wrote to Brusov about the incident:

> A. Bely lied sick with us before the operation and almost cried from pain, which tightly wove around his torso. Now all little by little has passed. The operation was a success and all went well, and Bely is lying contritely and happy. The Catholic nuns like Angels are taking good care of him in their austere manner. Hopefully he will be able to stand sometime next week. Everybody here seems to like him.

Gippius likewise wrote to Bely's mother to console her:

> His illness was much caused by this abnormal mode of life that he led prior to this incident. He would be at our house during the day, constantly, and the last time we begged him to go to sleep earlier, but he said that he has not slept now for a week. He sits up until morning, drinks tea and smokes. He has upset his nervous system to such a stage that his appearance is plainly horrible. He had developed a very weak will and could not take control of his life. I am very glad that he will continue to stay in the hospital for some time and under a strict regimen. This will really relax his nerves. We love your son very much, firmly and immutably, and all are thinking and guessing and counseling what to do for his future to be better.

In such a complex and critical situation the Merezhkovskys displayed their better human qualities. Bely spent almost a month in the hospital, to the end of January, but he quickly recovered from the attack and surgery and gradually returned to a customary but better mode of life. Apart from his poetry he started to write on the topic that was his most favorite: religion and socialism, ideas that were long ago formulated in his mind. He wrote on how the socialism of Karl Marx had the effects of a religion, although in reality they are inherently opposite to each other. Bely felt at the time that social-democracy was to the advantage of the proletariat, the terminal hope of humanity. On February 22, Bely read his treatise *Social-Democracy and Religion* to a group of Russian immigrants in Paris. (The presentation was so provocative that 3 months later it was published in the Moscow symbolist magazine *Progression*.)

Especially interesting was having Bely, a popular poet and symbolist, use such allegorical and mystical language in dealing with the topic, although the reaction was somewhat questionable. The concrete substance of what Bely defined as religion was still unclear, but he emphasized it as the sole religious truth of the future. As Bely wrote:

The class of the proletariat more and more becomes the class of humanity in generation. The creativity of the future belongs to it. Its religion will be the religion of humanity.

The symbol is the unification of something with something else beyond the limits of knowledge. In particular this world beyond our frontiers is one of eternal values and is the supreme reality attained by the route of inner creative activity, on the basis of art and religion, and specifically art where religious essence has been maintained from primordial eras.

The one symbolic life is disclosed to us, the world of value is not ascertainable completely, displayed in all of its simplicity, attraction and diversity, being the alpha and omega of all theory. It is the symbol of a certain secret. The approach to this secret is an all-growing, boiling creative aspiration that carries us as though we have arisen from the dust of the Phoenix's ashes, over the cosmic dust of space and time. All theories terminate under our feet. All reality flies away as a dream, and only in creativity does reality, value and the meaning of life remain.

The mountain pass through which humanity traverses consists in the new hours of life beating – knowledge, creativity, being. This is your great noon when the depths of the vault of heaven is illuminated by the sun. The sun rises. It has long since blinded us, and so comprehension, creativity, existence form their dark spots in our eyes. Presently the comprehension in front of our eyes is clearing these dark spots. It says to us in our language, "I am no longer here." Creativity presently before our eyes ruptures its dark spots. It says, "I am no longer here." Our mundane life before our eyes ruptures its dark spots. It says, "I am no longer here." The decision depends on us if there is something that can evolve from this. Our will speaks, "There is nothing." But we are not blind, we hear the music of the sun standing presently in the midst of our soul. We see its reflection in the mirror of the sky, and we say, "You are it."

The actual reaction to such allegorical language from the side of the social-democrats is unknown, although the reaction was positive from the side of those seeking something other than the emaciated and mundane philosophic thought they heard from others.

By this time the money assigned for Bely's trip to Europe was long ago exhausted and any that remained went to pay for his hospital expenses and other related medical services. He reached a dead-end as far as any further stay in Europe was concerned or even to travel to Italy. At the tail end of February 1907, Bely returned to Moscow. He spent the previous evening at dinner with Merezhkovskys, while Jean Jaures accompanied Bely to the train station for his departure after having breakfast together at a local restaurant.

Returning home to Russia Bely had to face the full size problem of the further financial security of his personal life and his mother who was now dependant on him. The regular source of income on which he was dependant until now were his royalties for his lectures, although not many. Crumbs were paid for his reviews of other writers' books and articles and he could not depend on them. As far as his volumes of poetry were concerned he was paid considerably less than other poets, for example, Feodor Sologub was paid 5 times more per line, Aleksandr Kuprin was paid 8 times more, and Leonid Andreev was paid 10 times more. But Bely did not consider that these men wrote what the public wanted and what publishers printed. By 1907, Bely's few volumes of poetry did not have the wide distribution as did these men and other poets, novelists and dramatists of the silver age of Russian literature. He was more of a novelty, a passing fad. It is obvious that due to Bely's philosophic and mystic attributes and his preoccupation with the materialization of fantasies, he did not have a natural capacity of handling money or knew how to do business. He just wrote and left the financial aspect to publishers and who then took advantage of him. Being naive in the area of finances he was also timid, Bely never asking for more money if he felt the royalty for his books were not adequate. He only requested funds when what he had was exhausted, not seeming to have a concept of what he needed for the future and some to save for emergencies.

Bely turned to lecturing, renting an auditorium somewhere, printing flyers and developing a script. Often the halls was filled to the point of turning away interested individuals. The themes of his lectures were very diverse: the theory of symbolism, the art of the future, modernistic theater, Friedrich Nietzsche, Henrik Ibsen, and etc. Bely loved an audience and always promoted a lively intercourse with his audience; he had an excellent ability to keep their attention and retain it to the end of his presentation. His natural public speaking skill drew his audience into his topic, making it interactive and so he was able to control their interest. His inherent ability to improvise under any conditions made him the best in his class, never at a loss for words or something to say, somehow able to continue the topic and deliver something to not break the continuity of his address.

On April 14, Bely lectured at the Poly-Technical Museum on the topic, *Symbolism in Contemporary Russian Art*, and then on April 17, *The Future Art*.

Bely was also willing to share his speaking skills with others, and so wrote in one article:

> When a person willingly devotes himself to improvisation, it is independent of the audience, since you are looking at it indirectly. I was always amazed at the decuple amount of attention to trivialities in the process of deliberating the details of my presentation, standing at this cathedra. You do not see a mass, but several hundred distinct sitting individuals, each one as though illuminated by your rays beaming from your eyes. You see the nuances in the impression of each listener. You notice their traits. And you momentarily read their face, take good note of them, and so simultaneously adjust your subsequent phrase. And you know who has the capacity of understanding you, and who is

rejecting your delivery. You see the effect of some misunderstanding or an agreement or agitation. You see a group of people grasping your concepts little by little. Sometimes like lightning you will mentally sum all of the diverse impressions and reactions and where necessary change your tragedy or conclusions or style of delivery.

The stupor of those not comprehending even one word will emerge just like a cork floating to the top of water and stay there motionless.

The initial 5 minutes you proceed with an ambivalent attitude in your thinking, not know whether *for* or *against*. The energy dedicated for the lecture is based on touch. You just as well be babbling in vain, but this babble is an introduction. Subsequent is the affect of touch, and having touched everybody in the audience you seek bases for your points. You draw yourself toward individuals that appear to understand you, and you read to them. They are an island in some unknown sea to you, and full of surprises. Standing on that island with your feet firm you are full of assurance in what surrounds you.

Other than this it is necessary to know when your audience is tired of listening to logic. Then discard the logic, now it is necessary to swing the listeners like on a swing, on something soft, images that are easy for their mind to absorb. Then you either speak from your heart, or you are laughing at the humor.

The lecturer needs to be able to speak not only to the conscious, but also to the subconscious. The lecturer's conscious needs to be 10 times that amount. At any moment while lecturing he must see the process of the advancement of his thoughts in the individual listeners. This loads on him unexpected tasks. He must be able to turn the static steadiness of his lectionary plan to a dynamic. This is why in the process of lecturing he needs to be an artist displaying himself in a number of roles during his lecture. He must present himself toward his enemies with the attitude of an angry Othello, and like a clever Iago.[64] He needs to become sorrowful for a lack of taste as Lear over Cordelia.[65] But these roles must somewhere enter the lecture so not to allow the variations to submerge the theme.

The lecture is not reciting abstract thoughts entering your mind. Its introduction needs to be a background setting, like buildings in a scene in a play, so that the paragraphs read in the lecture would be like the subsequent scenes of great acts.

Once ascending the cathedra it is a corporate body listening to what is emanating from your lips. The end of the lecture is the accumulation of the sum of the information your thoughts have provided, penetrating through the listeners and returning to you, and will always be unforeseeable. Here you enlarge yourself as the audience is now inspired by you. Now you will feel the crash and sense decline.

The lecture over the course of somewhere about 3 hours will experience all the stages of the growth of a seed: ploughing soil, planting, sprout of the blade, flower and ripening of the fruit, so that at the conclusion of the lecture you can eat some of the fruit which will be provided him from the audience, and this fruit is sweet, especially if it seems the audience may be stagnant initially.

The connection with the audience is mysterious, and not just once have I experienced a joy reading somewhere several lectures in series. The joy evolves from many who attended the initial lecture returning for the next and that some listeners return to hear the entire series. You will a acquire new circle of friends, people who earlier were unknown to you. This is what motivated me to dedicate much effort to lectures, although interrupting my work as a writer, but eventually they materialized again in several new books. Among them my treatise on Symbolism.[66]

I do not regret any of this at all.

---

[64] Characters in Shakespeare's *Othello*.
[65] Characters in Shakespeare's *King Lear*.
[66] Bely's book *Symbolism as a Ideology*.

Bely delivered lectures on an irregular basis and he could not depend on the royalties from them. They were unstable and after paying for expenses there was hardly enough on which to live. Often Bely and his mother were in a condition of malnutrition. Bely informed Gippius in a letter that his total income per month averaged 20 to 30 rubles. Then he was offered a job at a newly-forming newspaper with a promise of 150 rubles a month income, which is what he needed for he and his mother to survive, but the offer collapsed.

When Bely's mother became ill she was prescribed for treatment at minerals springs near the Caucasus Mts, and what remained in their account at the time was spent for her recovery. Over the next few weeks Bely went on 2 meals a day.

The primary jumping-off place now in Russia for a poet like Bely was the now flourishing magazine *Scales*, it was started a couple years earlier and published by Brusov. A new literary and artistic circle was formed about this time on April 10, 1907, called the Society for Liberal Aesthetics, created by the prominent doctor Ivan Ivanovich Troyanovsky.[67] Among a group of individuals the thought arose of creating a society that would unite activists of all the categories of art – artists, musicians, poets, dramatists and ballet figures – with the goal of a close association. Unlike the Merezhkovsky or Ivanov gatherings this one was semi-organized and held at the Vostryakov home on Bolshoi Dmitrovsky Street. Most of the previous group of symbolist poets attended, such as Bely, Valerie Brusov, Ellis, S.Solovyov, Vyacheslav Ivanov, Juirgis Baltrusaitis (also the publisher of *Scorpion* books), Voloshin, and A. Skryabin. A vast collection of activists in other areas of Russian culture also joined the society.

Bely in his memoirs did not desist in his laud of Troyanovsky for his love of the arts and his sincere desire to promote them for the cultural advancement of Russia. The president of the society from 1908 to 1920 was Brusov, as expected. The Soviet

[67] Ivan Ivanovich Troyanovsky, 1855-1928, Russian medical doctor, botanist, gardener, social activist.

nationalization of homes at this time forced the society to dissolve, although a few moved to Europe at this time.

Bely was active in this society until his next relocation to Europe. He did his best to associate with both groups of symbolists writers: those in Moscow, at whose head was Brusov and the Merezhkovskys whenever they were in Russia, and those in Petersburg, at whose head was Vya. Ivanov and Aleksander Blok, and later joining them was Georgy Chulkov. To further patch up the relationship between himself and Brusov, with the Petrovskaya matter still in the background, Bely wrote a letter to Brusov on April 19, 1907:

> Dear and deeply respected Valerie Yakovlevich!
>
> Presently my nerves have failed. I have fled Moscow for 3 days now. I do not know why, but I do want to tell you how much I love, value and respect you. Accept the word – respect, in its most sacred and serious meaning. You are for me an image of a genuine knight among a chaos of personages whom I disdain for the most part. Do not be surprised at my tone of voice or the motives of my letter. All of these days I have wanted to – and from my inner self and contritely – indicate my admiration of you.
>
> Sincerely loving you,
> Boris Bugaev

Bely needed the support of Brusov for the publication of his future volumes of poetry, continually working on his *Symphonies*, and this was a wise move on his part, now back in Russia from Europe for the distant future.

With the recent revolution of 1905, the writings of Mikhail Bakunin became popular and serious among the Russian intelligentsia and educated levels. He was considered the father of Russian anarchism and a social and political revolutionary. Some of the symbolist group, studying his writings, attempted to correlate or merge it with their fantasies calling the result – mystical anarchism. Georgy Chulkov especially was a promoter of this new genre of a combination of polity and philosophy. Bely likewise studied Bakunin at this time and his name appears occasionally in Bely's compositions and letters, but in general, the attitude of Bakunin was alien to Bely's nature and religious convictions, and especially Bakunin's history of revolutionary activism in Russia and Europe. The phrase – mystical anarchism, was repulsive to Bely's ears and seemed more of insanity than any indication of enlightenment.

The *Golden Fleece* magazine was published by Nikolai Pavlovich Ryabushinsky, lasting from 1906 to 1909, associated with the Petersburg group of symbolists. He was also the organizer in 1907 of the art exhibit – The Blue Rose. Also involved was Sergei Sokolov, who financed it, and he was also the publisher of *Grif.* Bely initially submitted articles, but then stopped when he dissociated himself from the Petersburg group in April 1907. Brusov was involved at its start but likewise departed at about the same time as did Bely. Blok continued as a regular contributor.

Bely took some time and traveled to Kiev to lecture. He arrived there the evening of October 2-3, 1907, and participated the next evening at an presentation at the Kiev City Theater on the topic, *Regarding the Points of Development of the new Russian Art.* On October 6, it was a lecture to a group of Kiev businessmen on the topic, *The Future of Art.* He returned to Petersburg on October 8.

Bely was now 27 years old and he wondered where so much of his life dissipated, but as in the past, the future was not stationary. This superficial altercation between the Petersburg and Moscow symbolist groups continued and Bely coordinated his effort with Brusov in Moscow, now gaining his trust after his letter mentioned above and any animosity of the past now forgotten history. Brusov called Bely his captain, while he was a officer. Bely still did not forget Blok's discrediting article in his *Golden Fleece* magazine, and so maintained animosity toward Ryabushinsky the publisher.

Bely wrote to Gippius August 7-11, 1907, explaining in detail the complex situation:

> Now regarding the *Fleece*. I am at war against the *Fleece*. It was back in April that I resigned from their group. Then Ryabushinsky asked me to return. I told him in a letter that as long as he was editor nothing of worth will ever evolve from the *Fleece*. Then Metner wrote an article against me. I responded with a Letter to the Editor. They refused to publish the letter, and if I wanted it published then I had to return as a worker but under conditions they dictated to me.
>
> I responded with my list of conditions, which included the following: 1. That the magazine not be inclined toward mystical anarchism. 2. That Ryabushinsky rearrange the company. They responded to me with a vile and insulting letter and all of this was accompanied by every kind of mean action. Finally I published a letter of protest in a local newspaper. No doubt this letter will also be the slogan for Brusov's departure. He promised me that in the event my letter could cause unrest, he will leave the *Fleece* in protest.
>
> Now the *Fleece* is a decaying corpse poisoning the atmosphere. What is now flourishing is the stupidity of Ryabushinsky together with the barbarian cretinism of a certain person name Tasteven[68] who runs the literature department and who likewise discredited me. All that is left at *Fleece* is Blok, Ivanov, and Gogodetsky.[69] Maybe Chulkov will return there.

Bely's confederates were impressed with his articles and letters, and he gained the attention of many readers. He was especially annoyed with the group that he identified as being epigoniums: those who joined after symbolism became popular to get on its bandwagon, and then imitated the poetry of others to acquire some fame and credit. He also called them riff-raff luggage. He

[68] Henrik Edmondovich Tasteven, 1880-1915, Russian art and literary critic, and book editor. He worked at the *Golden Fleece* 1907-1909.

[69] Sergey Gorodetsky, 1884-1967. Russian poet and a member of the symbolist group, close friends with Blok, Ivanov and Brusov. Eventually he abandoned symbolist concepts and joined with the new Soviet concept of socialist realism.

included these terms in an article titled *Voluntarily Terminated*, in the February 1908, issue of the Moscow symbolist magazine *Scales*.

> Truly, riff-raff luggage are the epigoniums of symbolism. They were not born in its uterus, but joined from the outside at the moment when they absolutely had nothing to lose. Truly, they are released slaves, weak-willed warriors, who are deceived by the flattery of those to whom they subject themselves.
>
> We the genuine symbolists do not recognize these literary clowns, prodigal cats and hyenas eating the corpses of fallen enemies. If they say that they are symbolists, they lie. We drive away from ourselves such a crowd of idle clowns. Gathering at some safe distance from us, they holler their cry for this field of Russian literature, installing their own covenants although stealthily appropriated from us.

Meanwhile the gatherings of the Religious-Philosophical Society continued at the residence of Margarita Morozova. The primary motivator of the conversations was her close friend Prince Evgeni Nikolaievich Trubetzkoi. At one time or another almost the entire society of Moscow humanists and intellectuals and philosophic thought attended. Bely likewise attended occasionally with a treatise to deliver or debating with others on such issues. There was always room for everybody and lasting the entire day.

One person who attended regular was Feodor Stepun, and he likewise attended the gatherings at the Morozov residence. In his memoirs he recollects Bely:

> During the described years of his Moscow life, Bely with identical passion raged foamed at the crests of all of his waves. I remember him not only at the meetings of the Religious-Philosophical or the Psychological Society, not only at Morozova's or at *Musaret*, but likewise at the comfortable evening dinner conversations at the Gershenzon residence,[70]

[70] Mikhail Osipovich Gershenzon, 1869-1925, Russian journalist, philosopher and

at the *Scorpion* office, at concerts starring the singer Olenina-D'alheim,[71] at the Astrov[72] salon (where the leftists would gather and he would passionately debate with the cadets), at anthroposophist evening dinners at the Kharitonov residence,[73] and finally at some little house deep in the snow outside of Moscow at halfway-legal gatherings of Tolstoyans, Stundists, Reformed Orthodox, or Orthodox Revolutionaries. There with the same enthusiasm he would dance and sing and cry his concepts and visions.

To recount the themes on which Bely spoke over these years is impossible and unnecessary. It is sufficient to say that his cognizance was listened in and noticed by everybody in hearing range. He would often refer to himself as a seismograph, seeming to feel subtle agitations of events in Russia and Europe that others did not. Whether it be some all-encompassing crisis of European culture or life, some approaching revolution in Europe, the subject of revolution circulating in Russia, it would all excite or disturb him. In his cognizance, all the trivia and incidentals of life would naturally and regularly turn into symptoms, symbols and signals.

Bely was most talented in the art of debate. He had the ability to bring life to some lifeless subject and the most emaciated of subjects grew in his lips and performed just as though he was holding Aaron's rod.

About this time Bely started studying the philosophy of Nikolai Aleksandrovich Berdiaev, a religious and political writer and activist whose initial major work was just published in 1907, in Russia. He also moved from Petersburg to Moscow, and Bely had the opportunity to discuss philosophical matters with him. From his side Berdiaev was able like no one else to penetrate the essence of the creativity of Bely, seeing in him not only a poet and

---

translator.

[71] Maria Alekseevna Olenina-D'alheim, 1869-1970. Russian chamber and concert singer.

[72] Nikolai Ivanovich Astrov, 1868-1934, Russian political and socialist activist.

[73] Pyotr Alekseevich Kharitonov, 1852-1916, state senator, high ranking Russian Mason.

writer of the symbolist class, but an original philosopher. The following is an example of what Berdiaev wrote about Bely. It is his impression of Bely's recent publication *Symbolism as an Ideology*, a collection of articles that he wrote and of which some were delivered at gatherings of the Religious and Philosophical Society at Morozov's residence.

> Simultaneously with *Silver Dove* the exceptional book of A.Bely was published – *Symbolism*. With striking talent another facet of A.Bely is unveiled, one that is not available in his poetry, in his *Symphonies*, in *Silver Dove*. This is A.Bely – philosophical, gnoseological, methodical, different, cultural.
>
> The verses of Bely are purely Russian, national, native, oriental. His verses on women are passive, enveloped by nightmare and premonitions, so near to insanity. So close and native are Russian fields and emaciated grandmothers, ravines and saloons. There is so much mystical slavophilism in A.Bely, a slavophilism that is disconcerting, catastrophic, tied with Gogol and Dostoyevsky (but not with Khomyakov, although the Logos was strong in his works).
>
> A. Bely as a philosopher is the most pure of the westerners and so cultured. He does not like Russian philosophy, the slavophile cognizance is alien to him. His cognizance is exclusively occidental. This is why Richert[74] is closer to him than Vl.Solovyov, Nietzsche closer than Dostoyevsky, Jacob Boehme closer than St. Seraphim,[75] a diversely methodical philosophy closer than a synthetic religious philosophy.
>
> So are the oriental-Russian mystical poetry of A.Bely and his occidental-European concept of philosophy contradictory? A.Bely seems to be experiencing nightmares and transparence of existence in his mystical poetry. This nightmary and transparency of existence remains in his philosophic cognizance. His book *Symbolism* is amazing and some chapter are ingenious, like the chapter *The Emblematic of Meaning*,

[74] Heinrich Rickert, 1863-1936, German philosopher in the Neo-Kantian school.
[75] Seraphim of Sarov (Prokhor Moshnin), 1754-1833, renown Russian Orthodox saint.

where A.Bely develops his original philosophic system, similar to Fichteanism,[76] but more artistic than scientific. In his personal reorganization of Fichteanism he senses a severance from existence and a fear of existence.

A.Bely deifies at least his individual creative act. God does not exist as an Entity, but the creative act is divine, so God is created, and He becomes the creative valuable as a result of necessity, but not because of solely existence. In the process of creativity there is no end, no termination in absolute existence. The creative process flows beneath the nightmary authority of a bad infinity.

I see in A.Bely a falsified union of slavophilism and Occidentalism, a falsified union of east and west. But he projects this problem in an extremely sharp and painful manner. He stretches toward oriental mysticism in his verses, while to the occident in other areas. The occident rejects the fundamental religious truth that mysticism is expressed in the Word – the Logos. The mysticism of anti-ecclesiasticism and anti-religiosity is inexpressible in the Word. As an artist, A.Bely defeats individualism and subjectivism, but only as an artist. As a philosopher, A.Bely remains severed from the universal Logos. This severance abandons him to an inescapable pessimism. A.Bely does not believe that it is possible to acquire the light of the Logos in the depths of the soul. He futilely seeks light at one time in the oriental national verses, at another time in the occidental cognizance.

The philosophy of the politically oriented Berdiaev repelled Bely due to his revolutionary activism and his liberal religious views.

Another prominent individual who moved from Petersburg to Moscow at about this time was Sergei Nikolaievich Bulgakov. Although he had not yet composed his philosophic works, he was recognized for his books on the future of Russian economy and polity. He also started to attend the Religious-Philosophical Society where Bely and Berdiaev would discuss issues with him.

---

[76] The philosophy of Johann Gottlieb Fichte, 1762-1814, German philosopher.

Bulgakov was far more of a conservative Orthodox Christian than Berdiaev who was more a political activist.

Bely wrote of his acquaintance and impression of Bulgakov:

> Conversations with Bulgakov were filled with berries, a fresh forest and the fragrance of resins, in the middle of which a hut of Christ's love is built. Not entirely a dogmatic person.

Both Bely and Bulgakov were fervent admirers of Vl. Solovyov, and who both counted Sophia the Divine Wisdom as one of their central theological categories and they both included the Cosmic concept of Sophia as the basis of ecumenical contemplation. To Bulgakov we are obligated the introduction of the actual meaning of cosmism in scientific and philosophic debate. According to Bulgakov Sophia shines in the world as the primordial purity and beauty of the universe, like a child's charm and an astonishing enchantment of a small flower, in the beauty of a star-fill heaven and the flame of the sun as it is rising. Sophism is the primary concept that unites all meaning, permitting a direct bridge to be installed between a person and the cosmos.

Although the conceptual and aesthetic aspirations of Bely and Bulgakov were not consistent in every aspect, they seemed to complement each other and learn from each other. Bely also records in his memoirs about Bulgakov's "captivating smile."

Another individual with whom Bely became acquainted and discussed issues in depth at the Society was Vasili Vasilyevich Rozanov, but their conversations inevitably led to verbal altercations and debates, most of it due to Rozanov's very conservative Russian Orthodox beliefs as opposed to Bely's allegorical interpretation of the Bible and church.

Bely's acquaintance with Mikhail Iyosefovich Gershenzon belongs to the same year of 1907. He was a Russian Jew and a representative of native philosophical and cultural thought. Gershenzon was also literary editor of the *Herald of Europe* and of the *Critical Review*, both very influential magazines, and he lived on Nikolsky Crossing not far from Bely and his mother's new residence. He was one of the few who without debate valued the diversity of Bely's talents as a writer, poet, critic, theologian, aesthetic and philosopher. As a result Gershenzon regularly invited Bely to submit articles for his magazines, and this started a tight and productive cooperation and sincere friendship between the two of them.

What especially made Gershenzon established in the publishing world was his publication in March 1909, of a collection of the best articles of the most prominent figures in Russian philosophy, called *Landmarks*. Within a year it went through 4 editions. In general the volume of articles decried Marxism as not providing an answer to the question of human purpose for existence and promoted Christianity in diverse religious and philosophical applications. Both Berdiaev and Bulgakov were contributors, as well as Gershenzon.

Other than some temporary excursions into neo-Kantianism and the contemporary Russian philosophers mentioned above, Bely's philosophic passion and preference remained as before. Of course of all those available it was Nietzsche who prevailed without competition. This motivated Bely to do what he liked best – to lecture, as well as accomplish a secondary motive – income from lecturing. Beginning December 19, 1907, Bely proceeded with a series of lectures dedicated to his idol at the large auditorium at the Poly-Technical Institute in Moscow, then the next month, on January 21, 1908, he repeated the same series, although with some improvements in content, at the Moscow Literary-Artistic Circle. Then he traveled to Petersburg where he delivered the same lectures at the Tenishevsky Institute,[77] and finally after returning to Moscow, he again delivered the same lectures to sold-out crowds and again at the Poly-Technical Institute. In between, on January 15, he also lectured on the *Art of the Future* at the Tenishevsky School.

As far as Bely was concerned Nietzsche in no way was a thinker of the past, he was the philosopher of today whose

[77] Built by Vyacheslav Nikolaievich Tenishev (1844-1903), in 1898, as a middle or junior high school, and lasting until 1918 when it was appropriated by the Soviet Commissariat of Education.

concepts belong first of all to the present and the future. Such an approach to a great extent impressed his listeners summing a genuine enthusiasm. Even Bely's former physiology professor, Kliment Timiryazev, an unbending materialist, came to listen to his former student, and then after the lecture complemented him on a job well done. How long did each lecture last? Probably in the area of close to 3 hours, and so was Bely's knowledge of his subject tied to his ability of keeping the attention of his audience and one very diversified in education, age and interest. Bely unfolded a picture and unleashed information on a cosmic scale that just about mesmerized his listeners.

So Bely recorded his understanding of these concepts and in the manner he delivered them to his audiences:

> All iterates. The sum of all combinations of the atoms of the universe terminates over the course of infinite eras, and even if one such combination is repeated then all combinations are repeated. But ahead and behind is infinity, and all combinations of atoms that arrange life and life in us have infinitely iterated, and we have also iterated. We have iterated and are iterating. The billions of centuries that separate our iteration are like zero [time], because with the extinguishment of cognizance time is also extinguished. We measure time only when conscious. And this infinite iteration of terminal fragments of time minus the course of time when we are not creates for us an immortality, but it is the immortality of his life. If we do not want to be immortally unhappy we must fill every moment of this life to the full with the wine of happiness.
>
> For the distant future humanity appends the name Friedrich Nietzsche to the names of the great teachers of life who created a religion of life. In essence, the route upon which Nietzsche summons us is the eternal route and which we have forgotten. The route that Christ traversed, the route by which the Raja Yogas of India walked and do walk. Nietzsche attained the supreme mystical consciousness that depicted him as the image of the New Person. In the future he became

> practical, presenting the route to corporeal transformation of the individual in *Zarathustra*. Here he affixed himself to contemporary theosophy and to the secret doctrine of antiquity.

At one of the lectures at the Poly-Technical Institute there occurred an encounter that would be fatalistic for Bely. After his presentation a fragile appearing girl walked up to him and reminded him about their acquaintance some 3 years prior at the apartment of her aunt, the singer M.A. Olenina-D'alheim, where Bely occasionally dropped by. The girl's name was Anna Alekseevna Turgeneva, although she went by Asya. She was studying drawing and graphics in Belgium, but occasionally she would visit her relatives in Moscow. In time this young woman would become Bely's wife, but for the occasion she just shared her respect for Bely and expressed a hope to continue further contact. Bely shared his admiration for Asya at the time after hearing about her art studies.

Even after the completion of the series of lectures, Bely almost every day was forced to worry about his daily bread. He was desperate and willing to have any of his articles published anywhere just for some royalty, and this just about caused a further rupture of association with Brusov. Bely responded positively to an unexpected request of the *Golden Fleece* for them to include in their magazine a collection of his new verses (although the magazine was to finally close it doors in 1909). Brusov counted this step to be nothing less than treachery. Bely was forced to explain the situation to him.

> When I agreed to give the verses to the *Fleece*, I was guided by an inner desire to only have 2 or 3 poems published. I had a large stack of poems and nowhere to publish them, since I was limited to publishing 7 or 8 poems a years.[78] I also have many introductory articles, those explaining my essential concepts,

[78] This would have been with *Scales*, the magazine published by Brusov.

> and *Fleece* took the effort to gather them for print. There was no place for them in *Scales*, and I do not write for any other magazine, and so I am forced to present them to the literary world outside of my present environment.
>
> What makes the situation more delicate is that so far I have not been able to close the deal with my estate in the Caucasus,[79] which would have provided me the possibility of almost becoming independent of the necessity of publishing my compositions.
>
> This is why I am destitute at present. Over the recent months I have been living exclusively on my income from *Scales*, but can I really (and you know this) exist on what royalties I have been receiving from you?
>
> This is a matter that has been very difficult for me so I have no choice but to proceed in the manner I have to find anybody willing to publish on my behalf.
>
> In addition to this, Valerie Yakovlevich, I do not even have funds to purchase the most necessary of items. I no longer have a decent suit, and I am in need of a new jacket, boots, galoshes, which I cannot afford. It is painful to my conscious if I have to turn to *Scales* and grovel for more royalty. I do have some pride.

Nothing hindered or postponed the plans for Bely's creative work as a writer and poet and so he continued to compose his verses. They were generated everywhere: Moscow, Petersburg, Munich, Paris, in the city and country, in the quiet effort in his private library or in the agony of a train wagon deafened by the repetitive noise of the wheels. At the same time he entertained the idea of a large novel. Best of all he liked to work at Serebryanni Kolodez. Bely's final opportunity to visit and live here in quiet and tranquility was in June 1908. In view of the deeper and more intense financial desperation that he and his mother were in, Bely's mother decided to sell the estate, although it contained his best memories and always would.

---

[79] The property the family still owned in Sochi.

While at Serebryanni Kolodez Bely completed a new collection of poems, titled *Ashes*. Most of the collection was composed during Bely's residency in Paris in January 1907, but it was finished that summer and finally published in Russia in December 1908. In the history of Russian poetry of the Silver Age, it was distributed under the moniker of *Nekrasovsky*, meaning that it followed the same vein as the poetry of the Golden Age poet Nikolai Nekrasov due to his theme of Russian tradition and love of his native land. Never did Bely write poetry as well as in this collection and he dedicated the volume to Nekrasov's memory.

A funny incident occurred to Bely that same December 1908, toward the end of the month. After a lecture at the Literary-Artistic Circle he received a letter from some unfamiliar girl whose name was of Armenian nationality – Shaginyan, and she called herself Marietta.[80] He divined a sincere intent in the letter and was impressed by the depth of her thinking, it was unlike the letters from other women and girls, all the many that he had received. She was 20 years of age and a student at the prestigious Moscow women's school of Vladimir Guerrier. Marietta had been studying the philosophy of Kant, adopted the modernist school of neo-Kantianism, and was fluent in the works of the fathers of the Christian church, and especially Russian Orthodoxy. A very impressive resume for a girl and of her age. She stated she was also acquainted with the philosophers Nikolai Berdiaev and Sergei Bulgakov – who were likewise acquainted with Bely – and the poet Vladislav Khodasevich of Moscow, as well at the Merezhkovsky couple Dmitri and Zinaida Gippius. She had a small income from working part-time as a letter and document copyist and so was able to get a ticket from an employer to attend one of Bely's lectures. She lived in Moscow with her sister Lina who also attended courses at Guerrier's. It was obvious from her letter that her intentions were not the same as most of the other women who were writing to Bely, but she portrayed a genuine

[80] Marietta Sergeevna Shaginyan, 1888-1982, Soviet writer of Armenian descent.

sincerity and dedication to philosophy and religion. Marietta mentioned in her letter that she wanted to become a writer.

Marietta Shaginyan described and recorded the subsequent event with Bely in her diary.

> He was slender with intense shoulders, incessantly changing places. While sitting he could not sit still or he would move to another chair. It seemed that he was always being blown somewhere by some wind fanned solely toward him, and this wind even lifted the hair of his head, even his voice cracked and yelped when he would start his presentation standing at the podium. This particular evening Andrei Bely had no grace, no aesthetic composure in his style.
>
> I saw at the podium a tortured human with a strained voice. Speaking he started to quickly look around himself, behind himself looking at his back, and then appeared frightened as though someone was overhearing him with a malicious intent. His fingers nervously shook. He cowered and squeezed the corners of the podium, then digging in his pockets, then looking over his shoulders again. It was physically difficult for me to watch him, and yet this was the author of *Symphony*, the amazing prose, light, gentle, and calming a person as would a nice dream. He seemed to be completely helpless, a naked soul thrown out of the defense of his body. I felt what he was like that evening. He was like an ill person in a ward accepting another ill person there, his neighbor in the next cot.
>
> Returning home and in a state of some kind of complete irresponsibility, I wrote to him a letter, right from my soul to his soul.

Not suspecting anything Marietta fell right into Bely's heart. By this time his soul reached a terminal crisis due to his regular torment from loneliness and hopelessness. He had been unable to develop any working relationship with a woman, and now this letter. Bely had no doubt in the sincerity of the writer of the letter. He could almost not believe it and had to respond, and he responded not just once, but with many letters. From that day and for a long while he wrote almost each day and they were long. He poured his soul out and passionately and without regrets, not even thinking about what would occur from all of this.

The first of his correspondence spoke on its own, sent sometime early January 1909:

> A calm clarity is needed, a serene dawn and, my God, not with any hysterics. It is good if you are not a decadent.[81] Nonetheless, the comic-dramatic tone of your words convinces me otherwise.
>
> We will write one to another about one another. Do you want to? It is good that you wrote about you mother, sister, about yourself and not bragging, and etc. The only reason I want to write to you is because I want to write to you. I will also write to you about myself, if you want. You can ask whatever your want about me, I will be open and will reply directly, but to the extent possible due to our absence and through letters. But paper only allows us 1/100th of the words necessary, and if there is a living tie between us we must see each other so not just to feel each other in space.
>
> I need to warn you. I am not much of a writer. Often I go out of control, I open myself, I talk through my teeth, but not due to any subtlety, but due to embarrassment. People are afraid of me. I am not formal with them or tactful, neither open to the end. It is a mask that I am long wearing.
>
> So farewell dear, my dear. You and your lilies of the valley are also dear. I await a letter. And I am already sorrowful. Are you departing somewhere? For long? And if you depart, send me your address. In any case it would be bad to ask me to write without us really wanting to be friends.
>
> Boris Bugaev
>
> P.S. Who are you? Do I know you? Where did we meet?

---

[81] As mentioned about, some of the traditional Russians labeled the symbolists – decadents, as they felt the new genre of literature was a decadence of the 19th century classic.

Bely's reply leads us to realize that his life was in psychological turmoil. Although prominent as a lecturer, writer, philosopher and conversationalist and very popular, he lacked success in terms of financial gain and with the opposite gender. Although there were many women willing and who attempted to physically draw close to Bely, none had the attributes or intentions that he hoped in a female friend. As a result, as mentioned above, he would shoo them away. Doubt of ever resolving these issues tortured him, and so he shared them with Marietta and grasped at her letter like to a straw.

The following is a selection of his subsequent letter to Marietta:

> My dear, dear, dear Marietta. I think of you and my thoughts are like a soft stream of pearls. Do not discard me, dear Marietta. Be my eternal Marietta. Forgive me for my foolishness and the brevity of my letter, my dear. It is difficult for me to write, it is a weakness of mine. Do invite me to visit you, but after 3 days.
>
> B. Bugaev

Marietta responded and invited him to spend Christmas Eve with her around their Christmas tree.[82] All the money the Shaginyan sisters had went for Christmas tree decorations and a package of candles, and a box of pastries made with marmalade, which is all they had to offer Bely.

Some 70 years later – this would be 1979 and she lived to 1982 – Marietta recollected the excitement of the event of meeting Bely and the time spent that evening:

> Standing excited at the candle-lit Christmas tree, our hands in a cold sweat, we waited, and Boris Nikolaievich arrived just as afraid as we were. Instead of extraordinary women in a fairy

[82] Christmas in Russia is still based on the Julian calendar which is 12 days behind the Gregorian calendar, so Orthodox Christmas is celebrated on January 6 of the year following corresponding to December 25, of the old calendar plus 12 days. So this day would be January 5, 1909.

> tale setting, which perhaps he was expecting, he saw 2 girls both pale as a corpse. One girl 20 years of age and the other 17, holding hands. Bely did not eat the entire day, excited wondering what was to occur Christmas Eve, and he was starving. So he started to talk and he talked and he talked about nothing while eating one marmalade pastry after another not noticing that it was already midnight. And then it was 2 o'clock in the morning and our box of pastries was empty.
>
> Maybe it was because he expected something else that the evening turned out the way it did.

One reason for Bely's agitation was that he found himself entangled in a bad relationship with Anna Mintzlova that day and the situation was bothering him.

Correspondence between Bely and Marietta soon turned toward a philosophic character, and then eventually slowed and stopped. She did visit Bely at his apartment at Nikolsky Crossing a few times, but she left no impressions of it in her memoirs and neither did Bely.

Bely's next letter to Marietta was not until 1928, when he was traveling through the Caucasus Mts.

Bely again took opportunity to travel to Kiev to lecture. On March 14, 1909, he lectured on *The Contemporary Era and Przybyszewski*,[83] at the Medvedev Theater in Kiev.

Bely spent that summer of 1909, at the estate of Sergei Sokolov, and then spent August with the Merezhkovskys at their estate near Petersburg, and then lived in Petersburg for a while.

During this interval, he completed his subsequent volume of poetry, which he titled *Urn*. It was published at the beginning of spring 1910. Distinct from previous collections of his poetry with clearly expressed Nekrasov-like themes, *Urn*, as Bely described it, was a book of philosophic meditations and disappointing passions.

---

[83] Stanislaw Felix Przybyszewski, 1868-1927, Polish novelist, dramatist, and poet of the symbolist school.

Three levels of his poetic evolution were inherent in it, signifying his 3 previous published collections. Bely explained it as follows:

> My first book of poetry had the title *Gold in Azure*. I could not entirely unite with this infantile book that was incomplete in many areas in its symbolic meaning, as its title indicated. Azure is the symbol of the highest sanctification. The gold triangle is the attribute of Hiram, the builder of Solomon's temple.[84] So what is azure and what is gold? The Rosicrucians reply to this. The world discards into the abyss the one who comprehends the gold and azure bypassing the occultist route. The world is consumed by flames, scattering ashes. Along with it the one who comprehends is also consumed in order to rise from the dead to proceed further on an activist route.
>
> *Ashes* is the book of self-immolation and death. But this death is just a curtain covering the horizon of the distance, so we can find our search nearby.
>
> In *Urn*, I gather my individual ash so it will not obscure the light to my living *I*. The dead *I*, I confine in the *Urn*, and the other living *I* is awakened in me and toward the truth. Yet the *Gold in Azure* is distant from me, in the future. The azure of the declining sunset is clouded by dust and smoke, and only the nighttime dark blue washes the dust with its dews. In the morning perhaps the azure will be clean.

The book starts with 4 poems dedicated to Brusov.

Subsequently were preparations for another series of lectures in Petersburg, titled *The Present and Future of Russian Literature*. The first lecture was delivered middle of January 1910, and an article was published on the topic in the magazine *Scales* in February.

Bely's prime goal was to underscore the development and preeminence of Russian poetry and prose, disclose its deep traditions, beginning with the most ancient of Slavic texts, *A*

---

[84] Referring to Hiram Abiff as the architect of Solomon's temple, based on Masonic tradition.

*Word about Igor's Regiment,*[85] which Bely called the alpha and omega of Russian literature, to the modern prophetic and Apocalyptic genre. As Bely noted in his article:

> From Pushkin and Lermontov to Brusov and Merezhkovsky, Russian literature was profoundly native. It developed in conditions quite different than did the literature of the west. It surfaced as the host of the religious pursuit of both scholars and peasants. More than any other type of literature it pertained to life's meaning and there was a certain preaching inherent in it: Russian literature of the 19th century was a continuous summons to a transformation of life. Gogol, Tolstoy, Dostoyevsky, Nekrasov – are musicians of the word. But they are immeasurably more than that as preachers, and the music of their words are the means of effectiveness.
>
> Our present is dark just as our past was dark, from the beginning, from primordial time. Darkness blends with darkness into a single night spread over a level plain, solid, icy, coffin-like – the plain of Russia.
>
> We writers are like theoreticians, having a premonition of the future, but like artists we speak of the future. We are just people that are just seeking also, not preaching but confessing. We only ask of one thing, for you to believe us.

Of course, Bely could not avoid promoting his symbolist group as being prophetic as opposed to the supposedly unilluminated authors of the Golden Age.

Gradually long intended plans were materializing in Bely's life. At the end of winter 1909, he finally sat still long enough to write his novel that he already composed mentally from beginning to end. It title was *Silver Dove.* Initially it was serialized – part but not all – in the final issues of *Scales,* but then was published by *Scorpion* in 1910.

---

[85] Also translated as *Tale of Igor's Campaign*

Meanwhile fate relentlessly brought Bely closer to Asya Turgeneva. He initially met the 3 sisters – Anna (Asya), Natalia and Tatyanna – when as girls they moved to Moscow in 1905. After the unexpected death of their father their mother remarried, but the girls were raised by their aunt, the famous chamber singer, Maria Alekseevna Olenina-D'alheim. Natalia would later marry Aleksandr Pozzo, editor of the Moscow magazine *Northern Lights*, while Tatyanna would marry Bely's friend Sergei Solovyov.

Although Asya was distinct due to her exceptional humility and quietness, she nonetheless made the first step to meet her fate and proposed to Bely that he pose for a portrait. The eyes of the 18-year old girl – and Bely was almost 30 at the time – with her long and hanging ash-colored hair could stare right into your soul. And Bely's heart vibrated from her radiant smile. As he described Asya in his memoirs:

> She represented living springtime to me when the two of us were left alone. This impression overwhelmed me, it was as though we again met after a long absence, and as though we were friends as children.
>
> An assurance rose in me during our initial meetings that this girl over the next 7 years would become the most indispensable soul.

Asya's attraction grew and strengthened day to day. During the last week of April 1909, the 2 of them took a ride to Savvinsky Monastery, near Zvenigorod, just outside of Moscow to the west. They went with her sister Natalia and her future husband Aleksander Pozzo, and Bely's friend Aleksei Petrovsky, staying at a hotel inside the monastery. After performing the expected ecclesiastical rites Bely and Asya went for a walk in the forest and tree climbing, regarding of their ages. At the top of one of the trees Bely asked Asya to marry him.

Some 25 years later Bely recollected the event and his feelings in his memoirs:

> I recollect our conversation. It was in a tree, we were hanging over a light blue, clear pond reflecting the sun with its sparkling. I recollect the reflections bending my head down. From the green clumps of leaves, at a certain moment of the breeze of the wind, I saw the curled locks of Asya's hair, her 2 eyes wide open and intensely paying attention to me. And I recollect the pink silk coat she was wearing. Suddenly the branches rubbed against her face. It was nothing. Under her feet the trunk was separating, splitting into 2 or into 3 branches. I recollect the backs of Natasha[86] and Pozzo against each other beneath us, sitting far below us, along the green bank of the pond.
>
> We stayed several days in the village, but they would be special for me always as opposed to my melancholy past. We gathered to leave, but when they gave us the bill it seemed we had nothing with which to pay. So A.Petrovsky had to go to Moscow for money. He left the 2 of us love-birds there with the monks, the hotel managers, as hostages until he returned.

Upon returning to Moscow Asya was compelled to immediately depart for Volin, in northwest Ukraine, to care for her dying grandmother Bakunin (on her mother's side). Then she was to return to Brussels in order to complete art school. The separation would be a trial of their love, in the meanwhile correspondence would be the link between the 2 of them. Bely wrote to her an immense number of letters, each longer than the other, and often he would sit up the entire night writing a letter. Unfortunately not one of these love letters has survived. They would be separated 1-1/2 years.

Bidding farewell to his bride, Bely immerse himself into the flood of Russia's literary life. That year was the celebration of Nikolai Gogol's 100-year anniversary. Although he was born April 1, 1809, the festivities were planned for April 26, 1909, with a wreath to be place on his grave by a group of symbolists. Bely of course had the

[86] referring to Asya's sister Natalia.

privilege of delivering an address on Gogol, and it was subsequently published in *Scales* magazine. Bely saw the forerunner of all the newest trends of Russian literature in his favorite writer, not only realism and romanticism, but symbolism. The conclusion of his address, as published in *Scales*, was the following passage:

> So what are images? Of what impossibilities are they formed? Everything is fit into them: flowers, aromas, sounds. Where are there more bold comparisons? Where can artistic accuracy be more unbelievable? The destitute symbolists: critics cannot desist from discrediting them for their *blue sounds*,[87] but find me an image from Verlaine,[88] Rimbaud,[89] or Baudelaire,[90] which were not unbelievable due to their boldness, as with Gogol. No, you will not find them, and meanwhile Gogol is read and they do not see, to this point they do not see, that we have no words in dictionaries with which to call Gogol. We do not have the capacity to measure all of the possibilities that he exhausted. We still do not know what Gogol is. And although we do not see him personally, all of Gogol's compositions are closer to us than all the Russian writers of the 19th century and available for us to receive.
>
> On every page and almost in every phrase does he traverse the border at what is some kind of new world that is growing in our soul.

Meanwhile on the Moscow literary front popular movements were progressing. That year Bely's old friend Emilie Metner acquired some capital and utilized it to organize a new book publisher, giving it the name of the ancient sun god Apollo – *Musaget*, based on Musagetes. Prior to this Metner worked as an Editor at the

---

87 Reference to a compilation of poems, published 1895, many of which were satirical and parodies, by Viktor Petrovich Burenin, 1841-1926, a Russian poet, novelist and dramatist. The statement by critics of the symbolists was intended to be discrediting.
88 Paul Verlaine, 1844-1896, French poet associated with the symbolist movement.
89 Arthur Rimbaud, 1854-1891, French poet and close friend of Paul Verlaine.
90 Charles Baudelaire, 1821-1867, French poet.

*Golden Fleece*. Metner hired his symbolist friends to work there and which likewise attracted them. The first publication of *Musaget* was Bely's collection of articles *Symbolism as an Ideology*. Bely worked furiously on the collection to prepare it for reprint and to meet the time frame that Metner demanded. Many of the articles written a few years back Bely felt needed to be rewritten, as well as adding some 200 pages of new commentary, and all done speedily. Bely also wrote his primary article, *The Emblematic of Meaning*, absorbing some 100 pages of final text, in just one week.[91]

Bely recollected his work with *Musaget* in his memoirs:

> The dawn caught me working, then I fell asleep until 2 in the afternoon. I went back to work, not even leaving for tea in the dining room (they brought it to me). At 5:30 PM, I attend church services locally. Then I went to *Musaget* and encourage my coworkers. Then I went home for a nap and was up at midnight to continue work until morning.
>
> For weeks my study looked like a horrible spectacle: the sofas were moved over to clean the rug. A fan hung overhead. About 20 opened books, notebooks, sketchpads, laid over the run. For hours I would lie on the run on my stomach. I would flip through my commentaries, my fingers flying through the pages. I worked insanely.
>
> The first half of my book was returned to me with heaps of corrections, while the other was still cooking in the oven. Under such conditions I was not surprised that they viewed my book as still raw. I am surprised that some people still read it.[92]

Bely and Metner were friends over these years at *Musaget* and Bely was a type of philosophic mentor to Metner, but until 1912. The rupture was due to Metner departing from the concepts of the symbolists and going in the direction of psychology, and

---

[91] Some of this is translated into English in the Appendix.
[92] This recollection was written about 1930.

specifically Carl Jung, with whom he became a personal friend, while Bely at the same time inclined toward Rudolf Steiner's anthroposophy, which Metner would not accept.

Regardless of his daily occupation and constant hassle Bely continued intensely working on *Silver Dove*. He was most successful writing during that summer of 1909, isolated at Sergei Sokolov's estate in Dedova. Bely wrote to his friend and fellow symbolist poet Feodor Sologub about his experiences of the time and work on his novel:

> I live outside of Moscow, I live in complete solitude with a friend.[93] The terrace extends directly into an unmown meadow, a forest is further. I live with flowers, with books, with days. The flowers are white, red, yellow. The books are scholarly or humorous. The days are golden, turquoise, and dark grey, and the days slip away. Time is forgotten, the days are forgotten. If I could submerge myself always in time and space this way. With deep fear I think about winter arriving with its snowflakes, and which causes me hysteria and aggravation. Anything not to step into mud, but I am referring to our literary circle. There is no need to order new boots that are higher, otherwise they will just dirty the mud.
>
> In the garden where I reside, there is a small, elderly woman. She is very self-educated and this is difficult for someone to achieve. The old woman is kind, but when the thunder begins, terror emanates in her eyes, then she calls to me. Unexpectedly she involves me in some intellectual conversation. I look around and the storm clouds are gathered. After the storm the old woman smiles at the flowers, rays and bees. And we are at peace.
>
> The sunsets this year are especially pretty, there have not been such sunsets now 3 years. Suffocating darkness obscured the view of the mountains, and now these new sunsets as if again provide me a promise. But of what? There was a time

---

93 This would be Sergei Sokolov.

when I did not skip even one sunset. For 5 years I tracked the sunsets and finally I learned to converse with acquaintances about the sunsets. Soul, what is the sunset? One is red, another resembles a tiger's fur, some other is opaque like a pearl. And so this is what happens, the dawn shines and then radiates like a familiar soul. So earlier I was able to fly on the sunset to my dear friends and close associates. And then the sunsets became dark and faded. You look and what remains is the fur of a carcass, like a pelt with blood on it. The sunset lies heavy on the heart, it tears at my heart, painfully and bitterly. I would then enjoy what occurred after the sunset: a translucent, dark blue darkness. Now it seems the sunsets are clear and again the nice voices call. You again await with excitement and hope. But why all of this?

Dear Feodor Kuzmich, It was precious when I received news of you. I was happy that you let me hear your voice. We know little of each other on the mundane side of life. This is valuable for me and I joyfully contemplate that there is between us the possibility of a mutual relationship. So few realistic people, but so many living in an elusive fantasy, so many over-sensitive in this world not even living a life. But I feel that the time is approaching when a union will sprout among those who carry high the banner of service, or at least – as in my case – they attempt to do so.

Affectionately yours and deeply respectful of you.

Boris Bugaev

Work on the novel was tedious and Bely intended to provide a new literary meaning to his latest and it being a novel, as opposed to the many volumes of symbolist poetry and collections of articles already published. *Silver Dove* contained several of Bely's personal memories and experiences of the countryside and the information he gathered about Christian mystical sectarians, and especially the Khlisti. He used Lubov Blok to form the character of the peasant woman Matryona Semeonovna. (The reader is urged to purchase a copy and read it and make your own conclusions.)

Bely's novel *Silver Dove* summoned a storm of excitement from the side of friends and symbolist adherents. Especially provocative but favorable reviews were provided from both Nikolai Berdiaev and Sergei Bulgakov. Berdiaev wrote a very frank review of the book that was published in a local magazine. The following is an except:

> A genuinely wide scope of themes are contained in A.Bely's novel *Silver Dove*. It delves into the width of traditional life, penetrating into Russia's soul. With the strength of his artistic gift A.Bely overcomes his subjectivism and penetrates into the objective element of Russia. I must decisively state that the new Russia art has not created anything of more significance. A return toward the traditions of great Russian literature is sensed in A.Bely's novel, but on the field of battle of a new art. In *Silver Dove*, in an originally manner, he unites symbolism with realism. Bely belongs to the school of Gogol and has surfaced as a contemporary continuer of the Gogol tradition.

Sergei Bulgakov offered his review in a letter to Bely:

> I am totally agitated by your book. You have succeeded in it, no, it is what you were given, to penetrate so far into the national soul in a manner we have not been able since the time of Dostoyevsky. The miracle of artistic clairvoyance is achieved in it. The clandestine secrets of the national soul in its unnatural state were ploughed up with your composition and as you have shown with all your strength, the demonic elements are inescapable. The deception of the Petersburg mystery services[94] is now clear along with the depths of the satanic mystic sectarians.

The novel was serialized in the magazine *Scales*, beginning with the March issue and through December 1909, while it was

[94] The Khlisti started their gatherings in Petersburg at the home of Baroness Tatarinova beginning 1817.

published in book form in 1910. Bely then had intentions of continuing with subsequent volumes to create a trilogy under the heading of *East and West*. However the effort expended in that direction led to his next novel *Petersburg*, and in a different setting and new characters and plot.

In June 1910, Asya Turgeneva completed her curriculum in art in Belgium, and then went to Bogolubi, a village near Volin, Ukraine, to visit her mother and family. Bely immediately traveled to meet her there. Beginning at this time, they were husband and wife, although they decided against a formal church wedding. Asya, as with her older sister Natalia, in principle did not recognize ecclesiastical ceremonies, although they were seriously interested when it came to religious mysteries, esotericism, occultism, and theosophy. They rented a room temporarily in a neighboring village to give them time to settle. Then shortly they returned to Moscow.

But there was nowhere for the newly-weds to live in Moscow, as Bely's mother Aleksandra Dmitrievna was categorically opposed to their marriage, and Asya could not tolerate her mother-in-law's disposition, any more than Bely's father was able. Aleksandr feared that Asya would cause Bely to abandon her in her old age, and he was her only source of support. The fact that the couple did not have a church wedding much annoyed Aleksandra, although a nominal Russian Orthodox Christian, and she wanted them to have one. Aleksandra's animosity toward Asya then carried over to Bely.

Due to the intolerance of Aleksandra toward her son and daughter-in-law, they concluded that a trip abroad would be the best measure to take and as long as their finances would allow them, and then decide a further course. Bely needed finances to travel, so he decided to renew his friendship with Blok, with whom he did not correspond for almost 2 years since their previous rupture, hoping he would publish more of Bely's poetry and so provide some income. It would be difficult for Bely but circumstances dictated.

Bely wrote the letter of reconciliation under the auspices of providing his opinion to a series of poems that Blok wrote titled *At the Field of Kulikovo*, and published in the magazine *Shipovnik*, and an article on symbolism published in the magazine *Apollo*. So at the end of August 1910, Bely wrote to Blok:

> Deeply respected and again a close associate, Sasha.
>
> First of all allow me to bring repentance to you for all that has occurred between us. I have already for a long while, over a year, have no animosity toward you. But it seems to be strange to speak to you about this. And why should we. Now, having just read your article in *Apollon*,[95] I felt an obligation to write to you to express to you my deep respect for the words of immense courage and noble truth, which almost no one bothers to hear except for a few individuals and those in Moscow.
>
> Right now I am deeply agitated and touched. You have found the words that I have been seeking for a year, but have not found. But you said them, not only for yourself but also for us. Again, thank you, dear brother. I call you my brother because I now hear you as though you are one. It is not so much that I want to see you or hear you. You can write to me or you can not write. We can be superficial to each other and at least not display any ill will, it is all the same. I am not writing for the sake of restoring our relations, but due to a duty I have to you. For the sake of rectitude I ask forgiveness of you, for into all that the devil got us untangled.

Blok did not hesitate to respond, and the setting for their reconciliation was the residence of Margarita Morozova in Moscow, where Bely was due to deliver a lecture titled, *The Tragedy of Creativity with Dostoyevsky*. On November 1, 1910, Blok attended the lecture along with a crowd that filled the residence, with not even standing room available. Blok and Bely spent time together after the meeting and were able to reconcile.

---

[95] Referring to *Musaget*.

The almost 2 years separation, as well as Blok having to settle his marital issue, played a beneficial part in his condescension.

A second item of discussion at the Morozova residence was the departure of Leo Tolstoy from his home at Yasnaya Polyana. For Bely such news was a personal tragedy. Over the recent years Bely acquired a high respect for Tolstoy, not only as a novelist, but as a profound religious thinker, although his study of Tolstoy recently started. Bely was agitated by this piece of news, so he proceeded to collect this thoughts in regard in to the conclusion of the life of Russian literary geniuses. Bely's article that evolved from Tolstoy's departure compared tragedy in the compositions of Dostoyevsky with the tragedy of Bely's 2 other highly respected authors – Gogol and Tolstoy – and tied them with the tragedy of Russia and the Russian people. The following is a selection from this article:

> Is it the tragedy of creativity or the tragedy of Russian creativity? Is every type of artistic creation either a religious tragedy or a Russian creation. In its supreme and completely developed intention, does tragedy become purely religious? A muse, a favorite woman, becomes Mother of our Native Land, just as she represented our Native Land for Dostoyevsky, for Gogol, for Tolstoy.
>
> For many years over Europe a question proposed by Tolstoy petrified like un immovable bolder. But he was the great pinnacle of Russian creativity and people stared at him with frightening perplexity. And this pushed the solid rock bolder and it rocked: the departure of Tolstoy out of the world, a silent thunder. The question is resolved in great sorrow, terror and fear for Russia. For some it is a premonition having a fragrant odor, while it is hope and joy for others. The rock, torn away and rolling, grows from snow attaching to it. The avalanche grows.
>
> The matter here is not just about Tolstoy. Tolstoy sat 30 years immobile: not moving forward or backward. For 30 years he lived through the tragedy of creativity. And now Tolstoy got up and went – he was affected. Can we know if Russia will be

> affected in the same manner, which is only sick. It is the roar of the avalanche that we feel in Tolstoy's motion. There is definitely something here for Europe to fear.

After news of the death and funeral of Leo Tolstoy, Bely supplemented and revised his report, and delivered it on November 1, 1910, at a meeting of the Religious-Philosophical Society. It was subsequently published as a brochure having the title, *The Tragedy of Creativity: Dostoyevsky and Tolstoy.*

# THE BELYS TRAVEL EUROPE, AFRICA AND THE MIDDLE EAST

After some negotiations Bely was eventually able to convince his employers at *Musaget* to loan him money in the amount of 3,000 rubles. It would be against future royalties to be collected on future books, and especially those published pertaining to his travels in Europe, Africa and the Middle East. But they did not give him all the money immediately, but promised to send it to him in proportion to the material as they received it from him. This complicated life for Bely and his wife abroad, always waiting for funds to be wired wherever they were staying. Nevertheless on November 26, 1910, they departed with a large crowd at Moscow train station. Alekandr Melentyevich Kozhebatkin, a secretary at *Musaget*, gave Bely a list of requirements they expected of him in regard to the books to be written based on his travels. As with all other such requests, Bely discarded them once on the train and with his own agenda for recording his experiences and putting them to paper, and in no hurry to do so, but to enjoy the opportunity to travel and with his new wife. Bely took no books with him at all for the trip, as he told Asya:

> You are the only book that I need.

Having visited Germany and France earlier, the Belys were just a short while in Austria, and then went directly to Italy, arriving there December 12, spending time in Venice, Florence, Rome, and

Naples. The art oriented Asya spent all the time she possible could visiting sites of architecture and history, libraries and museums, and so introduced and submersed Bely into another world of art he was not aware of, living in Russia all his life. They then went by boat to Sicily, arriving December 17, and stayed in Palermo for a short while, and then moved to a small town named Montreal, arriving December 24. Here they stayed for a couple of weeks, and then took a boat across the narrow pass of the Mediterranean Sea and landing in Tunisia on January 4, 1911.

There the couple stopped for a while at an Arab village called Rades, arriving there January 15. Here Bely wrote to Blok:

> I live in a small Arab village, it is blindingly white. Its blindingly clean houses have flat roofs and are high, similar to towers of 3 stories height, alongside snow white stone domes, beautiful minarets. It is next to the grave of some famous Islamic theologian surrounded by palm trees, olive trees and fig trees. Asya and I alive in a genuine Arab home, just us, and talk up the third floor with tiny, decorated and enchanting rooms.
>
> Asya and I have this majestic flat roof, and in the evenings we sit for a long while up there on rugs with our legs folded. Not far from here, only a 20 minute walk, the violet Mediterranean Sea sparkles. I have turned into a foolish and content epicurean. I gather cockleshells, read Arabian tales and say sweet nothings to Asya.
>
> But I am content, happy, I feel as if my strengths are surging back into me each day. Finally after 6 insane years consisting of continuous suffering, I am rested. I am only worried that this happiness sent to me will sadly tear apart.
>
> Dear Shura,[96] flee yourself from vanity, people, Petersburg, the literary scene. All of this is repulsive, greed, decay and unresulting hysteria. Life can be beautiful, but they ruin it, meaning people.

[96] Russian diminutive for Aleksander

Matters did not turn out as well for Bely as he expected due to homesickness. He could not stop dreaming of his home and Russia. However visiting many of these sacred and historical and distant spots did increase his feeling of oneness with the universe. Bely did compose some poetry while in Sicily and Tunisia, dedicating it to Asya. While there they visited Kairouan, and did some local touring.

After 2 months in Tunisia, leaving end of February, Bely and Asya traveled to Malta and then to Egypt. The captain of the ship offered to take them to his final destinations of Ceylon and then Japan, but funds were quickly exhausting for Bely and he had to reach Cairo soon, since money from Moscow was wired there and waiting for him.

Egypt was an incomparable experience for Bely and an unprecedented impression, compared to Russia and Europe. He read about the pyramids and other archeological sites in Egypt and now was his opportunity to visit them, as especially the Sphinx, since he earlier wrote a treatise on the object earlier.

In Cairo, Bely wrote to Blok on March 2, 1911:

> Dear Sasha:
>
> Yesterday was for me an unforgettable minute. I stared for half an hour, not moving away, at the eyes of the Sphinx. The Sphinx watches the sand with his immense living eyes, and each minute the expression of his monstrous eyes changes. Initially he was formidable, then humorous, then afraid, then nice, and then beautiful like an Angel. The moon is blindingly flaring, illuminating the desert. The dark skinned Fellahs are scattered in the area, and they all seem to look like one another. The conical design of the pyramids are insanely impressive.
>
> Affectionately yours,
> B. Bugaev.

Bely wrote a similar letter to his mother:

> I write to you, overwhelmed by the Sphinx. Such a living stare saturated with significance I have never seen yet anywhere.
>
> The gaze of the monstrous Sphinx in the desert flies straight to the stars in the dark blue sky. It is not an Angel, not a beast, not a beautiful woman.

Later Bely recorded in his memoirs his further impressions as he stood in front of the Sphinx:

> A limitation is expressed in the image. It is not an impression of unlimitedness, because the image of unlimitedness would be imageless.
>
> Egypt was a terrorist act struck at the contemporary soul of a person, the ineffable sculpture of the Sphinx throwing us out of the era. The Sphinx traverses all human means of measurement. It is a precise incarnation of immeasurability. And terrifyingly this immeasurability is installed in the image of something like a human, yet depicting something beyond our imagination. Staring at the monstrous expression of the Sphinx's head, we begin to feel how the bottom of human personality is broken in us. And on its own the *I* fails within us.
>
> For over half an hour I sat in the sand in front of the Sphinx. Together with it thorny rings of some kind of eternal route known from the primordial era overwhelmed me. A beast, corpse, Ethiopian, titan, then Angel – all gazed at me in order. But the beast and corpse and titan and Angel simultaneously resided in this face. The beast, corpse, titan and Angel formed the roundness of his head, out of which his ancestral era was force on us. His ancestral era forced upon me whispered to me that for him time no longer exists, that it – time – from now on is the alpha and omega. All of this resided enigmatically in the Sphinx simultaneously. And unfolding the eras, these fragments of the Sphinx's puzzle, I

> contemplated momentarily on my route and final destiny. This contemplation flew away in a whirlwind, slipped away, gone.

The Sphinx became for Bely one of the most significant of all symbols, a super-symbol, as already used above in one of his treatises. Bely likewise used the Sphinx to represent the city Petersburg in a poem he included in his novel:

> Russia is a Sphinx. Rejoicing and Sorrowing.
> And soaking in black blood.
> It looks, sees, watches you,
> And with hate and with love.

The Bely couple now had plans to traverse Africa through the Sudan desert by land, or travel to the Republic of Guinea by ship, and even to possible visit Togo and Liberia. What attracted the Belys, and especially Asya, was the claim of the German archeologist Leo Frobenius to have discovered remnants of the ancient civilization of Atlantis, which many identified with the region of the Yoruba people, primarily in Nigeria. However their financial difficulties forced them to reject such a wide scale expedition, so in the beginning of April 1911, they left Egypt for Palestine, hoping to spend Easter in Jerusalem.

Bely's visit of sacred places in Palestine increased his religious disposition. During Easter in Jerusalem he wrote to Blok, part of which is the following;

> Dear Sasha:
>
> We ran into the promised land from Egypt.
>
> I am tortured by the following plagues of Egypt: 1. Fleas. 2. Bribery. 3. The dirt. 4. The desert wind. 5. Toothache. 6. Englishmen. 7. The inability to leave due to lack of money.
>
> We were so amazed that Jerusalem is inexpressible, ancient, eternally arriving, legendary. The sepulcher of the Lord is not what you think from a distance, it is the incarnation of an eternal dream. And there is a unification of churches – Catholic and Orthodox – at the sepulcher of the

> Lord. We were touched by the Moslems in their turban who came to worship at the sepulcher. Not removing their turbans, they made the sign of the cross.
>
> Palestine is dearth of flowers, Jerusalem is a pale yellow, but migrates into a faded gold. I sat long at Solomon's temple.
>
> Jesus has resurrected! Hooray for Russia! May the European pagans perish.

The Belys returned to Russia by ship, leaving Jaffa, stopping at Constantinople, and then arriving in Odessa on April 22. From there they went to straight to Bogolubi, to Asya's mother and relatives, arriving April 25. They had to stay here for a while since there was nowhere for them to live in Moscow, Bely's mother still could not accept Asya as her daughter-in-law and refused to allow them to stay with her. They had no money to otherwise rent a place. Every day brought the couple into deeper debt, since the loan given them by *Musaget* was long expended, and the relationship with *Musaget* and the publisher Emilie Metner unexpectedly complicated. He categorically refused to advance Bely royalties on any books he intended to reprint. Metner was expecting new material from him.

In Bogobuli Bely and wife Asya settled in a small separate 2-room house built by some tree cutter off the side of some road. Surrounding it was a bare field filled with haystacks, in the distance was an oak grove. Bely's work on a narrative of his journey went slow, it seems his daily worries for survival continually interfered with his ability to think clearly.

After 10 days in Bogolubi, Bely left for Moscow, arriving on May 18, to see about a place to live and somehow established himself financially. After a few days in Moscow Bely wrote to Asya:

> Over the 9 days I have spent in Moscow I have turned into some kind of insensitive and impersonal robot. It is so difficult, so difficult.

Brusov's magazine, *Scales*, where the Moscow symbolists felt themselves so comfortable, terminated its existence, while Brusov himself relocated to the new magazine – *Russian Thought*. It is published by the popular economist and publicist Peter Berngardovich Struve, he was earlier a Marxist but now a leader of the liberal movement. Another old friend of Bely's also attached himself to the new publication – Sergei Bulgakov. It was he who suggested to Bely that he complete his impending volume or what Bely felt would be a successor to *Silver Dove* and have *Russian Thought* publish it as a serial. This would resolved all of Bely's financial difficulties. This became *Petersburg*.

Bely returned to Bogolubi for the months of June and July 1911, and returned to Moscow together with Asya arriving August 8, 1911. Bely and wife Asya then rented at a rooming house on Tversky Blvd. Bely's mother continued to ignore her daughter-in-law, but eventually she somewhat compromised due to their financial desperation and she lent 1,000 rubles to them.

Bely revived his previous association with Margarita Morozova as she, over the interim of Bely's absence from Russia, founded a new publishing house of philosophic and religious books, called *Pathway*. Bely proposed to write 2 biographies: one on the Russian poet Afanasy Fet,[97] and the other on the Russian cosmic philosopher and librarian Nikolai Feodorovich Feodorov.[98] Morozova extended an advance of 1,500 rubles to Bely on the future books and allowed him and Asya to spend the last 2 weeks of August at her estate in Mikhailovsky, in Kaluga province, northwest of Moscow. Sadly none of any of these books ever materialized as Bely immediately immersed himself in composing *Petersburg*, and afterward his subsequent compositions dealt with anthroposophy. They were back in Moscow the beginning of September.

Morozova in her later years recollected Bely in her memoirs, but the relationship could not be established with Asya:

[97] He lived 1820-1892
[98] He lived 1829-1903

> In August, Boris Nikolaievich and Asya arrived here at Mikhailovsky as our guests and they spend 3 weeks with us. Of course I was very interested in Asya. Boris Nikolaievich was obviously very carried away with her. She was rather impersonal, very calm, even cold and completely indifferent to what was occurring around her. She spoke little and almost the entire time she was silent and just smoked one cigarette after another. She very delicately held the cigarette in her thin fingers and after smoking it she would advertise her enchanting profile and as if stare at us from the corner of her eyes.
>
> Boris Nikolaievich never took his eyes off of her and when she got up and walked away he would literally drop what he was doing and run after her.
>
> For some reason there once occurred some disagreement between Asya and myself. It just seemed impossible to develop any kind of relationship with Asya or even to talk with her intimately was a failure.

According to the witness of those who knew her well Asya in general was a girl who talked little and even avoided people. She was silent in unfamiliar company and always had a cloud of cigarette smoke hovering over her. Even with acquaintances her social skills were shallow and she would often withdraw within herself. With Bely, and especially at the initial stages of their cohabitation, she did develop a trusting relationship. But gradually and slowly an alienation from her side materialized and this inevitably led to the dissolution of their marriage.

At the end of September 1911, Bely completed the work on his volume of his travels through Europe, Africa and Palestine and titled *Sketches of the Journeys*. It was difficult to write because such literature was not his love, and it was a matter of necessity due to the need to replenish his vacant bank account and pay his loans and other debts. But Bely received little income for the book from the publisher *Musaget*, as the advances went to pay for his debts first. Now he was ready to dedicate his time to *Petersburg*.

As Bely already orally committed himself, he was to have the initial 3 chapters submitted to the magazine *Russian Thought* by January 1912. The publisher, Peter Struve, did not maintain any special love for Bely or his symbolist creative effort, but he pragmatically ascertained that the publication in his magazine of a new novel composed by a recognized author might increase the number of subscribers. Even then no advances were made to Bely on the book. The senior editor of the magazine was adamant about he personally reviewing the initial chapters before allowing any funds to be routed to Bely.

Without a copek in his pocket after using whatever funds from his book on his journey to pay debts, Bely depended on the cordial involvement of Brusov, and who allowed Bely and Asya to stay at his winter estate in the village Vidnoi, near Moscow. The small house had 3 rooms. Asya immersed herself into the compositions of Helena Blavatsky and Rudolf Steiner, concentrating on them as though in a trance. Bely concentrated on *Petersburg* and once a week would travel to the offices of *Russian Thought* with a sample of his work and to discuss the business matters, but under no conditions were they going to provide funds to Bely until all of the initial 3 chapters of the books were final and ready to publish.

The idyllic life at the winter estate went fine until the first frost. The comfortable house had no insulation against the cold, the walls froze and were covered with frost, the small stove could not give enough heat to overcome the cold and warm the couple. Bely and his wife were forced to return to Moscow as a result and moved in with Aleksandr Pozzo and his wife Natalia, Asya's sister, and who just had a baby girl. The smallest room in their cramped apartment was allotted to the Belys with their personal belongings, books and papers, and clothes and suitcases. Work on the manuscript slowed temporarily.

Bely's financial state reached a point of almost inescapable destitution. As mentioned above Bely was not business oriented, yet his volumes of poetry were selling occasionally, but no royalties were forwarded to him. He wrote about this in a letter to his friend Emilie Metner at the end of December:

> Material deprivation, an avalanche of unpaid debts increasing over our heads, the recent months have exhausted me, I am horribly weakened, immeasurably weakened morally, and my moral exhaustion evolves from my inability to relax and due to an incessant search for money. No sooner do I turn around, no sooner do a series of scandals and moral blows impact me causing massive troubles for me. Then for 3 or 4 months I was fine and not thinking about money and finally relaxed,[99] and then I start to work on my book when they begin from every side to discredit me, saying I owe somebody something, or that I promised to repay and I did not and why not. In short it is a futile mundane existence. I pay what I can with what little I have. So here I am again.

For the most part by 1912, the symbolist or decadent movement of Russian literature was losing its audience. It was now viewed as a novelty that had run its course. Although Bely's volumes of poetry were occasionally sold, not enough for a steady income, and even *Silver Dove*, as popular it was, it was more sensationalism and popular reading than classic literature, and the income from it was an occasional royalty check to pay old bills, but he was still in a state of financial insolvency.

In total despair Bely turned to Blok for advice in a letter:

> Dear Sasha:
>
> I write not in the general vein of personal correspondence, but in the vein of a request for some advice. This is the matter: All of the magazines, all of the literary societies, in short, everything technological dealing with literature, is in Petersburg. Nothing remains in Moscow. I have one magazine in Moscow, *Russian Thought*, with which I deal. But Brusov has drawn me and hung me.[100]
>
> Since summer I have been badly in need of money. As far as personal savings is concerned I do not have even a copek,

[99] This is the time spent at Brusov's winter estate at Vidnoi.

[100] Referring to the game hangman's noose. With not enough letters the person is hanged.

there is no income from my literary works, and I am not invited to work at any of these magazines, the genre I am in does not fit them. I asked Brusov to give me some work, and through *Musaget* he asked me to write about Africa. All summer I wrote about Rades, [Tunisia] and Egypt, about 10 published pages, counting on living through the winter on income from *Silver Dove*. Now *Russian Thought* is telling me that they are overloaded with geography and travel. It seems my work is not needed. They have extended the deadline for the initial chapters of *Petersburg* to January 15, and right now I am in extreme destitution. I have nothing to live on while I write and I am already in debt 3,000 rubles to *Musaget*.

It will not be for another 6 months that the sale of my real estate will be complete and I will acquire those funds.[101] But I will be able to use those funds to pay all my outstanding debts.

Help in anyway you can.

Blok immediately responded and forwarded 500 rubles to him. What occurred was that Blok received a substantial inheritance after his father died and this was the portion that Blok saved for emergency purposes. Through Blok, Bely was able to receive some assistance from Grigori Alekseevich Rachinsky, one of the organizers of the Religious-Philosophical Society. He offered him a residence, and for as long as he needed, at his family estate in Bobrovka, in Tambov province, and where Bely had stayed in the past. Not losing a minute Bely packed his bags and left Natalia Pozzo's apartment. Asya followed him there shortly after, arriving November 30 .

The older mansion with its squeaking floors, mysterious rustling, and loud echoes in the empty half-dark rooms was not conducive to Asya at all. After tolerating the place a week she left her husband there alone with his novel and returned to her sister in Moscow. Isolated, Bely tenaciously worked from morning until

[101] The Russian source does not indicate whether this is the Serebryanni Kolodez property or the Sochi property.

late at night on *Petersburg*, and so by the end of December 1911, the coveted initial 3 chapters were complete.

Full of inspiration and further creative composition on his novel, Bely returned to Moscow on December 25, but he did not encounter what he expected. After reviewing Bely's submission, The senior editor of *Russian Thought* refused to publish it, he disliked the form of the novel. In general he doubted the success of the novel since it was so unusual in its plot and characters and structure. Brusov attempted to convince the senior editor by emphasizing the commercial advantage, since the popular name of Andrei Bely will draw a number of readers and subscribers to the magazine, and this was Struve's original thinking. The editor however was adamant about his position calling the novel – just based on the submitted 3 chapters – doomed to failure, immature and malformed, composed pretentiously, and so bad that it was just grotesque.

Now that he was run off the tracks Bely had no rest and could not sleep for a long while, it seems all his plans and intentions were railroaded, in addition to losing his faith in people, especially having been cheated time and time again by book publishers who took advantage of his naivety in financial matters. With no options at hand, Bely and Asya just sat and waited at Natalia's apartment for something to materialize.

At the end of January 1912, Bely and Asya left Moscow for Petersburg and moved in with the widowed Vya. Ivanov in his Tower; he had since returned from Europe after the Mintzlova affair. Ivanov took a liking to Asya and they would play chess together, while the residence continue to funnel people of all categories of philosophy and literature, and now with new writers of the Silver Age: Aleksei Tolstoy, Mikhail Kuzmin, Nikolai Gumilyov and his wife and poetess Anna Akhmatova, and Max Voloshin.

Bely took the opportunity to read the initial chapters of *Petersburg* to one of the gatherings. Ivanov in later years recollected the event:

> That evening in Petersburg is unforgettable, when Andrei Bely read his manuscript of his yet unfinished composition, over which he zealously worked and whose end represents, to the best of my memory, something more than what came out from under his pen. The author shook at the time just at the title of the book. I from my side assured him that *Petersburg* is the soul appellation that is worthy for such a composition, and whose principle character is actually the Bronze Horseman.
>
> And to this day it seems to me that the heavy weight of this monumental title of Bely's work will be easily maintained. So great is its inner pressure concentrated in it as spiritual energy and which convinces us of its significance. The style of this novel is a Gogol style from the aspect of a pure dynamism. And although it is just a dream and a personal upheaval, although all the static forms of verbal structure are as if directed toward one flowing dynamism of a musical-visual outburst, nonetheless there is something stable and solid in this sandy mirage. This poem of our history belongs forever to our artistic value and to our national cognizance.

As opposed to Bely's supposedly Moscow friends the Petersburg public overwhelmingly lauded the chapters read and shouted "Hooray," after the recitation, as though the novel was dedicated to their capital city. Rumors spread throughout the population of Petersburg of the upcoming new novel and Bely's spirit and mood uplifted and he no longer worried about the rejection by *Russian Thought* magazine. A new book publisher, Konstantine Feodorovich Nekrasov, who opened his own independent press in 1909, offered to publish *Petersburg*, with a serial of the chapters first in his magazine *Voice*. Bely was offered 2,200 rubles for the book with an initial and immediate deposit of half the amount. This was in February 1912. The offer was also considerably more than the amount that Struve promised initially for the novel. It was Bely's intention to use the advance to relocate to Europe with Asya and there complete the novel, but even then he was still short of funds.

Bely while in Petersburg met with Blok and thanked him for his financial assistance and intervention with Struve. However Bely was still in some financial straits, so Blok loaned him another 350 rubles. Blok was returning to Europe again with Lubov for medical treatments.

Nikolai Berdiaev was especially impressed with Bely's novel *Petersburg* and he wrote an article about it titled, *An Astral Novel*, and it was published in the *Financial News*. Berdiaev equated the book with a cosmic whirlwind and called it an amazing novel. He called Bely an ingenious writer, and the most significant author since the era of Feodor Dostoyevsky and Leo Tolstoy. Some of Berdiaev's article is the following:

> The style of A. Bely always at the terminating conclusion migrates into a violent circular movement. There is something of the Khlist element in his style. A.Bely senses this whirlwind movement in his personal cosmic life and found for himself an adequate expression in the whirlwind of word-combinations. The language of A.Bely is not a translation of his cosmic reactions to life into another, foreign language, as we seen in the colorfully-helpless Ciurlionis.[102] [Petersburg] is a unimpeded expression of cosmic whirlwinds in words. We can only reproach due to its intolerable style, it seems to always go off on a tangent.
>
> The ingenuity of A. Bely as an artist contains a coexistence of a cosmic flare and a cosmic whirlwind with a flaring verbalism and with a whirlwind of collocations. In this whirlwind growth of composition and sounds the growth of a vital and cosmic intensity is permitted.
>
> A. Bely tempers and heats the crystals of words, the solid forms of words that now seem to be eternal, and in this manner the tempering and heating of the crystals of the entire object is expressed, and so pertaining to the entire world. The

---

[102] Mikalojus Kostantinas Ciurlionis, 1875-1911, a Lithuanian painter, composer and writer. He is labeled as helpless by Berdiaev due to his depression in Petersburg in 1909 at an exhibition of his paintings, and he was then committed to a psychiatric hospital in Poland.

> cosmic whirlwinds are as if broken away and unleashed, and they temper our entire stationary and petrified, crystallized world.

Even with the above and the many other commentaries on the novel *Petersburg*, it is difficult to define one specific genre or category to place it, except in Bely's own genre of symbolism. (I will not further discuss the novel *Petersburg* or further provide quotes of commentators and reviewers. The reader is urged to purchase a copy and read it and come to their own conclusion.)

# ANDREI BELY AND ANTHROPOSOPHY

Bely was originally exposed to theosophy as mentioned above in studying Helena Blavatsky and Hindu texts translated into Russian, at the age of 16, this would be 1896, and some evidence indicates he was already attending theosophist meetings as early as 1902, organized by Ekaterina Kokhmanskaya. In 1907, Bely studied Anne Besant's books on Theosophy, also available in Russian. Sometime during the autumn 1908, Bely visited the theosophist circle of Kleopatra Khristoforova in Moscow,[103] and he became one of its members.

The other members of the group were: Bely's mother Aleksandra Bugaeva – who was a longtime friend of Khristoforova; Pavel Nikolaievich Batushkov – a prominent theosophist and fellow Argonaut; Alexsei Petrovsky – another Argonaut; Boris Grigorov – the future head of the Russian Anthroposophical Society;[104] Sophia Yurusova – who later became the president of the Moscow division of the Russian Theosophical Society; Ekaterina Kokhmanskaya; Ellis, Vyacheslav Ivanov, and others, including more Argonauts, and of course Anna Mintzlova. The circle of Khristoforova gathered at her home in Devichi Field in Moscow, and it existed until 1910. Total number of attendees or members would be about 30. Some of its members later organized a Rudolf Steiner circle that resulted in the Russian

[103] Kleopatra Petrovna Kristoforova, d. 1934.

[104] Boris Pavlovich Grigorov, 1883-1945.

Anthroposophical Society (RTO), and which materialized on September 7, 1913. Most of the names mentioned above, including Bely, were members. How large was the RTO? One estimate is less than one hundred serious members just before the 1917 Russian Revolution. In about 1932, it was suppressed by the Soviet government into non-existence as a anti-Soviet element and its members were sent into exile. (More will be discussed on this issue further.)

Some information needs to here be provided about Anna Rudolfovna Mintzlova. She was born in Ryazan province, Russia, June 10, 1866. Mintzlova spoke most of the European languages fluently and also had a mastery of Sanskrit, Latin and Greek, and so she became a translator of Rudolf Steiner's anthroposophical writings from German into Russian. While in Russia during her visits, she was the prime promoter of the Theosophist and Rosicrucian movements. From a young age she displayed an interest in occult and esoteric themes, and dedicated herself to their study. She was also known as a medium and performed chiromancy and graphology on her clients. Her spare time was spent in libraries where she became fluent in the ancient religions. There is no evidence that she ever married or even had a romance or any immorality. Much of what Mintzlova learned was from her close association with Annie Besant, the president of the Theosophical Society, and beginning 1905, she was one of the first Russian pupils of Rudolf Steiner, the head of the German branch of the Theosophical Society at the time. Mintzlova considered herself Steiner's emissary in Russia, as well as having her personal agenda of introducing the Rosicrucian Order into Russia and acquiring members.

The first of Steiner's books to be translated into Russian language by Mintzlova and published was in 1910, and it was *Theosophy: An Introduction to the Supersensible Knowledge of the World and the Destination of Man.* Mintzlova likewise attended international Theosophist congresses in London, 1905, Paris, 1903 and 1906, and Munich, 1907, and likewise traveled to Norway.

Mintzlova met with Brusov in 1900, and continued correspondence with him from this time on. She became acquainted with M.V. Sabashnikova and Maximillian Voloshin in 1903, while in Paris at a Theosophist congress and introduced them to Theosophy, and where she was able to introduce theosophy to Vya. Ivanov in November 1906. Voloshin was the first of the Russian symbolists to fall under her intellectual and mesmerizing influence. Shortly after, the Mintzlova and Voloshin made a sacred pilgrimage to the Rouen Cathedral in Normandy, France. It was through Voloshin that Mintzlova was able to access and attend gatherings at the Religious-Philosophical Society and she met Bely there in Moscow in late 1908. It was due to Mintzlova's influence that Bely abandoned Blavatsky's Theosophy in favor of Steiner's Anthroposophy.

Later Bely suspected Mintzlova to be psychologically ill. Bely described Mintzlova in his memoirs:

> She had a large face, she was obese, kind of like the cosmic expanse, toroidal having an immense scale in every direction, although much of it void. In her black loose overall[105] she forced herself at me for a moment. It seemed that her large body was inflating, pressing, overflowing and reaching to nowhere. But actually she would not be considered ugly.
>
> I remember the door was wide open and she flowed in, tumbled in, in her black sack (the overall she was wearing seemed to be a sack). The heavy horsehead pushed itself between us and her yellow braids stood up over her. And no matter how hard she tried to comb them, they stuck out like a bunch of snakes, in clumps over her huge forehead, and she had no eyelashes. And she would squint with her little, near-sighted and dirty-blue eyes. But her irises were like 2 wheels, not eyes at all, and they turned dark. It seems that they were bottomless. And her eyes, they would shred you apart.

[105] What she wore could be comparable to a muumuu.

Regardless of such an uncomplimentary description by Bely, Mintzlova had the capacity to entice people toward her. She displayed herself as the announcer of the world beyond our frontiers, and just like Helena Blavatsky she had contact with mysterious noospheric messengers called Teachers, members of the Secret Brotherhood in the Himalayas Mountains, and with much success she was able to convince people that she was here to fulfill their will. Supposedly they assigned Mintzlova the task and blessed her with the responsibility of building in Russia the Kingdom of the Spirit.

One of the first sacrifices of Mintzlova's mesmerizing charms at the time was Maximillian Voloshin, as mentioned above. Voloshin later was likewise not sympathetic in his opinion of Mintzlova. He recorded the following about her in a letter:

> In the Middle Ages she would of course have been burned as a witch in a bonfire. She is almost blind and recognizes people based on the aura around their head. She is almost always dying from some type of coronary illness. Her income is from her translations of Oscar Wilde from English. Not one person that once is drawn to her remains the same as he was before.

In another letter Voloshin plainly called her a female vampire.

It was during the years 1909 and 1910 that Bely and Ivanov fell into the clutches of this woman. Vyacheslav Ivanov was the worse because his wife, Lydia Dmitrievna Zinovyeva-Hannibal died recently, in 1907. Earlier she and her husband hosted a literary salon that had the nickname – the Tower, and where many of the symbolist adherents would gather. Now a widower the unmarried Mintzlova found it easier to manipulate Ivanov and they were about the same age, but the relationship was always on a platonic basis. Nonetheless, Mintzlova attended the Tower gatherings and utilized it to further herself as a channeler of the great Teachers. Mintzlova practically made Ivanov's apartment her home when in Petersburg and so had access to the symbolist adherents patronizing it. In Moscow she was close to the symbolist group, and Brusov published her translations of Steiner's compositions in *Scales*, and Sergei Sokolov published them in *Grif*.

At the end of January 1910, during one of his regular trips to Petersburg to deliver a lecture, Bely again came in contact with Anna Mintzlova who was living at the tower, the home of Ivanov. She intended to create a mysterial triumvirate – Bely, Ivanov and herself Mintzlova. But the first of the 3 potential candidates had a skeptical attitude toward her right from the start, and the second was not far behind him. Mintzlova did everything she could to keep the 2 of them under her influence knowing how valuable they were for her in her dissemination of anthroposophy and instituting her new Rosicrucian Order in Russia.

Bely admitted the following, recording it in his memoirs:

> I was brought to life in her atmosphere and she sanctified me in her nonsense. Here are a few words of her manipulation, "We are standing at the threshold of an unprecedented revolution of consciousness. Personages are already appearing, regulating moral regeneration, but devious occultists are not slumbering."
>
> She likewise approved of my bad opinion of the Masons and I was supposed to arm myself with her esoteric knowledge.

Bely nonetheless did not completely ascertain what it was that Mintzlova herself saw, but he did acknowledge that she was right in some areas, in her perspectives and visions, and that beyond all doubt there was something there. He did recognize her as genuinely occultist. Bely wrote of this also to Blok:

> The Rosicrucian route begins at that frontier of the soul beyond which begins either the deformation of health or the confirmation of spirit. The occultist method of development is the wise knowledge of the ability to confirm the region of human health.

Mintzlova wrote the following in one of her letters to Bely:

> The great war is presently being waged, a decisive war, in the sphere of nowhere else but in this world that is especially so close to you, Andrei Bely. In the celestial world, in the astral light.
>
> Yes, the Rubicon is in front of you. But the dice are already cast, you are already crossing the Rubicon, you are already at the world's border.
>
> I still do not know how all of this will occur, but I know that God is with you and the light will be with you.

Bely recorded the events in his memoirs:

> The Rosicrucian subject has its continuation in the circle of the former Argonauts. Mintzlova found eager listeners in the persons of Bely and Metner and decided to unite the symbolist circle into some kind of secret society. She influenced the former Argonauts: Petrovsky, myself, Ellis, S.M. Solovyov, E.K. Metner, Nilender,[106] N.M. Kiselov,[107] M. Sizov,[108] and Rachinsky. This was to form a new fraternity having the new appellation – Order of the Knights of Truth.

Mintzlova called her form of Rosicrucianism as Western European. Bely recorded his comprehension of her presentation in his memoirs:

> The Rosicrucians are divided into 2 directions: The Eastern Fraternity, an esoteric branch of the movement where the older generations are fully developed, such as Khunrath,[109] van Helmont,[110] and others. This vein, as they said, went

[106] Vasili Ottonovich Nilender, a poet and librarian. He worked at the Moscow symbolist magazines *Scales*, *Golden Fleece*, and *Musaret*, was part of the theosophist circle of Vya. Ivanov, and likewise a close friend of Andrei Bely. The 2 attended Moscow university together during Bely's second course of study. Later Nilender published the poetry of Marina Tsvetaeva.

[107] Nikolai Petrovich Kiselov, 1884-1965. An Argonaut and employee at Musaget.

[108] Mikhail Ivanovich Sizov, 1884-56. A Theosophist and devotee of Mintzlova.

[109] Heinrich Khunrath, 1560-1605, German physician and Rosicrucian.

underground. And this became the Eastern Fraternity which consecrated Novikov.[111]

Events of the future summons the appearance of a new vein of Rosicrucianism, as long as it is consecrated by the powers of the old Rosicrucianism. Now a new order of knights appears. This organization needs to be formed in Russia, and 2 persons must be found – one in Moscow and one in St Petersburg, in order to gather all those who are tied with the Fraternity and to create a type of a spiritual world out of those persons who prepare themselves through spiritual exercises. The exercise is the weapon of the future. There is an exercise of the helmet, another is the life of the heart, along is the life of the shield, and there is the exercise of the sword and the shoulder defense.

I have been summoned to help. I need to be immaculate and this will genuinely motivate the concentration of people. There is already such a person in Petersburg. Together with Mintzlova the three of us will compose the present triangle for the construction of the Temple of Knights.[112] The circle will gather around these two. Mintzlova will create a tie with the Sacred Brotherhood. Her mission consists in transferring to us whatever is important from the ancient traditions.

It was then Mintzlova's intent to travel with Bely and Ivanov to a small Italian city, Assisi, where a Franciscan monastery is located. They would meet with other Rosicrucians, and there or in the vicinity they would be consecrated for the mission. But Bely by now divined a devious and fantastical character of the entire matter. He consulted with Emilie Metner on the issue in June 1910, and decided against the honor of traveling to Italy. Bely's decision did not gain him any favor with others who were mesmerized by Mintzlova, and they turned against him.

---

[110] Franciscus Mercurius van Helmont, 1614-1698, Flemish Kabbalist.

[111] Nikolai Ivanovich Novikov, 1744-1818. Russian writer. He introduced Rosicrucianism into Russia.

[112] These 3 are Bely, Ivanov and Mintzlova.

For a long while, and after Mintzlova's disappearance, Bely still believed in his sacred selection and the need to travel to Assisi to execute it. But with Bely's later decision to leave Russia, the issue retreated into a latent form.

Mintzlova took another occasion to create a Rosicrucian-Symbolist Fraternity. But Ivanov, to detach himself from Mintzlova's grasp, left Russia in autumn 1910, for Europe on a vacation. Nothing more was done by Mintzlova, however she continued to circulate in the various theosophist circles. Shortly thereabouts Mintzlova realized her failure in executing the task she was assigned by these Teachers and which she promised Steiner she would accomplish.

About August 1910, Mintzlova wrote to Steiner:

> Beloved, dear, I received a second, unconditional confirmation of that news, of which I wrote to you in my previous letter. I must die. However I must once more, for the 3rd time, hear this summons, and then my hand will touch the Omniscient, the Blessed. I am now saturated with calm and joy, not one minute of turbulence or agitation resides in me.

After both Bely's and Ivanov's rejection of her propositions, Mintzlova realized her mission in Russia had failed and she had to somehow depart from the scene. She had no other choice. The dictate was issued apparently, if this can be ascertained correctly from the letter, from these messengers called Teachers, but she waited for a 3rd confirmation, and apparently received it.

In a subsequent letter, her last to Ivanov, Mintzlova still promised him a consecration. Knowing of Ivanov's departure to Europe, she mentions to him of her intent to travel to Moscow from Petersburg, where she will get a passport and then travel to Assisi, Italy, and meet him there. However none of this materialized. Mintzlova attended a meeting of symbolists in Petersburg in late August and left without an indication of her next stop. She was seen momentarily in Moscow – as she intended in her letter – and then was never to be seen again and there is no indication of what ever occurred to her. She just disappeared. Her final sighting in Moscow occurred early September 1910, Mintzlova was 44 years of age.

Berdiaev, who knew Mintzlova rather well, recording the following in his memoirs:

> She then walked into the street and no one and not ever saw her again.

Occultists in general viewed the postmortem world as part of a single reality. From their perspective all death in any form is viewed as a natural step from the world of a corporeal reality to another that is parallel but intangible. This action is as simple and painless as moving from one room to another. The conjecture is that Mintzlova, realizing that her mission here did not succeed, could fearlessly depart from this life and migrate to the other. Not long before her disappearance she disclosed to someone that "the depths of the ocean await her."

Bely summed up his complex and confused attitude toward Mintzlova in the following manner:

> Dear reader, I cannot explain anything concrete regarding these facts, it is all the same. It is so difficult to believe them, and they are not understandable to me either. I will just say a couple of words about it, what she relayed to me, I will state it abstractly, in general what she communicated: that she did not fulfill what was entrusted to her, and this was to fire hearts toward the light, unite us for the spiritual world. Her mission collapsed because her instability and illness along with the growing atmosphere among us of distrust in her loosened or undermined the entire bright activity of those certain unknown benefactors of humanity who were standing behind her.[113] Meanwhile she gave her word to them that a Brotherhood of the Spirit would be created among us. The lack of fulfillment of her words fell on her very heavily. Now they are exiling her forever and away from people and associations

[113] These Teachers from the Himalayas whose information she channeled.

> that extended around her. She disappears from that time for ever and no one will ever see her again. She beseeched us all, those who were close to her these years, to keep strict silence about the reasons for her terminating vanishment.
>
> I did not understand at the time what a vanishment specifically signified. Vanishment, where? To a monastery, to prison, to another country? Or did she mean to vanish from life? But she did make a hint that this time her supposed nonsense was not at all a myth, and that we will never see her. I guess this can happen. Literal opinions are released as paper snakes. Their tails twitch while on their back side lying under the sky. And now I take consideration of her words, as to something that is terrifying. Her secret, of which nothing is known to me, perplexes my entire soul. One thing is known: she was right.

Rumors circulated that Mintzlova did manage to reach Assisi, Italy, and the Rosicrucian monastery and lived their incognito for the balance of her life. But no evidence indicates she went anywhere after her final sighting in Moscow. Supposedly Mintzlova sent a note to Bely in Moscow that she had arrived, but no copy of this note exits. Others speculations are that she was institutionalized under a pseudonym, or had a sudden and unexpected death with no identification, or suicide. Of all the options, death as a result of some type of heart failure is the most veritable, as she earlier indicated having coronary disease, and then a burial as some anonymous or unidentifiable person. Mintzlova's fate was just as enigmatic as her mission.

On March 16, 1912, Bely and his wife left Russia for Belgium, to Brussels, where Asya still had to complete her studies in art. They traveled through Berlin, Cologne, and then arriving in Brussels on April 2. Once done their intention was to make one more trip to the East, and this time the couple wanted to visit Syria, Mesopotamia (the present Iraq), and India if possible.

Arriving in Europe both became ill, probably pneumonia from exposure to sudden cold weather, and they isolated themselves in a hotel to recover. During this interval Bely completed his 4th chapter of Petersburg. Bely wrote of his time in Brussels to Margarita Morozova:

> Now my working disposition is escalating. Asya spends her days at work, while I work on my novel. It is so nice here, quiet and well for us. I feel so strong, and I believe, believe, believe. I want to smile, work and the future burns with some kind of calm light.

It was in May 1912, that a fatal or destined encounter with Rudolf Steiner occurred, and Bely from here on would refer to him as – the Doctor. Initially both Bely and Asya had a dream at the same night of meeting with him, and then one of them saw an apparition of Steiner while on a streetcar. Finally through noospheric channels they were informed that they must immediately and indispensably meet with him. Bely had long studied Steiner's books and his educational activities to the extent they were available in Russia, and which were translated into Russian by Anna Mintzlova, and he associated with anthroposophists, such as his friends Ellis, Max Voloshin, Margarita Sabashnikova, and Vya. Ivanov, who followed Steiner in Europe, listening to him, and then bringing it back to Russia. Asya was also attracted to anthroposophy.

Bely's latent belief in his divine selection as part of Mintzlova's concocted Mystic Triangle and head of the new Order of the Knights of Truth could have led him purposely to find Steiner, and through him Bely could achieve this divine mission, rather than through Mintzlova. The new assignment was now Steiner's anthroposophy and it would be Bely to introduce and implement it in Russia. (But this is conjecture.)

At this time Steiner arrived in Brussels to meet with some of his adherents, as they were located in all of the European countries and in Russia. The Belys contacted Steiner's secretary and wife – his second and she was Russian also – Maria Sivers, and she permitted them to attend one of Steiner's private lectures. Ms Sivers had heard of Bely, so it was no problem for her to allow the couple to a private lecture that normally would only be reserved for dedicated anthroposophists. This was the first occasion for Bely to see and hear Steiner personally, and Steiner and his concepts would now be an indelible part of Bely's life to his demise.

Bely recorded the May 6, 1912, evening:

> We squeezed into the room and sat at a side door. We wait. The curtain is moving, but the area behind the curtain is still empty. Steiner will enter right now. All of a sudden a terrible turbulence envelops me, a discomfort, as if someone is staring at me from the side. I turn toward the door and within a minute I see the shallow edge of a cheek of someone's face, but the edge of the cheek is bright. Steiner showed himself momentarily and then disappeared into the background.
>
> About 3 minutes later Steiner walked out. He was short, emaciated, had sharp facial features, and with a stern expression, similar to what we saw on the streetcar. He walked to the podium and started to talk. What he said, I could write 10 pages on it and this would still not be enough. Steiner spoke austerely, dry, with a bass voice, and often would start to cry, often he would sing in a baritone key, but he spoke in such a way that each word flowed and became an indelible impression on your soul. Of all the people I heard speak in the past, they were just puppies in comparison to Steiner with his capacity to eloquently speak, and he was a master at his gestures. Often Steiner would project his palms at the audience, and it was as though you received a physical jolt right on the face at this gesture of his palms. Another face would evolve from his face, as though there was another looking at you from inside that one, and it even seemed that a third face would also unveil.
>
> Over the course of the lecture 10 Steiners passed in front of me, one surfacing after another, and not one like the one before, but all of them seemed to be permeated with some single item. Over the course of the lecture he was a Spaniard, and Brand,[114] and a Catholic Cardinal, and an educated

> scholar, and a Scandinavian Viking. He possessed such strength and authority in his gaze, and which I had not seen in anyone else. Surrounding him were beams of light; a bright cloud floated on his chest, changing colors. Asya and I saw the change in color at the same moment. His aura was unbelievable and was almost always apparent, and as his speech intensified it became blinding.
>
> His face maintained depth and displayed human suffering, along with a mix of kindness and insane courage. Such was our first impression.

The following day, May 7, Steiner gave a public lecture in Cologne and Bely and Asya attended.

Bely wrote to Blok detailing to his friend of the rebirth that occurred in his soul while absorbing the content of Steiner's lectures. Bely also included some biographical information on Steiner:

> He was at one time a disciple of Ernst Haeckel,[115] the naturalist. For 20 years he was married to a widow who had several children, and she was a vixen. He wrote human-interest articles for local newspapers and taught school for a living. Then for the next 20 years he was silent: said nothing, wrote nothing on his own. And suddenly he opened. These 20 years of silence were a route of reality he traversed.
>
> Not wanting to fragment the theosophist movement, he conditionally rejoined the theosophists and so meanwhile he functioned under the banner of Theosophy. Now becoming temporarily and conditionally a Theosophist, he motivated Theosophy in Germany. Speaking of Theosophy in general, he wanted us to remember that now there are 2 distinct Theosophies: the theosophy of Blavatsky and Besant, transmitting the wisdom of the yogas; and the theosophy of Steiner, transmitting the wisdom of others. For superficial

---

[114] The chief hero of the play by Henrik Ibsen.

[115] Ernst Heinrich Philipp Haeckel, 1834-1919, a German biologist, philosopher, physician, educator and artist.

people, both of them are superficially interwoven. So this is Steiner.

Beginning in 1910, and for several reasons (which I cannot relate to you in this letter), Steiner started especially intensive and intimate contacts with all of us. Some people blindly just threw themselves at him, like Ellis, others followed him with their eyes wide open, like Voloshin; a third group cautiously make pilgrimages to his lectures; a forth group, like Rachinsky and members of the Moscow Religious-Philosophical Society have been viewing him for 2 years now as an impending danger. (Bulgakov told me that Steiner is a genuine abyss.)

Beginning in autumn 1911, Steiner started to speak of the most astonishing stuff about Russia, its future, the soul of the nation and about Vl.Solovyov. [Steiner] sees in Russia a humongous and single future.

In 1911, there occurred in Moscow a genuine altercation regarding Steiner. The pros and cons of Steiner did not just once affected the existence of *Musaget.*

In general the anthroposophist-cosmic teaching of Rudolf Steiner was based on the theosophist doctrine of Madame E.P. Blavatsky and her famous treatises on *Cosmogenesis* and *Anthropogenesis.* Rudolf Steiner succeeded in uniting all of world history and the development of the universe into a single complete human life – past, present and future – meaning his own.

Anthroposophy according to Steiner is cosmo-centric, as is theosophy, but regardless of the appellation of anthroposophy, it is not anthro-centric. According to Steiner's anthroposophy the entire universe is built under the banner of the human and the cosmos is an inherent part of the human. The present state of the human is a cosmic transfer from a pre-human state to a super-human state. Akin to Christianity the human did not develop through evolution, but was created by God and bears the image and likeness of God. He can also enter into a divine life, but he will always be a person. For Steiner, the development progresses further, beyond a person retaining any aspects of humanity, into an angelic realm.

From the first occasion that Bely listened to Steiner about anthroposophy he was permeated with these concepts and his life took a change of course. It became more cosmic oriented and less terrestrial; more spirit and less corporeal. It seemed to Bely that he found the piece of the puzzle that he had been searching all his life to complete it, as though there was always something missing, and so running to the Argonauts, or to Merezhkovskys, or to Morozovs, or to Ivanov's Tower, or to the Religious-Philosophical Society, or other meetings including the sectarians outside of Moscow. Bely now acquired the assurance that Steiner would unveil to him the manner of possessing the clandestine strengths of his *I*, and with their help he could blaze a trail to the hidden secrets of the universe.

Bely was gradually replacing Blavatsky's theosophy with Steiner's anthroposophy. The reason being Blavatsky's version was heavily Hindu and with an oriental connection, while Steiner was able to provide a version of the same content having with a somewhat Christianized base and a European identity. The basic tenets of both were essentially the same. It was a matter of packaging the religion in a manner that it would be acceptable to his audience, so its superficial aspects were modified to make it more palatable to the occidental seeker, a Christian base replacing the Hindu base. The person of Jesus Christ was the pinnacle of the incarnations, and several of Steiner's lectures dealt with understanding the Gospels and other parts of the Bible. Reincarnation was interpreted in a sense of Christian resurrection. This was a positive benefit to his anthroposophy rather than the Hindu texts or their incarnations, which were distant from the people in Europe and Russia both geographically and culturally.

(This book will not delve any further into the tenets of either Theosophy or Anthroposophy, since these are available to the reader in other texts, and that this book is a biography of Andrei Bely.)

During May 1912, Bely and Asya had the occasions in both Brussels and Cologne to listen to several of Steiner's lectures and they made indelible impressions on the both of them. As a result, they were also able to meet with Steiner alone in person and have long and in depth conversations. Bely's inherent capacity to grasp mystic and symbolist concepts, and his philosophic depth, provided a natural sponge to absorb and digest all that Steiner had to offer.

Steiner likewise divined an acute cognizance in Bely and extended his trust to him, no doubt seeing in Bely a capable person to further and promote the concepts of anthroposophy in Russia, and as providing a mutual benefit. As a result, Steiner invited Bely and Asya to Munich in July, to there learn more from Steiner. Although by this time the Belys were running out of funds, they nonetheless agreed without second thoughts. As a result the Belys over the next 12 years were inseparably connected to the person of Rudolf Steiner and his concepts and intentions and his commune.

Ellis, who was in Berlin, heard the Belys were in Germany and he went to Cologne to their hotel. Ellis explained to Bely that he was living with an elderly Hassidic scholar and studying Hassidism and Kabbalism, in addition to anthroposophy. While with the Bely's, Ellis immersed them into the deeper concepts of anthroposophy that he learned from Steiner, listening to all of his lectures over the past couple of years and studying directly under him and reading all his literature.

Ellis' connection with Steiner was well for the meanwhile, but later the 2 would separate. One reason was that Steiner viewed him as a threat to his own position as sole possessor of such esoteric information. Ellis over the years became so advanced in the knowledge and application of all the concepts Steiner was teaching, plus Ellis' had an excellent knowledge of Hassidism and Kabbalism, in addition to knowing the theology of Russian Orthodoxy in which Ellis was raised, Roman Catholic theology and Marxist polity. A second reason was the concept of free association, which Steiner advocated, while Ellis had reached a point that he felt an attitude of asceticism and monasticism –

similar to Catholicism – should be demanded of the disciples of anthroposophy. So then the 2 of them parted ways.

Asya, knowing Ellis well all these years, noticed what occurred to him and recorded her summary:

> Ellis did not leave behind any significant effort by which to remember him, but he was an excellent conversationalist, exceptional, but a deep tragedy seemed to affect his individualism. He was always fervent due to some fire burning within him. From Marx he leaped to demonism, baudelaireanism,[116] and symbolism, from the Beautiful Dame to the Catholic Madonna. He sorrowed over the Doctor[117] not being a Jesuit, and after 2 years of a turbulent psychological drama, he finally found contentment in the bosom of the Catholic church, and where he died.

Ellis and Bely likewise went their separate ways shortly after. (Ellis eventually and in about 1917, converted to Roman Catholicism and joined the Jesuit Order. He resided in Locarno, Switzerland, near the border with Italy. Ellis wrote on philosophy in German until his death on November 17, 1947.)

Since there was still a few months until meeting with Steiner in July, Bely and Asya took the opportunity to travel through Europe, visiting Bruges in northwest Belgium and Charleroi in central Belgium in May 1912. Then they went to France, arriving June 4, to visit her aunt and one of Bely's favorite women: Maria Alekseevna Olenina-D'alheim, living outside of Pairs. Here Bely wrote his 5th chapter of *Petersburg* and took the time to edit the other chapters.

While in Paris, Bely wrote to Blok:

> Dear friend, where are you? What is occurring with you? I have no news of you for a long while. The longer I live outside

---

[116] A student of the concepts promoted by Charles Baudelaire, 1821-1867, a French poet. He promoted an aspiration toward infinity.

[117] Referring to Rudolf Steiner, as his followers referred to him.

of Moscow, the greater is the horror of thinking about that cursed place, boiling with hysteria and chimeras. I have the same desire not to live in Petersburg as not to live in Moscow.

I live in a modest place outside of Paris, but I do not go into Paris. I was there only a couple of times on business, but then I leave that plagued place as soon as possible. For many years I have dreamed of a content and tranquil life in a village. A village does not alter me; a city always does.

I am spending much time working on my novel Petersburg. The novel exhausts me, but I gave myself my word that I will restrain myself for a long while from any negative aspects of life. In the third part of my series *East and West*, I will depict the healthy and exalted moments of life and Spirit. Enough floating about in sewage.

Bely and Asya left France for Germany at the beginning of July, passing through Strassburg and arriving in Munich. While there, the 2 of them studied anthroposophy under Matilda Sholl, who herself studied theosophy directly under Anne Besant.

Several dozen of Steiner's close students gathered in July 1912, outside of Munich for their annual congress. First of all Bely and his wife Asya were initiated once and for always into the private life of the anthroposophist commune. Now started their education and immersion into Steiner's concepts beyond the elementary that they already traversed. The Steiner inner sanctum only consisted of handful of individuals, although there were about 600 that were considered serious students always attending his lectures and studies. They listened to his Munich course *On Eternity and the Moment*. While there Bely and Asya had the opportunity to meet and become close to Trifon Trapeznikov, an adherent of anthroposophy and art specialist. After meeting with Steiner Trapeznikov went with him to Dornach and helped build the Goetheanum, and where he became close friends with Bely. Trapeznikov was president of the Anthroposophical Society from 1921.[118]

---

[118] Tripon Georgievich Trapeznikov, 1882-1926.

Steiner made a decision at this congress to move his commune to Basil, Switzerland, away from Germany, to a more remote and tranquil environment, where meditation was more conducive.

Once relocating at the end of August 1912, Vya. Ivanov appeared and with his new wife Vera, likewise to become members of the commune.[119] But as with Ellis, Ivanov acquired much education in the various areas of religion and philosophy, very experienced in his efforts, and he had a special ability to influence people. Steiner felt a discomfort with Ivanov in his presence, considering him a threat to his sole rule. Steiner then requested his Russian friends to do what they could to keep Ivanov away from Basel and under any conditions. In any respect, he returned to Moscow in late 1913, and did not associate further with the Steiner movement. (Rejecting the Russian Revolution, Ivanov moved to Baku in 1920, and then to Italy in 1924. Ivanov converted to Catholicism in 1926, and remained in Rome, Italy, through his death in 1949.)

In Basel during September 1912, they listened to Steiner's series of lectures on the *Gospel of Mark*.

Enjoying vacationing, Bely and Asya traveled the area October 1-26, visiting Vitznau, along Lake Lucerne, then to Suttgart, and in November, to Degerlock, outside of Suttgart. On November 24, they were in Munich, and on November 30, again in Berlin, traveling through Nuremberg. On December 27, they were in Cologne to listen to Steiner's series of lectures on *The Letters of Apostle Paul and the Bhagava Gita*. They stayed in the region before returning to Berlin about January 5, 1913.

Steiner founded the Anthroposophical Society on December 28, 1912, in Cologne, Germany, and then reorganized it as the General Anthroposophical Society in Dornach, its new headquarters, in 1923. The inauguration of the Anthroposophical Society occurred as a result of the membership of Steiner's group being terminated by the Theosophical Society, much of it due to a

---

[119] After the death of his wife Lydia, Ivanov had a vision to marry his step-daughter, Vera Shvarsalon, she was 23 and he was 47.

struggle between Anne Besant, who wanted to keep a Hindu-based faith, and Rudolf Steiner who modified its fundamental concepts to a Christianized ideology and with a European façade. As a result the 2 groups parted ways.

In the meanwhile, Blok wrote good news to Bely. A new publishing house opened in Petersburg called *Lilac*, at whose head was Mikhail Ivanovich Tereschenko.[120] He was interested in publishing *Petersburg* and offered a far larger sum than any of Bely's previous offers. Bely agreed. A new person now entered Bely's life from the publishing concern: Ivanov-Razumnik (the pseudonym of Razumnik Vasilyevich Ivanov), one of the founders of *Lilac* and also the editor. The news could not have come at a better time, as by now the Belys were totally exhausted of all funds from the advance on the royalty for *Petersburg* from the earlier publisher and nothing remained. They were worried they would have to abandon Steiner's commune and education and return to Russia, now absent almost 2 years; the new amount was enough for Bely to pay all old debts.

The Belys made the decision to return to Russia for a while. Bely was traveling too much between France and Germany and Switzerland, and so involved with studying anthroposophy under Steiner, that he did not have the time to finish *Petersburg*. He hoped that by returning to Russia this would give him the time to complete the book and then be able to return to Switzerland. But neither Moscow nor Petersburg were suitable for Bely to complete his novel, so they decided to spend spring and summer 1913, in Bogolubi, and then return to Europe at the end of July.

So on February 26, 1913, the couple arrived in Volin. The spring thaw started and the road from Lutz to Bogolubi was all mud with scattered snow in the fields. Asya's stepfather rescued them and allowed them the same residence they had during their previous visit, after their return from Africa.

Bely wrote to Blok on March 20:

[120] Lived 1886-1958, a wealthy Russian business who gained his fortune in the sugar industry. In 1917, he was minister of finance and minister of foreign affairs during the interim government.

> I need to tell you about myself. I am inexpressibly happy with this village, sunshine and my diversions. The March winds blow, the lungworts are blooming, recently cranes were flying. My soul is so clear and calm, now that all these superficial upsets have passed, and my work is cooking away. How little is really necessary for a person: assurance of his safety and survival, some sunshine, and with the absence of argument and misconstrual, and so I am as happy as a child. The novel is progressing well, the doctor will lose nothing if I lose a year of my life to my own destiny, the sun shines and the lungworts are blossoming.
>
> This is not a nasty city like Berlin. There is no pagan a people like Berlin Jews (in Berlin they are all Jews, and even the Germans). Here in Volin even the Jew seems to me to be a Russian. It is well to live in Russia.

Bely now isolated and comfortable went to work furiously to complete chapter 6 of *Petersburg*. Once finished, the couple returned to Petersburg, arriving May 11.

Asya's intense immersion into anthroposophy now surfaced in a new attitude toward sexuality. She informed her husband that she finally realized her route in life and it was asceticism. Asya felt it would be difficult for her to continue normal marital relations with Bely, and so she no longer wanted to live in terms of husband and wife, but that they need to have a platonic relationship, one as brother and sister, although otherwise together. For the next 9 years and until the dissolution of their so-called marriage this was their new relationship.

The 2 of them then departed to Helsinki, Finland, spending the period of May 15-25, 1913, to listen to a series of 10 lectures by Steiner on *The Occultist Foundations of the Bhagava Gita*. The couple first stayed in Petersburg for a few days, visited Blok, the Merezhkovskys, and Berdiaev. The latter asked if he could accompany them to Finland, and the Belys agreed and he went. Berdiaev listened to the lectures, but made no indication as far as pursuing anthroposophy any further.

While in Petersburg Bely took advantage of the occasion to meet and become familiar with Razumnik, the editor at *Lilac*. The two were able to successfully resolve any problems connected with editing and publishing Bely's novel *Petersburg*. They hoped the book would be ready to release to the public within 6 months.

On the return trip from Helsinki the Belys again visited Blok, the Merezhkovskys and Razumnik. They attempted to visit Bely's mother, who was living in a rented cottage in Klin, in the countryside northwest of Moscow. But again an altercation occurred between her and Asya – she still retained animosity toward the girl Bely chose to marry. The Bely couple then went to Dedova, to the estate of their old friend Sergei Solovyov. However the 2 did not retain the same friendship and an altercation occurred on ideological differences. Solovyov could not accept Bely as an anthroposophist, and not just Bely, but Solovyov severed most association with anybody that was involved with Steiner. They hardly stayed at the estate and moved on. When the Belys attempted to visit another close individual, Margarita Morozova, she likewise was very cold toward them. Bely had written a letter 20 pages long expounding on Steiner's anthroposophy and sent it to Morozova sometime earlier, but all this did was turn her against Bely.

In June 1913, the couple were back in Bogolubi and there spent another month, and which allowed Bely to finish chapter 7 of *Petersburg* and deliver it to *Lilac*. They then left for Munich, Germany on July 31.

During the second half of August in Munich, the couple listened to Steiner's series of lectures, *On the Mysterials*. Then they departed for Norway on September 12, and visited Bergen. Then it was to Denmark. In Freetown Christiania, Copenhagen, On October 11-12, they listened to Steiner's lectures on *The Fifth Gospel*. The next stop was Berlin, arriving the middle of October. The 2 of them then traveled central Germany, returning to Berlin on December 25.

In Munich at the end of August 1913, Steiner announced to his adherents his plans for a new project, the construction of an anthroposophist temple, and to be named in honor of Johann Wolfgang von Goethe. It would be called the Goetheanum. It would be located in Dornach, near Basel, Switzerland. Planning for this project was long in the making. Steiner initially wanted to construct his anthroposophist Mecca near Munich, but too many local residents were against it, and the municipal authorities proposed too many obstacles for it, so it would be extremely difficult to start, much less complete. So the next option was Switzerland, and Steiner incurred no objections from them.

Rudolf Steiner placed the first stone in its foundation on September 20, 1913. The temple as proposed was to be displayed as an architectural miracle, from the outside and the inside it was designed to incarnate the most profound of the secrets of the universe, world and human soul. Every part of its inner and outer construction, its façade and interior, was fabricated from wood that possessed a sacred meaning. The essential areas of the temple would be two viewing halls or auditoriums of equal size with a dome over each of them. Anthroposophist activities would be concentrated here and symbolize the migration from the tangible and corporeal world to the intangible and supermundane.

Building this "higher school of spiritual science," as Steiner called the Goetheanum, would be achieved by the active participation of all of anthroposophy's adherents. Their direct involvement in its construction was also to be a step in their spiritual development. The spiritual energy of each adherent, as they worked on its construction, would be transferred into the building.

Bely, his wife Asya, her sister Natalia and her husband Aleksandr Pozzo, and Max Voloshin later, and many other adherents of anthroposophy, accepted Steiner's call to construction and to build the Goetheanum with their own hands literally. Bely personally worked on its construction over the next 3 years.

Bely described life in Dornach in detail in his memoirs. The cottage that Bely rented for himself and his wife as a residence was next to Steiner's villa. Steiner would often invite his neighbors over for tea and snacks in the evenings and to discuss divine issues, and the conversations would last late into the night.

Once work started each was assigned his role for the construction. Bely worked for 2 years as a woodcarver, he worked from dawn to dusk with his hammer and chisel.

Bely wrote to Razumnik and explained to him the work he was doing:

> From morning to evening, with a chisel in my hands, I work on the capitals and architraves.
>
> The building is a drawing on paper, but how majestic its form. This is something genuinely unprecedented, truly new, truly and original style, and not something contemporary. If there was something else to which to compare it, it would be Sophia of Constantinople.
>
> Never in my life did I work physically. But now it is apparent I can take a felled tree and work it into something, and how beautiful my craftsmanship. To physically participate in this work as a collective effort, and which will remain for a long while, is a monument. We are using seven species of trees, while those specifically for the columns and architraves are oak, ash, beech, cherry, birch and sycamore. You cannot imagine how wonderful an experience it is to carve a tree. When I am working on it, then each stroke of my chisel is a word, all of them corporately are a composition, poem, but it is composed collectively, because we, all the workers, are an orchestra, and our director of course is the Doctor. I leave for work in the morning, I return at night. My body emanates sounds of pain, my hands are stiff, but the blood pulses at this rhythm I never knew existed, and this new pulsation of blood composes within me some new song, a song of affirmation of life, hope, joy. I already possess in this rhythm of work a detailed outline of the third part of my trilogy.[121]

Bely, as with the other volunteer workers, gained physical strength and acquired the skill of a genuine master in woodcarving. Then in the evenings in the large hanger – although

---

[121] Referring to his next book after *Petersburg*.

the residents called it a shed – Steiner would read his lectures. Even while construction of the Goetheanum was in process, Steiner still traveled to other European cities to deliver his lectures on anthroposophy, and those with extra funds, or who felt the need to be relieved of the work for a while, would follow him. Over the 2-1/2 years from the time that Bely returned to Switzerland from Russia, he had the opportunity to listen to 30 courses, each on a different topic or tenet of anthroposophy. So including the initial lectures in Cologne and Munich, and those in Helsinki, Bely attended and listened to about a total of 400 of Steiner's lectures.

In November 1913, Bely concluded his writing of *Petersburg* with the *Epilogue* and sent it together to *Lilac*. By this time the first installment of *Petersburg* as a series was issued in Nekrasov's *Voice* magazine.

As Bely more and more immersed himself in anthroposophy, and especially the lectures in Helsinki and Dornach, it affected the composition of *Petersburg*. The final chapters of the book included some of its concepts, noticeable in a few of the conversations of Dudkin, and in other areas. Eventually Razumnik edited out some passages that were overtly obvious and that deviated from the subject of the novel, so not to turn it into a platform for anthroposophy. Readers were able however to notice toward the end of the novel the tendency of the characters to reflect anthroposophical concepts, and the book was saturated with symbolisms.

From this point onward Bely stopped writing, figuring there was now no obligation to have to, and so he completely immersed himself into an anthroposophist life. Now he saw the universe and all it contained through the prism of anthroposophy. Dream and reality sometimes merged into a single realism through visions that more and more cracked open doors into totally different worlds of the past, present and future. Steiner read a lecture on December 27, 1913, titled *Christ and the Spiritual Worlds*. Bely attended and he recorded his experience and apparition in his diary:

The Doctor read that lecture of the course that speaks of Apollo's light. As the Doctor was speaking of the light a strange occurrence transpired with me. Suddenly in the hall in front of my eyes, or more correct, it was light that flared out of my eyes, the light was so bright that I could not see any of the hall, it just disappeared from sight. It was shown to me, that it was not just my skull braking open, and not just the ceiling of the hall opening directly to display the kingdom of Spirit, that this was as though the descent of the Holy Spirit occurring. All was light, only light, and this light shook. Soon objects materialized through the light, the light of the chandelier still seemed dark to me. There only a contour of those sitting, the Doctor, the walls. The Doctor finished. When I moved from my spot I felt as though a continuation of my head over my head of about a distance of 5 feet. I almost fell into a state of apoplexy. I grabbed Asya with my hand and died for a few seconds. When I moved a second time, then the apparition vanished. This apparition did not even surprise me. It was just a reflection of my transcendent state.

On one of these days, the 29th or 30th,[122] I saw but do not know what: a dream or a continuation of my evening meditation. I was meditating and suddenly within and at the front of me a row of rooms opened, but not in my dream. The Doctor appeared in a strange pink-red suit, and he was himself a red cross. He grabbed me and led me through the series of rooms, and this was as though not in a dream. Then an interruption in my consciousness occurred but I immediately came to my senses. I discovered myself as though in front of a round table, one high and flat. A cup set on this table, and I realized that this was the Grail.

On December 31, 1913, Bely met with the German author and poet, Christian Otto Morgenstern.[123] He lived in Munich, was a

[122] Probably December 1913.
[123] 1871-1914

member of the General Anthroposophical Society and a close associate of Steiner.

The beginning of 1914 did not indicate anything formidable or tragic for Bely. First the couple traveled to Leipzig, Germany, to listen to Steiner's lectures on *Parcifal.* While at the lectures Bely had additional visions, and they continued shortly afterward while visiting on January 3, the grave of Friedrich Nietzsche, buried in Lutzen, near Leipzig. Asya and her sister Natalia and her husband Pozzo accompanied Bely. After placing flowers on his grave, Bely got on his knees and suddenly felt something strange enveloping him. He described the event in his memoirs:

> It was apparent to me that the spiral of history broke off of me. I exited from history into a frame of super-history. Time started to circulate around me and over this circle was a dome of a Spiritual Temple. And at the same time this Temple was my head, and my *i*[124] became *I.*[125] From being a human I became a Person of Time, and along with this I felt within me history emanating out of history: now history reached its culmination, all of its understandable eras ended. We grew into the non-understandable and now we stand at the edge of colossal political and cosmic upheavals that are supposed to occur in the years of the 1930s, with the consummation of the Second Advent, and which has already started in the individual consciousnesses of distinct people, as well as in my consciousness.
>
> At this minute when I stood in front of Nietzsche's sepulcher, a lightning strike through me caused a series of thoughts, and they were imbedded in me later as my four crises: the Crisis of Life, Crisis of Thought, Crisis of Culture, and Crisis of Consciousness. However at this minute I was my individual crisis, because my life as a existence, all of its earlier interests, ended and was destroyed. And so I do not know what I will be tomorrow.

---

[124] Small letter I

[125] Capital letter I.

This was one of several premonitions of the impending world war and the crisis of European War that Bely received.

After visiting Leipzig, the couple returned to Berlin, where they listened to another of Steiner's series of lectures, this one on, *Macrocosmic and Microcosmic Thought.* On January 31, they left for Basel, Switzerland, and then to Dornach, back to work on the Goetheanum. This was until the beginning of March, when the couple traveled to Suttgart to listen to more of Steiner's lectures. The couple then spent some time in Pforzheim, near Badin, Germany, and returned to Dornach about March 10, 1914.

In March 1914, Andrei Bely as Boris Bugaev and Asya Turgeneva registered as a married couple in Switzerland (they had been living to now as common-law husband and wife), even though their relationship had been platonic for some time. This was demanded by the Swiss government, as well as by the other residents of Dornach and their anthroposophist associates, so they married in a civil ceremony. Now they were able to get official documents from the Swiss government as a married couple.

During April 1914, the couple were on a circuit listening to Steiner's lectures in Munich, Vienna, Austria, and Prague, Czechoslovakia. They were back in Dornach from May to June. On July 10, they left for Norrkoping, Sweden, for a series of Steiner's lectures. While there, Bely and Asya and also M. Sabashnikova toured the region, visiting Malmo, Sweden, Rugen and Stralsund, Germany, on the Baltic Sea, then to Berlin and back to Dornach.

During this period, Bely worked on a condensed version of *Petersburg* to translate into German and publish.

A second and no less significant vision occurred on or about July 20, 1914. Bely was returning from Steiner's lectures in Sweden mentioned above, along with his wife Asya and a group of anthroposophist adherents. They stopped at the island of Rugen in the Baltic Sea along the coast of Germany. In the ancient past a majestic Slavic temple of Arkona, today known as Jaromarsburg, was here located. They were the Slavic tribe of the Rani. (It was destroyed by the Danes in the 12th century, but Russian historians viewed them as Germanic tribes.) Bely's subsequent vision was apocalyptic, depicting to him a soon resurrection of the Slavs – meaning the Russians – to take vengeance on the Germans for this early conquest.

Bely recorded the event in his memoirs:

> On the following day we traveled on a small steamship and arrived at Rugen and visited Arkona, the spot of an ancient Slavic village. According to what the Doctor said, at one time there was a center here of Slavic mysterials, but at the present they are replaced by immense radio towers. Arkona is at the edge of immense, white and bare cliffs. Grassy meadows surround it, the borders of the ancient village is identified by a long green mount. Beyond it are farmed fields. We gathered at the highest ledge over the sea and sat in the grass, and for some strange reason we stopped talking. Then something from the distant past overwhelmed us. And a series of bright and totally unbelievable images distinctly unfolded here in front of me. I could not ascertain from where they evolved. It seemed to me that the images arose out of the ground.
>
> This is the apparition I saw. What was shown to me were strange and potent powers surging out from earth's entrails, and these powers belonged to the Arkonans who lived here at one time in the past and were destroyed by the Normans. They – the Arkonans – descended underground, and now there, under the ground, and buried under strata of later Germanic culture, they continue to develop their awesome underground volcanic powers, erupting through the surface in order to overthrow all, to displace the work of centuries, to take vengeance for their destruction and spill their lava all over Europe.
>
> I overhear something like a voice, "We will again arrive. We will return. We are already returning, to take vendetta for our annihilation." And then some kind of barbaric power ascending from earth's entrails grabbed me and entered into me. And I as though spoke from inside of myself, although this

essence did not belong to the world of my cognizance, I said to myself, "The map of Europe will change. All will be turned upside down." And then in front of me flashed the place of the future horrible battles, where on the one side fought those underground natives incarnated into live beings, while on the other side were the representatives of the ancient Norman and Teutonic cultures, as if reincarnated knights.

Further I saw that the underground powers who cast a shadow of the past onto the future threatened Europe with formidable attacks where the present European peace will perish.

Then there stood in front of me a completely and distinctly alien figure, appearing like a Kalmyk.[126] He was an old man, with sharp squinting eyes, with large cheekbones, with a grey beard. He had large and wide shoulders, although slouched forward. He was arrayed in some type of oriental hat and wrapped in a long, multi-colored velvet robe. He stared intently at me with his penetrating eyes and as though said, "I am from the past. But I will again arrive." And then I understood that the image of this avenger for the past will soon incarnate, that he, this image, in his new incarnation will lead these underground powers against Europe, those that are presently squeezed underground due to the European world. They will be responsible for the change in Europe's map.

I pressed my head to the grass. I heard as though the echo of an underground city. I saw as though a city square and a large quantity of people crying and beating on drums. On a bed lay a Slav who was mortally wounded in the past, a champion warrior with a black beard. Now he regained consciousness in order to lead the regiments of the barbaric ghosts from underground and to battle and so avenge their past desecration.

---

[126] Indigenous tribe of the descendants of the Mongols who invaded Russian. Their residence is the republic of Kalmykia on the western shore of the Caspian Sea.

It is astonishing that Bely received this revelation at Arkona just 10 days before the start of World War I on August 1, 1914, the day Germany declared war on Russia. By this time, Bely and his wife were already back in Dornach. The day after war was declared Max Voloshin arrived in Dornach via Austria, he was able to cross at the last moment.

The assassination of Jean Jaures on July 31, 1914, a French socialist leader, by a French nationalist fanatic, Raoul Villain, especially effected the anthroposophist commune. Jaures was anti-militarist and was doing all he could to prevent war. The anthroposophists in general were pacifist.

The fervency of building the Goetheanum was interrupted by the First World War, and some fields of battle were not far from Dornach, and near the border with Switzerland. From their village the residents could hear cannon and artillery fire between French and German armies. The Swiss announced a general mobilization, fearing that the same could happen to it as did to neutral Belgium: the Germans invaded anyway.

Bely described the events of the initial few months of the war in a letter to Razumnik:

> We are severed from Russia. Letters travel through France. Around us is war. The entire preceding week we have lived in a region of cannon fire. We hear the battles in Belfort, Altkirch, and Mulhouse.[127] Our windows are shattered from cannon fire. In the event should either France or Germany turn their cannons in our direction, into the valley where we reside, we would be directly under fire. Alarming rumors have been spread these days that the French, gathering to surround the Germans, need to travel through our valley, which we call Arlesgeim. If the Germans barricade the road, then there is no other choice except for the battle to occur in our valley.

[127] Cities in north-west France, in the region of Alsace, near the border with Germany and Switzerland.

> For two days we lived in this manner: our traveling suitcases were packed and ready to go, so that at a moment's notice we could evacuate the place and flee into the mountains.
>
> But now the mobilization of Switzerland is complete. Our region is filled with soldiers. Patrols walk about, they beat on their drums, airplanes fly overhead, and there is artillery in the fields and cities. The chance of either France or Germany violating our neutrality is slim. As a result we continue to work overhearing the distant cannonades, the sound increasing and decreasing.

Although nationalist tendencies overwhelmed other regions, the members of Steiner's commune building the Goetheanum were international. There were citizens of almost 20 different nations together at Dornach, although the majority were from 4, and in order of number: Russia, Germany, Austria, and France. Steiner seemed to possess a special sympathy for those of the Slavic countries and especially Russia. He would often speak of the future messianic role of Russia in the world, foretelling a dawn of slavophilism and their impending important role in world history.

Bely and Asya took a break from working on the Goetheanum and during autumn 1915, they toured Switzerland visiting Lucerne, Brunnen, Fluelen, Goschenen, Lausanne, Montreux, Glion, St Moritz, Neuchatel, and Zurich.

However life in Dornach gradually became more and more difficult. Excerpts from Bely's letters to Razumnik testifies to the disposition prevalent at the time:

> Tough and hard is the life for my wife and I due to all the conditions here. Our situation is difficult in general. The conditions of life, even to be an anthroposophist is difficult and the pressure of life is so heavy on us. If you can imagine yourself for example the life of my wife and I, and she is very fragile and weak. She works all day cutting wood, for 19 months straight now, and is totally exhausted from such heavy

> physical labor. Since war was declared almost all the men have left and so for the most part women remain. It was almost intolerable the past winter.
>
> If there is any way possible, my friend, Razumnik Vasilyevich, with embarrassment do I ask my friends and associates in Russia to somehow assist me to regain our situation, maybe with literary work or books or an advance on future compositions. Anything you can possible provide us will help.
>
> There seems to be no way out of this and we are living on our final crumbs and to find more food is next to impossible and very complex. By the time you receive this letter our situation will be even worse and we may already be evicted from our apartment, and my wife will succumb to the cold. So she asks me, compels me, to set aside my pride, to ask you for some funds by advances on my books. It is dangerous what may occur to my wife.

Bely attempted to work on the Goetheanum while at Dornach during the war years, but was unable. The war seemed to have beaten out of him what motivation remained. Bely recorded in his memoirs:

> It has now been two years abroad since the start of the war. I have lived through the war especially difficulty. I could not work at all the first year of the war, this was due to communication being severed from Russia, then my depressed psychological state as a result of the events of the war. This forced me to fine work [outside the commune] at least as a minimum to provide me some psychological balance, otherwise it is difficult in general to live. I went back to physical work during the second year of the war and so I worked intensively to get my mind off of it.

Bely shortly after did receive an encouraging letter from Razumnik, to let him know that they did not forget about him. Although there was nothing they could do at the present to ameliorate his difficult circumstances. Bely wrote of his feelings in his memoirs:

> At this time I received a letter from Ivanov-Razumnik. He asked me a few things about my efforts in composing while here. His letter was permeated with warmth and the recognition of my literary merits. It indicated to me that it was definitely written from another world, one where they remember, love and value me.
>
> Here in Dornach, no one loves me as a writer. Many of them slash me apart and I do not know why. I was surrounded by strange apparitions of fate, not understandable to me. And I again wanted to run from all the Dornach abracadabra, noises that were an insult to me.

Bely wrote his response to Razumnik's letter and sent it March 11, 1916. Again he repeats the difficulty of his life with some personal details.

> Life is melancholy here. It has a tense effect on the nerves, sometimes I am out of breath, sometimes I suffer from heart pain. Starting recently I cannot any more tolerate the cannon fire in Alsace. And there is no where to escape.
>
> My novel is at a standstill. I have had many worries recently in my personal affairs, bitter experiences and pressure on myself. I cannot enumerate the discomforts and anxieties of life in this place. Our anthroposophists have become despairing people, we cannot seem to find any ballast to steady ourselves. The Doctor puts the brake on the entire effort. The dome has been ruined by sloppy work and poor craftsmanship. The Doctor has not been here in 3 months and the construction is in disarray. I and my wife are surround by troubles, trivialities and so much gossip. The workers barely drag their feet they are so exhausted. One person has heart disease, another had a splinter from a tree penetrate a tendon, one person became seriously ill, and all of this is like a nightmare.

The desisted and postponed novel of which Bely spoke was *Kotik Letaev*, and he was mentally contemplating a series of autobiographical fiction for a long while. It would consist of 7 parts, each one an independent novel: *Kotik Letaev* (years of infancy), *Kolya Letaev* (years of childhood), *Nikolai Letaev* (years of adolescence), *Leonid Letaev* (adulthood), *Light from the East* (about the orient), *Sphinx* (about the occident), *At the Threshold of the Temple* (World War 1). Bely composed this plan also with some general sketches of their contents during autumn of 1915. But as far as Bely got on the series by this time was the first chapter of *Kotik Letaev*.[128]

Of the series only 2 books materialized: *Kotik Letaev* composed in 1916, but not published until 1922; and then 4 years later he wrote *Nikolai Letaev,* except it was published in 1927, under the title of *The Baptized Chinaman*.

Soon after Bely's letter to Razumnik, he finally received some good news. Together with Blok he convinced the publishers of *Lilac* to gather the unsold copies of the installments of *Petersburg*, and then just publish as a complete book. They agreed and the book quickly went to press with a first run of 6,000 copies and put on the market. They then reserved 7,000 rubles for Bely, which would be his net income after all expenses were paid, except for 300 rubles for some miscellaneous items. Blok also intervened with the Literary Folder, officially called the Society for the Assistance of Writers and Scholars in Need, for some financial assistance for Bely. They used the reason as Bely's destitute condition in Switzerland and his inability to leave due to the war.

Receiving such good news from Russia, Bely immediately wrote back to Blok:

> Dear, dear, dear Sasha! When Razumnik Vasilyevich related to me that you intervened with him on behalf of my novel, that

---

128 The name of Letaev is based on the Russian word, le-tatz, meaning, to fly, as does a bird or airplane. So Bely's choice on an autobiographical fiction of himself flying in the sky through life.

you undertook the responsibility to have it published, even though there was not much income for you personally in it, but yet you intervened, and even more, you also intervened on my behalf with the Literary Folder, and so I am so obligated to you for this subsidy that was forwarded to me. When I found out about all of this, then I was so shaken – but not due to sentimentality – I was profoundly excited and a fervent wave of gratitude arose in me. I was so touched and almost to the point of tears. For a long while I was embarrassed of responding, and because I was at a loss for words since the feeling of gratitude could not be expressed in words, but only out of my soul.

It was genuinely the thought that I still have friends in Russia who love me and have not forgotten, you are such an immense moral support for me.

At the moment of receiving this letter from Razumnik Vasilyevich I was in a state of particular psychological devastation, stressed by the consequences of the conditions of the 2 years already spent here. I cannot explain to any of you any more because it is so morally horrifying, intolerable, disgusting, inescapable, regardless that my Guardian Angel, Asya, is with me, and the Doctor whom we adore resides with us. It is not that you have financially rescued me – although the subsidy from the Folder did rescue me – what excites me is that you were the valuable and precious news unto me and from a distance, from Russia, and that specifically you undertook this involvement for my intervention and which bail on my behalf serves as my peripeteia. It was you whom I incessantly love.

Further in the same letter Bely describes to Blok the same as in previous letters to Razumnik, regarding the unhappy and difficult life at the commune. By now Bely and Asya had turned into slave labor for the construction of the Goetheanum, and had lost their physical strength as a result of the hard work. People were now unfriendly and would stare at each other with spite, some would use the profanity of their language toward others of another nationality, Bely not knowing what was being said about him. Bely spoke of how the morality of the residents decreased, and some were delving into occult practices deviating from the tenets of anthroposophy and making it into something that it is not. Bely complained that the gossip among women does not seem to end, the social environment is now, as he states:

> Residing in a cloud of vile rumors and an atmosphere indescribably malicious and repulsive.

All of this occurring under the sounds of local cannonades from the battles between the French and Germans over Alsace, the war just continuing with no end in sight, worrying about their safely in such a dangerous region. He and Asya now felt doomed to oblivion and their high aspirations dissolved. The war had a cruel effect on the residents, economy, psyche and food supply of the commune. Steiner's absence months at a time to give lectures in other countries caused a lack of leadership at the commune and also a damaging effect.

From December 1915, to February 1916, Steiner gave a series of lectures that was especially to his close circle of intimate anthroposophists. It was titled, *Kant and Steiner in the Light of Contemporary Theoretical-Cognitive Problems.*

In March 1916, Bely and his brother-in-law Pozzo traveled by foot through Switzerland, visiting Olten, Solothurn, and Aarburg. In April Bely and Asya visited Lugano and Brunnen, returning in May.

The inescapable situation for Bely and Asya was resolved in an unexpected manner. On July 12, 1916, Tsar Nicholas II issued a supreme order for the recruitment for military service of all those in the categories that were considered earlier as exempt. Bely was initially assigned to one of these categories being the sole child and responsible for the care of his widowed mother, but now he had the obligation to return to Russia and fulfill his duty in the war as a soldier. Even though the concept of war and military service was against his essential convictions and character, nevertheless he accepted the summons and had to make the best of a bad situation.

On July 20, 1916, Bely sent to Razumnik the manuscript of his latest novel *Kotik Letaev*, except for the final chapter.

Bely left Switzerland on August 16, 1916 to return to Russia. The route home was complex and dangerous and he traveled via France, then England, Norway, Sweden and Finland, arriving in Petersburg on September 3. Asya decided against the trip and remained in Dornach as the best option. At least Switzerland was not in the war and considered neutral.

Steiner, hearing of Bely's departure, was sorrowed over it, but he also prophetically foretold to Bely before he left of the impending February and October 1917 Revolutions and that Russia would be engulfed in chaos.

In his later lectures in Russia Bely developed a theory regarding the similarity of anthroposophy to traditional Russian philosophy and the new sophiology. Bely also figured he was able to create the connecting link between the ideology of the revolutionary democrats and the mysterial revelations of contemporary thinkers, writers and poets. By following a route of a spiritual-revolutionary search the Russian cognizance approaches anthroposophy.

Anthroposophy, according to Bely, manifests as the natural inner exit from the tragic years of Russian life. It is the outline of the Russian future in the new culture. The contours of this culture are precisely described in anthroposophy and which will allow it to develop. Anthroposophical teaching does not sever the bond with freedom, but it will allow post-revolutionary Russian to find this route to the future.

Bely advocated freedom of religious thought as provided by anthroposophy, as he wrote:

> It is useless to ask yourself, "Do we have the ability to descend into the crater of the volcano of Russia? Are we capable of interpreting the profound aspirations of Russian toward culture, freedom and justice as also being the aspirations of

anthroposophy?" We must firmly keep in sight that with a stripped codex of dogmas regarding the essence of a person and karma, none of this will penetrate Russia. We must learn to speak with Russians in the language of their most beloved, philosophers and societal dreamers. Accepting the truth as disclosed in the writings of Herzen, Blok, Vladimir Solovyov, Bakunin, Gogol and Pushkin, we can be able to identify what it is that separated all of them – Bakunin, Herzen, Gogol, Pushkin and Blok – from the truth. Russians excessively love their heroes, in order to depart somewhere without them.

The Russian cognizance is not comprehended anthroposophically. Anthroposophists must initiate a familiarity with the specialties of Russia's culture and must speak in the language of this culture about the eternal truths of Sophia and Anthropos.

# ANDREI BELY

# LECTURER AND WRITER

Bely was back in Moscow at the beginning of September 1916. Conditions in Russia were not much different than conditions in Europe due to the war, and even worse in the light of impending revolution. Bely registered for military conscription and waited. Bely departed Moscow on September 19, to Kiev to visit some friends. He received a notice of induction into the Russian army and immediately returned to Moscow. On September 21, Bely received a 3 month postponement of his recruitment. He would utilize the time to catch up on his literary work and other personal matters, now absent from Russian 3 years. He first met with Razumnik regarding *Kotik Letaev*, and then went to Moscow, where he finished the final chapter of the book.

Bely concluded an agreement with V. V. Pashukanis,[129] secretary of the publishing house *Musaget*, and founder of Pashukanis Publishing after the 1917 Russian revolution. He had published Bely and Balmont in the past. Pashukanis' intention was to published the completed collected works of Bely. But nothing evolved from it.

---

[129] Vikenty Vikentyevich Pashukanis, 1879-1920. He was arrested in December 1919 for alleged counter-revolutionary activities and sentenced to be executed on January 13, 1920.

Bely spent about 3 months at the estate of Sergei Solovyov, near Sergeev Posad,[130] his friend and now brother-in-law, marrying Tatyanna Turgeneva. Sergei was attending the Theological Academy at the time and was ordained a Russian Orthodox priest on February 2, 1916. (Later in 1921, he left Orthodoxy and became a Roman Catholic priest.)

Bely also completed a treatise in November 1916, titled *Rudolf Steiner and Goethe in Contemporary Ideology*, and submitted it for publication. The book was Bely's summary of the lectures that Steiner delivered on Goethe and his influence on the philosophy of the era. It was published the following year.

Bely also intensely delved into materializing a new and large project – as though the *Kotik* series was not large enough – consisting of a series of literary-philosophical books, each one of them a collection of essays, to be titled *At the Pass*. These would be the 4 crises that were mentioned above and with which Bely had to deal. The first would be the *Crisis of Thought*, and which was almost already finished. The next 2 books would deal with *Life* and *Culture*. These 3 volumes were published in 1918. The fourth dealing with *Consciousness* was composed in 1921, but was never published.

In February 1917, Bely received a second reprieve from military recruitment, now for 2 additional months and he returned to Petersburg. Now without worry about the military Bely returns to lecturing. On February 12, he delivered a lecture on *The Alexandrian Period and ourselves in the Light of the Conflict between the East and West*, at the Petersburg Religious-Philosophical Society. Then on February 16, he delivers a lecture on *World Creativity*.

Now it was the end of February 1917, Bely is staying at Razumnik's estate at Tsarskoi Selo, or else with the Merezhkovskys. Here Bely experiences the events of the February revolution, with the abdication of the Tsar and the installation of the Provisional Government, but not without much bloodshed. The

---

[130] Also known as Zagorsk, about 60 miles north of Moscow.

Merezhkovsky apartment was directly across from the Tavria Palace where the new State Duma was conducting affairs and became the center of power struggles for control of Russia. Bely watched from the window as tens of thousands of soldiers marched the streets of Petersburg, and the fighting between the different military factions.

In the very center of the heat of events, on Tuesday, February 28, Bely was returning from Tsarskoi Selo to Merezhkovsky's apartment in now-called Petrograd, when he came under fire. Bely crawled on the sidewalk from the rail station to their apartment building, it took 5 hours for a couple of miles. Bely mentioned in his memoirs how he was under machine gun fire 5 times from soldiers stationed on the roofs of buildings. He would bury himself in the snow to hide, or in some alley, along a fence, huddled in his winter overcoat. He could not understand at what they were shooting or why.

A few days later, on March 9, Bely went to Moscow, the trains were packed with people leaving Petrograd and they ran at irregular schedules. In Moscow the conditions were the same: paper money devalued on the hour, administrative chaos – no one knowing who was in charge or what department had the authority, immensely long lines at bakeries, and soldiers flooding the streets. The city was piled with trash and the sewers were backed up. Belligerents overran Blok's estate at Shakhmatovo and burned it down, including his valuable library.

Bely shared his impressions in a letter to Razumnik from Moscow:

> I love Russia. I am Russian. I believe in the Russian people, but when they tell me that the wounded in the emergency wards threaten to throw the nurses out the windows, where the sanitation workers just wander about, as a result of which Moscow for 2 weeks now is dirty, and the unsanitary conditions are causing eye and throat diseases, and when the rain falls the sewers are clogged, Moscow is turned into a sewage dump. The streetcars stop running with drunks in their way, the soldiers act barbaric when they throw women

> out of the streetcars to get on, prostitutes line the streets proposing to the soldiers for money to survive.

Bely believed in the miracle of the February revolution, as he wrote in his memoirs on April 4, 1917. Beyond the chaos and collapse he saw and heard the "rhythm of a new cosmos." Once arriving back in Russia not for a minute did Bely stop work on more literary compositions: poetry, articles for newspapers and magazines, essays for his series of *At the Pass*. Again he started to advertise public lectures and the audiences filled the halls to overflowing as excited listeners. One attendee, S.A. Vengerov, wrote:

> The auditorium was totally captivated by the presentation, although three-quarters of them understood none of it. It was the personage [of Bely] that was mesmerizing, this prophet in the best meaning of the word. He was a lapidarian in lecturing.[131]

Possessing a gift of foreknowledge and realizing the potential fulfillment of his earlier revelations, Bely sensed a series of tragic impending events, and perhaps like nothing else in the history of Russia. At this time Bely recorded the following in his memoirs:

> Like an underground quake breaking apart everything on the surface, so is the revolution ahead of us; a hurricane in front of us to sweep away the old systems. Like statues of rock or sculptured images they are now petrified. The revolution will remind us of nature: thunderstorms, floods, waterfalls, beating all of it to the edge, beyond its ability to withstand.

Bely likewise attended political meetings, as did so many people wanting to voice their opinion on the new government, although none had any authority or capacity to do anything beyond

---

131 The reader will ascertain this as well after reading the translations of some of Bely's symbolist treatises located in the Appendix in this book.

providing their opinion, Bely included. Some were held at the Religious-Philosophical Society, which still gathered regularly at the residence of Margarita Morozova. As a result of his political views combined with his anthroposophist beliefs, Bely was labeled a mystic Bolshevik. Nikolai Berdiaev attended likewise and the 2 had several debates on the issues of polity and religion in the future of Russia.

Bely expounded his political platform in his memoirs, although permeated with anthroposophy:

> For a long while I have striven to impress on these magnificent people the following in particular:
>
> 1. We are residing at the beginning of a world revolution,
> 2. That Russia for the first time perhaps will enter its trail,
> 3. That the dual authority is the beginning of a completely new, unprecedented construction,[132]
> 4. That the rotation is changing based on dramatic dialogue,
> 5. That I await a trilogy, when the Council of Peasant Deputies enters the scene,
> 6. That Russia will stage mysterial plays, where the Councils will be participant of a sacred act,
> 7. That the present system of government in Russian will be transient, this will be a system in motion,
> 8. That if we are able to endure this system in motion for a few more months, then:
>     1. All the nations of Europe will be drawn into and be submerged into our Moskstraumen whirlpool,[133]
>     2. That within Russia we will hear the Voice, not the party, but the very soul of the nation,
> 9. That Russia will birth a child,
> 10. That we need to fracture into small single parts: a federated republic is the beginning of this movement,

[132] Referring to the Provisional Government.

[133] In the Norwegian Sea, a system of whirlpools, the most dangerous in the world.

11. But to separate is frightening, but if we do not terminate what we are presently, at least we will not die as a result, and we will not ruin the old peace of Europe; that we will resurrect and initiate the start of a new resurrection,
12. That through all the ugliness I hear, I see a cut for the breath of Manasa,[134] I see a cut for the new spiritual culture,
13. That this is counted as intelligent addresses in *Russian News*, I discard to the Social-Democrats,
14. That I rejoice in the truth of the new world epoch, seeing the rhythm in the course of events among us, and etc.

This is the reason other Muscovites count me as a bacteria.

Bely understood the revolution exclusively as a revolution of the spirit materializing in the name of the kingdom of freedom. The true European revolutionaries, according to Bely, are not Marx and Engels, but Nietzsche and Ibsen. As far as the revolution in Russia is concerned, Bely described it in the following manner, and typical of other symbolist passages:

> The revolution of the spirit is a comet flying toward us from the frontiers beyond reality. Its supremacy as indispensable in the kingdom of liberty is depicted as a socialist leap. It is the fall of the comet on us. But this fall is an illusion of the vision. It is a reflection in the sky of what is occurring in the heart. In our heart we already see the star-filled meadow[135] of our newly-born image in our future displayed by music. The expansion of the point of a star into the flying disc of a comet is already occurring in the depths of the knowledge of the heart. The flaming enthusiasm takes this star and develops it into a comet, and we hear sounds of stars about us, about our future.

[134] Sanskrit word for *mind* in a wide sense, often used in theosophy.
[135] Meaning the Milky Way.

The center of attraction for Bely in the area of intellectualism, art and ideology became Tsarskoi Selo, where his friend Razumnik organized a literary-political association that he named The Scythians. At the same time Razumnik was preparing a magazine having the same name. A significant portion of the initial 2 issues consisted of Bely's novel *Kotik Letaev*, and a series of his articles inspired by people's moods as a result of the revolutionary and their expectations. Razumnik, due to his political convictions and party affiliation, announced himself a socialist-revolutionary (SR), and he counted himself one of the primary ideologists and theoreticians of the SR movement.

Sergei Dmitrievich Mstislavsky, a close associate of Razumnik and member of the SR group, was also one of the ideologists of The Scythians and also author of the Scythian Manifesto. The 2 of them were able to attract several prominent Russian writers to join their association: Blok, Bely, Remizov,[136] Prishvin,[137] Zamyatin,[138] Lev Shestov, and others. The motto of the Scythians was: Life – Will – Truth – Beauty.

The publication of the first half of *Kotik Letaev* at the end of summer 1917, promoted Bely even further and higher with many positive reviews and from many influential publicists. The second half was in the next issue of *The Scythian*. Bely reflected on his book in the following manner in an interview, and symbolist as always:

> Self-realization, like a child within me, opened wide my eyes.
>
> I see there what was lived through, what I lived through, only mine, the consciousness of childhood fits into it, considering it at the age of thirty-two years. It was at this point that the moment of childhood became comprehendible. It blends with self-realization and all falls into place in it.

---

[136] Aleksey Mikhailovich Remizov, 1877-1957, Russian modernist writer and calligrapher.

[137] Mikhail Mikhailovich Prishvin, 1873-1954, Russian Soviet writer.

[138] Yevgeni Ivanovich Zamyatin, 1884-1937, Russian author of science fiction and political satire.

> Falling leaves carry a meaning of words. They shed from a tree and the words to me are indistinct, they rustle and flutter. I reject their thoughts. In front of me is the first cognizance of childhood and we embrace it, saying, "Welcome you, the alien."

(I will not deal further with *Kotik Letaev*, with selections of the reviews or an interpretation. The reader can purchase an English translation and make their own evaluation.)

Bely left Petrograd on the eve of the October 1917 upheavals. Before leaving he stopped to visit the Merezhkovskys and had a heated argument and serious quarrel with them. The reason was Razumnik who was considered by his symbolist friends to be a Bolshevik. Bely defended his new confidant and publisher, since was actually an SR.

Gippius recorded the visit the next day, on October 24:

> The pitiful lost child, Boris Bugaev, who came here and left yesterday, back to Moscow.[139] Deranged. Irresponsible. He associates with this Bolshevik, Ivan Razumnik, another lost child, and no different than Blok.
>
> We have many such rock-heads as Blok and Bely, and it seems they reside in some fourth dimension. They do not seem to realize this and so belch phrases that echo vilely in our three dimensions.

The association of both Bely and Blok with the Scythians, which the Merezhkovskys considered political and not philosophical, annoyed them. Bely and Blok became traitors to the many years they associated with the Merezhkovskys at their residence, where a conservative religious attitude pervaded the atmosphere, and now, as they felt the situation, abandoning the spiritual in favor of a secular agenda, the socialist. From this point forward the Merezhkovskys maintained spite toward both Bely and Blok and

[139] Zinaida uses the word – child, as a parody on Bely's book just published, about him as a child.

terminated all association with them. In December 1919, the Merezhkovskys would flee Russia for Europe and permanently.

The October Revolution caught up to Bely in Moscow. The city was in chaos, with troops of the various factions all fighting each other in the streets, food supply to the city interrupted, and people fearing for their life in general. Bely was able to stay with his mother at their apartment on Nikolsky Lane near Arbat.

Bely wrote to Asya in Switzerland about their situation:

> From Saturday to the following Friday,[140] an entire week, we, that is, our home, were severed from the world, because it was almost impossible to leave the place. Our quiet Arbat region unexpectedly became one of the centers of military action. The cadets, foot soldiers and white guard regiments are stationed along the Arbat, Povarsky, Prechistenka, and at all the street intersections.
>
> The regiments of the revolutionary committee and red guard have control of the Smolensk Marketplace and I think the Presnensky District. In short, our Nikolsky Lane is the border between the 2 fighting factions. They even shoot from the buildings. The cadets shoot from the houses on Arbat, the Bolsheviks shoot from Trubnikovsky Lane. The cannons roar, the shells fly, the walls shake from the noise. On Monday at 9 AM, I jumped from the sofa – I was sleeping in my green office – due to the deafening roar. Running to the window, I saw a pillar of dust from crumbling brick. It was apparent that shrapnel fell on the house opposite us and broke all the walls.
>
> Since Monday we moved our living quarters into the kitchen and bath, it is only here we can live. Bullets fly into the windows, breaking the glass. Shrapnel struck the balcony of our apartment, and good that mother and I were in the lower floor and were there saved. A fragment of shrapnel, breaking a window, flew no more than a couple of inches from mother's temple. Mother went into hysterics. The last few days

[140] From October 28 to November 3, 1917, Old Style calendar.

> were have been staying with the Makhotins. It is almost impossible to live, there is almost nothing to eat. My office is filled with bullet holes, all the windows are broken. The cold is infernal, and I cannot get myself to do any composition.

Bely had no choice but to abandon his destroyed apartment and seek a refuge with friends. Thinking about Asya all this time gave him no additional consolation. Much of Bely's time while in war torn Russia was consumed with worrying over Asya, but there was nothing he could do and he had no information on her living conditions.

Bely wrote to Razumnik about his concern for Asya:

> Without Asya, only wails emerge from my soul. I am definitely and entirely crumbling. And among the many reasons the primary is this feeling of being completely helpless while I languish over Asya. She is sick, she has no money. It is impossible to send her any or to travel there. This despair has increased in me for a long while.
>
> Against all obstacles I need to get to her. If she hungers, I will be hungry with her; if she is sick, I will be near her. For 1-1/2 months now I only think of one thing: to discard everything, discard it all, right or wrong, and get to her. She is my psychological and spiritual help. I cannot work without her, and my life just crumbles. This is enough. If I knew the obstacles that would be installed between us, I would never have returned to Russia. I would have preferred being a deserter as long as I was alongside Asya. I am plainly sick from worrying over her.

Nonetheless, about this time a new woman was gradually starting to enter Bely's life, Claudia Nikolaievna Alekseev, and her husband was Peter N. Vasilyev. She would become Bely's second wife. Claudia knew Bely due to their common involvement in the anthroposophist movement in Russia and Europe. Claudia likewise followed Steiner's schedule of lectures, traveling all over Europe to listen to them. She likewise went to Dornach with the others and worked on the construction of the Goetheanum at its beginning, but as soon as World War I broke she immediately returned to Moscow. Prior to this time their familiarity with each other was on a social basis and at a distance. It was at Bely's lectures at the end of December 1917, titled, *World of Spirit*, at the Moscow Anthroposophical Society, which she attended, when her acquaintance with Bely took a serious turn.

One of the members of the society, M.N. Zhemchuzhnikova,[141] who knew Claudia well, wrote of her:

> Claudia Nikolaievna Vasilyeva – Bugaev through her second marriage – was a small framed person, having calm movements of some kind of musical rhythm. One special quality was her beautiful rhythmic walk, and which she perfected in eurythmy.[142] She spoke calmly and plainly, but always right to the point She loved to joke, so humor was always playing around with her face.
>
> But all you had to do was look in her eyes and you would feel, and just by looking at them, all of what she consisted. I call this – fervency of the soul. She had astonishing eyes. There is only one word to describe them – beaming, that is, beaming eyes.

The Moscow Anthroposophical Society was founded in 1913, shortly after Steiner founded the general Anthroposophical Society in Cologne, Germany, in 1912. It lasted 20 years in Russia, until 1932, when it was closed by Soviet authorities along with other organizations whose ideology contradicted dialectic materialism.

In a large and somewhat heated hall on Sadovo-Kudrinsky St, where Moscow anthroposophists would gather weekly, Claudia

---

[141] Maria Nikolaievna Zhemchuzhnikova, 1899-1987, poet and anthroposophist. Arrested in 1933 along with other members of theosophist societies, but released, and then again arrested in 1938, and now sentenced for distribution of anti-Soviet propaganda, 5 years in exile in a concentration camp in Kargopol.

[142] Movement as an expression of art as developed by Rudolf Steiner and his wife Marie von Sivers. She learned this as part of her anthroposophist education.

would read her lectures and lead a seminar based on Steiner's popular book, *How to Attain Knowledge of the Higher Worlds.* Here Bely also taught a series of lessons on *The World of Spirit,* and other topics.

Bely wrote to Asya at Dornach:

> I have about 60 or 70 people listening to my series of lessons, most of them are women who also attend some local university, and a few young people. After each lecture I have the opportunity to hear some impressive statements from the side of my students, like, "If this philosophy is anthroposophy, then I want to be an anthroposophist."
>
> I seem to also have acquired a circle of friends as a result, although they are not anthroposophist. For the meanwhile this venture is still green and much work is needed in order to establish the philosophy of anthroposophy.
>
> Not long ago I delivered a lecture on the anthroposophical cognizance, *Light from the Future,* at the hall with 250 attending, and they all paid a high price for a ticket.

In February 1918, Razumnik sent Bely a copy of the SR newspaper, *Banner of Labor,* of which he was editor, and which included several poems composed by Blok titled *The Scythians.* After reading the article, there was no limit to Bely's ecstasy and he immediately wrote to Blok:

> Precious, dear and close Sasha. What a strange destiny. We have again crossed paths, I read your poems – *The Scythians* – with excitement, loudly and to the extent that my voice even echoed, just as it did with *The Field of Kulikova.* All that you write causes my voice to increase in pitch. I lived with such a high pitch in Dornach. I know this.
>
> What you write about Russia, as far as I am concerned expands to Europe. A crash is also impending there, as what occurred with us. I know this. Of course, even more will occur.
>
> Remember, all of us need you, and especially in the more difficult future. Be wise.

I embrace you strongly, and love you as I never have. Your involuntary brother.

B.B.

Bely corresponded with everyone regarding his personal life and events, in detail and openly, and it seems on a daily basis. The following is a selected passage from one of his letters:

> The picture of Moscow: in the evening gunfire. We have become so accustomed to the gunfire that none of us pay any attention. Recently someone shot at us from an automobile, then the automobile quietly drove away. Near the house where I am spending the nights, all day today I have been shoveling snow over the fence from the former school of art and sculpture. My history teacher V.E. Giatzintov still lives there. Many of the intellectuals of Moscow are making for themselves a living doing this. People are just walking into apartments and making themselves at home.
>
> One administrative department is running my mother into the grave. They want the last crumbs of bread she has in breadbox to pay her debts. They told her, "Go to work. Work and pay." Our door-keeper needs to receive 200 rubles a month, and yet he does nothing. I received a income of hardly 200 rubles a month.
>
> They oppress us with every law and illegal means. All that remains for us to do is turn to anarchy and coerce people for their money. When will this all end? God only knows. Along with this, such a complex life is causing my head to go in circles.

Bely's attitude toward Soviet authority from the very beginning was not simple, and he did not run to become an extreme or unrestrained anti-Soviet. As a result the Russian immigration of philosophers considered Bely to be a traitor, accusing him of capitulation for remaining in Russia. However Bely suffered emotional pain when he noticed any form of oppression or coercion. More than all Bely was cautious about a socialist development of Russia and tried to have a good perspective since the Soviets were now in power. But he was not about to sacrifice his individual freedom and the freedom of his creativity for the sake of Soviet socialism.

Bely's repulsion toward socialism as a standardization of people's lives, thoughts and residences was expressed some time earlier, in 1905, in a recorded conversation with Nikolai Valentinov:[143]

> This is so terrifying! Herd thinking, the estrangement of life's personal joys. All cling one to another. There are no partitions. From such spiritual stuffiness it is impossible to breath. A person cannot have a large vent, drill a hole in it, leave at least a small hole so fresh air can enter through it. Terrifying! It is not the individual, but it is the *we* that neigh, some kinds of strange Mayne Reid headless horsemen.[144] Without heads or without individualities, without testicles, it is one and the same. The herd mentality. At no time and in no place in history did a herd mentality accomplish anything. And I visualize clearly this society.
>
> I see dormitories. Thousands, hundreds of thousands, millions of beds, one alongside the other, extending somewhere into infinity. On these beds sleep the *we*. And all have the one and same kind of grey colored blanket. The color of their slippers are the same, the design of the nightstand is one and the same, and all are dreaming the same dream.
>
> The monstrous machine manufactured millions of identical dolls and placed the same kind of soul in each. It is frightening for me to be among them, as they are not people. I am suffocating from the respiration of these millions of dolls. I cannot be among them. I jump from my bed and I am crawling up the wall, to the vent, the vent with a screen is high up the wall. I jump, I fall, and again I jump, I fall, I grab at the vent,

[143] Nikolai Vladislavovich Valentinov, 1879-1964, Russian socialist and journalist. He was an advocate of the early policies of Vladimir Lenin, but with the rise of Joseph Stalin he left Soviet Russian for Europe in 1928.

[144] Reference to the novel *The Headless Horseman* by Mayne Reid.

> it slashes me and I wound my hand. Nevertheless I succeed in holding to the vent with my blood-covered hand, I lean my face to the vent. Fresh air is circulating through it. What happiness! I see a tender moon, a river reflects its light, the tops of the trees have a silver glow.
>
> There are no lifeless, alien, grey-yellow dormitories there, no millions of dolls that look like people. I cry, "I will no longer be among the *we*." If they lead me back to my bed at the dormitory, and there is one having my number on it, I will not go. I will hang holding the screen in the vent until I drop dead. I will die if they want to tear me away from here. They will carry only my body no longer breathing back into the dormitory. My *I* they cannot take captive.

However just as earlier, now during the years of the most difficult of experiences and unexpected upheavals, incomparable in Russian history, Bely continued to believe in Russia. He still had the concern over an income and survival and himself and his mother. The new Soviet administration were labeling philosophers and certain classes of writers as non-working elements or parasites of the economy, and it was next to impossible for them to get ration cards or have legal rights. A person needed to be working at some official place of employment to acquire them. So Bely went to the Government Archival office to get a job as an assistant archivist, but he did not last there very long, unable to adapt to their routine, and they discharged him.

Bely then went to the Proletkult, short for proletarian culture, a newly-created Soviet institution whose purpose was to develop and promote literature, art, culture, education, music and theater in the environment of the new Soviet Russia. He went to work there at the end of September 1918, and became one of the managers of the Moscow office.

This opportunity for some stability, as well as a place for Bely to continue his individual creative expression, fit him well, and he did his best to avoid the bureaucracy. Bely's responsibility was to interview and provide counseling to all of those wanting to join the new proletariat culture, working with novice writers, and welcome existing willing writers into the Proletkult and have them become members. Bely would read their submitted manuscripts and conduct seminars on poetic rhythm, aesthetic form and vocabulary. He also gave lectures on Russian literature in general. Bely noticed that right in front of him a new generation of intellectuals was being born, the legacy of the best traditions of great Russian literature. The prognosis of the Proletkult ideologues was that the new generation inheriting the old style would be counterproductive to the expectations of the Soviet administration, but with Bely's direct assistance in their development, he was able to prove them wrong. So many that joined the Proletkult were factory workers wanting to advance themselves culturally, and eventually membership at its peak was 400,000 individuals of all ranks of Soviet Russian society.

One of those who attached himself closely to Bely, and who later advertised Bely as being his mentor, was the young poet, Grigori Sannikov.[145] After Bely's death, he was one of the three who composed his obituary. Sannikov recollected Bely in his later years:

> Andrei Bely was my first – and actually my sole – literary mentor, a pedagogue in the literal sense of this word. I will not be exaggerating if I said that I was unable to write verses before I received tutoring from Bely. I remember, the year was 1918, the month was September, the passing of a hot year filled with great and formidable events. That month I was summoned to Moscow and assigned as military commissar of a regiment of foot soldiers of the Red Army.
>
> But Moscow was not just occupied with military affairs. Moscow's walls were scattered with announcements of various studios, schools, courses, events. Once I read an advertisement about the Moscow Proletkult, where they announced a welcoming event at the literary studio with departments in prose and poetry. I decided to enroll. What concerned me was

[145] Grigori Aleksandrovich Sannikov, 1899-1969. Soviet Russian poet.

whether I could fulfill my duty as a military commissar and still have the time to attend courses at this studio. I went to the Proletkult and enrolled in the class on prose, hoping this was more inclined toward literature, since I might be able to use my improvement in writing in my military reports.

I started to attend in the evenings. Our teachers were: Vya. Ivanov, Khodasevich, Bogdanov,[146] Polyansky, Shershenevich,[147] Sakulin,[148] and Andrei Bely. The course that Bely taught was verse composition and was the most specialized of them all and it seemed to me the most meager in attendance. The class initially was boring and monotonous, but this was because Bely was not a good teacher at the start, but after a few lectures he perfected his teaching talent and his subject matter became interesting and fascinating. In time he became my favorite instructor of them all.

If an opportune situation arose Bely would preach anthroposophical concepts, but accomplished in a very subtle and professional manner, and not often. This was his manner of countering those preaching atheism. Bely would explain that the materialistic ideology should be counted as the counter-revolution, which attempts to replace the discarded bourgeois culture. It is the teaching of Steiner that should be recognized as the actual revolution, as it breaks open the boundaries of human comprehension and indicates the new routes leading to the emancipation of spirit.

The audience of young people seeking a meaning of life was filled with fervent enthusiasm listening to Bely's lectures, but his uninhibited and original interpretations quickly provoked suspicion from the emaciated and cautious Proletkult Communist party members. They accused the anthroposophical lecturer of

[146] Aleksandr Alekseevich Bogdanov, 1874-1939. Soviet Russian writer and Bolshevik revolutionary.

[147] Vadim Gabrielevich Shershenevich, 1893-1942, a Soviet Russian poet and lectured on poetry at the Proletkult.

[148] Pavel Nikitich Sakulin, 1868-1930. Soviet literary scholar.

anti-Marxist propaganda and non-proletariat views. They warned him that he was not fulfilling his duty at the Proletkult.

Then in November 1918, he was moved from the literary department of the Proletkult to the theatrical department of the National Commissariat of Education (Narkompros). The matter was handled by Anatoly Vasilyevich Lunacharsky, the Soviet Commissar of Education, who felt Bely would be more of a benefit in the theatrical department instead. Bely would handle exhibits on scientific subjects. The sister of Leon Trotsky, Olga Davidovna Kameneva, had undivided authority over this department, and her husband was the infamous powerful president of the Executive Committee of the Moscow City Council of National Deputies (Ispolkom Mossoveta), Leo Borisovich Kamenev.[149] A very pragmatic, capricious and unsentimental woman, Olga Kameneva had no mercy for the symbolist poets or those people associated with them. As a result Bely's career at the Narkompros was short lived. (Her husband would make life difficult later for Bely.)

On November 7, 1918, the First Anniversary of the October Revolution, Bely walked about a festive and decorated Moscow with Margarita Sabashnikova. Always friends, she also worked at the theatrical department of the Narkompros, involved in the organization of children's theater. Occasionally she would attend meetings and lectures at the Anthroposophical Society. Moscow was a safer and cleaner city than a year before and life was settling for Bely and his mother.

In January 1919, Bely received a promising letter from Razumnik. He was informing Bely of the organization in Petrograd of the Liberal Philosophical Academy, later known as the Liberal Philosophical Association or Volfila. They decided to elect Bely as the president of their council. Along with him members of the council were Blok, Vsevolod Meyerhold,[150] Petrov-Vodkin,[151] Lev

---

[149] Kamenev, 1883-1936, was a communist revolutionary and a prominent Soviet politician, in addition to being Leo Trotsky's brother-in-law. Kamenev was executed on August 25, 1936, as part of Joseph Stalin's great purge.

Shestov,[152] with other popular activists in Soviet culture. Razumnik, who was founder, would be deputy-president. The cofounder of the association and a member of the council was Aaron Shteinberg.[153] For their meetings the Volfila was allowed a large building and financial support from the Soviet government.

Bely was forced to contemplate on the matter seriously before making a decision, since he would have to move to Petrograd from Moscow as well as leave his mother. They promised Bely a sizeable compensation, complete freedom in his presentations, and plenty of extra time for writing. Since nothing remained for him at Narkompros anyway, Bely was happy over the offer and decided to accept it, and at the end of January 1919, he arrived in Petrograd, deciding to settle in Detskoye Selo (formally known as Tsarskoi Selo).[154]

Bely arrived just in time for the first meetings of the new association and which were held at Razumnik's apartment, until the building was remodeled and available for use. However unexpected disturbing events immediately occurred. Soviet authorities and the Chekists[155] suspected them of organizing contra-revolutionary activities using a philosophy club as a façade. Arrests and interrogations followed. Blok was retained under guard at his Petrograd apartment for 2 days. After a search he was taken by the Cheka to the prison at the Police Department on Gorokhovoi Street. Blok was released only after a personal intervention by Anatoly Lunacharsky and Maxim Gorky's wife

---

150 Vsevolod Emilyevich Meyerhold, 1874-1940, Russian and Soviet theater actor, director and producer. In 1939, his theater productions were considered anti-Soviet and he was arrested and tortured. He was sentenced to death and executed on February 1, 1940.

151 Kuzma Petrov-Vodkin, 1878-1939. Soviet and Russian painter and writer.

152 Lev Isaakovich Shestov, 1866-1938. Russian existentialist philosopher. He immigrated to France in 1921, after the Russian Revolution, residing in Paris until his death.

153 Aaron Zakharovich Shteinberg, 1891-1975, Jewish Russian philosopher, writer and activist in international Jewish affairs. In 1922, he migrated to Germany, and when persecution against Jews began he migrated in 1934 to London.

154 In 1937, the name of the city was changed to Pushkin.

155 Members of the Cheka, the state security organization, similar to the American FBI.

M.F. Andreeva, who also held a high post in the Soviet administration.

Bely was able to escape arrest. After the initial meeting he became sick from the February cold and had a high fever. He returned to Moscow.

Who especially suffered was Razumnik. He was arrested as a continuation of a previous arrest for being a leftist SR, who were considered enemies of Soviet authority. After an interrogation and submission of statement under oath, Razumnik was released (following this incident arrests and incarcerations would continue).

The organization of the Volfila terminated for several months and had a hard time starting again. When it did start in 1921, it was under conditions that were more conducive to Soviet authorities, so to avoid any further suspicion. The association nevertheless continued its activities until it closed on September 4, 1924. Its property was then transferred to the Union of Soviet Writers.

The Russian Civil War erupted and again life was intolerable for Moscow residents. General Denikin and his White Army were attempting an invasion of Moscow. For Bely, again in Moscow, it was his and his mother's survival, not only due to the war conditions, but food was scare and people were dying from malnutrition. As regular Bely shared his problems with Razumnik in Petrograd.

> Any opportunity to appear in public is atrophied. I just cannot write books. There is no paper either. No reason to write letters as the cities are cut off one from another. I cannot work since the frost is so bad right now in the apartments that people hide under the covers all day to stay warm. There is likewise nothing to eat. What can we do? Just little by little.

No less of a tragic picture did Bely depict in a letter to Asya, during the years of the Civil War, through the end of 1921.

> Beginning January 1919, I dropped everything, crawled under my heavy and thick overcoat and I laid there totally prostrate until spring, when the thaw somewhat warmed my soul and body. Do not tell us, the old people, about Russia, who bear on our shoulders the years of 1917, 1918, 1919, 1920, 1921.
>
> I want to say, "Yes, here, when I laid for 2-1/2 months in fleas, then to me..." but my converser interrupts and tells me, "Yes, how bad, so you had fleas." I look at him and condescendingly say, "For 2 weeks I suffered while recovering from eczema that was caused by the fleas." Or I will start to say, "People just the other side of the fence moaning day and night from typhus." Then they interrupt, "Oh, you lived with typhus!" Again I will smile and say, "Yes, I lived through it and went to deliver lectures, and I prepared lectures through their cries."
>
> The temperature in my room reached a low of 8 degrees frost,[156] and no higher than 7 degrees warmth.[157] Moscow was dark. During the night they would drag away petrified people.[158]
>
> It costs at least 15,000 rubles [a month] to survive, while my mother receives hardly 200 rubles pension. She lived without a small stove in her room and the temperature was at freezing point. She went every day to the Smolensk Marketplace and sold some of her old stuff. I gave what I could, but this was still little.

All of this, the exhaustion and devastation, was imposed on a person who previously flared with an inextinguishable fire of tolerance of creative ecstasy.

Ilya Ehrenburg[159] remembers the Bely of the Russian Civil War era:

---

[156] 18 deg. F.

[157] 45 deg. F.

[158] meaning that they froze during the night.

[159] Ilya Grigoryevich Ehrenburg, 1891-1967. Soviet writer.

> Immense, wide opened eyes, a flaming bonfire over a pale emaciated face. A disproportionate high forehead with these islands of hair standing straight up. He reads verses, he screams as did the Sibyls, and reading, waves his hands. Emphasizing rhythm, expressing not the verses but his secret thoughts. It is almost humorous and after a while Bely seems to be a majestic clown. But when he is alongside you, it is alarm and then languor, the feeling of some kind of elemental misfortune that possesses everyone.
>
> Bely is higher and more significant than his books. He is a wandering spirit, not having found a flesh, a stream outside the banks.
>
> Why does the flaring word genius, when spoken of Bely, sound like a title? Bely could become a prophet, his weird insanity is illuminated by divine wisdom. So a six-winged Seraphim flew to him but did not finish the work.[160] It opened the eyes of the poet, gave him the ability to hear rhythms out of this world, gifted him with a sting of a wise serpent,[161] but it did not affect his heart.

Bely's poem, *Christ is Resurrect* is published at the beginning of April. On August 24, 1919, Bely is elected to the presidium of the All-Russia Union of Poets. For him this is a great honor.

At the end of 1919, Bely could be located most of the time at the Palace of Art, where he taught courses in literature for a while, gave lectures, and even spent the night. The Palace of Art was under the patronage of the Narkompros, beginning its work in early 1919, and Bely provided an active participation in its organization. Here literary and musical evening dinners occurred, discussions and lectures were delivered, new compositions of respected authors and novice authors were read. Here functioned 4 departments: literature, art, music and history-archeology.

---

[160] Reference to Isaiah 6:2

[161] Reference to Matt 10:16

Particularly here he invited a friend, Boris Zaitzev,[162] who would become Bely's closest friend for many years. He wrote of Bely:

> He always was from his earliest years, aspiring to the left. There was something in the revolution that he liked from a long while back. He foresensed it, awaited it. When it came, he accepted much that it had to offer. Bely did not suffer morally from the revolution as we did, and so he lived through it better. Nonetheless anthroposophy led him to the side. The spiritual principles of this movement had only a minute similarity to revolutionary thought in the manner Lenin viewed it.
>
> Bely met me very courteously, somewhere at a distance, in his room with a window that looked out to a garden. The room was filled with books, manuscripts, all disorderly, of course. On one side was a blackboard, as in a classroom.
>
> Very soon the conversation turned to anthroposophy, to the revolution. Perhaps, in regard to the death of Count Mirbach,[163] he seemed to incline to my position, as this helped him and his anthroposophy. Now even the blackboard seemed useful. He started to quickly sketch various circles, spirals, curls. The world was a cycle of history arranged in the volutes of the spiral. He explained this long and inspirationally. In any case this was a rarity, much less orderly, almost mesmerizing. Bely in general was an excellent orator and speech writer, full of imagery and color. But he had no stability. Something always seemed to possess him, but he did not control it.

While at the Palace of Art Bely met and became friends with the poetess Marina Tsvetaeva. She would later write a eulogy about Bely and include him in her memoirs. Another person involved in the literary world of Soviet Russia was Pavel Medvedev,[164] and

---

[162] Boris Konstantinovich Zaitzev, 1881-1972, Russian writer. Zaitzev moved to Berlin, Germany in 1922, to Italy in 1923, and then Paris in 1925, where he lived until he died.

[163] Wilhelm von Mirbach, 1871-1918. German ambassador to Russia. He was assassinated by Yakov Blumkin.

whom Bely met at the meeting of the Moscow Anthroposophical Society. Medvedev left his impression of Bely in his memoirs:

> Bely amazed me. An ashy grey face. His hair flared over his extremely large domed, solid and high forehead, definitely flared around his bald patch. Blue eyes: one laughs, the other weeps. A mouth with bloodless thin lips. He was thin. His mobility was strange. Just too many movements and all of which seemed to be disorderly. He could not sit still. It was difficult for me to converse with him, although once started he was mesmerizing. But it was not truly conversation, but listening to him. Bely spoke a whole lot, loved to speak and had beautiful diction. It was very cold in the room, it was disorderly and uncomfortable. On a small table piled with personal items and letters and tableware, under a bust of Dante, cigarette stubs and tobacco were scattered, and along with them were these manuscripts. He ate meagerly, always cold food.
>
> I reluctantly observed the poet and spoke little. Bely touched me with his hair and gazes. I did not ask him any prepared questions.

In autumn of 1919, Bely left the Proletkult, or as he said it, "They left me." In order to again quality for food ration cards and any kind of pension he went to work at another organization – The Department of Preservation of Monuments of Antiquity, a division of Narkompros. The head of it was Natalia Sedova, the second wife of Leon Trotsky. Bely's responsibility was the care of the museum collection and display of the French Revolution, and to arrange all the manuscripts of personal experiences for public use. This work brought Bely a large amount of moral satisfaction since he was involved in reading many rare books and documents in the original French language. He worked there from September 1919, to March 1920.

---

[164] Pavel Nikolaievich Medvedev, 1891-1938. Russian literary scholar. He was accused of anti-Soviet writing and arrested, and executed on July 17, 1938.

On January 28, 1920, Bely concluded an agreement with the publisher Grzhebin,[165] a second opportunity for someone to publish his complete works. But nothing more than one small book of poetry was printed.

Bely continues to lecture at the Volfila: May 30, on *The Old and New Testaments*, June 7, on *Culture and Race*, a series of lectures in June on *Anthroposophy as the Route of Self-Realization*. He returned to Moscow on July 10, and lived in a room at the Palace of Art while working at the archeological department.

At the end of August 1920, Bely moved to live at Peter Vasilyev's new apartment on Neopalimovsky Lane. Vasilyev himself was conscripted into the Red Army as a doctor and sent to the front as soon as the Civil War started. The apartment was better than what Bely had since Vasilyev was a doctor and so could acquire a better residence. Bely's room was relatively warm, with a table. He was able to get food easier, and especially now he had extra money for cigarettes – he was still a chain smoker. Between his new place of employment and a nicer residence, Bely was feeling his best since the beginning of World War 1.

Claudia however had a less positive perspective on the matter of life's comforts. She recorded in her memoirs:

> The conditions of life here are very severe. There is no heat in the homes. The streetcars do not run. Boris suffers intensely from the cold and is almost always sick. He came to us wearing someone else's oversized pants, in an uncomfortable undersized coat with a suffocating collar, freezing cold, weak. He sat in a chair and barely uttered a few coarse and upsetting complaints about his intolerable life, and suddenly he as if went silent and interrupted his statements and devolved into this strange state of a mute stupor.
>
> I hurried to give him some hot tea. After 2 or 3 glasses he revived, revitalized. He started to talk about where he was,

---

[165] Zinovii Isaevich Grzhebin, 1877-1929, Russian illustrator and publisher. He emigrated to Germany in 1922.

> whom he encountered, of what they spoke. Then he opened his portfolio, removed some clusters of scribbled pages. the last cluster was on what he was working, and he began to read, interrupting himself to interject some additional notes.

Under the conditions of a cold and famine-stricken Moscow Bely managed to work without stopping. A new magazine was being published called, *Notes of Dreamers*, by the Petrograd publisher *Alkonost.*[166] In the first issue of the magazine 2 of Bely's articles were published. The first titled, *Diary of a Writer* and the second was the first of a series titled, *Notes of an Odd Fellow.* As with all of the publishers of the symbolist genre, this one was also short-lived and the magazine only had 6 issues. It was closed in 1922 by the Soviet authorities. Much also had to do with the destitute conditions of the printing industry: a lack of paper, ink, distribution and difficulty with Soviet censors.

Over the course of the following year Bely was able to have many of his poems recently composed finally published, such as *Star*, and a series of tales having the title, *The Princess and the Knights.*

Nights at the library at the Rumyantsev museum, at freezing temperatures, and until his feet were almost numb to the knees, Bely was making excerpts and reading the treatise of Leo Tolstoy, *On Life*. The book was forbidden by the Holy Synod, and to get a personal copy was impossible, and the only one available Bely was able to access. The hand copy Bely made of the treatise became one of his altar books. In the past, Bely was not a fan of Tolstoy, but now with his immersion into anthroposophy deeper, Tolstoy became of interest to him due to his spiritual depth.

Bely wrote to Razumnik regarding the treatise:

> Read the astonishing book of Leo Tolstoy, *On Life*, and you will thank me for it. No doubt about it. Have your already read it? Then read it again and no doubt you will have another understanding of it. This book from here on has become for me

[166] The Alkonost is a woman-bird of paradise in ancient Byzantine and Slavic legends.

a book that accompanies me each day, just as does *Zarathustra*, just as the *Bhagava Gita*. I loved it. This book is the most epic, next to *War and Peace*. It is thoroughly permeated with the consciousness of a new era. Placed on one side of the scales, it will outweigh all the volumes of Vladimir Solovyov. And even if you were to add the sum of all the books written on the new religious consciousness – from the volumes of Merezhkovsky, Rozanov to Florensky, Berdiaev, Bely and others – to the scale, this book will still outweigh all of them.

Read the book and you will understand my excitement.

Life for the Merezhkovskys was very difficult in Petrograd. As writers and philosophers, they were unable to acquire meal ration coupons, and as a result Dmitri Merezhkovsky was assigned by the Soviet administration a job doing physical labor. He was emaciated, sick and weak, but from 6 in the morning he dragged wood, and another day he would dig trenches in the ground, although not thawed completely. But he had no choice in order to survive.

The Merezhkovskys left Petrograd on December 14, 1919, under the guise of lecturing to Red Army soldiers. First they traveled to Minsk, Belarus, then to Vilnius, Lithuania, and the next stop was Warsaw, Poland. They had made their escape from Russia. They eventually migrated to Paris, France, and which was their home until death. (Dmitri died in 1941, Zinaida Gippius died in 1945.) No sooner did the couple exit Soviet territory they started their anti-Soviet campaign, and which immediately brought them under condemnation by Soviet authorities, those who allowed them out of Petrograd in the first place.

Naturally many intellectuals saw a quick trip over the border as a means of deliverance from such a hopeless situation. Some of them used the excuse of a business trip or for necessary medical care in order get approval to leave. Bely likewise devised a reason to get approval to leave. He had been absent from Asya for over 4 years now, and the last correspondence he received from her was 1-1/2 years ago. He explained this in a letter to Razumnik:

> I decided to utilize what unbelievable strengths remain to leave Russia and at the first possible opportunity in order to find Asya. I have no news about her at all. On Wednesday I will turn to Lunacharsky with a petition for him to look into the unendurability of my situation, me having to live completely unaware of what is occurring with my wife. Once I leave for the west, please do not forget about me and keep me in view.
>
> In this blind attempt of mine to leave, leave, leave, under any circumstances, is this instinct to propel me forward, it is my lifelong task to accomplish, to write that series of books *Odd Fellow*. While in Russia, I will never write it. I will accept whatever terms the Narkompros dictates to me to somehow get to Asya, and once there, then we will together discuss plans for our future life.
>
> I hope to be able to leave this spring, or summer at the latest.

The assistance from Lunacharsky helped but was insufficient because of the amount of paperwork involved, and the time frame was not acceptable to Bely. On January 4, 1920, Bely wrote to Maxim Gorki, to solicit his assistance, explaining the entire matter in a long letter. Gorki decided to help Bely and so intervened and had a discussion with Lunacharsky the next day. The result was positive, except with considerable conditions, under the circumstances at the time, for Bely to receive an exit visa the waiting time was 17 months. Margarita Sabashnikova also applied and it took her 6 months to get through all the bureaucracy.

One reason that made it difficult for Bely and other writers to leave was the situation with Konstantin and Elena Balmont. Lunacharsky granted them permission to leave Russia, but only under the condition that he remain either positive or neutral toward the Soviet government. However, no sooner did Balmont reach Paris he was writing and publishing critical articles against the Soviet administration. This caused Lunacharsky to cancel or postpone the requests of others to leave Russia, including Bely's.

Bely considered taking the same route of escape as did the Merezhkovskys, but decided against it. Russia was his home and he wanted to continue to have the option of returning. The second was his mother. He did not want something bad to happen to her should he leave the country illegally, or he may not be able to return should he need to care for her in the future. Bely still had faith in Russia, yet his personal opinion at the time was very critical, as he wrote:

> It is terrifyingly miserable. It is miserable and difficult for me in general right now. Moscow is a lifeless dream. So is the chancellery and all the increasing idiocy of the government authorities. They have to dissect the entirety of the repulsive animal corpse. The time the contempt consumes is suffocating. You disdain not the revolution, not even communism, meaning what they have done with communism. You disdain the rudeness, the triviality, the tedium and the cruelty and slow motion of their officers.

The Volfila was given approval to continue by Soviet administration under the conditions that it be called an association, and not an academy. On February 17, 1920, Bely moved to Petrograd, where he lived through the beginning of July, dedicating all of his strength as president, and talent as an lecturer, to his new cause, and which he called – a second birth. In the summary of his treatise, *Why I became a Symbolist*, written in 1928, he notes the following regarding the years of 1921-1923 when he was active there:

> The Leningrad Liberal Philosophical Association became at one and the same time my personal and my individual matter. I became connected with all of its participants, and its slogans, and its expansive but organized auditorium, its diversity, and the tempo of its work. In the expansion of its anthroposophical presentations I encountered obstacles and evil suspicious eyes from the side of other anthroposophists. But also the opposite, as others who were not anthroposophists here offered me

> unforgettable fervent brotherly support. I will not forget the truly malevolent attitude of the anthroposophist Voloshina[167] toward me, who condescended to spreading malicious gossip about me. I will also not forget the brotherly attitude of Ivanov-Razumnik toward me, who acted like a natal brother.

For the Russian intellectuals Volfila, for a short duration, became a genuine island of liberated scientific and philosophical creativity in an ocean of dogmatic thought. At their weekly meetings, and which circulated in various prestigious buildings, such as the Russian Geographical Society, the best of Russian literature, science, philosophy, gave presentations. The younger and older generations disputed in turbulent and uncompromising discussions, displaying the sharpness and speed of their words and thoughts. In addition to Bely, others of Russia's best who gave presentations were Blok, Lossky,[168] Askoldov,[169] Razumnik, Petrov-Vodkin, Kropotkin[170] and Zelinsky.[171]

Nina Gagin-Torn, a young poet who was soon to be popular in Russia, attended the Volfila and became friends with Bely.[172] She also wrote a eulogy of their friendship and the following is part of it:

> On boards that covered the broken windows there were posters and advertisements glued. It was 1920, and I learned about the existence of the Volfila from this particular advertisement. I read it, it was to be held at the building of the Geographical Society, on Demidov Street, and Andrei Bely was going to read a lecture on the crisis of culture. I knew of this

---

[167] Margarita Sabashnikova

[168] Nikolai Onufrievich Lossky, 1870-1965. Russian philosopher.

[169] Sergei Alekseevich Askoldov, 1871-1945. Russian religious philosophy, spiritualist and pan-psychist, and professor at University of St Petersburg.

[170] Peter Alekseevich Kropotkin, 1842-1921, Russian scientist and philosopher.

[171] Tadeusz Stefam Zielinsky, 1859-1944. professor at University of St Petersburg in literature.

[172] Nina Ivanovna Gagin-Torn, 1900-1986. Russian and Soviet poet and historian. She was 20 when attending the Volfila. She was persecuted by the Soviet government, accused of being a counter-revolutionist, and spent the years 1936-1942 and then 1947-1952 in various concentration camps.

> writer, having read his *Symphonies* and *Petersburg*. I ran to listen to him. As with all the students of our dormitory I was hungry, but I sat on a bare bench and was not bothered by it, since I was enveloped with satisfying my hunger of knowledge. We were assured that we were building another world and an exemplary one for tomorrow will be built. I needed to really know how to do this.

Nina enrolled for 2 seminars taught by Bely: theory of symbolism and the culture of spirit. With basically young people Bely would conduct his lessons at a room at the hotel Angleter, where he happened to be staying on this occasion in Petrograd. One window looked out on St Isaac's Cathedral.[173]

Nina Gagin-Torn to the end of her life remembered how Bely would dart from his chair, walk and almost run about the room, expounding the creation of myths in a precise manner. He stretched his arms. It would not have amazed us if he flew away by embracing the sun's ray, and soar out of the room, and float over Isaac's Square, illustrating the world-wide movement. The girls sat mesmerized. Other students just taking notes angered at them, "Is this the place to venerate him?"

The issue was not excitement or emotion, but of attaining the unknown, what was vaguely guessed from long ago, about revelations of deep issues. However Bely during the course of his lesson did not take notice of this veneration or the deep impressions that his words caused on them.

At every possible opportunity Bely would make a presentation at some auditorium. Vera Bulich, who fervently venerated Bely, was a student at the university in Petrograd at the time and an up and coming poet.[174] She listened to one of Bely's lectures and the impression he left on her remained for the balance of her life. Vera wrote of Bely in a Finnish newspaper shortly after his death:

---

[173] Russian Orthodox Cathedral in central Petersburg dedicated to St Isaac of Dalmatia.
[174] Vera Sergeevna Bulich, 1898-1954, Russia poet living in Finland for most of her life.

My father proposed, "Why don't you go to the university to Andrei Bely's lecture on rhythm?" I greeted his request excitedly. What I remember clearly is that Andrei Bely read his verses, those which I especially liked, and for which I am grateful to him forever. Even though some were vague and indefinable, but they were significant, what was opened to me that evening and remained forever as reflective knowledge.

A classic blackboard, pieces of chalk breaking in the nervous fingers of his incessantly motioning hands, and formulas, equations, diagrams. What is this? My amazement, "Mathematics proves poetry?" Recently I took and passed some examinations on algebraic equations, and my head was still filled with series of numbers and letters, not yet erased by time, and I am attempting to focus my attention to catch the thread of his proof. But either this is higher mathematics that will always be unattainable to me, or Andrei Bely is distracting my attention from complex calculations of curves. I decide to stop using my mind and begin to just believe him at his word.

And how can I not watch him? Short, nimble, with stealthy and at the same time abrupt movements, at one moment bending over and as if dying under some heavy invisible load, the next moment ambling with his especially brisk walk from place to place. He somehow reminds me of a bird or a fast flying bat. He exuded this general colorful impression: bright grey, with a radiance from his fluffy, dusty, and almost gray hair over his high forehead. It seemed a stream of rays beamed from his almost transparent blue-grey eyes. These eyes would watch us but not see us. Andrei Bely would gaze not with his eyes, but as though from above his eyes. He does not see the world provided to us all, but what is following him and what is more significant than anything we know. In his gaze is a joy of a secret vision and only accessible to him and this is an illuminating sparkle of insanity.

Andrei Bely spoke, "Rhythm, rhythm is the soul of a verse." And again the chalk glimmers in his hand, the blackboard rotates yet untouched in its evening luster, so it can be further weakened under a load of new white-colored formulas. He whirls near it, he casts spells, chants, invokes, inspires, convinces us with his persistently waving hands, his fervent penetrating voice, the pulse of his heart and the radiance of his half-insane visionary eyes. And finally, as the terminal incantation, already concluding his summaries, this visionary and perceptive person already celebrating the victory over us who are aware of only three earthly dimensions, Andrei Bely reads his verses. His voice is soft and stealthy, as are his movements, he maintains no pathos, no metal parts, no wealthy modulating sound. His voice is also a pale grey and pastel set of tints, but this is the color of ash under which burn coals. And he creates miracles, he transformed verses, pouring into them his burning respiration, a echoing secret melody of rhythm.

Just like an antique brittle crystal carefully raised with a cautious hand, was each verse of his exalted above us. Here he weaves the drab dust of time and unveils a radiant frontier. Rhymes that we have known since childhood, that we learned my memory sitting on hard school benches, already monotonous from over-repetition, are suddenly unrecognizably new with bright images, filled with life and respiration, and they again enter my memory with inspiration in order to remain here this way and for always.

And through these images that were initially deaf to me and indistinct, now they all the more distinctly and intently appear leading their pace of an unknown commanding power – rhythm. Andrei Bely, as though from the cognizance of this great and inexpressible something that possesses him, stands on his tip toes while reading and grows, grows in our eyes, illuminated by this revelation from above.

He finishes and in front of us is again this short, grey person soiled from chalk dust who is fooling with the blackboard, clumsily erasing what was written. That night I understood the secret power of rhythm, not mentally, but sensitively. I felt the unheard melody represented as a verse that he carried and livened, and not only verses, but life itself,

> and the world is cosmic music. I understood that what is important is not what we see, but what is behind the seen: the unseen and still not deciphered, and that the incarnation of this indistinct vision is the transformation of the world and this is primary in art.
>
> So this is the 4$^{th}$ dimension. This is what is unknown, what is still not disclosed to all or accessible. There is no doubt in this, one just needs to experience it.

The compilation of emigration documents demanded Bely's constant presence in Moscow, and so about July 10, 1920, he left Petrograd. At the new capital – Moscow – matters were just as chaotic as before. For Bely it was busy: lectures, recitations at the anthroposophist circle, personal articles, work on the novel, *Nikolai Letaev*, later to be called, *The Baptized Chinaman*.

An unfortunate incident occurred in December 1920: Bely slipped in the bathtub and received a serious concussion, and for over the next 3 months he was hospitalized. He is released in early March after he recovers and travels to Petrograd and again immerses himself in the turbulent intellectual life of the Volfila. As always, material subsistence was at a high demand for Bely, so this forced him to assume a job that was totally absurd for such a famous writer as Bely, not to mention all of his other universities studies and related credentials: assistant librarian at the elementary library of the National Commissariat for Foreign Affairs. He settled in a room at the hotel Spartacus. Now it was early spring 1921.

While there, P.N. Medvedev arrived from Vitebsk and visited Bely. Noticing Bely's substandard living conditions, he invited Bely to spend the summer at a Belarus village where Medvedev had a cabin. Bely was overjoyed at the invitation.

While at his hotel room and during the Orthodox holy days of Pentecost and Trinity, Bely suddenly experienced an unprecedented creative burst, and over the course of 2 days he wrote his best autobiographical poem, *First Meeting*, where he described his adolescence and the formation of his Sophian-Cosmic ideology.[175] The recitation of the poem was dedicated specifically to a meeting of the Volfila, scheduled for July 24, 1921, at the large hall of the Geographical Society.

Marietta Shaginyan attended the poetic evening and wrote the following review for a local newspaper.

> A. Bely at the Liberal Philosophical Association read his new poem, *First Meeting*. He is a supreme reader. When I saw how this plastic artist wound his words using gestures, transforming the incomprehensible into music, the music poured into us with wide and harmonic movements. I enjoyed grasping the strength of genuine art. No bacillus or skepticism, spite or torpor will kill it.

After the fall of Leon Trotsky and the exile of he and his wife, the department of Narkompros was declared a Trotskyite nest and reorganized. The department passed to under the administration of the National Commissariat of Foreign Affairs.

Apart from some cooperative effort at the Volfila, Bely wanted to meet and spent some personal time with Blok and his wife Luba Dmitrievna. Their final meeting was on May 25, 1921, at the hotel Spartacus, where Bely was staying. As close an association they had in earlier years, with Luba playing the role of the Maiden of the Rainbow Gates and Bely was the Knight, nothing remained.

By this time Blok lost faith in the socialist revolution and the new government. It affected him both psychologically and physically. His earlier marital difficulties and loss of a child likewise exacerbated his condition. He lost his strength and several untreatable illnesses seriously affected his health. In addition, and as with Bely, it was difficult for Blok to acquire the basic necessities for survival, since he was a writer all his life and he never acquired an education or learned some trade or vocation in order to make a living. Depression affected Blok, he lost weight and he was having pains in his heart. Eventually he became

---

[175] Sophian regarding Sophia the concept of the feminine aspect of Divine Wisdom of Vl. Solovyov.

bedridden and refused guests to visit him. He petitioned the Soviet government to allow him to leave to Europe for medical care, but they deliberately procrastinated and the exit visa was not signed and issued until 2 days after Blok's death.

Aleksandr Blok died August 7, 1921, a Sunday, probably due to tuberculosis; he was 40 years of age. No newspapers were printed the next day, so friends printed a notice and glued it all over the city, announcing the death of the poet, and the schedule for the civil requiem and funeral. All in Russia realized what occurred: the brightest star of Russian poetry descended like a sunset. Few of his closest attended due to the Soviet repression of the funeral, no newspaper announcements. Marietta Shaginyan stayed the entire night at his side, reading the Psalms. Nikolai Gumilyov was arrested the night before, so he was not there. Kornei Chukovsky, the popular children's writer, was in a nervous hysteria. Bely was ill and lay prostrate on his bed, almost unable to move, but came the following morning. Anna Akhmatova attended also.

Blok in his casket was almost unrecognizable, he was withered, unshaven, with sunken eyes and cheeks.

The funeral was scheduled for August 10. Six carried the coffin: Bely, Vladimir Pyast,[176] Vladimir Gippius,[177] Evgeni Ivanov,[178] Evgeni Zamyatin, and Wilhelm Zorgenfrei.[179] The procession followed the streets that Blok enjoyed walking, until reaching the cemetery. He was buried at the Smolensk Orthodox Cemetery in Petrograd.

E.P. Kazanovich[180] recorded Bely at the funeral:

---

[176] Vladimir Alekseevich Pyast, 1886-1940. Russian symbolist poet. He later wrote a biography on Blok. He was arrested on February 6, 1930, for counter-revolutionary activities and spent 3 years in exile in the Russian far north, and another 3 years in the south of Russia, finally released in 1936.

[177] Vladimir Vasilyevich Gippius, 1876-1941, Russian poet, school teacher, and brother of Zinaida Gippius.

[178] Evgeni Pavlovich Ivanov, 1879-1942, author of children's books and author of a biography of Blok.

[179] Wilhelm Aleksandrovich Zorgenfrei, 1882-1938, Russian poet. He was arrested in 1938, for counter-revolutionary activities and executed. He wrote several articles for Soviet newspapers on Blok's life and poetry.

[180] Evlaliya Pavlovna Kazanovich, Soviet writer.

> He stood at Blok's grave holding in his hand the white cross to later place at the head of the grave. His large bald stop was surrounded with a crown of clumps of gray curly hair. He wore a camel-hair jacket, and his face was numb from the pain.

The closest thing to a requiem was a meeting at the Volfila on August 28, 1921, dedicated to the memory of Aleksandr Blok. The large hall of the Russian Geographical Society was overfilled.

Bely gave a eulogy regarding Blok and he spoke for almost 2 hours. The following is one passage:

> Remembering Blok do not extinguish within yourself that spark of spirit of all that was said about him. In order for matter to flourish ignite the spirit, otherwise matter will not remain in matter. Ignite the spirit means to proceed according to the route exemplified by Blok. He was his entire life a revolutionary, and with all his life, all of his attitudes to the future and past, that future which we create, that past which we are summoned not to forget like barbarians, but we are to value it in our creativity, plough it, refine and temper it.
>
> In all changes, in all searchers, a spark is maintained, but so are ashes. The fidelity of this spark will be for us the memory of Aleksandr Aleksandrovich Blok. He in his entirely was a spark; he in his entirety was a fire. He was the offspring of goodness and life. He in his entirety was the freedom of creativity.

Blok is considered by many as Russia's second greatest poet after Aleksandr Pushkin, and no doubt the best of all those in the Silver Age.

At the beginning of September 1921, Bely was informed that no obstacles remained for his trip abroad. This was 19 months after this initial application. Bely described his situation the passed few months in an un-sent letter to Asya:

> I again intervened regarding my exit and the Cheka again did not release the documents. Then I became neurologically ill. A neuropathologist had to treat me, a professor Troitzky. Then I decided to just flee, but then somehow the Cheka found out about it, so my attempt to run would have failed. Then Blok died, they shot Gumilyov, and my plans froze. Young people started to cry, "Let Bely abroad, otherwise he will die as Blok did." Friends imposed some pressure and they released the documents.

Nikolai Gumilyov was executed August 25, 1921, with 61 others.[181] He was also a cofounder of the All-Russian Union of Writers.

It was another 1-1/2 months until Bely actually received his exit visa. In the meanwhile he returned to Moscow and there participated in some of the Moscow division Volfila presentations. He gave a eulogy on Blok at a Volfila meeting at the Poly-Technical Museum on September 26, and then returned to Petrograd.

The Petrograd Volfila bid farewell to their president warmly and touchingly, and many accompanied him to the train station. It was early October 1921. One unknown girl shouted at him just prior to entering the train and her comment was documented:

> Dear Kotik Letaev. When you get lonesome there, abroad, remember that we love you here.

[181] This was the Tagantzev Conspiracy fabricated by the Soviet secret police to terrorize intellectuals.

# THE DISAPPOINTMENT EXCURSION

The train went first to Moscow, and there he delivered a lecture on *The Russia of Blok*, and then read his poem *First Meeting*, at the All-Russia Union of Writers. On October 20, 1921, Bely left Moscow for Berlin, Germany, he would be gone for the next 2 years. He arrived there November 18, after making stops in Riga, Latvia, Kaunas, Lithuania, and Konigsberg, Prussia (today known as Kaliningrad, Russia).

Over the years of Bely's residence in Berlin, Germany, it would turn into a haven for the Russian immigration, the majority of them philosophers, writers, religious dissenters, intellectuals, school teachers, professors, those in general disenchanted with socialist ideology, those disagreeing with atheism and the closing of churches, those persecuted for their convictions, whether political or religious, and those who felt life would be better somewhere else after experiencing the conditions in Russia after the October Revolution of 1917. Some census takers estimated 200,000 Russians in Berlin, with a total population of 4 million. Once settled Bely had on his agenda contacting and reconnecting with his wife Asya Turgeneva.

Several Russian writers of the Silver Age during the decade of the 1920s, resided at one time or another in Berlin: Maxim Gorky, Aleksei Tolstoy, Boris Zaitzev, Mikhail Osorgin, Vladislav Khodasevich, Ilya Ehrenburg, Sergei Esenin, Vladimir

Mayakovsky, Boris Pasternak, and Marina Tsvetaeva, and considerably many others lesser known. So Andrei Bely was added to the list and he found a small apartment on the 6$^{th}$ floor of a large complex of Russian immigrants, immediately he went to work on completing books started earlier, preparing books published earlier for reprint, writing articles for local magazines, and contemplating new projects. Bely assisted Gorky in the organization of a new magazine, *Conversation*, created to unite the immigrant writers scattered all over Berlin and other regions of Germany. Each would submit something from their perspective and initiate a communication between them all. It was a brilliant idea, except that it only lasted 6 issues.

The first issue of *Conversation* carried an article written by Bely having the florid titled, *About Russia in Russia and about Russia in Berlin*. The article had the purpose of defusing the extreme anti-Soviet element residing in many of the Russian immigrant population of Berlin, including those acting like rabid dogs toward Gorky. Bely did not hide or deny the unbelievable conditions, deprivation and suffering in Russia after the October Revolution of 1917, but as a dedicated Russian he still had belief in its successful future. Bely wrote in his article:

> In 1919, I lived in a room that was all of 2 or 3 steps wide and deep. Just enough room for a cot, table, and nightstand for my clothes. My manuscripts, papers, letters and drawings and books were piled high on the nightstand, the table seemed to have all else on it. I lived snuggled against a small stove that about 3 times a week would fill the room with noxious fumes and I would fall on the floor almost dead, but nonetheless it was still cold. I oiled the shutters to open them so to vent the room and opened the doors into the adjoining rooms (where others were living).
>
> I wore used felt-lined boots as I ran to the ice-cold museum in the mornings to assemble material for the history of the revolution collection.[182] I sat in the museum in a warm

[182] This is mentioned above when Bely was working on the project of the French

overcoat and hat and mittens. To warm my feet frozen to the knees, I would dance. Taking notes from the *Moniteur*,[183] I would ruin my eyes staring at the miniscule font of the letters. Also taking notes sitting in the Museum, the nausea and the coughing. I went to Petrograd once and left all my notes on the nightstand. Worrying about them, since I had no key to the door and so could not lock it, I returned and some of them were stolen by someone (they probably used them to wrap salted fish). At the time I was delivering a series of lectures on self-realization, at someone's private apartment.

Moscow at night was dark and lifeless and you would be robbed, the snowdrifts would stick to you and you would slip in the ice. After a working day, after ploughing through the darkness and snow, tired listeners would drag in the gloom. The room temperature was below freezing and was barely illuminated. They sat in their heavy overcoats and stomped their feet from the cold. I walked to the lecture slipping and falling.

I get to the auditorium, about 35 are gathered, the atmosphere is warm anyway. I read for 3 hours forgetting all else in the world. The ice cold auditorium has a warm spiritual environment and this also warms me. This I would do all week. Then we had to shorten the course, frost set in, at the lectures our brains would freeze.

I remember the auditorium of these lectures. It was not accidental for us to meet, feel. Among us an immense duty arose, culture sprouted, our self-realization materialized. I am connected with all of the listeners. The lector and listeners became brothers and sisters. The question of realization, its meaning.

Typhus spread at this time. Many were hungry, quivering in unheated buildings. Days were spent standing in line somewhere. We still had lectures.

---

Revolution.

[183] *Le Moniteur Universel*, French newspaper.

> There is no doubt: it is difficult to write in Russia: no paper, pens or typewriter. But nonetheless. Were there not scientific discoveries in Russia: Rozhdestvensky,[184] the academician Marr,[185] and others? And were there not talented people in Russia's Russia? I will say this frankly, the talent continued on and new were born there. There Sologub composed, Zamyatin grew up, the Serapion Fraternity was born,[186] Vsevolod Ivanov and Pilnyak sprouted, Khodasevich recited the best of his poetry, Marina Tsvetaeva was lauded, creators such as Gumilyov and Akhmatova lived, Mayakovsky, Pasternak, and Esenin and other achieved their aspirations. It was not in Berlin, but there.
>
> Here little talents appeared, but the great talents there. What did the immigration produce? A few interesting potentials, 2 or 3 names that might have promise. That is all.
>
> Russian poetry with one stroke achieved the greatest of cultures.

It was about this time that Bely became acquainted with Vadim Andreev, a Berlin student and up and coming poet.[187] Andreev in his memoirs recollects his first encounter with Bely:

> When I entered a rather large room, one with many corners and where the furniture was arbitrarily placed, Andrei Bely stood from behind a table piled with excerpts from newspapers, correspondence and manuscripts, to meet me. I then forgot all else. He walked a few steps toward me, amblingly and with unusual elegance. He bowed low and offered me his hand. All of his movements were flowing and

---

[184] Aleksandr Konstantinovich Rozhdestvensky, 1877-1940, Russian engineer specializing in underwater vehicles.
[185] Nikolai Yakovlevich Marr, 1865-1934.
[186] Or, Serapion Brothers, a writer's circle in Petrograd.
[187] Vadim Leonidovich Andreev, 1902-1976, poet and son of the dramatist Leonid Nikolaievich Andreev, 1871-1919, and brother of mystic and visionary Daniel Andreev, 1906-1959. Although born in Russia, he lived in Berlin and Paris most of his life; he returned to the USSR after World War 2.

> unexpectedly harmonious, as though he was performing some ballet steps while listening to music that only he can hear.
>
> Then I saw his eyes, glowing, bright-blue, blinding, and intently acute; they were not eyes but rays beaming out, radiating.
>
> Andrei Bely stood from the chair and walked about the room with an adolescent's agility, a harmony of gestures, he penetrated the air, accompanying each word with a new enigmatic movement. They were amazing. His soft face with sharp perceptible dimples, possessing a typical fleshy Russian nose, his head surrounded by puffs of white flaring hair, he could pass himself off as elderly, although at this time he was just 42 years of age. But as soon as he stood and started to walk about the room, this sense of age vanished.

Bely immediately became involved in the newly-formed Anthroposophical Society and continued to study under Steiner.

After some time, once Bely settled in Berlin, he traveled to Dornach, Switzerland. His intent was to find Asya, but she had left sometime earlier and no one had any information on her. Bely stayed for a while, but the records do not indicate exactly when or how long, but probably in autumn 1922, and Bely barely mentions this part of his stay in Europe.

Finally the reason for Bely's return to Europe materialized, and for which he was waiting and worrying for several years now: the reconnection with his wife Asya Turgeneva. When she arrived in Berlin in November 1922, and Bely met her, she was cold and distant. Immediate she told him that they can no longer cohabit, under any conditions. It was difficult for Bely to understand the reason for such a sharp change in her attitude toward him, someone who sincerely loved her and who was still formally her husband. She spent only a short while in Berlin and her visit there was not specifically to meet with Bely. Their encounter occurred in passing.

Rumor circulated that Asya was seen in the company of the poet and novelist Aleksandr Kusikov, who also migrated to Berlin, and where he met Asya.[188] This caused an emotional outburst and jealousy in Bely. Asya found someone similar to her husband in his absence and he filled the void in her life, and perhaps in a better manner, one more realistic, as Asya was also distancing herself from anthroposophy and had left the Dornach commune a couple of years earlier. This was the reason Bely was unable to further correspond with her, not knowing her location and she did not inform him of her whereabouts.

Asya left Berlin and then returned in March 1923, and stayed through April, and again accompanied by Kusikov. She met with Bely sometime in April and she confirmed the termination of any relationship between the 2 of them, a complete severance in their lives. Later, in 1924, Asya and Kusikov moved to Paris. (Eventually, Asya returned to Dornach and remained there until her death in 1966. She became an accomplished artist and her paintings decorate the Goetheanum.)

The incident psychologically devastated Bely, especially with all the almost 2 years of effort to acquire an exit visa and leave Russia. He felt that Asya betrayed him. As a result Bely devolved into serious depression and started to drink, and drink heavily, and then acting disorderly and embarrassingly in public. Bely became foul-mouthed when anybody attempted to speak with him. Many observers in Berlin remember Bely in this condition and so left their observations in their memoirs. Some wrote out of spite, while others out of compassion.

Bely took time to vacation while he was in Germany. He went to Swinoujscie, in northwest Poland on the Baltic sea coast on July 6, 1922, along with visiting Miedzyzdroje, Poland, Heringsdoft, in Western Pomerania, Germany, and then to Berlin, arriving there September 6. Here he stayed at a boarding house in the Victoria-Luisen-Platz area.

Bely over the previous 6 years had advanced considerably in the areas of philosophy and public speaking, not to mention composition. Under the conditions of post-war Europe Steiner was

---

[188] Aleksandr Borisovich Kusikov, 1896-1977, author of romantic fiction novels and a poet part of the imaginist movement in Russian literature. He escaped Russia in 1922, and spent the balance of his life in Paris, France.

doing his best to keep the construction progressing on the Goetheanum, which was completed in 1919. Now with Bely's return and ready with his immense acquired talent and zeal to blend back into the community, Steiner viewed him as a threat to his sole autocratic rule of the community and anthroposophical ideologist. Steiner's suggestion that Bely leave Germany and return to Russia shocked him. Steiner's excuse was that Bely could be of more use to anthroposophy in Russia than here, but Bely – and maybe as a result of his infantile mind – was devastated, since Steiner had evolved into a father figure for him and for whom Bely had devoted many years of his life and sacrificed much in the construction of the Goetheanum and studying under Steiner. Bely traveled to Suttgart March 23-31, 1923, and met with Steiner for the last time in his life on March 30 (Rudolf Steiner died March 30, 1925). This final meeting of Bely with Steiner resulted in the termination of their relationship. Bely returned to Berlin on April 1. He then visited Harzburg, central Germany, from the end of May to the beginning of June.

Bely described the terminating event in the following passage in *Why I became a Symbolist*:

> It is difficult for me to approach the final concrete stage of what it is I did not understand and which evolved into this social severance. The tragedy with the anthroposophical environment, my final refuge, prolonged for 15 years. And it surpassed other tragedies in length and sharpness. It is all clear to me now. The emotions still stir violently the surface of the water of life where my *I* was reflected.

The 15 years covered the period from 1907, when Bely first started to study Anne Besant, to this year 1922. Bely left Germany double devastated: not uniting with his wife and now suffering discard by Steiner.

Vladislav Khodasevich and his wife Nina Berberova were residing in Berlin at the time, and he visited Bely during this difficult period of his life, attempting to help him. Khodasevich recorded the following in his memoirs:

> The entirety of Russian Berlin was a curious and malicious witness to his hysteria. They saw it, were happy over it, joked excessively over it with others. Let me describe it. Here is one manner that he expressed his misery: he would go to the dance hall and drink and then dance. He was to start a poor dancer and now he displayed contortions in his movements. He would invite women he did not know to his room and they would go to humor him. Others would refuse him and so insult him. But this was not just some drunk person dancing and acting stupidly wearing this grimace, it was the entire symbolist movement that was being desecrated, made a mockery, since Bely represented it.

Nina Berberova, who associated much with Bely during the Berlin years with her husband, summarized his situation in her memoirs and from a woman's point of view:

> During this period of his life, 1921-1923, Andrei Bely was in deep crisis. Being from the day of his birth the "son of his mother," and not the "son of his father," he passed his childhood in search of a father, and he found a father in the anthroposophist Rudolf Steiner before the First World War. Returning to the west in 1921, after the destitute years of war communism, he had to face a tragic fact: Steiner rejected him, and now Bely, shaken by the disclosure of having to deal with orphancy, returned to his primordial defenselessness, and he could not overcome it, or grow out of it, or reconcile himself with it.
>
> I saw him once playing an old piano, *Carnaval* by Schumann. No one was listening to him, all were occupied with their own interests, with themselves. On the next day he did not believe me when I said that he played Schumann and I enjoyed listening to him. He did not remember anything. On the next evening he twice explained to Khodasevich and myself, in particular details, the entire drama of his love for L.D. Blok and his argument with A.A. Blok, and when without

even taking another breath he started to relate it a third time, I saw that Khodasevich was sliding down the chair onto the floor in a deep slumber.

That night Bely noisily beat on our door, he wanted to supplement the story with something more, and Khodasevich in a cold sweat whispered to me, beseeching me not to open the door, not to respond. He was afraid that this wild, strange story, one not having any substance or meaning or end, will be repeated.

At the same time as this was going on he wrote, often entire days, often nights. This was the time of composing *Recollections of Blok,* which was printed in the magazine *Epopee.*

During the winter we lived in Saarov, outside of Berlin, where Gorky and his family lived. Boris Nikolaievich was our guest often and wrote, while in the evenings he would read to us what he wrote. Yes, I listened to him reciting these pages of his recollections of Blok and I felt this exalted, unforgettable happiness. What would happen is that he would read his pencil manuscript until 2 o'clock in the morning, sitting at the table in his room, while we would sit, one on each side of him, and listen.

The strength of his genius was such: disregarding all of his dismal abnormalities, daily inebriation, the treachery he endured, the hysterical bouts with his past, and which he could not seem to relate in its entirety, disregarding his infected wounds or the healed scars, each encounter with him was a radiant and rich event in life.

Whatever the events were that occurred in Berlin these years, his capacity to write was phenomenal. He wrote without ceasing, all day and often all night, as mentioned above. The result was that over the almost 2 years Bely resided in Berlin on this occasion, he wrote and published 9 new books, and revised and reprinted 7 of his previous books, in addition to innumerable articles and reviews published in local as well as in Russian magazines and newspapers.

Bely described his health and his tedious work in a personal manner in a letter of spring 1922, to the editor of the magazine *Russian Book*, A.S. Yashenko:[189]

> Do not be upset at me. I am seriously neurologically ill. I have many troubles, and so many that would not fit into the pages of your newspaper. I have been neurologically ill for a long while. I work up to 20 hours a day, I write summaries of future books and sit on a pile of proofs I need to finish. Meanwhile I have suggestions, requests, demands, raining on me from every side. Meanwhile, with the help of dozens of letters of mine my books are slowly being exported from Russia. Meanwhile, I have regular attacks of pain in my heart. Meanwhile, I am completely alone and have no one to even sew a button for me. Meanwhile, as soon as I stick out my tongue I end up running through a series of places only so that "they" do not get offended. Meanwhile, my neurologist said, "Unless you do feel yourself emancipated from all of your responsibilities within 3 months you will die. You cannot live in such moral stagnation."
>
> So right now, believe me, I am sick. But I still work the entirety of days. And if I work, then I work a constant stream: I have 10 things going at the same time: verses, a novel, reminiscences, human interest articles, or serious ones, or half-way, and so forth. Based on my neurologically conditions, all of this signifies, as the doctor told me, that I am going out of my mind.

One item to interject at this point is the burning of the Goetheanum. On the night of December 31, 1922-January 1, 1923, arsonists destroyed the Goetheanum. Because it was constructed primarily of wood, the entire edifice was consumed in flames over 2 days of burning. Eventually a replacement was construction, but this one of cast concrete. The new Goetheanum was not completed

[189] Aleksandr Semeonovich Yashenko, 1877-1934, Russian lawyer, philosopher, teacher and publisher. He taught law at Petersburg University, then migrated to Berlin in 1919, to teach there, but stayed until his death.

until 1928, after Steiner's death in 1925. (Whether this event had a influence on Steiner's decision to terminate relations with Bely just a few months later is not indicated anywhere.)

While in Berlin Bely was able to find someone so interested in his work that she was willing to translate it into Italian. She was Olga Resnevic-Signorelli.[190] After Bely's death she wrote an article recollecting her time with him in Berlin:

> I had a personal meeting with A. Bely in September 1923. The atmosphere of those days seemed to be strange pages evolving from under his pen. This was also a time of immense inflation in the economy, the value of the mark in paper money decrease in a swirling manner. On November 20, 1923, the mark reached it lowest value: one dollar could be exchanged for four trillion marks. Many of the Russian intellectuals migrated out of Germany. Bely, burned just as his hero Daryalsky,[191] unable to endure his lonesomeness for his homeland, was ready to return.
>
> He found out I was in Berlin and wanted to meet with me, and so invited me for dinner with 2 of his Russian friends in a modern restaurant. We came before he did. I remember the large hall was already filled with thick tobacco smoke. Bely entered quickly, propelling his body forward like a sailboat penetrating the sea of smoke. He brought me a copy of each of his books as a gift, those that were published in Berlin, and said that he was happy to meet personally with me. Then he repeated to me what he wrote about earlier to me, that he would be happy if I were to translate his *Reminiscences of Blok*, when he finished it. At the time he gave me a shorter version.
>
> While in Berlin he had to suffer many deprivations, but now he was receiving royalties from his publishers. His

[190] Olga Ivanovna Rezniewicz Signorelli (Sinorelli), 1883-1973, born in Jelgava, Latvia, died in Rome, Italy; writer, biographer, translator of major Russian authors into Italian, actress.
[191] Character in *Silver Dove*.

pockets were full of white banknotes, in millions of marks, that he had to quickly spend, so he paid the meal for all of us. He said he did not need this money as he was getting ready to leave in a couple of days.

> What is retained in my memory is the lightning flash of his eyes, a bright blue, then violet. It seems that they were sparkling from the inside. I remember his turbulent voice when he spoke of Michael-Angelo, of the creation of the human, and his words reached into my consciousness and impressed on me: not so much the strength of their logical meaning, as much as the strength of his living rhythm and the fiery conviction of his voice.

Initially the Soviet consulate made the decision not to allow Bely to return, so he considered Prague, Czechoslovakia. Marina Tsvetaeva was living there at the time and he wrote this letter to her in November 1922:

> My little dove! My dear sister! It is only you! It is only to you! Find a room alongside yours, wherever you are but alongside yours. I will not interfere, I will not enter yours. I only need to be assured that on the other side of the wall is living – yes living – warmth.
>
> I am thoroughly tormented! I have been tortured! To you I go, under your shelter.
>
> My life this year has been a nightmare. You are my sole salvation. Create a miracle! Build one! Hide me! Find, find for me a room.

Marina replied that she was able to acquire a room for Bely, but by the time he received her letter he changed his plans: he decided against remaining anywhere in Europe. Bely again went to the Russian consulate in Berlin and gave them notice of his intent to return to his homeland, and an entry visa was granted on August 1, 1923. Nonetheless the decision affected him inwardly, having to leave Germany after both of his reasons for arriving were blatant failures: his reconnections with wife Asya and with Rudolf

Steiner. Regardless his return was inevitable, he could not remain absent from Russia forever.

While in Berlin, Bely's mother died about October 20, and this added to his psychological difficulties, not being with her at the end of her life.

The young daughter of Marina Tsvetaeva, Ariana, was living in Berlin at the time and so had the opportunity to meet Bely. She left a short note in her diary about him:

> He was not a very large person, but he had these fox-like, almost insane, speedy eyes, like a cat. I really liked the man.

Claudia Nikolaievna arrived in Berlin in January 1923. Rumors reached Moscow, the next worse than the previous, of Bely residing in a critical state and there was no one there who could save him. Claudia felt she was the only person who could. Her exit visa to travel to Germany from Russia took six months. A quiet woman but now feeling she had more of a right to the man than anyone else, she helped with the paperwork. However her visa expired in July, before Bely was able to get his documentation together, and she had to return.

Before Claudia left the 2 of them did some traveling together: July 14-17, in Ahlbeck, northeast Germany, and then back to Berlin. Then on July 22, to Szczecin, northwest Poland, near the Baltic Sea and border of Germany, across from Ahlbeck, and all the cities in between. Claudia left Germany on July 31.

Bely enjoyed the Baltic sea coast so much that he returned during August, visiting Ahlbeck again, then Swinoujscie, a seaport on the Baltic Sea, and Szczecin Lagoon in northwest Poland, then back to Berlin.

Other than the typical bureaucracy, the Soviet consulate was not allowing any person suspected of anti-Soviet activities while in Europe to return. By October 1923, Bely was able to acquire a return visa.

Before his departure a group of the Russian emigrant writers staged a festive farewell dinner. But not everybody's mood was the same. Some were glad for his decision to return to Russia, while those who escaped and could not return, or who were jealous that Bely was returning, had a malevolent attitude. Bely felt he would have to face repercussions in Russia on behalf of those who escaped or were in Europe illegally, and perhaps face incarceration or execution, as with other Russian authors who did not capitulate to Soviet demands and remained there, and this frightened him. So he let them know this.

The evening did not end without a scandal. Nina Berberova attended the dinner and witnessed the event:

> The evening festivity was a well populated, farewell dinner. But Bely arrived at this dinner in this state of anger I had never seen before. His immense fists were clenched between his legs, his oversized suit jacket, one of different shades of grey, hung on him, and he just sat not looking at anyone. But at the end of dinner when he stood with a glass in his hand, he stared with his white eyes odiously at those sitting about his table, and there were about 20. He announced he would deliver an address. I had the impression he would give a toast about himself.
>
> He demanded that they drink on his behalf because he was leaving to be crucified. "For whom? For all of you, gentlemen, sitting in this restaurant, for Khodasevich, Muratov,[192] Zaitzev,[193] Remisov,[194] Berdiaev, Visheslavtzev."[195] So he was going to Russia to allow himself to be crucified for all of Russian literature, Bely was going to shed his blood for all of it. So he compared himself to Christ.

---

[192] Pavel Pavlovich Muratov, 1881-1950, Russian essayist, novelist and playwright. He was banished from Russia in 1922, and lived in Berlin until about 1930, when he moved to Paris. He died in Ireland.

[193] Boris Zaitzev, mentioned above, not to be confused with Bely's later friend Peter Zaitzev.

[194] Aleksei Mikhailovich Remisov, 1877-1957, Russian modernist writer and calligrapher. He moved to Berlin in 1922, and then to Paris in 1923, and where he died.

[195] Boris Petrovich Visheslavtzev, 1877-1954, Russian philosopher and religious thinker. He migrated to Berlin from Russian in 1922, and then to Paris in 1927. He died in Geneva, Switzerland.

> All started to shout at him, converting the fact of crucifixion into a joke, into a metaphor, into a hyperbole, into an eloquent toast. But Bely held his ground.

Bely let them unequivocally know that those who remained in Europe were taking the easy way out, not willing to face the consequences of their writings. But he was willing, and even willing to face the repercussions for their abandonment of Russia.

# ANDREI BELY AND THE RUSSIA HE LOVES

On October 23, 1923, on a rainy autumn day, Bely left Berlin. Only a handful of friends accompanied him to the railway station. Bely was in Europe not quite 2 years.

Razumnik received a letter from Bely on November 3, filled with optimism.

> I want to share with you a great joy: the joy to be in Russia. I have been in Moscow now over a week, and I cannot remember being this happy to be in my homeland. Never has a stay outside of Russia been such a burden to me as was the previous year. Never has a return to Russia seemed to me to be so solid an event in my life. All personal matters take a place far in the back with this opportunity to breath the air of Russia. How I pity those who cannot return to Russia.
>
> Berlin is the place where I received the worst of all of life's possible blows. It remains in my memory as a nightmare. I also died there, and I do not know what would have happened to me there if I did not escape in time. I do not idealize contemporary Russia. This is how it is: there in nice conditions of comfort blood bled out of my heart and my soul languished in indescribable discomforts, while here in Russia I acquired calm and inner happiness. It is quiet and joyful for me here. My trip abroad is now behind me.

> I had to endure a serious operation on my soul, one that almost deprived me of life. The operation finished and my wound healed, I returned emancipated, not dead. Ahead of me is the unknown, and my voice confirms, "You need to enter a new route." I am not premeditating a route, it will ripen on its own. The future will tell. I view it impartially. But I know that for a long while, that I will not leave Russia for a long while for anyplace.

Bely again wrote to Razumnik shortly after his return. The following passage is part of his letter:

> My encounter with Asya created a series of heavy blows and agitation. The 24 months of my life in Europe were a life without Asya, and we just met momentarily as she was passing through Berlin. Other than this she died in my soul, and the process of her dying in me saturated my soul with poisons for over a year, causing me to run to wine to quench the pain. I journeyed to Dornach, then sat in Berlin, in the most tasteless, vile, lonesome and cynical city in the world.
>
> When I realized that they would not allow me to return to Russia, I was ready to escape back over the border, to appear in Moscow and say, "I have nevertheless returned. Put me in prison if you want, send me to the Narimsky region,[196] but do not send me back to Europe."
>
> Yes, Razumnik, I returned with a firm realization of the conditions here, but also not to return to Europe for a long, long time. I know it will not be easy.

The homeland did not meet Bely with fanfare and a band. Not long before his return the newspaper *Pravda* published a short article composed by the still-powerful Trotsky. He called Bely a former symbolist and who had died, and he will never resurrect,

---

[196] The northern portion of Tomsk region, on both sides of the Ob River, in central Siberia.

no matter how hard he tries. He is just lying prostrate in this path of a new life while interfering with social construction.

Returning to Moscow Bely had no residence of his own, so he moved into a spare room with the Anninkovs, staying with them through November and December.[197] Although their apartment was not far from the Arbat, Bely felt uncomfortable there. Although home now, he did not even have a crumb in his pocket. What money he had when he left Germany devalued considerably and all was spent on the journey, and now again he worried about his daily bread. Still he had mental plans evolving for another novel, this one to be titled *Moscow*, and he compiled some sketches of the book. He went to several publishers with his idea but with no results, since at this time all the publishers had become socialized, meaning, government operated and financed and anything published had to pass censorship. Finally a private publisher who had a magazine titled *New Russia*, agreed. He was I.G. Lezhnyov, but the agreement was conditional.[198] Initially the book was published in installments in the magazine, and then later as an individual volume. Lezhnyov knew Bely's financial destitution, as well as knowing that the book would be promising in sales, and he did take advantage of Bely's situation, but Bely had no choice but to go along with any terms that Lezhnyov dictated.

Bely turned to lecturing to supplement his income, however at first his lectures were rejected and the audience of young people booed and hissed at him. This new post-revolutionary generation in Russia was totally alien to the earlier value of symbolism, and its foremost representative – Bely of course – presented them with something that was a part of the unreal and obsolete past. Bely realized he had to modify his theme if he wanted to gain his audience.

The next lecture was titled, *One of the Residents of the Realm of Shadows*, dealing with his life in Germany. Some of the previous audience attended and no sooner did he start that they

---

[197] Yuri Pavlovich Annenkov, 1889-1974, Russian artist.
[198] Isai Grigoryevich Lezhnyov, 1891-1955, magazine and book publisher.

started to hiss and boo and stomp their feet in the gallery. The balance in the lower section waited patiently and Bely was finally able to get his audience's attention and control it to the end of his lecture. It was a success.

A new friend entered Bely's life at this time, one who would stay close to him through the end of his life and after: Peter Zaitzev.[199] The 2 were acquainted since 1911, when the young poet was a member of the staff at *Musaget*, and he worked under Bely, and after the Russian Revolution they both worked together at the Moscow Proletkult, and now they were again together. Zaitzev would become Bely's unselfish assistant, secretary and literary agent, as well as a devoted and reliant friend and Bely's closest confidant. As a result Zaitzev almost venerated Bely, now his mentor, considering him one of best writers of the 20th century.

In January 1924, Bely was invited to Petrograd for the 40th anniversary of the literary activities of Feodor Sologub, one of the original Russian symbolists. It was originally scheduled for January 28, at the Aleksandrovsky Theater, but was interrupted due to the death of Vladimir Lenin on January 21, and his subsequent funeral. The festivity was then held on February 11, Sologub was 61 years of age, his first poem was published when he was 21, in 1884.

Bely gave the primary address at the honor for Sologub to a crowd that filled the hall, and of course filled with much allegory. The conclusion of his address is the following;

> You are a name highly valued by all Russians, and following at the end of the series of other names highly valued: Tolstoy, Pushkin, Lermontov, Dostoyevsky, Turgenev, Gogol, and now Feodor Sologub, and all of them were, are and will be our mentors. You are especially precious to our generation, Feodor Kuzmich, with your combination of boldness, flight, new

[199] Peter Nikanorovich Zaitzev, 1889-1970, writer. His memoirs include many of the Silver Age writers.

> routes of composition, which you opened to us, combined with the best traditions of great Russian literature. You are precious to us, as an austere sentry of our covenants of art, insisting on the best traditions of literary forms.
>
> You are close to us not just as an artist, but as an indispensable person in the highest meaning of this word – a man of the century. You are the measure of form and style.
>
> Endlessly precious, beloved, respected, Feodor Kuzmich, permit me, your admirer from early days and your disciple in many respects, let me clench your hand here in public and simply embrace you, and on this day so joyful for all of Russian literature I wish for you further productive effort.

As Bely settled in Russia and developed a routine of writing, lecture, study and a social life, his mind again generated many interesting thoughts. Among them were his opinions of the political situation, now with Vladimir Lenin gone, and the future to be decided with a power struggle between those of Joseph Stalin and those of Leon Trotsky. Bely frankly voiced his hopes and doubts that pertained to the present state of conditions in Soviet Russia.

> At one time, and this was during epoch of the beginning of symbolism, I lived with the sensation that the great future was approaching. I lived with the feeling that lilac-colored exalted days were to surround us. The future seemed to be great but enigmatic, and this future has passed. It did not deceive us, but perhaps another future will also seem gloomy. But it will be great. You live in the great present, this is a fact. But just because it has manifested does not mean it is understandable. But on the contrary, it is not understandable.

Bely returned to Moscow on February 20, but then departed for Kiev on February 24. There he visited his cousins V.A. Verter and E.A. Zhukova. He delivered a lecture on *The Creativity of Blok*, on February 25, and *Rhythm of Life and the Contemporary Era* on February 28. On March 7, he returned to Moscow.

Maximillian Voloshin arrived in Moscow the initial days of March 1924, where he had not been since before the world war. Overwhelmed by the concepts of anthroposophy he left Russia in the summer 1914, for Dornach, where he worked on the Goetheanum. When he received a notice of conscription Voloshin requested exemption from the military during World War 1 as a pacifist, but it was denied. Voloshin then refused military service and any participation in war, and so he secluded himself in Switzerland until after the war. He returned to Russia after the revolution and settled in Koktebel, on the east coast of the Crimean Peninsula, where his family had a summer home and estate and where he remained the balance of his life.

Voloshin and his mother intended to convert it into a haven for Russian poets. They had been living in Koktebel in an apartment on and off since 1893. In 1913, the house was completed, however during the First World War and the Civil War it was used as a safe haven for those escaping the horrors of both wars.

It was not until 1924, that their personal home in Koktebel was converted into a guesthouse for fellow poets and symbolists, and members of the later Union of Soviet Writers, wanting to escape the city life and to vacation. Voloshin married a second time in 1922, to Maria Stepanovna Zabolotzka, and who continued operation of the guesthouse after her husband's death.

Now in Moscow Voloshin went to the National Commissariat of Education, to Lunacharsky, to get his permission to transform their estate at Koktebel into a guesthouse for writers. The request was granted, but for the most part it extended to Voloshin's friends of the past and present. As a result and because of the continuing friendship between Voloshin and Bely – both poets as well as anthroposophists – he invited both Bely and Claudia to spend the entire summer at Koktebel.

The invitation could not have come at a better time, as it allowed Bely a relief from having to worry about a residence, until after summer. Secondly, Bely hoped the retreat would be a tranquil isolation to provide him the opportunity to work on his newly-conceived novel, *Moscow*. Seriously intending to concentrate on it, his suitcase was filled with heavy bundles of papers and notes, sharpened pencils, pens and ink. They left Moscow on May 28, and arrived on June 1.

The conditions however were quite the opposite when Bely arrived at the writer's guest house – no rest, no isolation. So many guests arrived at Koktebel that the Voloshin's two-story house was tearing at the seams. The local residents did not cease funneling through the facility the entire summer. Every talent available made the writer's haven their stage for display: writers and poets, artists, musicians, dramatic actors and actresses, and some ballerinas. From early morning until late into the night – noise, movement, laughter, recitations, announcements, music and instruments playing, singing, games of fun and risk, theatrical scenes, and of course, strolls along the beach and mountain climbing. During that summer of 1924, some 300 managed to funnel through the place, and the number was more for 1925. Some came for a few days, while others – like Bely and his new wife Claudia – for the entire summer. They lived in a communal style, and the work was divided among all the residences. Bely was assigned the role of sweeping and disposing of the trash after every event. For him the work was an enjoyable distraction.

After Max Voloshin's death on January 29, 1932, Bely recorded the following recollection of him at Koktebel that summer:

> The entire environment of life at Koktebel at the house artistically designed by Voloshin, and the manner that he traversed his life, exposed a M.A. Voloshin a second time, one in a new light. And I am obligated to him at least for this, that having seen his Koktebel through his eyes, deep in my soul I attached myself to this place.
>
> He taught me to gather rocks, he educated me in the meteorology of this corner of the Crimea, I watched him provide counsel to biologist scholars who visited him. They told me how for the first time he was able to predict the eccentricities of the winds that blow in that region, their

> direction and impact. He artistically impressed on my mind the manner the lava flowed through the area. He had interesting prognoses on the effect of excavations on the region and identified for me the cultural monuments that were vanishing from the area. He gave us a personally tour of the surroundings and these strolls were accompanied by his interesting lectures, not only for the artists and poets, but equally for the scholars. For a long while before the revolution he maintained a love for the physical culture of that corner of his life.

One young writer, Nikolai Chukovsky, son of the famous children's story writer, Kornei Chukovsky, was vacationing not far from Koktebel and visited the guest house that summer. Chukovsky recorded his impressions of Bely at the retreat:

> Bely, disregarding his grey hair and bald head, was at the time still lean and strong. Looking at his face he appeared to be significantly older than his 44 years, but his body was still one of an adolescent, and now with a good brown tan from exposure to the local sun. He walked fast, briskly, was agile, active and talkative. He spoke rapidly and sometimes with a whistle, with many gestures, and his small blue eyes were like gimlets boring right into his conversationalist.
>
> He rose early in the morning, went to the beach for a swim, and off somewhere apart from others, then he would wander about the shore for several hours gathering pebbles. He did not go to the men's beach, and he was not inclined toward the contemporary liberal morals of Koktebel. I remember how he returned from the beach on one occasion irritated, and he said how 2 unfamiliar women went to where he was sitting and made themselves comfortable just a few steps away and then disrobed. While Max, an admirer of antiquity and freedom, just stared at him affably and smiled through his beard.[200]

[200] Koktebel in the decade of 1920, was a haven for nudists, and much of the Crimea is a popular region for clothing optional beaches.

With women Bely was polite to the point of prudishness. But what become quickly notice was that he was an excellent and passionate dancer. He brought a new dance with him from Berlin – the foxtrot, and none of them had heard of it before. He decided to teach the foxtrot to all of us in one of the large rooms. They we had a evening of dancing. He wore a domino as a costume, just like he describes it in his book *Petersburg*. He danced vigorously, fervently and oblivious to what surrounded him. My 20-year old wife clearly preferred him as a partner over the other 5 anthroposophists.

It was only apparent that [Bely] was intensely enveloped by anthroposophy. Soon after my arrival he gathered us and read lectures on anthroposophy to us. He spoke rapidly, with every outward display of inspiration, he walked about talking and gesturing, and his words would whistle. But I do not remember even one word of his lectures, since all of it alien was to me, all that he said. In the corner of the room stood a school blackboard and he sketched a circle on it with an arrow piercing it to explain his thoughts. The circle was supposed to signify existence, while the arrow – realization. Nevertheless I just do not remember and maybe I do but do not want to. We listened respectfully but cautiously, and the lecture made no impression on anybody, except one person – Nikolaven. While Max would openly laugh.

Anna Lebedeva[201] also came to Voloshin's retreat for the summer, and left her impression of Bely:

He was ostensively original. Sunbathing he became so burned, almost like a Indian, with a dark reddish-brown skin. And this caused his blue eyes to be more brilliantly prominent on his face in the center of his dark and thick and short eyelashes. His gaze was extremely acute and extraordinary. He has a large balding forehead and on each side were these clumps of

---

[201] Anna Petrovna Ostroumova-Lebedeva, 1871-1955, Russian and Soviet painter famous especially for her water color painting.

> grey hair. For the most part he walked about in bright red clothes.

In the evenings Bely read his novel *Petersburg*, his poem *First Meeting*, and other poems and writings to the audience there attending. He also gave lectures: one on the *Philosophy of Concrete Knowledge*, and another was an *Address on Vladimir Solovyov*, in memory of the Russian religious philosopher. He was fervently involved in regular debates and discussions, and one especially with young people there after his lecture titled *Russia and the West*. Bely compared the value of Russian culture to European culture, which he felt was a lower quality. This forced Bely to take the role of a neo-Slavophile, insisting on the originality of Russian art and literature, for the sake of argument, and then deal with the response of his listeners.

As far as working on *Moscow* was concerned, it did not progress at all. There was just no time with all the activities that summer at Voloshin's guest house.

A few days before his departure Nikolai Chukovsky had the opportunity to speak privately with Bely. Chukovsky was laying on the sand and looking at the stars that evening and Bely, strolling at the time, sees him and sits next to him. Bely then explains to Chukovsky one of his coveted cosmic meditations, one that did not seem to give him rest:

> Right now we can establish that the construction of the atom is similar to the construction of the solar system. Following this concept we are in the right to suppose that all the constellations visible to us are just atoms composing – to use as an example – the heel of some kind of giant Ivan Ivanovich who is sitting in his terrace and drinking hot tea. So now understanding this much we can proceed to further seek the meaning of the universe.

One incident that occurred at Koktebel that summer that had a tragic result pertained to Valeri Brusov. His arrival was enthusiastically greeted by all and was followed with much recitation of his writings. While in the Crimea Brusov went to visit Kara Dag, a volcanic rock formation not far from Koktebel. Brusov was caught in a summer rainstorm and caught a chill. He returned to Moscow but fever set in and his health quickly deteriorated. He died within a month, on October 9, 1924. Valeri Brusov was 50 years of age.

September 10, 1924, Bely and Claudia left Koktebel for Moscow after a wonderful and unforgettable summer. But now Bely had to face the bad situation of not having a residence and not having a regular employment, his philosophical and symbolist writing was not considered a vocation by the Soviet administration. So Bely complained in his memoirs:

> These are the superficial aspects of my life: On the other side of Moscow River I work 18 hours a day, sleepless nights, short rests, headaches. Moscow is one discomfort, another discomfort, more discomforts. Then I rest at the Vasilyevs.

Returning from Koktebel, they could no longer live in a room at the Annenkovs, and due to the marital scandal of the wife Vera Georgievna making it uncomfortable. Claudia, now divorced from her husband Peter N. Vasilyev, needed to also move out from her husband's apartment, and especially since Bely was also staying there occasionally. The 2 of them decided to rent something together and make the best of the situation, they considered their marriage common-law. So Bely and Claudia rented a room for a month or so at the estate of the wealthy Ryabushinsky. Later professor M.A. Belikanov offered the homeless writer and Claudia a small house on the premises of a hydroelectric station outside of Moscow. Belikanov had connections with the supervisor and so was able to make these arrangements, but only temporary.

In March 1925, Bely and Claudia settled into a small summer cottage in Kuchino, it was the second story and not far from the train station to allow them easy access to central Moscow. It worked well for them through the summer of 1925. When autumn came along, an elderly couple, the Shipovs, also in Kuchino, offered them 2 rooms in their small two story house. The Shipov couple were impressed with Bely and Claudia and took a liking to them, associating with them during their earlier residence in Kuchino. The husband worked in Moscow as a accountant, while the wife was a homemaker, although taking local jobs regularly cleaning and maintaining the homes of others in the area. One room was a kitchen that also served as a bedroom, and the second room became Bely's study where he would work. They finally found stability here and fate secured them a residence for almost 6 years.

Bely finished the initial 2 chapters of his novel *Moscow* at the end of 1924, and submitted it to his publisher Lezhnev for his evaluation. But some of Bely's friends – and specifically Aleksandr Voronsky and Boris Pilnyak – got involved and were able to terminate the contract with Lezhnev, since it was heavily in favor of the publisher, and to get a new contract with a state publisher on terms that were very favorable for Bely.

Financial matters were now improving for Bely with Claudia taking the role and responsibility of his advisor and agent. They were able to vacation much, with several excursions to the Russian south, the Caucasus and Crimea. In general life had now reached its best for Bely in every area.

Interesting that Pilnyak wanted to start a new magazine called *The Three Borises*, named after himself, Boris Pasternak and Boris Bugaev (Andrei Bely), with their articles and themselves as editors with the inclusion of other's articles. But it never went past the planning stage. It was also about this time that Bely and Pasternak became close friends and to the end of Bely's life. They knew each other somewhat and from working together at *Musaget*, but now a new friendship developed.

With the popularity of the novel *Petersburg*, it caught the attention of Michael Chekhov.[202] From 1918, Chekhov was a student of anthroposophy under Bely until he left for Berlin in

---

[202] Mikhail Aleksandrovich Chekhov, 1891-1955, Russian and later American actor, director and theater producer. In the late 1920s he migrated to Europe, and then to America just before World War 2.

1921, and the two of them continued to be close associates. Chekhov considered anthroposophy the source of spiritual regeneration as well as being a means of developing his mastery of performance. Michael Chekhov became head of the First Studio in 1922, and which was transformed in 1924 into the Second Moscow State Artistic Theater.

Contact between the 2 resurrected with Bely's return to Russia. In 1925, Bely rewrote *Petersburg* into a play and titled it, *Death of a Senator*. It was performed by the Moscow State Art Theater on November 14, 1925, with Michael Chekhov playing the part of senator Apollon Ableyukhov. Chekhov considered this one of the best roles he played in all of his years of being an actor.

On May 2, Bely departed Moscow for Kiev, where he delivered lectures on *The Culture of the Word*, and *The Poetry of Pushkin*. He left Kiev for Moscow on May 11.

Now and again Bely returned to continuing his novel *Moscow* and which would take him several years to complete. Due to the immense content of the volume, Bely decided to separate it into a series of small novels, each with its own title. As a result he succeeded to write three of them: *The Moscow Eccentric*, competed September 1925, and published June 1926; *Moscow under Attack*, published late 1926, and *Masks*, published 1932, although all 3 of them under the heading of *Moscow*. These encompassed the era up to the First World War.

(As with Bely's other novels, the reader is urged to purchase an English translation and read them and make his own conclusions, rather than reading my opinion.)

The publication of *The Moscow Eccentric* became an instant sensation and it immediately gathered a group of admirers. Among them was Vsevolod Meyerhold, who literally flared with a passion to transform the novel into a script and perform it as a play in his experimental theater. Bely was contacted to begin arrangements. Of course the 2 of them were associates from an early date, before the Russian revolution, and Meyerhold already modified Blok's *Balaganchik* (*A Puppet Show*) for the stage (and it is still performed to the present).

Bely, recovering from a illness in Kuchino, outside of Moscow, wrote to Meyerhold on March 5, 1927. It was Bely's response to a letter from Meyerhold:

> Dear Vsevolod Emilyevich, my little dove, do not be angry at me. Just listen to me, and if you will hear me out, then you will understand me fully.
>
> My health is weak. For some time now I barely move my legs. I do not like living in Kuchino and believe me I would go elsewhere if I could. You cannot imagine how difficult it is for me to reside outside of Moscow. Otherwise you would not have been so easily critical of me.
>
> Let me describe to you my life. In front of me right now are two unfinished books. One is titled, *History of Self-Realization of the Soul over the Previous Five Centuries*. This is a crucial volume demanding extensive rework of material.
>
> I need to place myself in that position toward life, one that resides outside of that world that I drag along with myself. I seem to materialize as a person dragging a large load not seen by others, but genuinely tangible to me, and this load is regularly and totally trampled.
>
> The second is this other book that my heart is heating, and it is not yet composed. I am meditating over it, and figuring how to acquire time for it.
>
> The third issue is the fact that the time for me to get the third volume of *Moscow* into gear is long past as my thoughts on it are gone. I have migrated into another domicile, while in two domiciles I have these two contemplated books that are two nice and beloved entities. Even if there were 48 hours in a day to divide my time, it would not be sufficient to fill my daytime and nighttime meditations.
>
> My dear friend, do not be angry. I am tired today. Exhausted. I so much want to see you. I will be at the theater with you on Saturday, the 13th in the evening, for the presentation. On Sunday I will drop by to see you. Give regards to Chekhov.

I remain sincerely devoted to you.
Boris Bugaev

Nourished on Henrik Ibsen and Maurice Maeterlinck, Bely admired theater, both dramatic and musical, and always maintained its possibilities in artistic expression. In Dornach Bely participated in Steiner's mysterial performances. But Bely as a playwright only started with an adaptation of *Petersburg*, which was a success, and now with *Moscow*, a failure and which was never performed in public. Nonetheless Meyerhold invited Bely to join his theater, to be a type of producer for Gogol's comedy, *The Inspector General*. After the initial performance Bely acknowledged that he was not adapted to such work, and decided to return to writing.

With no interferences Bely wrote furiously and fast, almost at lightning speed. He can only be compared with the striking working capacity of Honore de Balzac or Alexandre Dumas, except in the general genre of philosophy and not so much fiction. The Soviet writer Vladimir Lidin[203] knew Bely well and recorded the following about him in his memoirs:

> Andrei Bely writes. He wears a sweater and which causes him to be narrower at the shoulders. He always appeared disheveled, as through wrapped in some kind of vortex, with an aureola of hair surrounding a bald skull.
>
> He would discard on the floor alongside his desk page after page of scribbles nervously written in large letters and often slanted. Page after page would fly out from under his hands with just a short interval between each one. Bely's slender emaciated hand could hardly keep up with the expression emanating from his thoughts. How much time was consumed to write this immense pile of papers lying on the floor? A week? A month? No, just one morning. It is as though he is an

[203] Vladimir Germanovich Lidin, 1894-1979. Russian Soviet writer and teacher at the Literary Institute in Moscow.

> impetuous composition machine. The technology of writing by hand is old fashioned and cannot keep up with Bely's mind. What he really needs is a dictating machine of some sort, but even then, it may also not keep up with his mind's expressions soaring.

One of Bely's publishers had him compose directly on a linotype. Time was consumed with copyists transcribing every word of Bely's scribbles into a legible form and then pass it to the typesetter. Bely was likewise a fluent typist, although a typewriter was not always available. One reason dictating the need for this was trying to get Bely to read the proofs, and then he would append or correct or supplement the text and this would slow the work of publication with a new set of proofs and again waiting for Bely to proofread them and approve. Bely's direct operation of a linotype was successful on a meager few of Bely's compositions, a few articles in their magazines, and only if he was there at the typesetter's office, which was rare. Otherwise it was longhand. But the linotype of the era was complex and not otherwise efficient with someone like Bely.

Bely nicknamed his new Kuchino residence – my clandestine island, and once settled and relaxed from central Moscow turbulence he was indescribably happy with the isolation. Nearby was a nature preserve with a forest adding to the tranquility. Peter Zaitzev would frequent Bely and Claudia at their Kuchino home, acting as an unofficial secretary and always keeping Bely on track with completing what he was starting, without going on a tangent on another contemplated book. Zaitzev recorded in his memoirs his recollections of life at Kuchino:

> Life in Kuchino progressed relatively normalized. He was able to have meals and they were planned on a strict schedule every day – breakfast, lunch, dinner. After dinner Boris Nikolaievich would return to his study for half-an-hour to stretch out – as he stated – on his cot, and even with guests attending that evening he would excuse himself and leave. So would he prepare himself for work that evening. At about

> 10:30 PM, he would sit at his desk, nibble on a few snacks and drink a glass of hot tea. He would work until 4 o'clock in the morning, or in the winter he would sit until 6 or 7 in the morning. He would lie down to sleep just before daybreak, but even in his dreams he would visualize images of characters and changes of scenes and events. He would sleep up to about 1 or 2 o'clock in the afternoon, then Boris Nikolaievich would awake but he was still not rested. It is not difficult to imagine the effect such a routine had on him.

Regardless of the disorder or discomfort of his life, there was no where else to go. The Kuchino house was old, and the winter cold blew right through the windows and cracks. To heat the house they needed wood, and which forced Boris Nikolaievich to hew it himself. As a tenant, he had the responsibility to shovel the snow that would pile on the house and the wood. The worst worry was getting kerosene, and its availability at the local cooperative store was irregular. It seems that right in the middle of fervently working on a book late into the night the electricity would go out, and even then electric service was periodic. On a regular basis Bely had to stand and walk about to stay warm. Zaitzev, aware of this, would bring a can of kerosene to them when possible.

While at Kuchino, Bely composed his three volumes of memoirs: *On the Frontier of Two Centuries*, published 1930; *Beginning of the Century*, published 1933, and *Between the Two Revolutions*, published 1934.

Bely also composed his volume pertaining to Rudolf Steiner during this period in Kuchino: *Recollections of Rudolf Steiner*, completing it on January 29, 1929. Although it was never published in Russia, it was published in Paris, France, in 1982. The volume covered the years Bely lived in Germany and Switzerland – 1912-1924.

The couple lived unpretentiously. Once during a winter, Bely was at the public square next to the Kurst Railway Station waiting for a streetcar and he bumped into a familiar person who was also an artist, V.A. Milashevsky.[204] Bely stood in front of this exceptionally well-dressed and dignified painter while wearing a disheveled cotton-lined jacket with a shabby fur collar raised as high as possible and with a women's shawl tied around his neck. He wore repaired felt-lined boots and had a hat pulled down just above the eyes. No doubt Bely looked like something from another world. Milashevsky remembered the occasion, as he later recollected:

> From under his women's shawl, sparkled some kind of Seraphic gaze, a gaze of an archangel or a character from one of Pushkin's takes. He was at the same time excited and raptured and as though for the first time descending like a homing pigeon, now seeing and watching these people, as though they were insects from his heights, who were all pulling something, squirming and chasing, dragging something decayed, but not edible.

Claudia from here on was almost always at Bely's side and again he started to sense poetic inspirations. All of his previous female acquaintances were history: Margarita Morozova, Luba Blok, Nina Petrovskaya, Zinaida Gippius, Marietta Shaginyan, and his first wife Asya Turgeneva. But now he had someone for the balance of his life and his inspiration for survival and future writings and a promise for success. And even if the 2 of them together would not be eternal, at least his poetry would be, and Bely dedicated his subsequent collections of poems to Claudia. His final large collection was titled, *Summons of Times*, and consisted of old poems rewritten and improved and many new poems. But this volume was never published.

On September 14, 1925, Bely became a member of the Moscow Society of Dramatists and Composers.

On December 28, 1925, tragedy stuck Russia with the unexpected death of Sergei Esenin, a very popular poet and only 30 years of

---

[204] Vladimir Alekseevich Milashevsky, 1893-1976. Soviet graphic artist, book illustrator and portrait painter.

age. The cause of death was suicide, as a result – as many felt – of depression and a neurological disorder due to pressure brought upon him by the Soviet administration and other Soviet writers. (He was married 3 times with his final wife being Sophia Andreevna Tolstoya, granddaughter of Leo Tolstoy, but it did not last long. Esenin was also a close friend of Mayakovsky, and whose wife Lilya Brik was a secret agent of the Soviet secret police.)

Bely was invited to the memorial dinner by the widow Sophia and delivered a eulogy on Esenin. The following is a selection:

> The image I have of Esenin, the one he portrayed in my presence, is very precious to me. This was before the revolution, in 1916, one characteristic of his struck me and which permeated through all of my recollections and all of my conversations with him. This was his extraordinary kindness, unusual softness, unusual acuity and exalted congeniality. So did he pivot himself toward me, a writer of another school, a different age. So did he portray himself all the occasions we were together until our last conversation a few years ago, it was 1921. We worked together at the Proletkult, where I was an instructor, but Esenin looked for something more than what was available there, just as with myself. The difficultly of being a poet in a socialist country is that he becomes the megaphone of the collective, once he is tied to it he blends into the atmosphere.
>
> I will not speak of the immense and inspirational talent of Esenin, others knowing him better will do this. It was always his immaculate human character that struck me.

Bely was never able to reconcile with Esenin's tragic death, but he did attempt to justify it: that it occurred due to pressure from the Soviet administration on independent and liberal writers for them to conform to socialist realism as they defined it, and Esenin could not, and noting that others died relatively young also or else made the decision to immigrate to survive. Perhaps Bely had in the back of his mind that something like this or similar may also occur to him.

On August 13, 1926, Bely arrived in Moscow on some business. After finishing he was on his way to the railway station when he was hit by a streetcar on Chistoprudnoye Street. The impact caused a light brain concussion and a temporary loss of consciousness, and a serious dislocation of his shoulder. For Bely this was one more stroke of bad luck, but it was serious enough for him to stop and review his life and attempt to understand the hidden elements of his fate and his connection with the world around him.

Following this unfortunate incident Bely sensed the need to review the years he lived, and to utilize the experiences along with the realization of the temporality of life, to plan and determine his life's path for the future. This would affect both his literary and his personal life.

Over the next year Bely especially wrote on the anthroposophical attitude toward reality. These were in the form of lengthy letters to Razumnik, and included topics such as: a philosophic-cosmic analysis of the novel *Moscow*; an attempt to reconcile the dominating political theory in Soviet Russia of Marxist ideology with the basis principles of anthroposophy (but Bely failed to prove that anthroposophy can be equated with dialectic materialism); an analysis of his individual life; and the evolution of creativity in his life. All the letters combined consisted of enough material for another large volume, although never published.

Claudia in her memoirs described those fortunate moments when Bely would enter into contact with the noosphere. He would be enveloped with inspiration, unconscious and oblivious to the environment surrounding him, or even his own maneuvers during this withdrawal from reality.

> He sat complete rested, almost motionless. On occasion he would scribble something quickly and then again withdraw.

Not once did I see him jump out of his chair to find some necessary word, or beat with his foot to a rhythm, or drop his pencil from his fingers, or write lines haphazardly. No incidental movements at all. He was pale and focused on some point of concentration. It seemed he forgot that he was in a body.

It was because of the growing quiet of the surroundings that indicated he was distant, distant from our cottage. And there, in whatever worlds disclosed to him he was now developing the energy of his activities, and which caused the quiet to intensify and strangely grow and without interruption.

Yes, quiet. But what type? How can I qualify it? It is unusual as it is a saturated quiet, what pours into our rooms and summons a turbulence to the point of agitation in our souls, while compelling the heart to increase its pulse and blood pressure. So it is at the time of a mountain storm where the elements approach their incarnation in you, where the atmosphere intensified by electricity takes away your breath.

The silence of the room is interrupted only by an echo of turbulent rhythm. Through the slippery muteness the thunders of some kinds of extraterrestrial organisms audibly but dumbly roared. They flamed and they extinguished, the flares of alien dawns.

Meanwhile, B.N.[205] became all the quieter. He sat like a statue. But it seems that now he was the center of some immense whirling vortex drawing into itself the entire fire of his life, the entire heat of his words and casting them out as a spiraling hurricane.

He quieted, but the spirals flew all the wider, all the higher, carried away, and carried away fare, and then descended. They traveled to the edges of the universe, to the ancient fires of the limits of the Zodiac. There in the immeasurable distance, all rotated, swarmed and churned. They became entangled in the singing dances of the anapests,

[205] Initials for Boris Nikolaievich, that is, Andrei Bely

iambs, and trochees. They proceeded in the festive level of the molossus. The resonance sparkled as an oscillating wire, as a polished pattern of a precious brocade, and the pearly flickers of the lights gently burned: turquoise, lilac, pink. It was as though the distant sun played on the snow-filled faraway crowns.

He spilled his sounds and rainbows upon the white sheets of paper. I could barely breathe. Meanwhile B.N. was just as calm and concentrated and austere. The shadow surrounding his eyes deepened and his face become more pale.

I could not read, not even think. I sat down with my feet on the cot opposite the door in B.N's room. From there I could see his profile as he bent over his desk. I did not want to rustle, not to gesture, but just to freeze and hush so not to annoy him, not to frighten him. I watch and listen. But what?

In front of my eyes was this hunched and deliberating profile, the lamp's light shined on the felt of his hat, the gentle sketch of his shoulder, and his hand holding a cigarette. Rarely would he suddenly stand, just like being raised by an inner whirlwind. He would swing in a circle in his chair and then walk casually about the room, with firms steps, looking straight ahead of him, but not seeing. He walked with an impersonal expression on his face, stiff like an arrow, straight and firmly, appearing to restrain himself as though an unreleased storm resided within him.

He took two or three steps in each direction and then returned to his desk, bending over to a sheet of paper. Still standing he writes rapidly. After a while and in a mechanical manner he slowly descends into his chair.

Once I asked him after, "Why did you rise and where were you so decisively going, even though there was nowhere to go?" He answered, "Did I stand? No way! I just do not remember."

He thought equationally like the sages of ancient Greece; paradoxically like Nietzsche, intuitively like Goethe. But the gestures evolving from his thoughts were based on Kant, Aristotle, Socrates, Vl. Solovyov, Leo Tolstoy. They entered into him like yeast.

Now he started to write. Waves of light poured and it seems that a gigantic sun arose illuminating the landscapes of eons: tens of tens[206] of worldwide kilometers – nations, cultures, centuries and worlds – back to the beginning of beginnings, or the atom where the frontier from the start became boundless and where – as chemistry teachers – the sun as a proton with its electrons of satellite planets unveiled as a point so infinitesimally small that it was unseen to the human eye.

He spoke and a depiction of the epochs materialized. Figures of warriors and the builders of knowledge came alive. The voices echoed, "This and this was done at this time." They disclosed the treasures they carried, and then just as fast rescinded and hid in the shadows of fleeting eras. But in their place others entered the scene, more and more, beginning at Heraclitus,[207] Thales,[208] Roger Bacon,[209] Abelard,[210] and further and further, approaching us.

B.N. meditated on the institution of culture. It alone and in its entirety was generated from the centuries in the fire of contemplation, and was arranged in a living and growing humanity, as an original rhythmic gesture unrepeatable in the same manner at any occasion, but repeatable in a new attire over the immense spans of historical process over the many centuries, and which B.N. called the spiral of history.

On April 8, 1927, Bely and Claudia left Moscow to vacation in Georgia, visiting the Caucasus Mountains. This was a personal celebration of his 25 years as a writer.

Arriving in Georgia Bely and Claudia rented a summer cottage in the resort village of Tsikhisdziri.[211] The cottage was located on the mountain slope and they were able to get 2 rooms in the

---

[206] Russ: decalin, a colloquial numerical word based on deca or ten, meaning tens of tens.
[207] Heraclitus of Ephesus, 535-475 BC, Greek philosopher.
[208] Thales of Miletus, 624-546 BC, Greek philosopher, mathematician and astronomer.
[209] Roger Bacon, 1219-1292. English philosopher and Franciscan friar.
[210] Abelard, 1079-1142. French scholastic, philosopher and theologian.
[211] 10 miles north of Batumi along the Black Sea.

highest floor with 2 balconies and from there have a good view of both the sea and the mountains. The slope descended to the Black Sea shore, but it took time and endurance to walk the distance down and then back up. They stayed there April 14 through May 19. They traveled to Borjomi, in south-central Georgia, staying there May 24-27, and then back to Tsikhisdziri, through June 26.

Bely's attitude was that he finally arrived at the region of Colchis, an important place in Greek mythology, as well as the destination of the Argonauts and home to the Golden Fleece, it was an adolescent dream come true for him. In addition to this was the identification with the novels he read by Mikhail Lermontov and Aleksandr Pushkin regarding the Caucasus region. Bely also remembered the stories his father told him about the region, as he was born near Tiblisi. Bely was exuberant over the opportunity to spend time in the region. A few of the days were sunny and enjoyable, while the rest were rain and fog.

While Bely and Claudia were in Tsikhisdziri, theater director Vsevolod Meyerhold and his wife Zinaida Raikh came by to visit. They were vacationing themselves in Tiblisi, connected with a theater performance for the residents, they heard the Belys were local and came to visit. Their purpose was to try again and resurrect a theater version of *Moscow*, the initial being a failure. Meyerhold described his better intentions for a screenplay and scenery. Bely was willing to give it a second try, and the play would have a new title, *My Spiral*.

From Batumi the Bely couple went to Tiblisi and stayed May 19 through July 3, at the same hotel as the Meyerholds. They attended a performance at the theater, again watching Gogol's *The Inspector General*, with which Bely was involved in producing while in Moscow. While there Bely had, as he described it, the privilege of meeting the 2 famous Georgian poets: Paolo Iashvilli,[212] and Titsian Tabidze.[213] They already considered Bely to be a living

[212] Georgian poet, magazine editor, and one of the leaders of the Georgian symbolist movement, 1894-1937. His writings were later condemned by the Soviet government and he was threatened with exile and incarceration. Prior to his arrest Iashvilli committed suicide on July 22, 1937.

[213] Titsian Yustinovich Tabidze, 1895-1937, Georgian poet and a leader of the Georgian

classic, a genuine Russian poet, and their mentor. As a result Bely and Claudia were treated the most respectfully during their stay in Tiblisi. The two were given a tour of the region by automobile by some of the younger Georgian writers, also taking advantage of his presence with some of his advice on composition. While there Bely took the opportunity to rent a hall at a local music conservatory and deliver 2 public lectures, one titled, *The Reader and the Writer*, and the other, *Personality and Poetry*.

Titsian Tabidze wrote an article regarding Bely's visit and it was published in the local newspaper, *Light of the East,* on July 1, 1927. The following is a selection:

> The traits of genius is often noticed in Andrei Bely, and not just in this narrow circle among the symbolists – where it seems now he has more enemies than friends – but fully among literary genres. Andrei Bely's novel *Petersburg* to this time remains unsurpassed in Russian literature.
>
> The influence of Andrei Bely on contemporary Russian prose is great, and hardly will you right now find a prose writer who has not traversed through Bely, just as the others earlier traversed through Gogol and Dostoyevsky.
>
> So did the Moscow writer celebrate here his 25 years of literary activity.

To return to Moscow Bely decided to take the Volga River. Leaving Tiblisi on July 4, they traveled along the Georgian Military Highway by automobile over the Caucasus Mountains to Vladikavkaz. The couple stayed there until July 10, also visiting Mount Kazbek. Then they took a train to Stalingrad on the Volga River. From there it was a riverboat north, passing through Kazan and Nizhni-Novgorod. This trip – from Batumi to Moscow – opened Bely's eyes to immense regions of Russia to which he was never exposed, especially the size and length of the Volga. They arrived in Moscow on July 24, 1927.

---

symbolist movement. He became a close friend of Pasternak. He was arrested for anti-Soviet propaganda at the beginning of 1937, and then executed on December 16, 1937.

On his return to Moscow Bely immediately shared his experiences with Razumnik:

> Claudia Nikolaievna and I sailed along the Volga from the Caucasus (from Tsaritzin[214] to Nizhni it was 7 days).
>
> The Volga opened a picture to us: Russia is a depiction of large fields, shores, parcels of land, villages, cities. And this immaculate contemplation in its own manner displays the concept of Russia. The visualization of Russia past Kazbek,[215] located on the summit of the highest peaks, for us signifies Russia's expansiveness and cut in half by the Volga.
>
> I lived in the steppes, fields and forests and rural regions of Russia, absent from the silent regions. I needed these 7 days so that for the first time I could traverse the expanses, an experience that penetrated deep into my soul. When I descended from the Caucasus ridge I understood the contour of Russia's immensity.

The Caucasus made an indelible impression on Bely. He was among the snow-covered peaks, the deep and steep canyons, the shore of the Black Sea, the blinding penetration of the sun, and surrounded by enjoyable people, and so felt himself liberated and unburdened. It was so good an experience that Bely and Claudia would travel there the next 2 summers, and these times not just in Georgia, but also Armenia. While there Bely had the famous Armenian artist Martiros Saryan as his guide, giving him a tour of the country.[216] Bely also took the opportunity to find and renew his former friendship with Marietta Shaginyan, who was earlier infatuated with Bely. She was now a popular and respected Armenian writer. Before Bely left Tiblisi he wrote a letter to Marietta on May 20, 1927, thanking her for the renewed memories:

---

[214] Tsaritzin up to 1925, then name of the city was Stalingrad 1925 to 1961, and now Volgograd.

[215] Today known as Stepantsminda, a small town along the Georgian Military Road, in north-east Georgia near the border with Russia, at an of elevation of 5,700 ft.

[216] Martiros Saryan, 1880-1972, Armenian painter.

> Dear Marietta, thank you for the meeting. The feeling we had after such a long departure brought you close to me and K.N.[217] I would have like to speak more with you and longer, but not with superficial words, but with our essences. Although not seeing each other so long, even in this unseen and unspeaking interval we communicated in the rhythm of search and aspiration. But at least here in Erivan I sense that all went well, each of us on this parallel path.

It was over the period March 17-26, 1928, and as though in one breath, that Bely wrote his *Why I became a Symbolist.* And this treatise stood at the forefront in describing the concept of symbolist creativity. At no time in his life did Bely deny or regret even one word of all that he composed. As he stated in his treatise:

> In regard to the question as to how I became a symbolist and when this happened, I consciously answer, "I never became one, I never established myself as one. I was always a symbolist."

Simultaneously Bely never denied or withdrew from his identification with anthroposophy. He was likewise always an anthroposophist.

The summer of 1928, the Bely couple were back in the Caucasus. They left Moscow on May 4, arriving in Tiblisi May 7, staying there through May 15. The couple toured Georgia: Kojori, 15 miles south of Tiblisi, and then to Imereti and Sachkhere, in central Georgia. They visited with Paolo Iashvilli and Titsian Tabidze.

The second half of May they toured Armenia, staying in Erivan, Etchmiadzin, at Lake Ayger west of Etchmiadzin, Lake Sevan, Delizhan and Karaklis, traveling by automobile. The couple had the opportunity to visit with Marietta Shaginyan and Martiros Saryan. They returned to Tiblisi at the end of May and

---

217 Claudia Nikolaievna

remained there until the beginning of June. Then it was to Skhvitor in central Georgia, near Sachkhere, to Kutaisi in western Imereti, and then back to Tiblisi at the end of June.

The couple spent all of July through August 9, in Kojori, and then back to Tiblisi. They leave Tiblisi for Moscow on August 10.

Meanwhile in Moscow at the Meyerhold Theater preparations were in the process of a production of a screenplay of *Moscow*, but the higher party dignitaries could not grasp its concept. As a result the censors evaluated the play as being no more and no less than an anti-socialist endeavor, and so it was terminated, and a second time.

One censor wrote his opinion in an unofficial letter and forwarded it to Bely:

> Bely again has displayed how alien he is to the understanding of the era in which we reside. His caricatures of the Bolsheviks, and providing them such names to ridicule them, only indicates that he has not recognized and does not recognize either the working class or the revolutionaries.

Black storm clouds were released over Bely's head, and even such a person as Meyerhold, having considerable influence in the Soviet administration and authority in the theater, could do nothing about it. So both of them – playwright and producer – had to throw up their hands and with a pain deep in their hearts abandon any prospect of materializing a stage production of *Moscow* or *My Spiral*.

(But Bely and Meyerhold were not isolated. The censors likewise killed Saltykov-Schedrin's *History of One Town*, at about the same time.[218] It was being produced by Razumnik. Also 2 plays by Vladimir Mayakovsky that were produced by the Meyerhold Theater – *Bedbug* in 1919 and *Bathhouse* in 1920 –

[218] Mikhail Yevgrafovich Saltykov-Schedrin, 1826-1889, Russian novelist with many satires on Imperial Russia. *History of One Town* was composed in 1870, the city was named Foolsville.

caused a storm of criticism from Soviet writers, and they were both short-lived.)

Those who held Bely in high respect and valued his novels objected to the Soviet censors termination of the play. One repercussion that occurred which was to Bely's benefit was the offer to print the 3 volumes of Bely's memoirs, the first being *At the Frontier of Two Centuries*, which was complete and ready for print. It would be followed by *Beginning of the Century*, and then *Between the Two Revolutions*. The offer was made at the end of 1928, by the Leningrad State Publisher of Fictional Literature (Lenotgiz).

Bely could not refuse the offer and he signed the contract on February 6, 1929, and went back to work on editing his memoirs. The first volume, *At the Frontier of Two Centuries,* was ready to go to press on April 11. But it was another year before it was released to the public, as slow as Soviet publishing was at the time.

It was only obvious to all, and they were expecting this, that Bely's memoirs would have the same effects as the shrapnel and fragments of an exploding bomb. Much of the book deal with the era of Russia at the end of the $19^{th}$ and beginning of the $20^{th}$ centuries, the pre-Revolutionary period when the population was discontent and disenchanted with the government and administration of Imperial Russia. As with all else in Bely's life, he was clear and unabashed about his treatment of history. Especially important was Bely's explanations of literary trends and new forms of art evolving at the time, and his experiences with real people: politicians, writers, artists and religious figures, many of whom emigrated from Russia and became irreconcilable enemies of Soviet Russia. This did not gain Bely any favor with much of the Soviet administration, regardless that his book was published by the Leningrad State Publishing House.

Parallel with his memoirs, Bely was working on the $3^{rd}$ volume of his *Moscow* series – *Masks*. Although dramatic in style, as were the previous 2 volumes of the series, it was a grotesque satire of Soviet society, a concept continuing from the other 2 volumes.

As with the previous 2 summers Bely and Claudia are back in the Caucasus the summer of 1929. They left Moscow April 26, arriving in Erivan, Armenia on April 30. All of May they toured Armenia visiting: Kanakep north of Erivan, Ashtarak and Geghard in central Armenia. They also had the opportunity to travel to village Dara-Chichag (today known as Konstantinovka), Azerbaijan. They returned to Erivan and traveled to Tiblisi arriving on May 28. The couple toured Georgia: Batumi, Sukhumi in Abkhazia, Gagra and Adler on the Black Sea coast, and Krasnaya Polyana near Sochi. Then it was back to Tiblisi. July is spent vacationing, and again, in Kojori, and they returned to Tiblisi about August 12, and remained there until leaving for Moscow on August 21. Then back at the Kuchino home by August 26.

On April 14, 1930, the entirety of Soviet Russia was agitated by the tragic news of another death of a talented and popular writer. Vladimir Mayakovsky committed suicide by shooting himself. He was only 36 years of age. The situation of Mayakovsky was much the same as with Sergei Esenin: psychological pressure by the Soviet government for his plays and poems, he refusing to capitulate to their demands to write of Soviet realism as they defined it. His funeral was on April 17, 1930, and some 150,000 attended. (There was some controversy regarding Mayakovsky's death after some investigation, that it was a murder arranged by the Soviet government and then announced as a suicide as a cover. This was not unusual during that era. Mayakovsky's wife Lilya Brik was an undercover agent of the Soviet secret police. Brik acquired a vast inheritance with her husband's death and then remarried shortly after Mayakovsky's death.)

As with Esenin, Mayakovsky's death had a devastating impact on Bely. Peter Zaitzev visited him and recorded how Bely was himself filled with terror with his situation and relationship with the Soviet administration and especially Soviet writers, as he did not consider himself one, but still a symbolist. Bely described Mayakovsky:

> I was in ecstasy from Mayakovsky's verses *The Person.* I lauded his verses. Regularly I had public debates with him at the Poly-Technical Museum and we both read our poetry to the audience.

Bely and Claudia again vacationed in the Crimea during the summer of 1930, mainly in the city Sudak, not far from Koktebel. They left Moscow June 11, arriving June 14, and staying there until September 9. From there it was to Koktebel, to the Writer's Guesthouse through September 11, back to Sudak for a couple of days, then to Feodosia, and leaving Feodosia to Moscow on September 20. The couple were back home in Kuchino on September 25.

Here he finished the second volume of his *Moscow* series. The couple also visited with Max Voloshin in Koktebel, and this would be Bely's last occasion to be with him. The poet Vsevolod Rozhdestvensky was also vacationing there at the time and witnessed the close association of these 2 old friends, and he recorded this in a letter:

> Bely was a guest here for several days, and what struck me was the fiery youth of his spirit, an extraordinary outer vitality, and his flaming blue and totally adolescent eyes, that seemed to be placed somewhat slanting. His ability of discernment was paradoxical. An insanity and ingenuity exuded out of his individuality.
>
> He told us of his travel through the Caucasus, and debated with Maximillian Aleksandrovich about his recent book *Rhythm as a Dialectic.* Not since the time of Blok have I encountered such a brilliant soul that is a whirlwind bonfire. The final occasion of the epoch of great symbolism in its reality passed before my eyes, with its breath flamingly consuming my viscera that are accustomed to the normal atmosphere.

Bely turned 50 years of age on October 26, 1930, and a circle of associates send him their good wishes on the anniversary. Pasternak wrote to Bely in a telegram:

I congratulate you from my soul and fervently thank you for the happiness that you have gifted and are gifting us. I am glad I have the privilege to directly correspond with you. I am exuberant over the thought that perhaps the better part of your literature is ahead of you. May nothing affect your health.

Pasternak

The year 1931 was one of the most tragic of any in Bely's life. The upheavals begin with one that is repeated in his life: residency. Shipov, the owner of the cottage where Bely and Claudia had been living for 6 years now, died unexpectedly. His wife was sorely affected by his death and within a moment her attitude toward her tenants became malicious. She then made life hell for the Bely couple and demanded their eviction. Since Bely was not considered properly employed as far as the Soviet administration was concerned, he was unable to register for housing. The apartment of Claudia's first husband Peter Vasilyev was not an option, as he already remarried and had a family.

Touched by the situation Razumnik offered them 2 rooms in his house in Detskoye Selo. The couple moved on April 9, 1931. It was a benefit in another manner as other writers also lived in the vicinity: Petro-Vodkin,[219] Aleksei Tolstoy, Shishkov,[220] Chapigin,[221] and of course Razumnik. The couple were allowed the rooms as long as Bely continued to write.

Matters went well for a short while and then on May 30, 1931, the Soviet secret police arrested Claudia and without any notice or explanation she was taken to some unknown place.[222]

---

[219] Kuzma Petrov-Vodkin, 1878-1939. Soviet and Russian painter and writer.

[220] Vyacheslav Yakovlevich Shishkov, 1873-1945, Russian and Soviet writer, engineer, writing mainly about Siberia.

[221] Aleksei Pavlovich Chapigin, 1870-1937, Russian and Soviet writer of historical novels.

[222] This was the United State Political Directorate (OGPU), headed by Felix Dzerzhinshy, essentially to replace the earlier Cheka, similar to the American NSA (National Security Agency). Larger matters were conducted by the National Commissariat for Internal

This was the beginning of Soviet oppression of suspected foreign elements in the country, and in this situation it was the anthroposophists. There was regular correspondence between those in Russia and those in Germany and Switzerland allowing more justification for Soviet secret police to suspect anthroposophists of counter-revolutionary activities. In addition to Claudia, also arrested were her ex-husband Peter Vasilyev, and her sister E.N. Kezelman, and others. Bely was not arrested, in Petersburg at the time, however his Kuchino residence and previous Moscow apartments were searched and all of his available papers and diaries were confiscated and they disappeared. They did not hesitate to take his typewriter either. Peter Zaitzev immediately went to Detskoye Selo and told this to Bely.

What occurred in Bely's mind with the arrests and especially Claudia, her ex-husband and sister, was devastating. He also had so few people connected with the Soviet administration on whom he could depend to somehow intervene on his behalf and rectify the matter. Bely decided to take the best and proper channels: he wrote to Maxim Gorki and requested his intervention, and this achieved Bely's purpose. After incarcerated without cause for 6 weeks, Claudia and her ex-husband Peter Vasilyev were released July 3, and only after signing under oath a document that she will not leave the Moscow region under any conditions.

Bely, isolating himself in Detskoye Selo to protect himself, wrote of his excitement to Zaitzev:

> It is accomplished. I am writing to you because it is worth it. As soon as I explain this to you I am on my way as she is in Moscow.
>
> I am not writing about myself, as I am not important. I feel so close to her that here in Detskoye Selo I can already touch her. It was like being a body without a soul, building without a foundation under it. She is not just life to me, but a million lives to me.

---

Affairs (NKVD), similar to the American Federal Bureau of Investigation (FBI).

> After she was arrested, for days I laid as a corpse. But for her I will be solid in the future. Shred this letter after reading.

As to why Bely was not arrested can only be conjectured. He was never shy to disseminate the concepts of anthroposophy and openly advocated its philosophy as well as making sure all knew that he was anthroposophist and a symbolist, and not a Soviet writer. One reason is that Bely even at the age of 50 years was the oldest of the active symbolist writers in Russia; the balance either died or migrated to Europe. The population would have formidably protested his arrest. Bely was also supported by the influential Maxim Gorky and Vsevolod Meyerhold, who both had indirect means of communicating with some of the officials in the Soviet secret police, one of whom was Genrikh Yagoda.[223] The intervention of his friends allowed Bely to have a personal audience with Yakov Agranov, the secret police officer who arranged the execution of Nikolai Gumilyov.[224] The meeting was held at the Lubyanka Prison in central Moscow and no doubt Agranov wondered whether he could do the same to Bely, although Bely in his typical naivety had no clue what was occurring. Interestingly Agranov had an aristocratic background and their conversation consisted of literature and philosophy on a rather intellectual level. Agranov for the meantime decided to not prosecute Bely and he released Claudia.

One situation that was not in Bely's favor in his intercession on behalf of Claudia was that they were still not legally married, only common-law, and as a result Bely had to refer to Claudia as his secretary. As a result on July 18, 1931, Boris Nikolaievich Bugaev and Claudia Nikolaievna Turgeneva, by mutual agreement, were married in a civil ceremony, and she became Claudia Bugaeva. Simultaneously while at the courthouse Bely assigned his wife sole authority and heir of all his possessions and

---

223 Genrikh Grigoryevich Yagoda, born Enoch Gershevich Yegoda, 1891-1938. Soviet director of secret police. Eventually he would be himself arrested and tried for treason and executed.

224 Yakov Saulovich Agranov, 1893-1938, chief of Soviet secret police and a deputy of Yagoda. As with Yagoda, he would be arrested and tried for treason and executed.

books and publications and royalties, and all related rights, after his death. This was just a week after her release from incarceration.

But due to her signed statement of agreeing not to leave Moscow, Claudia was unable to go to Detskoye Selo, to their present home. Bely turned to writing letters to officials to have this restriction rescinded.

The Soviets proceeded with its investigation regarding the matter of the anthroposophists, and Bely did not hesitate to provide his written apologies for his beliefs. He sent several letters to the office of the secret police where the explained the essence and concepts of anthroposophy and the goals and intents of the anthroposophists, as well as justify himself as an adherent of this movement and provide an ideological defense for the arrested persons. Part of one letter consisted of the following:

> I consider the articles, those in the Soviet Encyclopedia and others similar to it, that characterize anthroposophy as a "display of German militarism," to be an illiterate conglomeration of words as well as a distortion of facts. Steiner has suffered persecution in German magazines as published by fascists, whose intent is to discredit his activities, and including their arsonist destruction of the Goetheanum. Such articles create preconceived notions causing unpleasant consequences for the former members of the Russian [Anthroposophical] Society, and which is non-political. The International [Anthroposophical] Society presently numbers over 10,000 members, all of whom are innocent of such malicious slander, and many of whom are my closest of friends.

The several letters sent to officials of the secret police were insufficient to turn their attention to assisting Claudia and intervening into the matter of the remaining incarcerated anthroposophists. Bely then turned to marshal Joseph Stalin. In his letter, Bely capitalizes on Stalin's spite toward Leon Trotsky, claiming that the anthroposophists are victims of Trotsky's unsubstantiated persecution. Bely refers to the uncomplimentary article that Trotsky published in *Pravda* about a decade earlier. Bely's letter is the following:

Moscow, August 31, 1931.

Most highly respected Joseph Vissaronovich! Life's penetrating difficulties, and after serious contemplation and a series of unproductive interventions, compel me to write this letter to you. If the accountable charges are not serious enough for your attention, then just discard this request and ignore it.

What I have been experiencing is crushing. It has been forced upon me as a result of my difficult situation in literature and which was caused initially by an article composed by Trotsky back in 1922, who distorted right to the root my reputation in the literary world and suppressing me as a writer. Prior to this time there were no doubts regarding my activities because everyone knew that I compliantly encountered the October Revolution and worked with Soviet authority during its initial stage. I worked at the Proletkult, and now some of my former students are visible proletariat writers, and working at the Theatrical Department of the Narkompros, and at other Soviet institutions. Rejecting war and sharing many of the slogans of the kernel of the Russian Revolution, I incurred a series of altercations with those literary figures with whom I earlier associated: Merezhkovsky, Gippius, Berdiaev, and others. After Trotsky's article I was banned from the literary world for two years.

Even though my books were acceptable to the censors and even met approval, a malevolent attitude toward be developed as a result of Trotsky's article, and it increased to the point that it deteriorated my health, my capacity in associations, and deprived me of the capability to further compose.

My wife, Claudia Nikolaievna Bugaeva, just after we relocated to Detskoye Selo and settled in our new residence, was arrested, as well as Vasilyev, at Detskoye the night of May 30-31, and she was finally freed on July 3, and the matter terminated, except that she was forced to sign an agreement to not leave Moscow until the entire matter pertaining the formers members of the Russian Anthroposophical Society was finished. Their excuse is that that this temporary restraint is merely a formality.

In order not to leave her isolated and defenseless, I came to Moscow and now for two months have been living in the residence of her former husband, Dr P.N. Vasilyev, also still under arrest, and our situation is becoming very desperate. Away from my study, I am not able to do much work.

All of this was caused by the falsified discredit of myself in Trotsky's article, and to force this restraint on my wife – for her to remain in Moscow and not be able to return to Detskoye – as merely a formality will accomplish nothing. This only makes conditions for my wife the more difficult.

This sorrowful plea arises: should this be the terminal point of a thirty-year career in literature? This situation being caused my wife exacerbates our condition and into simply a tragedy. Perhaps you will ascertain that this gesture of mine through this letter is a cry of despair and exhaustion and helplessness, so do accept it as such. So if you can assist us in this predicament – the situation with my wife – it would be a help to me and a stimulus to overcome our other obstacles, and there are many.

Again I ask you to forgive me for troubling you. I remain with deepest respect.

Boris Bugaev (Andrei Bely)

Bely's letter to Joseph Stalin is a prime example and testimony to his literary excellence, as well as his ability to utilize a subconscious animosity of Stalin toward his enemy Trotsky. This was a means of placing himself – Bely – as an innocent victim of Trotsky's arbitrary insolence, although innocent of all accusations, and at the same time lauded by his readers and approved by Soviet censures. So Bely presented Claudia as being the result of the repercussions Bely faced a few years earlier.

The order for Claudia's restraint was rescinded and she was allowed to leave Moscow, and the couple returned to Detskoye

Selo, and where they resided until the end of 1931. Visitors shortly after Claudia's return included Meyerhold and his wife Zinaida Raikh, and later the poets Paolo Iashvilli and Titsian Tabidze arrived from Georgia and visited. In addition to this, what made Bely extremely happy was the retirement pension granted to him by decree of the Council of Ministers of the USSR, now reaching the retirement age of 50.

Matters went well through the end of the year 1931, until a rupture occurred between the Belys and the Razumniks who lived alongside each other. The secret police had been trailing and investigating Razumnik over the years due to his correspondence with people outside of the USSR, and mainly writers and anthroposophists in Germany. The Soviet administration was gathering information on Razumnik, attempting to find evidence of disloyalty to the Soviet government.

It was shortly after Bely moved from Detskoye Selo back to Moscow that he was secretly warned to terminate further correspondence with Razumnik, one that had been continuing without interruption for almost 20 years of close association. The final time that Bely visited Detskoye Selo was at the end of March and beginning of April 1932, and after that he never again saw Razumnik.

The balance of Razumnik's life was a series of upheavals and he never returned to normality. At the beginning of February 1933, Razumnik was arrested on false and fabricated charges of having intentions of forming a center for a national uprising, that he was an anti-Soviet element, as the charges read. Of course, there was no evidence that the secret police could discover for any such clandestine activity on his part. Nonetheless in June 1933, a secretive decision was made by the OGPU and Razumnik was sentenced to three years exile in Novosibirsk. He resided there for some time and was then relocated to Saratov, and then released in March 1936. He was again arrested on similar spurious charges in September 1937, and was incarcerated until 1939, and then he returned to Detskoye Selo, now Pushkin. He managed to escape out of Soviet Russia and lived in Munich, Germany until his death in 1946, and he never again returned to writing or publishing.

As always in the past during times of stress or difficulty Bely would find consolation in Gogol, his favorite of all Russian novelists, as in his adolescence, so at the present. Bely's newest volume was titled *Mastery of Gogol*, and he devoted all his time to it. After its publication, this book was considered a brilliant effort in constructive literary criticism of the 20th century. The State Publishing House approved the publication of *The Mastery of Gogol* on June 19, 1932, although it was not until April 1935, over a year after Bely's death, that it was released to the general public.

As Bely wrote:

> Gogol is the epopee of prose. His cognizance reminds a person of a dormant volcano. In lieu of the Doric phrases of Pushkin and the Gothic vocabulary of Karamzin, what he has is an asymmetrical baroque. Gogol's phrases begin the period whose productivity we unearth.

Bely's book on Gogol was composed solely during the period of the uncomfortable circumstances related to Claudia's arrest and incarceration. The Belys were unable to continue living in Detskoye Selo and so moved to Moscow, to an apartment that was a half-way basement, where the windows were at street level, and no different than others in which Bely lived. This one located on Plueschikh St in central Moscow, building 53. It was a communal apartment and for which Bely was able to qualify, now as a certified pensioner as approved by the Soviet administration, as mentioned above. It would have been one room while sharing a kitchen and dining room with other residents. Again Bely and Claudia were able to receive guests and acquaintances. What would continually annoy Bely was the view through the windows of the feet of a continuous stream of pedestrians and the noise of their footsteps and the bustle of street traffic. Shadows incessantly broke the little sunshine that penetrated the windows into their room.

Above their room was a department store. Bely mentions in his memoirs how he would shout at people when they would stop to look at the displays in the windows of the department store and stand in front of his small window and block what sunshine was penetrating:

> Get away from the window! I ask of you. Please step back from the window at least a couple of steps if you can. A writer lives here! Do not interfere with him working!

The one group would comply, but then another group would stand in their place and Bely would shout at them. It was never ending. Bely complained to his friend the artist Vladimir Milashevsky about this in a letter:

> You know that even the great Bosch could not even under pressure visualize such ugly feet and their clothes.[225] This is a dirty hell, but instead of flames, it is basement dampness. You know that when certain legs appear, they have an ugliness or abominable evil totally incarnated in them. The feet of these witches stand long in front of my eyes, and it seems that no longer does a Dante or Botticelli[226] or Shakespeare or Pushkin exist in the world anymore. One pair of feet belong to a clumsy witch.

Again vacationing, Bely and Claudia arrived on August 8, 1932, at the city Lebedyan, about 250 miles southeast of Moscow in Lipetsk Province and along the Don River, at the home of Claudia's sister Elena Kezelman. Elena was exiled there by edit of the Soviet administration for being a member of the anthroposophical society. They spent August and September there and leaving to Moscow on September 30. The expanses of central

---

[225] Hieronymus Bosch, 1450-1516, Dutch painter.
[226] Sandro Botticelli, 1445-1510, Italian painter of the period of the early Renaissance.

Russia, the tranquil creative situation had a benevolent influence on Bely's personal disposition and mood. Every day just before nightfall he would depart with his 2 companions on a long stroll, watching the sunset and each day it was a different route. This was likewise a new region of Russia to which Bely was not yet exposed and he inwardly compared it to the depths of the infinite universe.

Elena Kezelman recorded the time spent with Bely and Claudia:

> When the sun started to set and its rays streamed into the skies, flaring lights played with the colors of the sunset, B.N. seemed to quiet even more, saturated with this silent conversation with nature. Something quiet, austere, very, very concentrated and profound emanated from him during such minutes.

In order to improve conditions for Soviet writers the administration decided to build a cooperative house on Naschokinsky Lane, and which still stands to the present. Bely realized the benefit such a place could offer him in the future and where Claudia could also live, and he could not foresee anything better than this. So Bely sold his archives to the Literary Museum and gave a considerable donation to the construction of the cooperative writer's dormitory.

Subsequent to this the Central Committee of the Communist Party issued an edit titled, *Regarding the Restructure of the Writer's Organization*. The edit dealt with the preparation of a new organization: the Union of Soviet Writers. The idea of uniting all writers into one union was long blowing in the literary atmosphere. Many writers suffered due to arbitrary censorship, a lack of publishers, no support from the government, without finances. Writing on non-productive subjects up to this time was not considered a vocation benefiting the Soviet state, and so they were at the mercy of publishers and whatever royalty they would pay, and Bely was a prime example of this. As a result writers in general suffered, not having adequate financing, housing, medical care and help in general with daily responsibilities.

Recollecting the difficulties of the early years of Soviet censorship and the lack of help from the Soviet administration, Bely sincerely made the decision to become a member and forwarded his application on June 19, 1932, through the proper channels. On October 30, Bely's application was approved by the highest party officials and he became a member of the plenum of the organizing committee of the Writer's Union. Even at age 51, he was among the eldest of the members and so felt he had the right to voice his opinion, and considering it to be authoritative, in regard to questions of composition and language.

One of his addresses to the organizing committee was recorded:

> More than any other I know how immense is the potential energy and creativity in the working masses. In 1918, I had the opportunity to work with young representatives of proletariat literature at the Proletkult. And I was amazed at how rapidly they were able to grasp the subtlety of our classics. This speedy perception of understanding the specifics of art is similar to the voltage in electricity, to the force of water in the Dnepr, to the force of the wind.
>
> I would want the enthusiasm of feeling to become the enthusiasm of will and cognizance in the processes of daily work, and which will bind us all together and so we will sharpen ourselves using each other.

On February 11 and 27, 1933, at the large hall of the Poly-Technical Museum, a tribute on behalf of Andrei Bely was held. The first evening festivity was directed by Vsevolod Meyerhold, and the second by Sergei Eisenstein.[227]

The newspaper *Moscow Evening* recorded the events of the first tribute and published the following article:

---

[227] Sergei Mikhailovich Eisenstein, 1898-1848, Soviet film director.

> After a long absence Andrei Bely again entered the world with a recitation of his artistic compositions. The large hall of the Poly-Technical Museum was filled to overflowing. Among those present were many representatives of the literary and theatrical world. On stage were Vse. Meyerhold, B.Pasternak, M.Prishvin, Vs.Vishnevsky. The presiding chairman of the tribute, Vse. Meyerhold delivered a short introductory address. He characterized Andrei Bely as a writer who "right now actively joined the advancement of our new genre of literature and is proceeding with great enthusiasm and fervency."

Bely's personal addresses at both tributes were preserved. The following is his introduction at one of them:

1. The Uniqueness of my Prose:

As an explanation of my prose, it is intonational. I do not compose at a desk, but while walking. My novels are poems where the lines of verses are continuous for the sake of economizing paper. But the phrases are composed in the same manner as a lyrical poet composes lines. He needs feet to keep a beat and even hands for gestures. I need to declare, not just to write.

2. Why am I so not Understood?

Not understanding my prose evolves from what is stated above. This is a fictional object where each word is constructed and where each stroke of the composition is predetermined. They want to abstractly swallow it like adventure novels, in immense doses. But try reciting *Evgeni Onegin* rapidly. Listening to someone doing this will cause your eyes to crawl up your forehead.

3. Why do I not Write at a Desk?

Why do I not write at a desk, but instead recite my novels aloud as I record them on scraps of paper, while in the fields, in the forest, while strolling? Because this is how I speak with the reader from my platform. I am a writer-performer, and I

> hold to the opinion that the life-providing book of the future is not a book at all, but an auditorium, or a talking movie.[228]
>
> 4. How to Write and How to Read:
>
> The writer and the reader learn from each other. The writer learns to understand the public demand, accepting it into his hand. The reader learns the ability to read. The art of reading requires literary grammar, and must be very extensive, just as political grammar is at present. Alongside the mobilization of scientific knowledge there must be the mobilization of writers. They must teach readers using their oratorical ability.

During this period Bely was continuing on his memoirs, volume 1 already published. He was as though reliving and experiencing anew the distant and recent past, the initial landmarks of the history of symbolism and the events tied with the literary activity of its more brilliant representatives. Since the death of Feodor Sologub in December 1927, Russian symbolism as if collapsed under the history of its development, losing the person that so vividly characterized the genre. Although several of its visible representatives were alive and writing, but they were abroad, and severed from their homeland and just as well be on another planet as far as Russian symbolism was now concerned. As far as the symbolists were concerned, it was Bely who remained as its final defender, and of which he was well aware.

The few standard-bearers of the Silver Age remaining alive in Russia were Bely, Anna Akhmatova (although her creativity ended with her husband's death in 1921), and Osip Mandelstam (he would die in 1938). Bely was fortunate to spend time in Koktebel with him in June and July of 1933.

[228] Talking movies were still a novelty in the USSR at this time.

# THE DEATH OF ANDREI BELY

# PART 1

Andrei Bely died in the 53rd year of his life – January 8, 1934. His death was preceded by pain and continual anguish for several months.

On May 17, 1933, Bely and his wife Claudia departed for a period of rest and vacation in Koktebel. Maximillian Boloshin had an estate in the city, where they stayed for a while, but for the next 2 months they were mainly at the Writer's Guesthouse. Bely and Claudia planned to end their vacation July 17.

Mandelstam and his wife Maria and Bely and Claudia arrived in the Crimea together, traveling from Litfonda, near Bichvinta, Abkhazia, Georgia. The men were unable to create an attachment although both were poets. The reason was the skeptical attitude of Mandelstam toward anthroposophy and he was tactless in his disregard of its concepts when discussing the matter with Bely. Otherwise the shallow conversation of the 2 of them concentrated on poetry, their plans for future publications. Bely spoke of his just concluded memoirs and his *Mastery of Gogol.*

Bely climbed to the top of the mountain Kuchuk-Enishar, to visit the grave of Max Voloshin who died August 11, 1932. His widow Maria Stepanovna placed a memorial stone on his grave with the inscribed words:

> This grave of his soars to the summit of this mountain, as though expanding upwards into the cosmos and transforming his personage.[229]

The days prior to July 15, Bely was in a state of extensive agitation and psychological stress and pressure. He would speak on end without a clear indication of purpose and move about the room and guesthouse without ceasing. But this was just a warning of what was next to occur.

On July 15, at 6 o'clock in the evening, Bely suffered what appeared to be a stroke. He and Claudia and friends were sitting and conversing in the guesthouse. Bely was lively, happy, and then all of a sudden he started to fever. According to Peter Zaitzev who was present, his coloration turned dark like a Negro. He immediately became nauseous, sick and faint. Bely first suffered a severe heat in the nape of his neck and back of the head. He stood up, stumbled and then fell. Bely was unconscious for several hours. When he gained consciousness, he was vehemently agitated. He wanted to take a walk along the seashore and then talked incomprehensively. Bely then started to feel a tightness in his neck and in the upper half of his back and spine. His movement was now even slower than before and he seemed to lose complete track of time. Later Bely would claim he had a sunstroke, knowing well what it was but trying to mask its severity. The Soviet doctors who examined him diagnosed it as arterial sclerosis. However based on the symptoms he displayed and the testimony of later physicians, it was obviously an aneurysm of a blood vessel in the brain.

Maria Stepanovna, Max Voloshin's widow, took Bely from his room at the Writer's Guesthouse to her home, where together with Claudia she made arrangements to keep him safe and called for medical help. It was on the following day, July 16, that 3 doctors arrived to her home and examined him (the 3 were either working

---

[229] Maria Stepanovna Zabolotzkaya would be buried next to him upon her death December 17, 1976.

or vacationing in Koktebel). Their diagnosis was that Bely suffered a heat stroke combined with the effects of sclerosis. On July 20, Dr M.S. Slavolubov, from the city Feodosia, not far from Koktebel, who worked in the department of physical therapy of the Central Council of Trade Unions, visited Bely. He knew the Voloshin family, having earlier treated Max for his asthma and heart irregularities. He confirmed the diagnosis of the previous 3 Koktebel doctors and concluded also that Bely was affected with extreme nervous exhaustion. The report that he issued on July 23, stated:

> I affirm the present conclusion, that Comrade Bugaev, Boris Nikolaievich, suffers from exhaustion of the nervous system to a severe degree.
>
> During the period of his rest and recovery in Koktebel, I observed a short-term period of headaches and fainting spells, due to hyperemia of the brain.
>
> I recommend that the ill person continue his stay here and rest until August 1, of this year.
>
> After his return home, I consider it indispensable that he make changes in his work habits, as far as amount and intensity. He needs to work calmly and in a tranquil environment, in the environs of a normal working period, and with relief of any worries or difficulties.

Bely was disturbed with having to acknowledge that he was ill. He was exceeding irritated over what occurred. However the oral conclusion of Dr Slavolubov sounded a bit more optimistic and even conducive to Bely:

> Your illness consists in you being considerably [psychologically] younger than your actual age.

Having accepted the doctor's words of his youthfulness literally, on July 21, Bely, overcoming the regular pains in his head, back and legs, attempted to raise himself and institute a lively and active routine. As Claudia recollected in her memoirs on July 23:

> He avoids the sun; takes long walks from sunrise and until after sunset. As in the past, he is very sociable and does not tire from conversation. Otherwise, I do not know what to say about B.N's condition. The pains in his head continue, although they are weak. But pains in his back now accompany them, and his [temperature] which was 100 deg.F, yesterday evening, this morning was 99.5, and then 99. It is apparent he has some kind of abdominal illness. But no one seems to be able to exactly define what kind. There is a good doctor in Fedosia and he did come here once. But this is such a complex issue and I do not see any need to repeat his visit. In general, to be sick under the conditions of being here is extremely difficult. I am attempting to bring him to Moscow as soon as possible. The doctor said it would be best not to move him anywhere until at least the end of July. I am troubled as to how to travel alone with him and what will I do if the shaking of the railroad car causes him some kind of disturbance. He has not slept one night normally since the 15th. Or else he finally falls asleep at daybreak, turning in his bed all night or just not sleeping at all. All of this upsets me, knowing B.N. is in this condition, and I cannot seem to get calm.

After a week, on July 29, the Bely couple decide to leave Koktebel for Moscow, the train departing from Feodosia. The train arrived at the Kursk-Moscow Train Station. The couple went first to their residence in the half-way basement on Plueschikh St. (The writer's dormitory on Naschokinsky Lane was not yet completed.)

Zaitzev recorded in his memoirs:

> They arrived on August 1. G.A. Sannikov and I met them and later stayed a while with them at the Dolgi residence. Looking at Boris Nikolaievich it was obvious he was seriously ill. His dismal impression made it seem to us that he is succumbing to something worse, as if again expecting a stroke like a spear piercing him.

Bely struggled with his illness all of August 1933, displaying excruciating attacks of pain in his head. Of course, the specific cause of his malady could not be explained at all by Soviet doctors, or so they said, and as a result Bely was confounded as to what was occurring in him. He concluded only that the alleged sunstroke caused some long-term latent or dormant nervous condition, or his exhaustion from working, to erupt.

Desperate and perplexed, Claudia first of all, after their arrival in Moscow, turned to her ex-husband for advice. She had to write to him, since he was not in Moscow at the time. Her former husband, regardless of how insulted he felt by the entire situation of his divorce and then subsequently having to provide housing for his ex-wife and her new husband, changed his attitude toward one of a concerned friend and took an active interest in Bely's condition. Bely was then moved to the apartment on Dolgi Crossing, the new home of Claudia's first husband Dr Peter Vasilyev. The apartment was hardly 500 sq.ft. in area, and included Claudia's piano, and Bely's desk and bookcase. They hid the bed vertically behind the bookcase. For Bely in his condition it was hardly comfortable. Dr Vasilyev wrote to Claudia on August 11, with his indirect evaluation of Bely's problem and then provided a medical recommendation. He wrote:

> Dear Claudia:
>
> It would be best for B.N. to make a visit to the neuropathological professor, Ivan Yuryevich Tarasevich, who resides at Dolgi Crossing, House 23. Because, based on what you wrote to me, it is obvious the matter is neuralgic pain evolving from the region at the top of the spine, and what is also possible, is a neural cause. I think that he can recover from it. It would be best to not delay any longer to visit the specialist that I recommended.

A few days later Claudia took Bely for a visit to Dr Tarasevich. His report on August 16, explained his diagnosis and conclusion. This is noted in the following:

> Bugaev, Boris Nikolaievich, suffers from encephalopathic arterial sclerosis, with paresis of the left side of his brain. He is in need of complete rest, systematic treatment, and a strict therapeutic routine.

Dr Tarasevich then continued to recommend a routine for Bely to follow in order to improve his condition and with the possibility of a good recovery, however it was too difficult for Bely to fulfill. He complained about it in a letter to Claudia's sister, Elena Kezelman, on September 1, 1933, as follows:

> This routine keeps a tight hand over me and it is not easy. I need to rise at a certain time; I sleep at a certain time; I can only smoke so much; I can only drink at certain intervals. If I take a step, it is in a methodical manner. I endeavor to observe all the doctor has prescribed me and live according to this austere regimen: 5-1/2 cigarettes a day, my tea is limited. Eating is strictly at certain times, same with strolling. I have kept statistics, notes, as to when and how many cigarettes I smoke.

No doubt Bely wanted to passionately recover from the illness, and so strove with all his capacity to adhere to doctor's orders.

Another important assignment by Dr Tarasevich as part of Bely's routine was long daily walks. This prescription, as opposed to that of quitting smoking, was very conducive and pleasurable for Bely. He enjoyed what he saw as a new Moscow, since now he was exposed to its environs. The groups of apartment complexes in the new style, and especially the gardens, parks and squares that now covered previously deserted areas of the city, captivated Bely.

Bely's struggle against tobacco became one of his most difficult tasks in order to orient his life to a new routine. The most difficult was that he was forbidden to work, meaning, he could not write or read or even think. Prior to Bely's initial stroke, according to Zaitzev, he would smoke an unhealthy amount of cigarettes, up to 60 a day. According to wife Claudia, it was 50 a day, and she noticed that her husband would provide the cigarettes an aroma by adding a few drops of naphthalene into a pack. Bely enjoyed the somewhat pleasant aroma, although hardly any more healthful than the tobacco itself. Bely then gradually weaned himself day by day from his addiction, although it was more a psychological than a chemical dependence. The following is the table he create:

CROOKED SMOKING
(my struggle against smoking)

Earlier I would smoke 50 cigarettes a day on the average.
Beginning spring of this year, I reduced my normal consumption to 25-30 cigarettes.
During the summer it was an average of 20 cigarettes.
Once I got sick, it went even lower.
Smoking for the month of August 1933:
August 24, I smoked 6-1/2 cigarettes.
August 25, I smoked 6 cigarettes.
August 26, I smoked 5-1/2 cigarettes.
August 27, I smoked 5 cigarettes.
August 28, I smoked 6 cigarettes.
August 29, I smoked 5 cigarettes.
August 30, I smoked 4-1/2 cigarettes.
August 31, I smoked 4 cigarettes.

It is obvious that it was the doctor who motivated Bely to create such a table, and due to Bely's inner nature, he quickly accommodated the request, rather than contradicting it. It is no wonder he named the table Crooked Smoking, referring to a distorted medical graph. Once cutting down on his daily consumption of cigarettes, a rather large accomplishment on the part of Bely, he became very proud of it, although occasions occurred when he would break the trend. On September 1, Bely wrote to Elena Kezelman that he reduced smoking to 3 cigarettes a day, although his average was actually 4-1/2, and this was the best he could do. Bely never actually quit smoking, but a few days prior to his death he was no longer able, now lying in the hospital.

In September 1933, Bely went for one of his daily walks and had the opportunity to be accompanied by Nina Gagen-Torn, and they went to the cemetery at Novo-Devichi Convent. While there he showed her the graves of the Solovyovs, and told her of his recollections tied with Novo-Devichi. As Gagen-Torn later recollected:

> Perhaps he was not totally conscious of this, but he did feel that the terminal point of his life was nearby. This was terrifyingly clear during this final stroll with him.

Bely's final notation in his diary of a visit to Novo-Devichi Convent is dated October 18, 1933.

Even through all of August and September 1933, those who were close to Bely, and even himself, still hoped for a successful recovery of his illness. Or perhaps they just all gave this impression that it was still hopeful. Other than hope, there was nothing that practically remained for them, even with Dr Tarasevich's systematic therapy for Bely. It was obvious that the famous professor and neurologist underestimated the severity of the situation. In the middle of September, Bely did start to feel better and his conditions somewhat improved, and it was due to the reduction in smoking, a better diet and the strict routine of rest and walking, but by the time October came along, it was a turn for the worse. It was only at the beginning of October that Bely started taking medication for the pain in his head.

Quickly Dr Tarasevich changed or modified his recommendation to another famous neuropathologist, V.K. Khoroshko, and a specialist in physical therapy, S.V. Marsova, and other doctors. In addition to Bely's therapy routine and pills, medicinal liquids and a massage of the head was also supplemented. The beneficial effect of this was negligible. The more effective medicines that were prescribed for Bely were not available for purchase at any pharmacy in Moscow, and Gagen-Torn had to send him some from Leningrad. At this point any hope in recovery was dependent on access to the Kremlin pharmacy and the Kremlin medical clinic. But Bely's right to entrance for purchase of medicine and treatment at this facility was at the whim of government officials and the intervention on his behalf of people with authority. Although Bely did begin to petition for the privilege of medical services provided by Kremlin doctors sometime in August, shortly after his return from Koktebel, it was not until sometime in November that Kremlin doctors did visit him. The report that the doctors issued did not include any diagnosis or indicate the extent of the illness. All they did was recommend a stay at a local sanitarium, but by the time Bely received the doctor's recommendation, he had little strength remaining to do much at all.

During October and November Bely's illness was aggressive and his life turned into total agony with the intolerable pain in his cranium. December 2, was the final day Bely was able to write. December 4, was his final stroll in public. Later that day Bely suffered another stroke.

On December 8, Bely was hospitalized in the Psychiatric Department of the First Moscow Clinical Hospital. This psychiatric clinic was the oldest medical facility of this type in Moscow. By this time Bely was no longer able to stand on his own. By December 22, in addition to the pains in his cranium, Bely no longer had the ability to utilize his hands, his brain had deteriorated so much.

Nonetheless, no diagnosis was yet provided by Soviet doctors. Zaitzev recorded in his memoirs the following on December 18.

> To this time doctors are unaware as to what occurred in Koktebel and what is presently occurring. Two propositions exist: first is that at Koktebel he suffered a heat stroke, a blood vessel ruptured and he is bleeding internally in his cranium. This is evidence of sclerosis. The second is that he has a tumor in his brain. The second is more dangerous and frightening. He can survive the former, but with the risk of ceasing to be a writer. The latter threatens him with physical termination. I do not know which is the worse for B.N. and for his friends.

It was not until December 29, that Soviet doctors finally concluded that Bely was suffering from internal bleeding in the brain in the region of arteriosclerosis.[230] However their definition could not change the progression of the deterioration of his health: the aneurysm had ruptured.

Claudia incessantly sat at her husband's bedside from this time on. She would stare at his face and eyes to ascertain what he wanted, whatever to make him comfortable. He spoke rarely and with difficultly and it was difficult to ascertain what he was saying. Bely had to be spoon fed soft food and liquids were given to him right to his mouth in a cup. Regularly his friends sat alongside him and on a rotating basis: Peter Zaitzev, Petrovsky, Ms A.M. Krasnovskaya and Ms L.I. Krasilschik.

Sannikov visited Bely several times the few days before his death, and recording the following in his memoirs:

> I gazed at his face. It was pale, motionless, a yellow tint of an incurable serious disease penetrated the surface of the skin on his face. His eyes were opened and stared straight into space. He was weak and tranquil, but attentive and coherent. I felt that he already thought all that had to be thought, acknowledge his fate and not with a weary stare he gazed at those surrounding him, at the white walls of the ward, at his emaciated and strange-looking and heavy hands that he could not hardly move without intense difficulty. But his face showed no anxiety, no fear. All was clear to him, all was plain and all was natural. Even the tops of the frost-covered Christmas trees visible through the window shutters did not attract his attention, did not summon him as they would have earlier, a love and greed for life, all was now terminated.
>
> The final period of his life, from the time he entered the hospital, he shared his condition with his friends. He was able to figure it from hints, from what little the unknowing doctors disclosed to him, the gestures of his associates, and how they

[230] The Russian word is also atherosclerosis.

> looked at him. Of course there was no need to disclose to him that you were aware of his doom. I listened to his words, the intonation and he just gazed at me, knowing that I did not believe in any recovery of his. He was tranquil and lay straight.
>
> We spoke a few words, about the ordinary and shallow and unessential. We avoided speaking of literary themes.
>
> It was difficult for him to speak to Claudia. In a whisper he uttered a few words, and so I or Claudia would catch the drift of his thought and then continue it, and if we had to guess at what he said, he would approvingly gesture with his eyes. We did not state anything of any significance to each other, but the minutes of our silence were more significant than any words spoken. This time we bid farewell to the ordinary in an ordinary fashion, as if we were not thinking about the inevitable. We both created an illusion, and it was frighteningly unavoidable to the both of us. I told him I wanted him to quickly recover, and he, as though having no doubt in this, answered with a kind and believing gaze. And this gaze was one of friendship and wisdom and was a quiet warm sadness. The motionless head rested on the pillow, above the blanket lay white emaciated hands with long fingers. The yellow tint covered the skin of his amazing face. I left him the way that neighbors leave the room. I preserved the tranquility of a person convinced in the definite and soon recovery of someone ill. But when I left him I wept.

Zaitzev visited Bely in the hospital on January 6, 1934, 2 days before his death, and Zaitzev noted in his diary the following:

> I arrived at 3 o'clock in the afternoon. Boris Nikolaievich was very quiet, courteous, and he displayed a bright smile. I fed him some buckwheat porridge with huckleberry jam. He was significantly weaker than earlier. Finishing his porridge he asked for a cigarette. But he could not hold it in his hand, so he just took 2 or 3 puffs from my hand.

For the most part Bely was in a condition of clear consciousness. Occasionally he would experience delirium and would talk nonsense. Occasionally he would speak of interesting and provocative and subtle subjects. In his final conversations with wife Claudia, he relived his birth on the nights of January 3rd–4th and 4th–5th. As she recorded the event in a letter to her friend E.V. Neveinova:

> He relived [his rebirth] with immense strength and joy and happiness. He whispered to me about happiness, about joy, about birth. And some kinds of unbelievable waves of love emanated from him. Then over the next 3 days: the 5th, 6th and 7th, he became weaker and weaker. Then on the morning of the 8th, the pain in his head started and it was the last.

In Claudia's memoirs she mentions that on the night of January 7-8. 1934, his thoughts were occupied with light and Bely made the nebulous statement:

> Time has departed from light.

Andrei Bely died on January 8, 1934. As Claudia announced:

> He died at 12:30 in the afternoon. His death occurred due to a paralysis of his breathing passages, although his heart was still beating, and in the presence of his wife and doctors. His death was quiet and tranquil. He died as though he was falling asleep.

Actually, no doctors were present, and the cause of death was the statement of Soviet doctors to be related to the newspapers to satisfy their curiosity. Based on the symptoms Andrei Bely died from internal bleeding in his brain due to the rupture of a blood vessel.

At 2:30 PM after Bely's death, he was taken to the morgue, specifically the anatomical division of the Sechenov Medical University on Abrikosovsky St, building 1.

Zaitzev recorded his visit there in his memoirs:

> The orderly led me into a light empty room. There on an immense galvanized table I saw the dead body of a person. This was what remained of the writer Andrei Bely, and the person Boris Nikolaievich Bugaev. This was my impression: this body did not seem to be a corpse, but was similar to a perfected sculptor of a genuine artist of some ancient era. But the artist was Nature itself who created this perfect body.

Then Pasternak, Pilnyak and Sannikov from the organizing committee of the Union of Soviet Writers arrived to inform them of the removal of Bely's brain and its transfer to the Human Brain Institute. The morgue already received the instructions, but the 3 came as a formality, since the decision for this manner of immortalizing Bely – by preserving his brain – came from a significantly higher level of Soviet authority and not from his friends. Such an honor was usually reserved for high ranking party activists, exceptional scientists and other people of some superior talent or capability.

Aleksei Ivanovich Abrikosov, a Soviet professor and pathologist, removed Bely's brain on the morning of January 9.[231] After embalming, at about 12 noon, a group of close associates gathered in the hallway, one of them being Claudia Nikolaievna. Zaitzev along with Claudia and Vasili Nilender, helped the orderly dress Bely and place him in a simple oak casket that was internally lined with newspapers. A few bouquets of white flowers with green branches of spruce and cypress that people brought were placed inside the coffin. At 1 PM, Bely's body was taken to the Dolgi St residence, where a month back he spent some time.

Zaitzev recorded the event in his memoirs:

[231] He was also the person responsible for Lenin's brain removal and embalming Lenin's body for preservation.

Friends and associates started to arrive at the apartment. Chulkov,[232] Rachinsky,[233] Pasternak, Pilnyak, Sannikov, Tzyavlovsky,[234] and Bely's cousin Oleg Georgievich Bugaev.

Sometime mid-afternoon the casket was taken by a horse-drawn carriage through Moscow snow-covered streets to the building of the organizing committee of the Union of Soviet Writers. Sannikov recorded the procession in lyrical form in one of his poems as though talking to Bely in he coffin as the horse was pulling the carriage:

The half-dead old horse forced to move forward.
You remember, my friend, the road to the Writer's Institute.
Among a crowd of friends and devotees
We walked with you behind the coffin.
We walked, our hats pulled down deeply,
We walked and so silently.
Evening was starting.
Novinsky Boulevard, covered with snow,
Cast a shadow of a blue tint,
In front of us on a catafalque the coffin rocked.
The exhausted horse hardly stepped,
Often just standing –
Since no hurry for the dead to go anywhere and no reason anyway –
And do you remember that you and I started to urge it on, annoy it,
As though this horse from its own philosophical perspective,
Was doing something wrong?

---

[232] Georgy Ivanovich Chulkov, 1879-1939, Russian symbolist poet, creator of the concept of Mystical Anarchism. He was a close associate of the Mereshkovskys.
[233] Grigori Alekseevich Rachinsky, 1859-1939, philosopher, president of the Moscow Religious-Philosophical Society, a publisher of the works of Vl. Solovyov. He was part of the symbolist group and close to Bely. He was also arrested several times and incarcerated for his religious publications.
[234] Mstislav Aleksandrovich Tzyavlosky, 1883-1947, famous for his biographies and the publication of the writings of A.S. Pushkin and Leo Tolstoy.

> But for this horse the entire event was impersonal, and it did not care
> That the lifeless load carried on the catafalque was
> The famous writer and our friend.
> She pulled the wagon as a duty, just as she would any other,
> As she does every day.

The coffin arrived at the hall of the Union of Soviet Writers on Vorovsky St. at about 5 PM, where a civil requiem and a solemn farewell was planned. Efim Vikhrev[235] recorded the event in his diary:

> The civil requiem for Andrei Bely was held at the former location of the organizing committee, the hell where party purges were conducted, A former Gothic-style Masonic Hall, and somewhat identifiable with Andrei Bely.
>
> They carried the heavy oak casket into the hall. When they placed it on the stage, the boards of the stage creaked with a sound resembling some human. The cluster of lilacs on the top of the coffin were turning orange from the winter cold. They lifted the lid and all gazed at the beautiful, intelligent and marble face, and it seemed that purpose was written all over it. Two silver strands lay on his immense forehead.

The orchestra consisted of a stringed quartet and were located in an adjoining room, and they played disconsolately. People gathered: writers, anthroposophists, friends, old acquaintances and several whom Bely never personally knew. Pasternak, one of the members of the funeral arrangement committee, was depressed because of the few who attended relative to Bely's popularity. Pilnyak was also disappointed with the attendance.

Vikhrev also mourned the dearth participation, as he later recorded:

[235] Efim Feodorovich Vikhrev, 1901-1935, Soviet author, journalist, and poet, and compiler of several volume on Palekh miniatures.

> I arrived when the coffin was en route to the hall from his apartment. At the entrance were some ladies. Semeon Fomin,[236] Ezersky.[237] And no one else. Then Victorin Popov arrived.[238] We went with him to greet the carriage. Those few who accompanied the procession also arrived: Pilnyak, Pasternak, Klichkov,[239] Sannikov. Much conversation in lobby. Several I expected did not show.

Even then, Zaitzev counted a total of 600 attending.

An honor guard of some distinguished person in the literature field rotated at the head of the casket every 5 minutes. As the Soviet newspapers noted, there stood Veresaev,[240] Gladkov, Leonov,[241] Pilnyak, Lidin,[242] Pasternak, Kamensky,[243] Prishvin, Evdokimov,[244] Inber,[245] Sannikov, Milashevsky,[246] Spassky,[247] Mandelshtam, Petrovsky,[248] Chulkov, Nilender, and several others. Zaitzev handled the rotation of the honor guards.

---

236 Semeon Fomich Fomin, 1903-1936, a Chuvash poet, novelist and literature translator. He was also a member of the Union of Soviet Writers.

237 Mili Vikentyevich Ezersky, 1891-1976, Ukrainian and Soviet author of popular historical fiction.

238 Victorin Arkadyevich Popov, 1900-1949, Soviet author dealing with socialist development in the USSR.

239 Sergei Antonovich Klichkov, 1889-1937, Russian and Soviet popular fiction writer and translator of Georgian literature into Russian. He was arrested on spurious charges, and sentenced and executed on October 8, 1937.

240 Vikenti Vikentyevich Veresaev, born Smidovich, 1867-1945, Russian writer and medical doctor, originally of Polish descent.

241 Leonid Maxsimovich Leonov, 1899-1994, Russian Soviet writer, a master of Soviet realism, and then in his later years he wrote of Christian morality in the tradition of Feodor Dostoyevsky.

242 Vladimir Germanovich Lidin, 1894-1979, Russian Soviet writer and bibliophile.

243 Vasili Vasilyevich Kamensky, 1884-1961, Russian futurist poet and playwright, and an aviator.

244 Ivan Vasilyevich Evdokimov, 1887-1941, Russian Soviet writer and dramatist.

245 Vera Mikhailovna Inber, 1890-1972, Russian Soviet poet and prose writer and journalist.

246 Vladimir Alekseevich Milashevsky, 1893-1976, Soviet artist and painter.

247 Sergei Dmitrievich Spassky, 1898-1956, Soviet poet and novelist, dramatist, literary critic. In 1951, he was for writing anti-Soviet propaganda and was committed to a concentration camp until 1954.

248 One of the initial members of the Argonauts and he later worked at the magazine *Musaget.*

In addition to writers, artists attended, a total of about 20, and some of them making a sketch of Bely in his coffin. This struck some of Bely's associates as unnecessary and inappropriate. The majority of the visitors arrived that evening of January 9, but the amount on the following morning was considerable less. The viewing lasted 5 hours, until 10 PM, and then the hall was closed. A few artists stayed the entire night, leaving at 6 AM the next morning. The sculptor S.D. Merkulov, a specialist in constructing post-mortem masks, made one of Bely's face and hands.

Viewing continue the next day, April 10. At 1:30 PM, at the sound of the funeral march the lid was closed on the coffin and it was taken out of the hall. Among those who carried the coffin were Pasternak, Pilnyak, Sannikov, Spassky, Grossman,[249] Zaitzev, and others. The casket was placed on a catafalque pulled by a horse harnessed to it and the funeral procession began its long route from the Writer's Hall to Donskoi Monastery, about 7 miles away, where the crematorium was located. Several hundred people left the hall following the coffin, but many left along the route due to the distance to the monastery. Claudia Nikolaievna along with her aunt, E.A. Korolkova, walked the entire distance.

(Interesting that the Church of St Seraphim of Sarov at the Donskoi Monastery was converted by the Soviet administration into a crematorium and he was Bely's most beloved saint, and having made a pilgrimage to his monastery in early years.)

They reached the crematorium at 3 PM, and gathered inside the main assembly – where ecclesiastical services were earlier held – and there the coffin was opened. Nina Gagen-Torn, who accompanied the procession recorded the event as the lid of the coffin was removed:

> For the final time they walked up and bid farewell. They bent over to the flowers. Arranged them and rearranged them. The music was very quiet.

[249] Leonid Petrovich Grossman, 1888-1965, Russian Soviet writer and language professor.

The orchestra played one of Frederic Chopin's *Preludes*. Claudia Nikolaievna whispered something into Bely's ear, and then the coffin was closed and moved through the doors to the area of the crematorium where the oven was located. According to the Soviet newspaper *Pravda*, Andrei Bely's body was cremated at 3:30 PM, that afternoon, April 10, 1934.

Now they had to find an appropriate place at the cemetery at the Novo-Devichi Convent to bury Bely's remains, since this location was already decided by the organizing committee of the Writer's Union, or most likely, by a decision of even higher authority in Soviet administration. (Due to the scarce available room for cemetery plots in central Moscow, only individuals of exceptional merit, significant for the nation, or government leaders, were allowed to be interred at the Novo-Devichi Convent.) Initially the widow Claudia and her friends wanted to bury the urn with Bely's remains alongside Nikolai Gogol, who was brought there from the Danilov Monastery in 1931. But no room was available in that area. There was also some room available in an area reserved by the Moscow Artistic and Theatrical Group. Pilnyak had discussions with V.I. Nemirovich-Dachenko, the theater director, on January 14, but with no success.

The cemetery administration located a place in a new section of the cemetery across the wall from the old section and convent: Section 3, Plot 60. Claudia was not upset over the new location and recorded the following:

> His grave is located in such a sunny place. Much light and air. We wanted to bury him near Gogol, but that area is completely occupied. Anyway, it is damp there and dark and right under the wall. But here he is right in the sun, and which he liked so much.

On January 16, the urn with the remains of Bely were given to his widow Claudia Nikolaievna. She went to the crematorium to retrieve it personally. The internment of the urn was on January 18, at 2 PM. The only people present at the internment were

Claudia, her sister E.N. Kezelman, and Bely's most devoted friend, P.N. Zaitzev. A secondary and not a very reliable source mentions additional people attending: Petrovsky, Sannikov, N. Bruni,[250] G. Chulkov, Leonid Grossman and Nadezhda Pavlovich.[251] But this may have been published for propaganda purposes. L.M. Alpatov-Prishvin[252] took a photograph of the grave for the family's sake.

Valeri Brusov is buried just a short walk away.

[250] Nikolai Aleksandrovich Bruni, 1956-1935, Russia artist.

[251] Nadezhda Aleksandrovna Pavlovich, 1895-1980, Russian poet.

[252] Lev Mikhailovich, 1906-1957, son of the above mentioned M.M. Prishvin, a popular fiction writer of his era who wrote under the pseudonym of Alpatov.

# THE DEATH OF ANDREI BELY

# PART 2

It is important to note that the illness and death of Andrei Bely is as much a medical and physiological matter as much as a psychological matter, and for us what is interesting are the social and political effects on his health.

During autumn of 1933, Bely had to make arrangements to move the third volume of his memoirs, *Between the Two Revolutions*, from the State Publishing House, which was slow in the release of the book, to the Writer's Publishing House in Petersburg. However such interventions did not progress in comparison with Bely's experiences connected with the preparation for publication of his research, *The Mastery of Gogol*, and the 2nd volume of his memoirs, *Beginning of the Century*, at the State Publishing House.

Leaving for Koktebel in May 1933, Bely requested friends, and first of all Zaitzev, to keep in touch with the publisher on the progress of the books and inform him of what was occurring. Zaitzev naturally agreed to take the role of intermediary and made preparations to regularly write to Bely about his visits to the State Publishing House and of the situation. Bely was grateful for his accommodation and so thanked him in a letter of June 19,

1933. What did agitate Bely was the schedule for the release of the 2 books, and the corrections that they seemed necessary to make on the texts. Even more than that, what especially upset Bely was the person who was selected by the publisher to write the prologue of both books: Lev Borisovich Kamenev.

Kamenev was a communist revolutionary and a prominent Soviet politician, in addition to being Leo Trotsky's brother-in-law. He was one of the initial members of the Politburo and in the years 1923-1924, the last year of Vladimir Lenin's life, was acting premier of the USSR. After Lenin's death, Kamenev opposed many of Joseph Stalin's policies and so was removed in January 1926, from all of his posts in the Soviet government. It was not until June 1928, that Kamenev had some of his authority restored to him. In May 1932, he was assigned as director of the publishing house, *Academia*, but this only lasted until October when he was exiled, but then returned to assume responsibilities again at the beginning of April 1933, and which post he held until he was expelled from the Communist Party and arrested in December 1934. Kamenev was executed on August 25, 1936, as part of Joseph Stalin's great purge.

This short biography is provided so the reader can understand the anxiety or even repulsion on the part of Bely of such a person composing the prologue to his 2 books, he being a devoutly religious individual and a dedicated anthroposophist, while Kamenev – an atheist and communist party ideologist with no sense of compassion. Even with such a low level position as a director of some low level enterprise, Kamenev's influence was still immense. It was also Kamenev who authored the prologue to the previously mentioned *Sixteenth Year* collection of articles. As a result Kamenev's prologue to Bely's books was very important: it would either open the door, or close the door, to Bely's future involvement and success in Soviet literature.

Bely's internal turbulence was fully shared by his friends. Zaitzev wrote to Bely in Koktebel on June 14, 1933.

> Kamenev's prologue is already composed and included in the book *The Mastery of Gogol.* I went there again yesterday. They

promised to give me a copy of the text of the prologue for me to send to you.

Entrusting Zaitzev to deal in its entirety with the editing and publication of his books, Bely nonetheless wanted to become familiar with the prologue to *The Mastery of Gogol*, and so sent him a letter to hurry and forward him a copy. However a copy never did reach Koktebel. Zaitzev responded in a letter of June 18, explaining that this was the fault of the publisher. As he wrote:

> Forgive me, I am not sending the prologue. Somehow they have misplaced the second – the other controlled – copy and they cannot seem to find it to give to me. They promised. For some reason I feel they will do what they promised after your return.
>
> The prologue is written favorably. The author recognizes the great worthiness of the book and its necessity and value, especially for Soviet readers who are involved in writing fiction. In general the prologue is acceptable considering the sequence of obstacles.
>
> So you, dear Boris Nikolaievich, do not be upset. Several of our friends have read it, and they all found it to be acceptable. Nakoryakov[253] is saying the same.

Sannikov wrote to Zaitzev regarding the matter:

> Only yesterday I brought up the question about the prologue to *Beginning of the Century*. L.B. Kamenev wrote the prologue but it is very piercing. It needs to be ameliorated. I had to talk to the person in charge and then they gave the article back to L.B. to softened the text, and so he did something with it, corrected it, changed some of it. Today or tomorrow they will show it to me, how it appears at present. First *The Mastery of Gogol* will be released. Its prologue is significantly better than

[253] Nikolai Nikandrovich Nakoryakov, 1881-1970, Soviet book publisher, member of the Union of Soviet Writers, editor of the Soviet Encyclopedia.

> the one in *Beginning of the Century*. It is possible that both books will be released in time for the congress, scheduled for September 10th to the 20th.

Both Zaitzev's and Sannikov's intent was for Bely to relax, knowing the prologue to both of his books was reviewed by them, but the manner that the correspondence reads, the prologue to *The Mastery of Gogol* is acceptable only when compared to the horrible prologue to *Beginning of the Century*. In conclusion, neither one of Kamenev's commentaries could be considered positive, and none of his Moscow friends were in any hurry to provide a copy of the prologues to Bely. They were obviously afraid that once reading them, it would ruin his vacation, and so they wanted to postpone the unpleasant news until his return from Koktebel.

Bely's stroke, as mentioned above, restrained him in Crimea until the end of July, and once returning to Moscow, medical attention was more of a necessity for him than to intervene in the publication of his books. According to Bely's diary, Kamenev's prologue to *The Mastery of Gogol* was not provided to him until October 20, when Zaitzev finally got a copy of it from the publisher. Attending that evening were also Paolo Iashvilli and Boris Pasternak, whom Bely considered his friends. After reading it, and in their presence, Bely acknowledged the article to be properly written and acceptable to him.

Other archival information indicates that Zaitzev received a copy of the prologue considerably earlier, maybe several months prior, and did not want to worsen Bely's illness with its negative content. Waiting for a good opportunity to present it to Bely, the visit of Iashvilli and Pasternak provided an ideal setting, and so Bely read it in their presence. It was obvious he had no choice but to not disappoint his 2 fellow poets with a criticism of the prologue, and especially with both of them important members of the Union of Soviet Writers.

The following is a section of Kamenev's evaluation of *The Mastery of Gogol*:

> The conclusion is that even the most liberal of all literary tribunals have no choice except to sentence the author to the most severe of literary capital punishment. Bely has prepared for himself this unpleasant fate exclusively because presently during the epoch of the division of the atom and synthetic rubber, he continues to utilize obsolete methods of alchemy, meaning that he has disdained the most valuable discovery yet attained – dialectic materialism.

With the prologue to *Beginning of the Century*, the matter evolved into something more complex. Bely never read an advanced copy, but only read it when the initial copies of the book came off the printing press. It was not until November 23, 1933, that Bely acquired a copy of *Beginning of the Century* and read the prologue. Of course it had a depressing effect.

Kamenev presented his conclusion beginning right at the first paragraphs of the prologue:

> A tragic-comic occurrence affected the author Andrei Bely during the years 1900-1905. It was comical if we look at it from one side, and tragic from the point of view of what the author himself has experienced. This tragicomedy consists in that during these years he sincerely considered himself a participant and one of the guides of the massive cultural-historical movement, a writer who indeed got lost and wandered this entire period through the most disheveled backyards of history, culture and literature. This is the tragicomedy that Bely has presently composed in his book *Beginning of the Century*.
>
> It reflects his literary bankruptcy, conceptual chaos and a mental rambling through the backyards of culture. He seems to be deaf to the accomplishment of the revolution and just doomed himself to oblivion in the process.

It is apparent as to why Zaitzev hid the prologues from Bely as long as he did, perhaps several months. From another aspect, Bely probably expected such from Kamenev, but there was not anything that Bely could do, since the publication of his books was in the hands of the Soviet publisher. If there was a primary reason for Kamenev to discredit and destroy Bely in this manner, it can be ascertained from later conversations of Kamenev with other writers who were likewise discredited. It was because Bely was an anthroposophist. The content of the book meant nothing to Kamenev, if he even read it. The fact was that Bely held anthroposophist convictions and Kamenev as a ingrained atheist and dialectic materialist had to ruin him.

To protect his own reputation, Boris Pasternak dissociated himself from Bely immediately after the release of *The Mastery of Gogol.*

The attempt of friends and associates to calm Bely provided no results. His reaction was not only predicted, but more painful than they suspected. The trauma caused by Kamenev worsened Bely's medical condition and psychologically devastated him. Bely told his wife:

> The prologue to *Beginning of the Century* has paralyzed me. I could not even take it as a joke, but now it has made a joke out of me. How can I ever show my face at the State Publishing House? I cannot bear having to recall the text of the prologue. All I can do is return home as a devastated person, lie on my sofa and wrap myself in a blanket. I will never know why Kamenev hurt me this way.

Claudia shared her husband's grief and cried incessantly. She likewise wondered why this occurred, and viewed it as a malicious joke. Bely related to his friend Sannikov on November 28:

> Kamenev dug my grave for me and buried me.

Just a few days later on December 4, Bely had a second stroke and which for the most part incapacitated him.

Interesting that in time the situation of Kamenev's prologue and Bely's reaction would grow with the inclusion of fictional events and turn into a myth. One of these was told by Nadezhda

Yakovlevna Mandelstam[254] to her friend Emma Gregorevna Gerstein,[255] and who recorded it in her memoirs:

> Andrei Bely died. A turbulent Nadya turbulently related to me what particularly led him to have this stroke and his death. As soon as his book of memoirs was released with the prologue of L.B. Kamenev, who called all of the literary activity of Andrei Bely a tragic-farce played in the backyards of history, then Andrei Bely went and bought all the copies of his book available and tore the prologue out of it. He went from one bookstore to another until he had his next stroke, and this one killed him.

The first half of the narrative does contain the truth of the matter; the second half is purely myth or legend built around Bely who developed a bigger than life reputation.

All of the above recorded history of Kamenev's prologue that led Bely to the grave summons some perplexity. The reoccurring question again surfaces: why would Bely's reaction, and he being a famous polemicist tempered in literary campaigns and fully capable of enduring attacks by Soviet critics, cause not just a minor illness, but an illness of such severity? Why was Bely not able, just as were P.N. Zaitzev and others of his Moscow friends, to perceive that this horrible prologue was just a disguise implemented regularly that was necessary to secure the book's public distribution, as an unavoidable evil that would serve in the end as a benefit? Zaitzev compiled the logic of a sound mind in a letter to Ms L.B. Kalikina:

> The prologue if written by another critic and editor could have been worse and more irreconcilable. They told me this at the State Publishing House, when I pointed out to them last summer that such a prologue should not be allowed. But

---

[254] The wife of poet Osip Mandelstam.

[255] Soviet author, also a member of Union of Soviet Writers, 1903-2002.

> without a prologue of this type the State Publishing House could not release the book, and so it would never have been released. Their hands were tied in the matter.

Noticeable was that these specific rules of the games were solidly installed in the relations between writers, the publisher and Soviet authority. So with the understanding in January 1934, a Warsaw, Poland, newspaper reacted to the inclusion of Kamenev's prologue in *Beginning of the Century*, in an article titled *In Memory of Andrei Bely*:

> Not long before the death of Andrei Bely the volume of his memoirs, *Beginning of the Century*, was issued. The book encompasses the years 1900-1905 while in Moscow and Petersburg. The pages consist of recollections of a series of personages whom Andrei Bely encountered, and who for the most part knew him at the time as Boris Nikolaievich Bugaev. One recollection is 20 pages long. The memoirs are introduced by a prologue by Kamenev who saw the primary value in the book that it serves as though proof of the helplessness, historical impotence, and spiritual handicap of an entire strata of pre-Revolutionary intelligentsia.
>
> This kind of prologue is an object absolutely necessary in the USSR. The majority of valuable memoirs would not have been released if they were not accompanied by a party-line prologue or notation.

However Bely for some reason did not want to comply with such an argument so obviously reasonable, although he knew about the practice of such prologues, and he should have been happy that his books saw the light regardless.

It is self-deceiving to blame the extremely sickening reaction of Bely on Kamenev's prologue. However a series of facts permits if not the matter to be completely explained, at least to understanding some of Bely's reaction. To do this we need to look at the situation in the context of the approaching First Congress of Soviet Writers and turn our attention to the preliminary arrangements, the retirement of Gronski – Bely's promoter, and the increase of the influence of Gorki – Bely's antagonist.

In 1933, Kamenev was one of those on whom Gorki bet and so assigned him an important role in the preparation of the First Congress of Soviet Writers, and this began Kamenev's flight toward a high career (although short lived). Gorki nourished the thought of assigning Kamenev the position of chief lecturer at the Congress, and so expended all effort and did his best to materialize it. So at the beginning of August 1933, Gorki wrote a letter to Joseph Stalin, where he unambiguously proposes this idea to him:

> Dear Joseph Vissarionovich:
>
> With excitement did I notice the article of L. Kamenev in Pravda, titled *Socialism in one Country and the Economics of the USSR*, published July 31, 1933. If we were to postpone the Congress, then perhaps could we assign him the position of lecturer?

Now Bely who felt he would be the primary lecturer at the First Congress realized that he was usurped by Kamenev through the manipulation of Gorki, and this was a second blow to Bely by Kamenev, the first being the prologue. Although Bely was unaware of Gorki's letter to Marshall Stalin, news however quickly circulated of the change in itinerary with Kamenev now taking such a leading role.

Under such circumstances Bely's painful reaction to Kamenev's prologue to *Beginning of the Century* was further provoked and aggravated by Kamenev's ascendance at the Writer's Congress simultaneous with Gorki removing Bely from the scene. Essentially both agents of Soviet authority and personal advancement did what they could to publicly discredit Bely as a symbolist writer to the Writer's Congress. The fact that *Beginning of the Century* was published and released was insufficient to redeem the damage done by Kamenev and Gorki. Bely now concluded that he had to say good-bye to any ambitions in regard to acceptance as a writer by Soviet literary censurers and any plans for participation at the first Writer's Congress. Now the reason for Bely's loss of health becomes more understandable.

In the long run, Bely's fears were insubstantial, just as were the hopes of Kamenev. If Bely did not take the matter so seriously, as with other unconventional writers of the era, he may have survived and lived beyond the first Writer's Congress and perhaps have been participant in others and so continue to write and be published. (After Bely's death Kamenev became director of the Pushkin House and Institute of World Literature. However as mentioned above, Kamenev was arrested, sentenced and then executed on August 25, 1936.)

Some writers associated with Bely attributed his illness to the arrest and incarceration of anthroposophists. Mikhail Osorgin[256] was familiar with the dramatic events that occurred in Bely's life and those who encircled him in 1931. This pertained to the arrest of Moscow anthroposophists and Bely's intervention into the release of Claudia Nikolaievna and her first husband P.N. Vasilyev from prison. Osorgin wrote in a Paris newspaper:

> Bely resided in destitution during his final years, he participated little in general literary life. They tolerated him, but only because the balance of the anthroposophist environment was broken apart and scattered. But he was only successful enough to save hardly a few of them – those with whom he had personal ties – from persecution, prison and exile.
>
> We really do not know what drove Bely into the grave. There was no news of his illness, and he was not that old, just 53 years of age.

Bely's friend Zaitzev was convinced that Bely's health was aggravated by the arrest of anthroposophists in 1931, culminating in a stroke after the events of a political nature causing additional

[256] Mikhail Andreevich Osorgin, 1878-1942, Russian Soviet writer and journalist. He was incarceration several times for his non-conformist views and eventually immigrated to Europe in 1922. He was residing in Paris when Bely died.

stress and pressure. Spassky likewise noticed a decline in Bely's health beginning in spring of 1933.

During his final summer at Koktebel, Bely was seriously occupied and worrying over a long list of problems that were a negative influence on his psychological state and health. There were many and various items that agitated him: the fate of his anthroposophist friends arrested in 1931, his personal homelessness, the complexity surrounding the publication of his books submitted to the State Publishing House of Fictional Literature, and of course the preparations for the first congress of Soviet writers.

Bely's removal from participation at the future Writer's Congress provides another perspective for the cause of his stroke.

After the successful conference in autumn 1932, of the first plenum of the Organizing Committee of the Union of Soviet Writers, Bely, as he indicated in his diary and letters, wanted to make a presentation at the First Congress of Writers, to be the primary lecturer. He supposed this would guarantee him, a symbolist and anthroposophist, entrance into the mainstream of Soviet literature and allow him access to social and political and other privileges. Above all of this, Bely has been dreaming for a long time of becoming if not the single, then at least one of the developers of a different concept of Socialist realism in literature, and it was particularly this task that he had to achieve at the congress.

The political situation, as it initially seemed to Bely, would assist in the materialization of his dream. Bely portrayed himself as a loyal subject of the Soviet state in his address at the 1932 plenum, and it became a trump for the officials in their reports of the successes of Soviet polity in the region of literature. In his report to Joseph Stalin and Lazar Kaganovich, Ivan Gronski[257] stated:

[257] Ivan Mikhailovich Gronski, 1894-1985, a Soviet social activist, journalist and book editor. He was eventually arrested in 1938 by Soviet police and spent the next 16 years in prison.

> Noticing at the first plenum a turnaround of the intents of writers and toward the side of Soviet authority, and specifically Andrei Bely, M.M. Prishvin,[258] Panteleimon Romanov,[259] Ryurik Ivnev,[260] Boris Pilnyak, some Ukrainian writers and others, it seems this is more significant than we initially supposed.

Bely with satisfaction even started to notice some gratitude toward him from the side of the Soviet literary and political leadership. It seemed to him that a close association with Ivan Gronski would be important. He was a solid party activist, a member of the governing commission on the liquidation of the RAPP,[261] the responsible editor of the newspaper *Izvestia* and the magazine *New World*, and in May 1932, become the president of the Organizing Committee of the Union of Soviet Writers. It was particularly the Organizing Committee that was supposed to guide the literary life of the country, and during the pre-congress period it was to prepare the agenda of the congress of writers and to develop – and again pertaining to the congress – the definition of socialist realism.

All of this inspired Bely, firmly taking the course for cooperation with Soviet authority – optimism. What did embitter him was that the agenda scheduled the congress initially for the beginning of May 1933, and then rescheduled it for June 20, which was particularly during the period that Bely already scheduled for his vacation to Koktebel and stay at the Writer's Guesthouse. However once arriving in Koktebel Bely realized that the weather was not the best and that the accommodations likewise were less than he expected. He then thought about terminating his vacation

---

[258] Mikhail Mikhailovich Prishvin, 1873-1954, Russia and Soviet writer.

[259] Panteleinon Sergeevich Romanov, 1884-1938, Russian Soviet writer, very popular, but his books were taken out of circulation due to their parody of the Soviet socialist system.

[260] Ryurik Ivnev, born Mikhail Aleksandrovich Kovalyov, 1891-1981, Russian Soviet poet and novelist.

[261] Russian Association of Proletariat Writers, originally established to persecute non-socialist writers and censure literature that failed to meet Soviet ideological requirements. It was disbanded in April 1932, and replaced by the Union of Soviet Writers.

and returning to Moscow. The self-deception Bely posed on himself to make such a radical decision consisted in that he felt he would be an active participant in the work of the congress. But the disruption with his vacation was not necessary in the end. On May 29, 1933, Bely received a letter from G.A. Sannikov with the latest news from Moscow, that the congress of writers was postponed to September. This was significant for Bely. Zaitzev likewise informed Bely of this in a letter of June 2, but only that it would be held sometime in autumn and a date was not yet scheduled.

The change in the date for the congress initially overjoyed Bely, and then he immediately responded to Sannikov in a letter on June 3:

> I am very happy that the congress is postponed and since I have much to write and it seems to me that it would have been out of place at such an early date anyway, and that it was the effort of I.M. [Gronski] to postpone it. I really believe I.M., his tactfulness. And other than this, I am now able to attend the congress, although just as a silent spectator. Much depends on him, and it would be better to postpone it 7 times than to summon it without sufficient preparation.

Let's suppose from Bely's perspective that the single reason for his joy was the revelation of his definite presence at the congress. If he was just recently prepared for a disruption of his vacation for the sake of participation in the congress, then the possibility materialized for him to rest and later participate in such a politically important event.

As far as the balance is concerned Bely's arguments seem to be plainly dreamed up. For the meanwhile he did not know anything about the course of events for the congress preparation and justified his situation with statements like, "It seems to me," and, "I really believe." But the situation for the postponement to autumn was not up to Gronski, but was connected to his political collapse, his estrangement from the position of president of the Organizing Committee. Even though the decision had been made by superior officials back in May, it was not until August that it was announced.

Bely quickly received details of what was occurring in Moscow in a letter from F.B. Gladkov,[262] dated June 3, 1933.

> In literature there are changes. Even though Gronski remains president of the Organizing Committee before the congress, but this is the case in reality. At the head is now Fadeev[263] with his group. Gronski lost sight of the congress' intentions and ruined the entire effort. And what possibilities could have been achieved. He never created a group to surround him, but just played with individual personalities. For 2 days straight he absent-mindedly had conversations with me and could not at all understand my comments regarding the direction of his course. But now the RAPP is in a new form. The congress will be held in September. Until then a new arrangement of officials will occur.

Having received this information from Gladkov in an unambiguous form, Bely was now scared and realized this was no joke. He bitter wept over the termination of Gronski and the fate of the congress. Bely wrote back to Gladkov:

> I know that for many it was a necessity to estrange I.M. [Gronski] and not because he understood in simple terms the task of the Union of Soviet Writers, but because he was fervent, truthful, and incorruptibly honest. And I am very, very sorrowful. In addition to this, why should some not believe that certain people faithful to the socialist future and having right motives in their soul will provide the necessary atmosphere to the congress?

---

[262] Feodor Vasilyevich Gladkov, 1883-1958, Soviet writer promoting socialist realism. He was at the top of recognized Soviet writers during this era.

[263] Aleksandr Aleksandrovich Fadeev, 1901-1956, Soviet writer and socialist activist, 1934-1939 vice-president of the Union of Soviet Writers. He committed suicide on May 13, 1956, due to his alcoholism.

These "certain people" to whom Bely referred were those "individual personalities" that Gladkov said Gronski "just played with." But Bely felt he was one of these "individual personalities." Bely ascertained the situation with the perspective that now with the installation of another candidate in the role of the head of Soviet writers, his personal future with the Union was very gloomy, and Bely views Gronski as well as himself as sacrifices of the RAPP, suffering on behalf of humanity, justice and belief in the socialist future.

In a practical manner Bely identified his fate with the fate of Gronski, now fallen from grace, and indicated that both are on the same plain in terms of a departure from the Union. Bely concluded the above letter to Gladkov with the following passage:

> In fear do I draw a picture of myself at the congress: to attend or not to attend, to speak or not to speak, to participate or just be a spectator. The terminal conclusion is that it is best if I am absent.

Bely's fears, although expressed in somewhat an exalted form, cannot be called completely premeditated, although he considered Gronski to be his benefactor. But parallel with the speedy fall of Gronski's influence was the proportional speed of the increase of Maxim Gorki's influence, and whom Bely vehemently considered his critic and malevolent enemy. From his initial nominal position of president of the Organizing Committee, Gorki reverted into a genuine politician, practically single-handedly and authoritatively directing the preparation of the congress. This scared Bely. Gorki started to install his own people in key posts, and first of all the former officials of the RAPP, those who worked earlier from a position that had posed a danger to Bely due to his symbolist style of composition.

Gorki openly demonstrated his negative attitude toward Bely in 1933, in the article, *Regarding Prose*, published in the first edition of *Sixteenth Year,* a collection of miscellaneous compositions by various Soviet authors. In this article Gorki promoted a simplicity and clarity of the language to be used in Soviet fiction. The article stated:

> The Soviet reader has no need of the superficiality of cheap embellishments. He does not need the refined gaudiness of verbal pictures... In the person of Andrei Bely we have a writer who is completely deprived of any sense of responsibility toward the reader.

Over the course of the article, Gorki selected Bely's novel *Masks* as an excellent example of how literature is being soiled with verbose verbal garbage. Similar attacks were made against Bely, but not so much of a literary character, as much as political. He hoped for the support from the circle that was not literary, but from party officials. Bely recorded the following in his diary in August 1933, naively imagining his actual importance in the area of Soviet literature and imagining foolish premonitions:

> A series of communist activists stands directly or indirectly for my defense from the attacks of Gorki. These are, from what I heard, Gronski, Stetzkii,[264] and Kaganovich, and some others. In short, I encounter support and attention from party circles.
>
> Even then, Gorki and Averbakh[265] ridicule me.

Bely lived this period of his life, the spring and summer of 1933, under a self-imposed duress imagining how and when Gorki and his confederates will strike their next blow against him, and then wondering if his advocates will defend and deliver him. So Bely was here living with an unjustifiable premonition of impending danger. The pressing alarm summoned by the reassignments of officials prior to the congress, the termination of Gronski, and the

---

[264] Aleksei Ivanovich Stetzkii, 1896-1938, Communist party member and socialist activist, and magazine editor. Executed by a firing squad on August 1, 1938, on charges of counter-revolutionary activities.

[265] Leopold Leonidovich Averbakh, 1903-1937, literary critic, member of Union of Soviet Writers, magazine editor. Arrested and executed during Joseph Stalin's Great Purge on August 14, 1937.

activity of Gorki, promoted for the most part the development of Bely's fatal illness. At least it was this, as Bely himself complained what had occurred to him, recording it in his diary over the months August and September 1933:

> If my sincere break from working in a Soviet manner and writing with political goals will ahead of me incur malicious ridicule, clandestine hate and "dagger eyes," I just as well lie down and die. At least this way I can exit the literary field. No matter how much they may support me, they still have the capacity to destroy me with their intrigues and effectively and unexpectedly.

However Bely was not yet ready to lie down or die, or exit from the literary field. In order to effectively oppose the intrigues he realized it was necessary to take a stand and restore his status. In fact, at the end of August and beginning of September Bely claimed he felt better and even imagined himself completely recovered, like the recharge on a dead battery. So at the beginning of September, as soon as Bely felt somewhat a recovery from his aneurysm, he returned to recording items in his diary, responding to correspondence, reading, drawing, accepting social invitations, inviting guests to his residence, listening to music, and even gained the strength to once attend the Bolshoi Theater.

Bely attempted to not withdraw from a social life or especially from his activity at the threshold of the congress of the Union of Soviet Writers now in preparation. Ms Krasilschik recollected that in September Bely expressed a strong desire to reenter society, to show himself at the state-run book publishing house in Moscow, but Claudia restrained him. This would not be without some danger to Bely's health, since any type of disturbance to his head could trigger the rupture of the aneurysm and kill him. It was already impossible during the months of October and November to stop him, although each time Bely would show himself in public, he would return home with severe pain in his head.

Overcoming his weakness and the intense pain in his head, Bely aspired to return to writing, although this particular type of activity was strictly proscribed to him by doctors. But at the first opportunity he began to plan his intents for future compositions. Claudia recorded this in her memoirs:

> During spring and summer of 1933, Andrei Bely spoke on several occasions about a piece of literature he would compose different from his previous types. He would write a novel in the traditional manner. In one of the illustrated magazines he read about a planned construction of a railway through the Mamison Pass,[266] and he decided to use the construction of this road through this region as the theme of his novel: Mamison Pass–Shovi[267]–Gori.[268]

On September 11, 1933, Bely noted in his diary:

> I clearly feel better after drinking some alcoholic beverage. Again I feel an active movement of the germs in my brain. I would like, if my health permits, to write an article on the theme of Socialist Reality. It would have to be dictated to some kind person, as it is too exhausting for me to write it on my own.

However Bely's health worsened and he was not able to even start of either of the above projects, however he did attempt to continue on his memoirs. This would be a 4th volume and Bely's intent was to make it a 2nd part of the last volume, and he worked on it heroically. Claudia noted in her memoirs:

> September 22. He started work on the 2nd part of the 3rd volume of his recollections. It is noticeable that he tires quickly.

---

[266] A high mountain pass between Russia and Georgia through the Caucasus Mountain range, located at about 9,000 ft elevation.
[267] A village and health resort along the Kutaisi-Alpana-Mamison Pass in Georgia, near the border with Russia.
[268] A city in central Georgia. The highway from Shovi to Tbilisi passes through Gori.

Zaitzev likewise complained about Bely as he recorded in his memoirs:

> What poor shape he is in! I fear for him. He has sclerosis, insomnia, and nightmares every night. Professor Tarasevich forbids him to smoke, drink tea, occupy himself, or even think. But he incessantly thinks about a fourth volume of recollections. It will be so difficult, very difficult for him to write this fourth volume! And not only because the author is ill, but primarily because he has reached this certain period in his life where he stands in sharp contradiction with the concepts now prevailing in the contemporary era. Boris Nikolaievich has reached an impasse.
>
> The years he has planned to reflect in the fourth volume – 1912-1916 – are connected with his spiritual quests, with Steiner. To write about them and expect it to be published is foolishness, it will not happen. The censurer will never approve it, plus is it alien to the contemporary era and not needed by the wide circle of Soviet readers. He should delete all of this from his next volume of recollections. What can remain in the book from the experiences of these years is his journey to Africa, his effort in the literary world, and distinct moments of his life abroad. Even then this would be of little interest and undynamic. In addition, the other events of these years through 1921 are still not an easy theme.

The difficulty of the subject matter did not stop Bely. Even though he could not write himself, he would dictate the text to Claudia. But this did not last long, as Claudia noted in her memoirs:

> On the morning of December 2, he finished dictating the final section of the second chapter. That evening he explained how the third chapter would begin. That evening, between the 2nd and 3rd [of December] a new attack of pain started. On December 3, he did some editing on the text, but toward the evening of the following day even harder attacks of pain in his head occurred.

This final incident terminated any further work of Bely on his recollections or any literary composition at all, and for all practical purposes he was incapacitated from here on.

# POST-MORTEM

The first meeting of the Organizing Committee of the Union of Soviet Writers occurred on January 8, 1934, the same day as the death of Bely. The presiding minister of the meeting was Pavel Feodorovich Yudin, a Soviet ideologist and senior editor of the magazine, *Literary Critic*. The committee selected another committee to take charge of organizing Bely's funeral, the members selected were: Boris Pilnyak, Grigori Aleksandrovich Sannikov, Efim Feodorovich Vikhrev, Vladimir Vladimirovich Epmilov, Boris Pasternak, Nikolai Vasilyevich Krutikov and Nikolai Yakovlevich Simmen. What is obvious is that the selection of the funeral committee was perfunctory, held quickly as just a matter that had to be quickly disposed at the meeting and that the only 2 members that were Bely's associates were Pilnyak and Sannikov. They others were Soviet writers, magazine editors or book publishers, who either did not know Bely or else – as with Pasternak – were not favorably inclined toward him.

Pilnyak, Sannikov and Pasternak went to the clinic to view Bely's body at the morgue, and gave orders for his brain to be removed and taken to the Human Brain Institute. Then they visited Bely's wife Claudia Nikolaievna. Afterward they sat together to compose an obituary. By the end of the same day they also decided that Bely's body would lie in state at the hall of the Union of Soviet Writers on Vorovsky St., house 50, and he would have a civil memorial with assigned speakers and some musicians.

Then the body would be cremated and the ashes interred at the Novi-Devichi Monastery.

Based on the information available the text of the obituary was quickly composed and was delivered that evening to Grigori Evgenyevich Tzipin, for publication in the newspaper *Izvestia* (News). Tzipin was a member of the Organizing Committee so was easily available. During the decade of the 1930s Tzipin was a visible figure in literary circles and up to 1932 was the head of the newspaper, *Evening Moscow*, and now an associate of I.M. Gronski, the responsible editor of *Izvestia* and who specifically had to confirm the submission for publication in the newspaper.[269]

The next morning, January 9, the 3 met with Tzipin and discussed the obituary with him, and although he had some reservations about the text of the obituary and some resistance from other editors at *Izvestia*, he was able to single-handedly force the issue of its publication in that day's issue. Gronski was not very enthused about the test and initially demanded a revision, but Pilnyak's response was that time was insufficient to revise and resubmit. Gronski's next suggestion was to publish the obituary in another newspaper to wash his hands of the matters. But Tzipin's intervention at this point was sufficient for Gronski to approve the obituary, although reluctantly. Gronski's apprehension cannot be completely ascertained, apart from Bely being a high profile figure and at odds with the organizers of the Writer's Congress, since the obituary was typical of Soviet rewriting of history. Little of it was factual and a good part was just legend and embellishment that would mean little to the typical Soviet reader, while the balance was purely the creation of Soviet propaganda to portray Bely as something he was not – a Soviet writer, and to discredit his early compositions.

On January 9, 1934, the day following Bely's death, the official obituary as composed by Pilnyak, Sannikov and Pasternak was published in *Izvestia*.

---

[269] Later in 1934 Gronski was terminated from Izvestia and replaced by Tzipin, and then in 1936 Tzipin was promoted to director of Det-Izdat, the branch of children's books at the State Publishing House, but in 1937 he was terminated from that position and in 1938 was executed by a firing squad.

On January 8, at 12:30 PM, Andrei Bely died of arteriosclerosis. He was a significant writer of our age, whose name in history will stand alongside the names of not only Russian writers but also those known worldwide. The name of each genius is always associated with the creation of his particular school of composition. The creativity of Andrei Bely is not only an ingenious arrangement of Russian and world literature, it is the creation of an immense literary school. Bringing to mind Marcel Proust, who was a master in the world of creating first-person expressions, A.Bely more fully and perfectly developed this method of composition. James Joyce likewise was a pinnacle and master in contemporary European literature, but we must remember that James Joyce was a disciple of Andrei Bely. As pertaining to Russian literature, even though Bely was a younger representative of the school of symbolism, he created more than any of the older generation of this genre: Brusov, the Merezhkovskys, Sologub, and others. He outgrew his school and displayed a decisive influence on all the subsequent trends of Russian literature. We, the authors of these post-mortem lines about Bely, consider ourselves his students.

As with many ingenious people Andrei Bely was woven out of colossal contradictions. He was of a father who was a scholarly Russian mathematician. Bely concluded 2 faculties, studying philosophy and sociology, while his favorites were chemistry and mathematics, not to mention his no lesser love for music. As a result he displayed himself as belonging to that socialist and scholarly stratum that was not in correlation with the revolution. If we can add to this, that while he was abroad Andrei Bely studied under Rudolf Steiner and whose disciples became devolutionists. But we also need to particularly note that – and although it was not immediately after the October Revolution – Andrei Bely defined his political views in an active manner by taking a place on our side of the barricade, so the essence of his compositions must be attributed to the series of effects of the revolutionaries. This migration is defined by the entire substance of Andrei Bely. He was not a communist writer, but it was easier for him to present himself in the capacity of a socialist, than as something else. This activity, in his aesthetic and moral influence, was always nourished by influences of specifically knowledge. This aspect of his was not some daydream, but had as its terminal goal the liberation of a person from every type of inertia, instincts of self-advancement, inequality, coercion, and every type of barbarism.

From the initial days of the revolution, Andrei Bely heard its integrity, because Bely was always able to listen to history. From 1905, A.Bely was a worker in the socialist-democratic press. In 1914, A.Bely was a raging opponent of the enemies of the people. In 1917, before the October [Revolution], A.Bely together with A.Blok were organizers of the Scythians. Now after the October [Revolution], A.Bely became a worker and organizer of the Theatrical Department of the National Commissariat of Education, as a result a guide in the literary studies of Moscow Proletarian Culture, nourishing a series of proletarian writers. From 1921 to 1923, A.Bely was abroad, and while in Berlin surfaced as a literary watershed, defining and confirming Soviet literature and exposing anti-Soviet propaganda. He took our banner abroad.

The final ten years was dedicated to the effort of writing, reviewing the past in a series of recollections, working on Soviet themes, filling one volume after another. All in all, Andrei Bely wrote 47 volumes of composition. He led a very complex life. All of this is a field of greater memories of him, his studies, and a greater collection added to our Soviet culture.

The obituary is so typical of Soviet rewrite of history and any reader knowing anything about Bely would be able to recognize the propaganda in converting Bely into a socialist after his alleged acknowledgement of his mistakes of early eras. There is no evidence of Bely involved in exposing anti-Soviet literature in Europe, or promoting Soviet literature there, or any promotion of socialism, or being any type of raging enemy of the Soviet nation (since he was a pacifist for the most part), or the past 10 years of his life writing on Soviet themes (he was writing his memoirs and giving lectures on anthroposophy), or that he excelled Brusov and the other symbolist writers, or becoming a socialist activist after the October Revolution, or how socialism influenced Bely's writings in a positive manner, or how he added to Soviet culture. This is all typical Soviet redefinition of a person to have the reader view Bely in the perspective that the Soviet authorities want.

Another area of gross manipulation is the inclusion of 2 writers of whom Soviet readers have little or no knowledge: Proust and Joyce. Proust was next to impossible to find in Russian translation and was unknown in Soviet Russia for the most part, while Joyce was not even yet translated into Russian, and was only known through a handful articles and commentaries composed about him, and likewise not available to the general Russian reader. As a result the typical reader would have no idea of the intent of the mention, or how Bely excelled some French writer, or how he could have been a mentor to some Irish writer, or was in any manner identifiable with either.

The obituary's discredit of Rudolf Steiner essentially serves no purpose, as few of any in Russia were aware of the man and his teachings and religious philosophy, or of Bely's association with him, or how Steiner's disciples would have caused any type of devolution in any area or lowering any standard of any area.

Mentioning the Scythians is also another manner of manipulation. They were an extension of the original Argonauts of Bely's early days, and a philosophic discussion group, more of a legitimate form of the Religious-Philosophical Society, than any type of socialist organization.

From another respect, the 3 authors of the obituary had no other choice but to compose and publish a panegyric of this type, and for the sake of their own future in the Union of Soviet Writers and as participants in the impending Writer's Congress. Any disclosure of the truth and reality of Bely as a symbolist, an independent thinker persecuted by Soviet authorities for refusing to capitulate to their demands and so write on the theme of

Socialist Realism, a person with deep religious convictions – although not a strict Russian Orthodox but from the perspective of theosophy, a person more inclined to the superterrestrial than the mundane concepts of materialism, would pose a hazard to their own reputation and future as writers subject to Soviet censorship.

Even then the obituary was not completely agreeable to Kamenev, so he composed his own. The day following publication of the above obituary, on April 10, 1934, Kamenev's was published in *Izvestia*:

> Andrei Bely – poet, romanticist, philosopher, literary critic, publicist, a historian of literature and poetry – was first of all a dreamer. All of his work is permeated with searches of the single and wholeness of the contemplation of the universe. His flaring and anxious thought process lived as some type of synthesis of his dreams.
>
> He entered literature at the moment when the country, rocking from an underground resonance indicating impending revolutions, lived in an atmosphere of progressing catastrophes. Intellectual thought aspired to comprehend the so complex weave of events and while it naturally fragmented into a total series of trends, schools, groups, sub-groups and factions. Andrei Bely was tightly involved in these divisions into small parts. He sought something else: some kind of wide all-encompassing system that would assimilate within itself all of the diverse currents of life and would permit a glance at its contradictions form one point of view. Such a system existed and gathered around itself a large and then even larger circle of defenders and preachers. This was the system of proletariat socialism. But as a typical scholar, a son of a Moscow university professor, a person who traversed his entire life among books and circles of the intelligensia, Bely remained alien to this single system that could satisfy his unquenchable thirst for that single synthesis of this grasp of the universe. This is where his tragedy begins.
>
> Andrei Bely was not just a dreamer isolated in his private library, but an artist, striving to not just understand the world

and history, but to materialize the reality unfolding in front of him in realistic artistic forms, and after having profoundly lived through the contradictions. His attitude toward books and life was not like a librarian or book collector, but like a passionate seeker of truth. His discoveries however manifested as fruitless. An individualist due to his nature, born deaf to the truth of socialism, he as a result entered truthless paths.

In his most recent book, *Beginning of the Century*, in the narrative of his wanderings while seeking the character of the condition he considered his ideal, as he explained them in 1905, he could not find another word other than – slime.[270] "I deliberately created for myself an entanglement of the maximum size." "And from 1905, arriving in Petersburg, for several years I eventually got entangled in Merezhkovsky's circle."[271] Such words are dispersed throughout the entire book – entangled, stumbled, web, confusion, the incompatibility of my concepts. "In the final end this was a complete bankruptcy of the scene that promised I would consume the world, but in place of this I was caught like a bird in a cage and which held me over five years."[272]

Alas! This continued not five, but thirty years, from the beginning of his literary activity to its end. The cage where this bird was captive, and which promised him the ability to consume the world, was the bourgeoisie culture. For Bely this was definitely a cage. For his entire life he beat against the sides, shredded himself apart as a result, wounded himself against its bars, but he could not get out of its confines. His books, poetry, novels, critical essays, and attempts at philosophical generalizations, preserve within themselves the reflection of these impulses, these aspirations, to break out of the cage, and they thunderously witness to their fruitlessness.

---

[270] "The end of the year for me was like slime. The word in all of its applications." Quoted out of context from *Beginning of the Century*.

[271] Additional quotes taken out of context from *Beginning of the Century*.

[272] Another passage quoted out of context. The 5 years from 1912 to 1916, the time Bely spent in Europe for the most part with Steiner. But Kamenev did not view the matter in this context.

We will not in front of an opened grave underscore what is so often contained in the books of our deceased poet – these aspirations of his that are expressed in a tongue-tied manner. Not willing to give account of himself in the genuine content of his tragedy, the tragedy of individualism, he could not explain it to people in simple and clear terms, using precise and real terms.[273] We will underscore the event that no matter how tongue-tied the concept of symbolism in expressing this tragedy, it is right in front of our face in Andrei Bely's books.

For many years it seemed to him that an exit would be found, and as soon as he finishes the theoretical argument on behalf of the symbolist view of the world. It was necessary to utilize Kant as a basis for this. Kant at the end of the 19th and beginning of the 20th centuries was a refuge for all anti-socialist thought. And it had to be a person who was absolutely deprived of any capacity to grasp the general struggle in its genuine depictions in order to seek in Kantian philosophy a direction to the exit of the cage of bourgeoisie civilization. Bely in the final end sensed this. However he attempted to break apart the iron rods of this cage, where his cognizance was struggling for survival, by using other means, more ancient implements: mysticism as a principle having the capacity to liberate a person's spirit from the reality of concrete existence.

The world is elemental, chaotic, turbulent, and not subject to measure or quantity. The mind is powerless, linear on one plain, and pathetically fruitless in its attempts to subject to itself the element of existence. Under such conditions history is inane and purposeless. The reconciliation of existence and cognizance – the justification of history – needs to be sought outside of nature, outside of humanity, outside of history, meaning, in deity. Such is the frontier to which the poet's thoughts were pushed. Such is the philosophical thought of the poet that provides us a picture of the complete exposition of the ideology, the despair in the strengths of humanity's mind, the distortion of the proper meaning of history, right at the

[273] A discredit of the concept of symbolism.

moment when the collective efforts of the working humanity for the first time turned history into a consciously guided process.

However the discredit of history by mysticism, and it causing the collective mind of humanity to be neglected, twice delivered the poet.

The first time was the revolution of 1905. Under its direct effect Bely, and truly for a short moment, found new themes and in a new manner perceived the world. This was the period when the collection of verses titled *Ashes* and the novel *Petersburg* were created, the most substantial period of Bely's compositions, standing but not unexpectedly under the banner of Nekrasov. A reflection of the shifts of immense historical strata are clearly felt in the verses and prose of this period. A tangible feeling of an impending immense historical catastrophe exists in them. In *Petersburg* an image of the royal empire at the moment when the very foundations of its existence are crumbling is artistically impressed. Let the author perceive his depictions in a mystic plain: Gogol also wanted to interpret *The Government Inspector* and *Dead Souls* on a plain of religious symbolism. The history of literature will notice Bely's compositions of this period as one of the most valuable reflections of the revolutionary era of Russian history. And the compositions of these years of 1906-1909, were not futile as Andrei Bely eventually promoted them as his right to an involvement in the creation of a new Soviet genre of literature. Sadly this incentive was only maintained in Bely's compositions for a short while.

The mystic draw and intellectual individualism again overflowed in the cognizance of the poet and abandoned him to captivity in the sect of the Anthroposophists. He sought god and found him – Rudolf Steiner! [Bely] would definitely have finally perished on this fruitless route if it were not for the October Revolution. It again motivated Bely and he composed a series of books where, disregarding all of their shortcomings, the bestial face, the poverty and doom of the world of bourgeoisie culture was artistically impressed. What the old symbolist poet left behind in the country where socialism was now being installed was not accidental. His wanderings along the roads of mysticism and religious theory were prompted, not by the self-interest of a simpleton, but by the thirst for a completion of his concept of the world, encompassing a disseverance of contradictions. And he could not but see in his final years that particularly what was alien to him ideologically – proletarian socialism – victoriously resolves these problems against which he so fruitlessly struggled all his life.

Andrei Bely was and remained a person of the obsolete perishing world. His aspiration to declare himself one of the early forerunners and builders of socialist culture is incorrect and groundless. In the questions of a general view of the world he finished the trend of Gogol and Dostoyevsky, but did not start something new. But he did not reconcile himself with the world of the bourgeoisie mundaneness, but did not laud it either, and did not attempt to create for himself in this doomed world a comfortable corner for himself, where he could have calmly and magnanimously observed the impending tragedies of history. He struggled while caught in the webs of bourgeoisie culture, tangibly felt its misery, temporality, doom, and sought an exit, and so strove toward a new view of the world, one that he instinctively felt, that this new truth grows in the collective strengths of the people who are building socialism. Here is the right he has for their attention. Here is the pledge that his books will not remain fruitless while gathering dust on the shelves of libraries, but that they will be taken off of them and studied even when what is reflected in them – the tragedy of idealism and individualism – becomes for humanity a long-passed bad dream.

This article is Soviet propaganda and rewriting of history at its pinnacle and well done by Kamenev, whose goal was to route all literature along the channel of socialist ideology, even if it was to the complete discredit of the subject writer and opposite to his convictions.

The description of what occurred during the days of the funeral cannot be counted as totally valuable without taking into account 2 important factors: the first is the human or emotional, and the second is the political. As far as the first is concerned there is not a whole lot to say. An atmosphere of sorrow prevailed, many wept, felt empathy for Bely, understanding that Russian culture suffered a great loss due to his death. All felt as though they were experiencing some historical event. As a result the amount of books, memoirs, recollections, obituaries, biographies, commentaries, newspaper and magazine articles, and reflections of Bely, surpass any other single person in Russian and Soviet literature of the 20th century. (Pushkin has this honor for the 19th century.)

The majority of personal witnesses noticed a special expression on the face of the deceased Bely, as noted in their memoirs:

> A totally child-like smile, which on the following day when they brought him to his apartment and then to the hall of the organizing committee transformed into a joyful, victorious radiance. (Claudia Nikolaievna)

> The face of Boris Nikolaievich was solemn, soft and majestic at the time. His mouth almost smiled. He had the face of a leader. Liberated from constant motion that constantly changed his position all his life, the face of the thinker was filled with content and an austere beauty. (S.D. Spassky)

> He became majestic and austere. Radiating light and softness. (Zaitzev)

As far as the political factor of Bely's death and post-mortem events are concerned they began immediately with his death, as reflected in the initial obituary composed by the 3 men mentioned above. The matter continued after the coffin was placed in the hall of the organizing committee, at 6 PM, on the evening of January 9.

Yudin, Kirpotin,[274] and Ermilov[275] came early to the civil requiem and immediately created a list of those who would speak. As soon as the coffin was brought to the hall and set in place and opened, Sannikov read to the audience the obituary that was published the previous day in *Izvestia*, being one of its authors.

Yudin, who was secretary of the organizing committee of the writer's union, opened the memorial services later that evening. He spoke himself and then asked the following individuals to speak: Ermilov, Hakoryakov,[276] Pasternak, Sannikov – again, and Grossman at the end.

No record is available of what Yudin or Nakoryakov had to say except they were impersonal and pallid. Grossman did better in his eulogy speaking of Bely's ingenuity and comparing him with Dostoyevsky and Tolstoy.

Some record of Pasternak's eulogy was made by Spassky, including the following:

> The face of Boris Nikolaievich was like a medal. Death is only a stage in the existence of Bely. We arrived at his coffin not to speak of his work, but to sorrow. He now views life with a different set of eyes, a rebirth to experience and now to further journey.

The words were not to be taken in terms of reincarnations, as some felt, due to Bely's convictions of anthroposophy, but that his books would be the next stage in Bely's life, to remain long after his funeral, and a rebirth of his literature would continue his memory. Pasternak's eulogy was considered the best of all the speakers.

The text of Ermilov's eulogy was published in the Moscow newspaper *Communist Enlightenment*, on January 11. No doubt

---

[274] Valeri Yakovlevich Kirpotin, 1898-1997, secretary to Maxim Gorki and one of the creators of the Union of Soviet Writers.

[275] Vladimir Vladimirovich Ermilov, 1904-1965, Soviet writer.

[276] Nikolai Nikandrovich, Nakoryakov, 1881-1970, book publisher, revolutionary activist, and member of the Union of Soviet Writers. He was at this time director of the State book publishing house.

it was also annotated by the editors to comply with Soviet requirements.

> No need to say much about how significant a loss this is. Andrei Bely was a poet, prosaic and art theorist. He traversed a path of life that contained an immense capacity and education.
>
> Disregarding that with his philosophy he affirmed an ideology that is hostile to the working class, to him was given, just as to Blok, a genuine ability to understand the barbarian face of bourgeois culture. It is sufficient to recollect the character of Mandro,[277] created by Andrei Bely, a monkey-like monster, generated by vile effusions of an imperialistic war. This passage is a premonition of the barbaric character of fascism. Both the image of Mandro and that of contemporary fascism are identical.
>
> Andrei Bely was not able to create a new school of literature, although he did achieve having several students who became established writers.

The reader can only obviously see a eulogy that would not have been delivered at a memorial service of such a famous and talented person, regardless of circumstances surrounding it, but something rewritten for the purposes of propaganda.

After Ermilov delivered his eulogy at the requiem, a journalist reviewed it, added annotations as necessary to meet the requirements of Soviet censors, and published his review of it in the newspaper *Evening Moscow*, the next day, January 10.

> [Ermilov] stressed the immense loss that Russian literature bore in the personage of the deceased poet, romanticist and art theorist.
>
> Andrei Bely traversed a creative route of immense capacity and immense education.

---

[277] The hero of Bely's novel *Moscow*.

> He was an artist connected with the trends of Russian bourgeois decadence and with religious and mystical dispositions, and he reflected them in his compositions. Being formerly a disciple of the head of anthroposophy, Rudolf Steiner, he at the time was able in a series of significant compositions to display the genuine face of bourgeois society. For example, in his exceptional novel *Moscow*, A.Bely exposes those bestial characteristics of the bourgeoisie, which are presently being formidably expressed in German fascism.
>
> This artist who confirmed the philosophy of bourgeois idealism in his composition was then given the opportunity to feel the impending catastrophe and annihilation of the bourgeois world and to see its doom.
>
> The route traversed by A. Bely shows how the best people of bourgeois society, who confirm their philosophy in their compositions, eventually attain the realization that genuine culture is only possible on the path of proletariat revolution.

As with the previous obituaries published in Soviet newspapers, the review of Ermilov's eulogy was likewise rewritten to something it was not.

A meeting of the organizing committee of the writer's union was held the morning of January 11, to decide on a speaker at the crematorium. The problem was that all of the speakers at the memorial service did not comply with the requirements of Soviet censors in their eulogies and so they had to be all rewritten for the press. They needed an orator who would not deviate from party lines, not deliver some true evaluation of Bely's compositions or any laud on his behalf. The result of the meeting was the selection of Vladimir Kirshon, a Soviet playwright, and on whom they could depend.[278] He would be the only person to speak. Of course, having to speak that afternoon, not personally knowing Bely, but

---

[278] Vladimir Mikhailovich Kirshon, 1902-1938, Soviet writer and playwright, a former secretary of the Russian Association of Proletarian Writers, member of the Communist Party, and early favorite of Joseph Stalin. But later he was accused of being a Trotsky sympathizer and was arrested in 1937, and executed the next year.

only knowing second-hand information, and primarily the obituaries already published in Soviet newspapers, his eulogy definitely followed party lines and did not do justice to Bely.

When Kirshon stood in front of Bely's fans and relatives at the crematorium his initial words were:

> The Organizing Committee assigned me to say a few words in regard to the occasion. Andrei Bely was a unique character alone in his class...
>
> Of course, we could say more that is significant about Andrei Bely, but nothing remains to be said after that vile article in *Izvestia*.

As one person who attended later related, his speech caused a despondent and melancholy atmosphere to prevail. He spoke in broken and disconnected phrases, doing his best to appear sorrowful. But no one was listening, then suddenly Claudia Nikolaievna left the room.

Kirshon knew himself he was in a difficult situation and was uncomfortable, but he was also angered at the article in *Izvestia* by Bely's 3 associates who did laud him for his literary capacity (of 47 volumes), comparison to European writers, travel through Europe, philosophic comprehension, promoting a new genre of Russian literature, and vast education.

Zaitzev also left his impression behind:

> The dramatist Kirshon delivered a speech on behalf of the Organizing Committee. He spoke very poorly. No one else gave a eulogy. The silence through the tears when he was not speaking were the most eloquent parts of his speech.

After the services at the crematorium concluded, F.A. Berozovsky[279] calmed Kirshon and told him:

---

279 Feoktist Alekseevich Berozovsky, 1877-1952. Russian Soviet novelist, Communist party activist.

> You brilliantly achieved accomplishing your task.

Even though *Izvestia* subsequently published Kamenev's obituary on January 10, it was still not to be outdone by *Pravda*, who published another obituary on January 11, and in order to mitigate the amount of credit offered to Bely earlier in the area of philosophy, education and symbolist literature, as well as defuse Kirshon's statement of their earlier obituary being – vile. Their terminal purpose was to officially evaluate Bely's life, literary creativity, and assign him his merited spot in Russian literature. Since the author is not noted, it would have been composed by a group of *Pravda* editors and journalists, and of course, it would have complied with Soviet intentions:

> Appearing as the foremost representative of bourgeois literature and idealistic contemplation, A.Bely during the recent past sincerely aspired to adopt the concepts of the epoch of socialist construction. The rotation of the expansive circle of the obsolete intellectualism toward soviet authority also enveloped A.Bely. At the end of the year 1932, he entered the plenum of the Organizing Committee of Soviet Writers with the announcement of his preparedness to present his compositions to the service of socialism.
>
> In the person of A. Bely, the last of the foremost representatives of Russian symbolism descended into the grave. It is important to note that he did not share the same fate as other leaders of this trend of literature – Merezhkovsky, Gippius, Balmont – all of whom skipped away into the swamp of the White Guard immigration.
>
> A. Bely died a Soviet writer.

The 3 mentioned above all migrated to Europe due to persecution by Soviet authorities for failing to write in accord with their definition of socialist realism.

The newspaper *Literary News*, in their January 11 issue, likewise included their version of a Soviet-inclined obituary of Bely, part of which is the following:

> Boris Nikolaievich Bugaev – Andrei Bely – one of the final representatives of Russian symbolism passed away. Somewhat more than a year ago at a plenum of the organizing committee Andrei Bely delivered a speech on Soviet literature and of his role in it, and which he has played up to this time, and of his intentioned role in the distant future.
>
> He said that he intends to dedicate the entire strength of his mastery to the building of socialism. He spoke of the immense work that stands ahead of him on this route. He spoke of that stance of accomplishment that he attained as a result of his many years of effort and of his preparedness to devote this stance on behalf of the proletariat.
>
> There was much the final representative of symbolism did not understand. He did not understand that the stance wherein he worked to this time ceased to be applicable for the new work under new conditions, that the objects developed while on this stance are objects indefinitely distant from the objects that now surround him and that now define this structure of a stance.
>
> The author of brilliant novels regarding the beginning of the century, he was helpless during the final years of his life. He continued to write of the past, of people long passed away, of objects that once existed. He lived among us as a relic of antiquity, as a participant in the construction of the famous tower of ancient times that was supposed to become the shelter of single individuals isolated from life – the apostles of symbolism. Andrei Bely only during the final years of his life perceived that a writer cannot be by himself. But the desire to not be alone never did manifest. It is difficult to say whether he would have succeeded at this since his death was rather premature. An analysis of his work may lead to an answer.

This eulogy is more appropriate and applicable than those above, although still heavily tainted by socialist propaganda. His brilliant novels are the 3 volumes of his memoirs, of which one is mentioned not by title but by subject, and so it was not edited out.

But they fail to mention that it was not due to Bely's recognition of any truth in socialism that he wanted to be part of the Soviet Union of Writers, but that this was the means for him to be able to continue writing what he had been writing in the past and have it published. He had no intent of changing his stance or theme, but to conform to the requirements of the new government in order to be recognized as a writer and so be able to continue. He was an anthroposophist within a socialist environment, but the author of the eulogy could not state this, as with the other soviet-style eulogies.

Longer and more information biographies of Bely were quickly published. Constantine Loks, a journalist and friend of Pasternak, in the January 11 issue, and Aleksei Bolotnikov, a socialist philosopher and newspaper editor, in the January 16 issue, of *Literary News*. Both of them were attempts to be more objective and ameliorate the rash content of Kamenev's obituary in *Izvestia*, although still slanting Bely toward having a socialist tendency in his later years. Both of them tended to concentrate more on Bely as a poet and symbolist novelist and his positive impact on Russian literature, and less on his religious or political inclinations.

What was missing in all of the obituaries and editorials about Bely were the many lectures he delivered in Moscow and Petersburg on symbolism and anthroposophy, readings of his poetry and novels at the various meetings of different societies, and there were hundreds of them. These were to packed crowds at different halls, each lasting 2 to 3 hours, and motivational to all the audience and participants. The most prominent of Russian philosophers and authors gathered to listen to him. Yet, all that was provided to Soviet readers after his death was their political agenda: to turn Bely from an independent thinker and symbolist failure into a half-way achieved socialist success.

Having this ideological groundwork a committee to immortalized Bely's memory was formed immediately after his burial, but under the circumstances it was unable in any manner to fulfill its purpose. The following individuals are listed by Zaitzev as forming this committee:

Claudia Nikolaievna Bugaeva (Bely's wife)
Victor Victorovich Goltzev[280]
Vladimir Vladimirovich Ermilov
Peter Nikolaievich Zaitzev
Nikolai Vasilyevich Krutikov
Vladimir Germanovich Lidin
Nikolai Nikandrovich Nakoryakov
Aleksei Sergeevich Petrovsky
Boris Leonidovich Pasternak
Boris Andreevich Pilnyak
Grigori Aleksandrovich Sannikov
Sergei Dmitrievich Spassky (from Petersburg)
Titsian Tabidze (from Tiflis, Georgia)
Sergei Mikhailovich Eisenstein[281]
Anatoli Tarasenko[282]
Paolo Yashvili (from Tiflis, Georgia)

In general the responsibility of such a committee consisted in first, memorial services after a short interval following the person's death, with appropriate speeches, and second, the assembly and publication of a compilation of the author's writings. The intent being to immortalize the individual in Russian history.

Bely's friends hoped that a series of such evening dinners with memorial speeches would occur in several cities on the same day. But this idea failed. Spassky wrote to Zaitzev on February 18, 1934, regarding its failure in Petersburg:

> Strange things are happening regarding the evening dinners on behalf of Andrei Bely. There was one at the Writer's Club,

[280] Victor Victorovich Goltzev, 1901-1955, Soviet journalist and writer, chief edition of the magazine Friend of the Nations.
[281] Sergei Mikhailovich Eisenstein, 1898-1948, Soviet film director.
[282] Anatoli Kuzmich Tarasenko, 1909-1956, Soviet novelist and poet.

> but no advertising was done, so it had a meager attendance and a blatant failure.
>
> There is supposed to be a second one, and real soon, and where I was invited to speak, and open to everybody, but for some reason it was postponed. Now it is unknown whether there will be anything at all.

In Moscow arrangements for such an evening dinner were started by Zaitzev immediately after the funeral. He met with O.E. Mandelstam who offered to speak and who also wrote a poem special for the occasion of Bely's memorial, and he gave Zaitzev a copy of it. Mandelstam also met with Pasternak on January 26, and read the tribute to him for his approval, and all seemed fine at the time. However the fact that Mandelstam was Jewish was not to the benefit of Zaitzev, and the Union of Soviet Writers did not care for him at all since he composed poetry critical of Joseph Stalin and the Kremlin. (Mandelstam would be arrested later in 1934 as a result and with his wife exiled. He died in 1938 en route to a concentration camp in Siberia.)

It seems that the initial effort for the organization of an evening dinner and memorial in Moscow proceeded satisfactorily. On January 29, the State Book Publishing House had a conversation with Zaitzev regarding a list of participants, and the number rose to some 15 men and a couple of women of mostly the literary field and a few in the art field who would deliver a short tribute or read passages from Bely's novels and poetry. A couple more would play a piano recital, and a couple of others would sing for the occasion. None of them however were affiliated with anthroposophy or any of the symbolist gatherings which Bely earlier attended, those at the Ivanov or Merezhkovsky residences, or any of the remaining Argonauts or the Golden Fleece publishing concern. All of the proposed participants were expected to route their tribute to Bely in a manner that would promote him as a socialist.

On February 1, a proposition arrived from the State Book Publishing House to Zaitzev, that because Bely was admitted to one of the sub-committees, becoming a member of the bureau in

June 1932, then it is the responsibility of the State Publishing House to honor Bely, rather than one of his associates. Zaitzev of course took offence at the suggestion and to salvage the effort expended so far and his involvement, he immediately compiled a new protocol for the memorial dinner and a new list of participants. It was not approved.

It was not until February 15, that Zaitzev realized the organizers of the Congress of Soviet Writers, which was to be shortly convened, were working together with the State Publishing House. The intervention was to suppress the honor that Bely was publicly due and replace it with some emaciated schedule, not much different than the rewritten eulogies and biographies published in Soviet newspapers, so not to distract attention from Soviet writers who would be making their presentations at the Congress.

Yet this was still not going to stop Zaitzev, and he rewrote his schedule for the tribute and the list of participants, hoping this would be agreeable to the State Publishing House and Congress. The musical portion was deleted in its entirety, as they requested. On February 15, Zaitzev presented his itinerary to the State Publishing House for their approval, as follows:

THE DIRECTORS OF THE STATE BOOK PUBLISHING HOUSE AND UNION OF WRITERS INVITE YOU TO AN EVENING TRIBUTE DEDICATED TO THE MEMORY OF ANDREI BELY

The tribute will be held February 20, 1934, at the Publisher's Hall, October 25 Street, Building 10.

PROGRAM:

Tributes: F.V. Gladkov, L.P. Grossman, P.N. Zaitzev, N.G. Mashkovtzev,[283] N.N. Nakoryakov, B.L. Pasternak, B.A. Pilnyak, G.A. Sannikov, T.P. Simson,[284] A.Tarasenko, Titsian Tabidze, G.A. Shengeli,[285] Paolo Yashvili.

Osip Mandelstam will recite his poetry dedicated to the memory of Andrei Bely.

Readings of the poetry of A.Bely and selections from his novels *Petersburg* and *Moscow*: P. Antokolsky,[286] E.P. Garin,[287] D.N. Zhuravlov,[288] Maria Sinelnikova,[289] E.G. Spendiarov,[290] and V.N. Yakhontov.[291]

The presentation will begin at 7 PM.
Organized by the State Publishing House.

[283] Nikolai Georgievich (Egorovich) Mashmovtzev, 1887-1962, Soviet art expert, author of several books on Russian and Soviet art.

[284] A medical doctor who specialized in children's diseases. (I do not know why he is here included.)

[285] Georgi Arkadyevich Shengeli, 1894-1956, Russian poet.

[286] Pavel Grigoryevich Antokolsky, 1896-1978, Soviet Russian poet and theater director.

[287] Erast Pavlovich Garin, 1902-1980, Soviet Russian actor, director of theater and film. Part of the Meyerhold Theater.

[288] Dmitri Nikolaievich Zhuravlov, 1900-1991, Russian Soviet actor, a professional public speaker and reader.

[289] Maria Davidovna Sinelnikova, 1899-1993, Soviet Russian actress of theater and film. Also of the Bakhtangov Theater.

[290] An actress of the Kamerni Theater. No information is available on her.

[291] Vladimir Nikolaievich Yakhontov, 1899-1945, Soviet Russian actor, professional speaker and reader.

All was arranged by Zaitzev, but it was not approved by the State Publishing House. The selected participants did not supply a sufficient ideological promotion of socialism. Of course the participation of Mandelstam also played a role in their decision. The entire matter was postponed for a few months. Zaitzev continued work on a new schedule and list of participants should the matter again be given consideration by the State Publishing House.

In early May the State Publishing House suddenly remembered about the cancelled tribute and memorial service and they quickly assigned a new date: May 14, 1934. They wanted to hurry and have this done and out of the way before the First Congress of Soviet Writers in August that year. Of course, this was a whitewash to cover their circumvention of immortalizing such a famous and creative author. Zaitzev along with widow Claudia Nikolaievna went to work on a new schedule and list of participants, and a list that would be acceptable to the Soviet administration. But 2 weeks was hardly enough time.

Zaitzev contacted the previous individuals he felt would be approved, but most were not available. Most declined in order to protect their reputation and did not want to risk their participation in the forthcoming Writers Congress, or were just afraid of repercussions: Sannikov, Lidin, Pasternak, Grossman, and Pilnyak. The only 2 that would volunteer were Gladkov and Antokolsky, but this was insufficient.

The Union of Soviet Writers insisted on the inclusion of Kamenev and Bolotkinov, the authors of the obituaries published in January on Bely, knowing they would follow party line in their tribute and not provide an objective evaluation of Bely and his writings. Of course this would turn the memorial service into a superficial display of Soviet propaganda. Kamenev refused, saying he had other commitments. Zaitzev thought about asking Georgy Chulkov and Sergei Shervinsky, but he was afraid they would both be rejected.

Mandelstam was rejected categorically by the Union of Soviet Writers, and even then he was arrested the night of May 13-14, 1934, and would not have appeared anyway.

By May 3, Zaitzev realized that he was in a catastrophic situation: none of those approved to speak would speak, and the balance were not approved to speak. The Union approved a few others, such as Vladimir Mayakovsky, but time was of the essence and one week was not enough for him. Another was Marietta Shaginyan, but she was in the Russian south and next to impossible to reach.

The evening dinner and tribute on behalf of Andrei Bely never happened. Zaitzev was unable to organize it and could not acquire sufficient speakers from among those approved by the Union and within the time frame provided. He likewise had no support from either the State Publishing House or the Union of Writers, and this caused the effort to stagnate until it died. They had the forthcoming Congress planned and were promoting its success, and something like a tribute to Bely would take away from its impact. Their goal would have been to protect their own reputation at the expense of Bely anyway.

From another perspective, this may have been best for Bely, not to have such a tribute, especially with the people approved as speakers. If they would have spoken they would have made Bely something he was not: a Soviet writer.

It is not surprising that other projects with the intent of immortalizing Bely's memory, more complex and impacting than a memorial dinner, likewise never materialized in the period after his death. The most important of these was a reprint of Bely's compositions. Plans for the assembly and publication of the entirety of Bely's immense and wealthy collection of novels, poetry, articles, essays, lecture notes, memoirs and recollections, were already in process among his friends as they were standing alongside his coffin. They considered this project as an important legacy for the Russian people, and one that was not just possible but natural for such an effective writer.

On January 11, 1934, Spassky was already discussing the issue with Olga Forsh,[292] and later met with Pasternak. The same day Zaitzev discussed the matter with Ms L.V. Kalikina. He also considered a subsequent volume of photographs from Bely's collections.

Of course, Sannikov was not to be left behind, and provided his opinion on what should be included in the collection, and he concluded that it would take 10 volumes or more for all that Bely wrote of value to the Russian reader to be published. It would be titled, *Andrei Bely Memorial Collection.* Over 25 of Russia's writers, artists, musicians, journalists and producers volunteered their assistance, most of them mentioned above who attended his funeral and memorial service.

Although they all wanted to participate, in reality it was not so, few took the matter seriously and even less were willing to risk their reputation to actually put their name on the project. The circle was now just a meager few of Bely's friends: Zaitzev, Sannikov and Spassky.

The preparation for print of Bely's immense collection began immediately after the internment of his remains and initially proceeded smoothly. What is noticeable is that the only publisher that announced it willingness to print the series of Bely's collection was *Academia,* and which was headed by Kamenev. Perhaps no surprise to anyone, and Kamenev of course would write the prologue, a biography, an article on Bely as a Soviet writer, an analysis and application of his writings to the contemporary Soviet reader, and of course an epilogue, all totaling about 50 pages of text. Some illustrations would also be included. What motivated Kamenev to volunteer his publishing house to accomplish this task is conjecture, but more than likely to rewrite Bely's history and portray him as a Soviet writer, which he was not.

Kamenev discussed the issue on January 28, with Zaitzev: setting the price, number of volumes, quantity to be printed. Since

---

[292] Olga Dmitrievna Forsh, 1873-1961, Russian Soviet novelist. She also played an important role in the 1934 Congress of Soviet Writers.

they figured this would be the first and only publication of a complete collection of Bely's popular compositions, they agreed on 10,000 copies, with perhaps an increase to 15,000, should preliminary sales look promising. Any net profit from the sales and all royalties would go to Bely's widow Claudia Nikolaievna.

However, the project was unsuccessful and never materialized beyond the planning stage. In December 1934, as mentioned above, Kamenev was arrested. What few were fervent enough to want to finish it continued working on the project for another 6 months. Then it stopped. Any hope for a post-mortem edition of a collection of Bely's writings died with Kamenev.

In April 1935, both *Between the Two Revolutions* and *The Mastery of Gogol* were published.

It was not until 1966, some 32 years after his death, that a collection of solely some of Bely's poetry was published in Russia, and not until 1978, that *Petersburg* was published.

Outside of Russia, and specifically in Germany, the 3-volume series of Bely's recollections were published in 1966, his 4 *Symphonies* in 1968, and a 10-volume collection was published in 1969.

Claudia Bugaeva never remarried and led a low profile life in Soviet Russia until she passed away February 22, 1970, at the age of 84 years. Over the 2 years after Bely's death she wrote an extensive biography of her husband and her memoirs of that era, but it was not published until 1960.

# APPENDIXES

## Symbolist Writings of Andrei Bely

(translated from the Russian)

# SACRED FLOWERS[293]

God is light and there is no darkness of any type in Him.[294]

Light is distinct from color due to the completeness of all the colors contained in it. Color is light, in one or another respect it is confined by darkness. The phenomenon of light is based on this. God appears to us: first, as a unconditional entity; second, as an infinite entity.

He is unconditional in regard to light. The infinite can be symbolized by the infinity of color confined in a ray of white light.[295] This is why God is light and there is no darkness of any type in Him.

"I saw," says Daniel the prophet, "thrones being placed and the Ancient of Days took His seat. His attire was the color of white."[296]

We are creatures created according to the image and likeness of God: from this most profound principle of our existence we are turned to the light. This is why the terminal contradistinctions of divinity are disclosed to us conditionally, within the limitation of light and even to the point of its complete absence. If white light is the symbol of the incarnation of the completeness of existence, then black [light] is the symbol of non-existence, chaos. "Then they

---

[293] Bely was 23 years of age when he wrote this treatise.
[294] 1 John 1:5
[295] This is the basis of the name Bely, Russian for the color white.
[296] Dan 7:9

were struck with blindness, and now encompassed by thick darkness, each sought an exit."[297] Black light categorically defines evil as the principle violating the completeness of the existence that assigns it transparency. The incarnation of non-existence in existence, assigning the latter transparency, symbolizes grey light. And to the extent grey light is created based on the relationship of black to white, to that extent the possible definition of evil can also consist in a relative grayness for us.

Departing from the character of grey light, we reach the actual effect of evil. This effect consists in the introduction into the substance of an attitude without the objects affected by the attitude. Such an attitude is zero, like a machine manufactured from whirling dust and ashes rotating for no known reason or purpose. The logic of this middleness is the following: suppose that something irrelative exists, then the surfacing of something irrelative occurs and needs a special measurement, we will call this measurement – depth, while the opposite to it is flat. When we institute 3 coordinate axis for the measurement of objects, then we have the responsibility to call one of the 3 axis – depth, while the axes lying perpendicular to the plain are planes with the measurement of width and length. The opposite can also be stated: the measurement of depth can be called the measurement of width. The choice of coordinate axes depends on us.

We can compare ourselves to a point at the crossing of coordinate axes. We are the start of the coordinate system. This is why the account from our perspective following the lines of depth, width and length is arbitrary. Such logic flattens every depth. It shreds it all and expels it, but does not take it anywhere, just like the Kantian noumenon, which limits the translucence of realism, but itself is non-existent. The world appears as an unnecessary picture where everyone is running having distorted pale-green faces, smoke the factory smokestacks hangs like curtains, they run, in some unnecessary outburst they gallop away on horses, and completely just as in the cities. It seems to be one single flight and right into themselves. But the *I* is the single salvation and it

[297] based on Gen 19:11 and 2 Kings 6:18

is displayed solely as a black crevice to where dust-filled whirlwinds return, oriented as ugly depictions that are all so familiar to us. And so now you feel as though you are eternally failing with all of the hallucinations, a hallucination with all the zeroes of a zero. But you do not fail, because there is no place into which to fall when all uniformly is flying, uniformly is decreasing. Following them these zeroes run confined in their paleness, in hats and caps. I want to shout, "Open your eyes! Why this disorientation?" But with the shout you only gather a crowd of spectators and perhaps some city official. The stupidity rises, vengeance for the attempt awakens. You remember what Nietzsche said, "The desert grows. Woe to him in whom the desert is secluded." And something detestable grasps the heart. This is the devil, the grey dust settling on everything and everybody.

Only when a cry of despair blares from the soul will the grey mirage be incited, the extinguishing light. It will shred the phantasmagoria:

In that day they will roar over it
Like the roaring of the turbulent sea.
And if one looks at the land,
There is only darkness and distress,
And the sun will be darkened by clouds.[298]

This is of what the deceit of unexpectedness consists. It will disclose as if an abyss at your feet. The one who says this is actually an abyss, he will accept this attitude as the substance. Contemporary lovers of contemplating every abyss existing in art, almost all of them are located at this stage. Next is to remember that here there is still no abyss of any kind. This is an optimistic deceit. A cloud of dust has extinguished the lamp in their hands, having hung an impenetrable wall in front of eternal light. This is the black wall of dust that at the first moment will seem to be a crevice, in the same manner as an unilluminated closet can seem to be a bottomless black world, when gloom will blind the eyes, not

[298] Is 5:30, modified by Bely

allowing you to glance into its frontiers. There is no reason to fear the rebelling chaos. What is necessary is to remember that it is a curtain, a trial that must be defeated. You need to enter the darkness in order to exit from it.

The first brightness to break the darkness is surrounded by a yellow and turbulent, ominous attack of dust. This ominous burst is well known by all those awakening, those halfway between sleep and reality. Woe to him who does not scatter this ominous burst by defeating chaos. He will fall, crushed by an illusion. And Lermontov, not being able to ascertain the route about which he was dreaming, always shorted his deep visualization.

And Lermontov was doomed to a total lack of understanding the essence of the disposition suppressing him, which could have surfaced as a posture of a benevolent pessimism, a sorrow for the world, a poetic grief, since upon all of this lives an impression of a sacred prophetic anxiety. But such a fate opens the eyes for the first time. They were far from sleep and from victory.

The destinies of individual famous personages reflect the fates of entire epochs, as though in a hall of mirrors, and now finally [reflects] the destiny of worldwide history. These individual personages all the more often are presented as actors playing the tragedies of our future. Initially they are actors and then perhaps the initiators of events. The mask they wear grows to cover their face. Such faces often surface as points of attachment and detachment of worldwide historical powers. These are the windows through which the wind of the future blows on us.

Soiled treatises are encountered in all of Dostoyevsky's novels. In them occur the most important abstract and awesome conversations of its primary heroes regarding the final destines of Russian and worldwide history. And you can feel that it is particularly this trivial, this ignoble and decomposing situation that provides these conversations a special contemporary Russian – formidable and ominous – apocalyptic burst, as the sky being struck by thunder.

The ray of eternal light here provides – and one not offensive to view – a moderate drabness to this terrifying color and one appropriate for it. Overcoming this stage, being draws near to another temptation, suddenly everything is colored by a fiery brilliance of a red sunset. So the impression of red is created as a result of the relationship of white light to middle-grey. Relatively the transparency of red light is its type of theosophical revelation. Here the enemy is revealed to us in his final accessible essence: in a flamingly red sunset of infernal fire. Now we need to remember that this – the final frontier of relativity – is an illusion of an illusion that is capable however to appear more real than reality, having accepted this description of the snake: Behold a large red dragon with seven heads and ten horns. And on his heads are seven crowns. His tale drew the third part of the stars from heaven.[299]

This is a mirage. Here burn the remains of the dust that landed on a person. This is right in front of our eyes, as it says in the Wisdom of Solomon.

> There appeared to them a bonfire in flames, only it was ignited on its own, filled with terrors. And they, fearing the unseen apparition, imagined that the reality was even worse.[300]

Love at this stage is surrounded by a fiery color of an all-consuming passion. It is filled with devious enchantments and an evil corporeal fire. Such a love is capable of displaying the type of image described in the Book of Revelation: And I saw a woman sitting on a scarlet beast. And its name was inscribed on its forehead, "Mystery, Babylon the Great, mother of prostitutes and abominations."

We cannot stop at this point, otherwise here you will be consumed by fire. You need to proceed forward. Know the words of the Apostle Peter who sufficiently clearly says that this is a trial:

> Beloved, do not be surprised at the fiery ordeal that has come upon to you to test you, as though something strange were happening to you. But rejoice inasmuch as you participate in

---

[299] Rev 12:3-4

[300] Wisdom 17:6, as in the Russian version of the Bible.

> the sufferings of Christ, so that you may be overjoyed when his glory is revealed.[301]

And as the prophet Isaiah says:

> Though your sins are like scarlet,
> They shall be white as snow;
> Through they are red as crimson,
> They shall be like wool.[302]

To extinguish this fire, to transform it into the scarlet of suffering, depends on our will, our blood. Or else we will be consumed and the wind will sweep the gray dust and will create illusions out of it. Prayer to the point of blood exuding from us will support us at the hour of suffering, it will destroy the enchantment of red terrors.[303]

> It would be better for me to die than to stop prayer.

Spoke the prophet Daniel. It was only Daniel's prayer that quenched the severity of the fiery oven.[304]

Zechariah said:

> And he showed me Joshua the high priest, and satan standing at his right hand in order to contradict him. And the Lord said to satan, "The Lord rebuke you, satan. The Lord, who selected Jerusalem, may He rebuke you." Is not he a brand plucked from the fire.[305]

Here the Savior is called: a brand plucked from the fire. It was necessary to incarnate Jesus in a concentration of struggle and

---

[301] 1 Peter 4:12-13
[302] Isaiah 1:18
[303] Luke 22:44
[304] Bely has two events in the book of Daniel mixed: the 3 youths in the fiery oven, and Daniel in the lion's den.
[305] Zech 3:1-2. Bely applies this verse to Jesus, as the Russian word for the names Jesus and Joshua are the same.

terror, descend into hell, into the red region, so that after the winning the struggle, He would leave a route for all of those freed. He gained the victory. Temptation rose to the surface as a fiery river which, according to the words of Daniel: A river exited and flowed in His presence.[306]

The terror of fire and the thorns of suffering are focused in the color red.[307] The theosophical duality of the use of red is understood. Is this not the reason that among the Manichaeans they maintain two creator gods: a good and an evil? Or Sataniel among the Bogomiles as Christ's elder brother. All of this will not fill the abyss between good and evil. Christ remains contradistinctive to satan as in the vision of the prophet Zechariah.

Blood did not turn Him red without a cost. They clothed Him in red but not without a cost. This cup is the new testament in His blood that He spilled for us. Not without a cost did he suffer fear and worry, turning his grieving gaze to His slumbering disciples, "My soul is sorrowful unto death." So His sweat as blood soaked the ground. And they suited Him in scarlet and weaving a crown of thorns they placed it on Him. It was the third hour and they crucified Him. At the sixth hour darkness started. At the ninth hour Jesus cried with a loud voice, "Eloi, Eloi, Lamma Savakhthani."[308] The cross erected on Golgotha is always awesome due to the impending happiness of the second arrival when He will come with the armies of heaven, all clothed in white linen.

The cross erected on Golgotha is completely soaked with drops of blood, and it wears a crown of aromatic imperishable and white mystical roses![309] Christianity was scarlet from blood over its initial centuries. The summit of Christianity is white as snow. The historical evolution of the church is the process of making robes white using the Lamb's blood.[310] As far as our church is concerned,[311]

[306] Daniel 7:10
[307] John 19:2
[308] Mark 15:33-34, Matt 26:38, 27:45-46
[309] This is an allusion to the Rosicrucian sign of a cross with roses.
[310] Rev 7:14

it has still not won, but is already tasting the sweetness of victory characterized by all the tints of the glowing pint color of our expectation. The pink color unites red and white. If the theosophical definition of the color red has a relationship to the struggle between God and the devil, and where the victory clearly expresses the luminosity of divine humanity as white, and this is compared to the pink, then the subsequent stage of spiritual experience is decorated in a pink color.

Approaching the unconditional we comprehend the concept. The realization of the concept produces life. In art the concepts are the source of enjoyment. When it is transformed into a banner that leads to the goals, art adjoins religion. Then the concepts are double life-producing. The ascent to higher spheres of existence require an inner knowledge of the route. Our trustworthy guide is prayer. It penetrates through opaque glass, and through which we can see. The blinding brilliance of the ideal occurs after tears are spilled. Prayer is the condition that allows us to sail across sorrow and to joy. Ecstasy is joy over these concepts and prayer uninterruptedly leads concepts into the soul.

In prayer the summits of art are united with the mystical. The unification of mysticism with art is theurgy.

Theurgy transforms the attitude toward concepts. The concepts are a display of divine principles. In the religion of Zoroaster concepts are identified with the nine angelic principles. In Christianity there are nine angelic ranks. In art the concept is passive. In religion it is influential. The contemplation of the concept in art liberates from suffering. Theurgic creativity communicates love. We begin to love the display when we notice its concept. We begin to love the world of ideal love. Feelings are the activity of the will. Love is the most profound feeling, the most profound activity of the will.

> If I distribute all of my property and abandon my body to incineration, but have not love, there is no benefit in this for me.[312]

---

[311] The Russian Orthodox Church

This is what the apostle Paul said. Diverse are the displays of love. Often the kernel of love is obscure. Often its true root is lost to us.

If the activity of love must be organized by rationality, then the question of the level of influence of rationale or feeling transfers the definition of love to the province of philosophy. But the harmony between rationality and feeling is not attained with compromises between one and the other. The unimpeded influence of feeling on rationality appears as the source of deception. Overcoming rationality and feeling through their unification immutably expands the types of comprehension even to the most common items. Wisdom is especially the widest level of comprehension. Symbolism is the province of its application. Every love from this point forward is exemplary, symbolic, representative. Symbolic love transmits the point of its attachment into eternity. The incarnation of love is theurgy. Love is theurgic in essence. Subsequently mysticism is inherent in it. The organization of love is religious.

If true love is contained in unorganized sensation a new series of questions now have a place here. What is the relationship of love to morality, to justice, to law? Some socialists say that morality is the appraisal of interests. Justice, according to Solovyov,[313] is historically a progressing definition of the compelling balance of two moral interests: personal freedom and the general welfare. Justice needs to comply with morality. The law – this obligatory organization of justice – is subjected to grace. Grace is the display of divine love. Love is the burst of brilliance of the essence that is outside of justice, morality, law, and must not nullify one or the other or the third. Its essential indications for this must be all-encompassing and constant – eternity. Eternity is incarnated in theurgy. As a result the unimpeded feeling of love must include something religious. It is unimprovable. Concepts can be natal and transmittable. The concepts of the world and

[312] 1 Cor 13:3

[313] Vladimir M. Solovyov

humanity are for the most part common to all. In the visible world the person forms the highest stage of objectification out of observations accessible to us. In it is the essence of worldwide progress. The concepts of the world and humanity conditionally coincide for us. We can call the concept of the world – the soul of the world. The soul of the world – Sophia according to Solovyov – is the perfect humanity eternally maintained within the divine essence of Christ. Here the mystical essence of the church is interfused with the image of eternal womanhood, the bride of the Lamb. Here the Alpha and Omega are true love. The relationship of Christ to the church – the groom to the bride – is a fathomless worldwide symbol. This symbol illuminates every consummate love. Every love is a symbol of this symbol. Every symbol in it terminating width displays the image of the Groom and Bride. The sound of the trumpet summons echoes out of the New Jerusalem. The pinnacle of every symbol pertains to the consummate, the terminative of all. The terminative essence of the final symbol is disclosed where the new earth and new heaven will manifest. The Revelation to John is consummated by the voice of the bride, "Come." The pinnacle of all styles of love converging due to this common symbol, prepare us for Eternity. That which begins here will conclude there.

The brilliant burst of religious love descends at the wedding. At the wedding, according to Solovyov, we have a figure that is sanctified by God's word, it signifies the union of Christ with the Church. As Solovyov writes:

> The primary significance of the wedding belongs to the pathos of love. A person views the wife not in the manner as she appears from an external observation, but gazes at what she represents, what it is that she was primordially designed to be, how God wanted to view her from the beginning of time, and what she must terminally become. She is confirmed as becoming her goal, her purpose.[314]

[314] From *Justification of the Good*

The gradual materialization of the wedding is the task of worldwide history. Its meaning is solely mystical. Every other attitude of the wedding is perfunctory. Such an attitude is the origin of a hope that will never materialize.

An eternal star-filled love will not radiate without a martyr's crown. Only when sharp thorns shred the suffering body and the discarded crown of crimson stars illuminate the sky with pink rays, then the current of marriage – beaten against walls – will ascend and sparkle like stars. Marriage and romantic love only then will acquire their proper tints when other symbols, those still not accessible due to their relationship beyond humanity's comprehension, appear.

So does the Groom speak to the Church his bride, in the Song of Songs, "What the lily is among the thorns, so is my beloved among the other girls." And so does the Bride the Church respond to the Groom, "What the apple trees is among the forest trees, so is my beloved among the young men."[315]

The image of the mystical church is at the frontiers of time and space. The expanses melt. The beginning of time merges with its end. What forms is a circle of time – a ring of rings is a ring of return. Solar light emanates from it. Now it discloses its image and raises its voice from timelessness, "Behold, I will arrive soon."[316]

Christ – the incarnation of Eternity – is the fullness of our day's time. The incarnation begins it and the symbolism concludes it. We must incarnate Christ [in us] just as Christ was incarnated. Our love for Christ is the second realism of reality.

> Truly, truly I say to you, I am the bread of life. Who eats My flesh and drinks My blood will reside in Me and I in him.[317]

This is the incarnation, the theurgy, so that we the children have hope to become what He is. And just as we reach for Him in the transformation through love, so He is incarnated in every type of transformed love. The day of the eternal noon when the

[315] Song 2:2-3
[316] Rev 22:20
[317] John 6:35, 53

superhuman appears was and will again be, and it will return again.

> Soon you will not see Me and again quickly you will see Me. And no one can take away your joy from you. And on that day you will ask Me of nothing. This I told you so you will have peace in Me. You will have sorrow in the world, but be courageous. I have defeated the world.[318]
>
> I tell you brethren, the time is already short. So he who has a wife should act as though he does not, and the one sorrowing as though he is not sorrowing. Because the scene of this world passes away.[319]

To traverse the form of this world is to depart to the place where all are insane in Christ: this is our route. We are at the pass and still do not know where to pass through. The end of forms leads us to accepting other forms. This world sprouts in forms during time and space. The changes of these forms for our interminable consciousness will erase the form of this world. Then there will be a new earth and new heaven. This will now be the end of this world. The endless line of causes unfolding in time, with the estrangement of time, turns into a point. Standing at the beginning and end is the same. "I am the Alpha and Omega, beginning and end, who is and was and is coming, the Almighty."[320]

Who of us will proceed outside of time will say with Christ, "I am no longer in the world, but they are in the world, and I go to You, holy Father.[321] We will gaze at Him. And the azure clear gaze will indicate nothing. And so from two different worlds we will look at each other.

The soul is awakened and again speaks of the end. We do not know whether our pass will be the beginning of the end or some illusion of it. But at the first snowfall that smothers us we read sacred promises. At the voice of the first blizzard we heard the

---

[318] John 16:16, 23, 33
[319] 1 Cor 7:29-31
[320] Rev 1:8, 22:13
[321] John 17:11

joyful summons, "Return, again return." Often enclosed in isolated streets of deep midnight, we stand in front of a crimson light of a street lamp, praying that our entire life will be illuminated with a scarlet light. The crimson flickers on the silver-white snow dust, while the dark blue sky with its gold lining is clear. And the sorrowful and kind tales of the blizzard continue and continue, and someone's voice rises from outside of time, "I will see you again, and your heart will rejoice, and no one will take away your joy from you. You will not ask Me of anything." The culmination of Christianity, the New Testament thought of the end, the unexpected consolation and joy which is immutably maintained in this thought – here is the light entering us, into our soul. From where did it arrive? Why?

When the remains of the dust fly away and the whiteness of the air starts to shine, and so immediately light blue will take over. In the middle of broad daylight we will learn to recognize our joy, watching the clear azure sky so full of joy. The white radiance on a colorless worldwide abyss will become blue. Such an optimistic law: this occurs always, whenever the white defeats the colorless abyss. And so looking into the azure we see that the impossible view of the abyss of the world has an air-white veil hung over it. Only a concentrated stare will unveil the abyss, opening into a transparent sea of white atmosphere like a background covering the ocean.

Departing from the colorful symbols we are in a state to reestablish the image of the victorious world. Let this obscure image scatter the fog, as we believe it will. Its face must be white like snow. Its eyes are two bridges to heaven, amazingly bottomless and blue. Like honey overflowing is the ecstasy of the saints in heaven and their gold thick hair. Eternity will shine on immaculate infant faces. Shine and then extinguish, but they will never know sorrow. Comprehending the reflecting radiance of the Eternal we believe that truth will never abandon us, that it is with us. Love is with us. Loving we will conquer. The brilliance is with us. O if when I awaken I can arise. Calm is with us. And happiness is with us.

1905

# SONG OF LIFE

Art is the art to live. To live means to be able, to know, to have ability. Knowledge of life is the ability to preserve all life – mine, someone else's, a relative's. But the preservation of life consists in its continuation. The continuation of whatever it might be is creativity. Art is the creativity of life. The instrument of creativity materializes as knowledge. Knowledge severed from creativity is an instrument without the person who possesses it. Such an instrument is an aimless instrument. Such knowledge is lifeless knowledge.

Meanwhile, this form of knowledge without creativity reigns in our culture.

So what is happening is that death is threatening it.

Our culture does not know life, does not want life, cannot live. But our culture is the crown of humanity's knowledge.

This crown is a mortal crown. Death threatens humanity.

And this is not a fantasy. Humanity is degenerating. Everywhere a bad breed seems to be dominating. The very condition of egoistic regeneration, the normalcy of the genders, is disintegrating.

Finally, there is certain data forcing us to see degeneration in the changes of the structure of human skeleton. All of these external symptoms are a sign of the degeneration of the human's soul and its rhythm of life.

The original art, as the creative basis as to what is valuable in life, is the creation of a healthy posterity outside of yourself or the accumulation of vital strengths in yourself. Its initial route is the transformation of the species. The second route is the transformation of the individual. As far as art and religion are concerned, their routes are the same.

The first route, the transformation of life outside yourself, is the route by which humanity traveled, and this route brought humanity to denying itself.

How did this occur?

The root of art is the creative power of the individual growing toward a struggle against the darkness surrounding it. Fate is this darkness. The task of the individual is to defeat fate, no matter how fate is expressed, whether it be in the form of a bear attacking the person, as it was undoubtedly in the caveman era, or in the form of an evil spirit threatening him, as it was during the prehistoric and dark ages. The creation of a harmonic individual, that is, the individuality of a strong hero, is an indispensable condition of life. Here life is a drama, the individual is its hero. Here life is creativity; here art is life. And the artistic form is the individual; he is constructing a ladder in life where the step taken is momentary. Subjecting the moment to itself, the individual carries self-realization through a series of instants. The form of the materialization of the individual then separates from the individual. The sum of these instants is the sum of artistic forms: the individual is still the same. So do the forms of life, that is, the artistic forms, separate from the individual. The person is an artist of many forms. The understanding of form becomes more complex. Form in the personal sense – the *me* expressed in the body – manifests as the creative principle of form in a transmittable sense: instrument, clothing, residence, intellect. Here art as we define it is united with the applied character of the instrument of production: the spear that is decorated, clothing that is woven with feathers, a residence that is designed. Thought is clothed in the form of songs, myths, images. The process of creativity, that is, life experienced as the creative song of the hero, is exchanged for the article of creativity.

Art becomes technology.

Articles are exchanged, but products now become goods. The exchange of creative forms institutes a circular shield of creativity: the hero defeating fate through the creativity of life becomes the warrior in a certain regiment that is barricaded by creative objects used as a common barricade. The form of life as a shield clothes the rhythm of the individual. Fate, chaos, a bear or evil spirit, will not break through due to the defense of the group. Creativity becomes the manufacture of an idol. The idol defends the group from the gloom of night. The idol now brings the individual and his rhythm as a sacrifice. As the basis of the sacrificial offering, it is fear, that if the hero, or the soldier in our case, wants to return to his heroic past, this past turning into a hero, threatens to shatter the defense made of images and release the darkness – whether it be a bear or evil spirit – into the residence which is presently safe: courage emaciates, life's rhythm begins to decay. As much as there is a hero in each of us, each endures some unknown force: not the force of a demon, but the force of a fetish, an idol, and the name of the idol is – the security of the group. The images here are goods and are replaced by creative value. Fetishism of the production of goods, the creation of idols and forms of art, force imposed on the hero – all of this is a personification of the extinguishing of one type of life's rhythm.

The substitution of creativity by comfort generates a release of the means of production – thought, objects of utilization, and etc. All becomes coordinated for general use. The source of creativity, the individual expressing himself in movement, is replaced by what the individual generates, by a lifeless seal. And unnoticeably the corpse – the fetish – ascends a place over life. So is the government formed with its rights and ethics, so does the nature of religion and creativity die. Within a person the living *I* becomes an unproductive contemplation of the surrounding nature and even nature becomes impersonal. This second step in the participation of life is an inflated development of philosophy and science.

Earlier the creativity of life, guided by rhythm, not only healed the nature of the artist, but also created in him a staircase of renovations. An allegorical picture of these renovations are reflected in biology as the evolution of animal forms, while religious images, songs, dances, prayers were the means to sculpture new steps of life in the staircase of the universe. A person walks from the land to the sky, and he would already be in the sky if his intellect did not turn the song of the land and sky into contradictory abstractions: the land into the understanding of the law of nature, and heaven into the norm of contemplating cognizance.

This dual decomposition of rhythm initially manifests in rights and ethics, then in science and philosophy it will fetter life with its solid armor. Life's creativity terminates existence. True that in history titans have risen shaking the environment like heavyweights, soon they no longer surfaced at all, because the heavyweights did not possess strength as did the hero. Humanity ceased to stir the volcano of personal creativity. But the group as a sum of enslaved individuals grew decrepit without creative gymnastics, and the mechanism – an invisible corpse in place of people – discarded millions of marionettes. The individual falling asleep surfaced as a marionette, its life was the type of life seen in a movie. Every personification of the image and form of a hero disappeared from culture. The fetish even disappeared, disintegrating into the rank of logical deliberations – the norm hanging in a vacuum. Science sprayed the fetish into atoms and power lines. Philosophy evolves laws of education of strength from laws of education of words. Humanity today is just alphabet letters. The heroes are the letters X and Y. Society is just a word arranged to form a conclusion. The world is a bundle of conclusions. The result of contemporary philosophy is reaching a conclusion not based on something to think or something to create; it is the culmination of dissolution. Even interest toward knowing something, what it is that is invisible that causes us to think, is forbidden. The result is what we inevitably end up as.

This great but limited dissolution of the world is not a dream. This short abstract view of the world was discussed by the foremost pillars of the researchers of gnoseology – Cohen[322] and

[322] Herman Cohen, 1842-1918, German Jewish philosopher.

Husserl.[323] As far as they are concerned, all that remains is to fold your hands, comfortably sit in your living room, fall asleep and die. This is to what we have converted creativity of life. As long as we thought that the struggle against fate was our destiny, tragic power was scattered on the surface of the land as fiery-breathing lava of religion and form of art. Now we submissively fold our hands. If the supra-individualistic norm of knowledge draws a picture for us of time and space, and in time us traversing time, according to the laws of contemplating cognizance, which in general just meditates within itself, then the struggle against fate is predefined by fate. So then fate already consumed us before the creation of the world.

* * *

Existence surrounds us with thousands of items of luxury, defending us from attacks of invisible bridges, towers, railways. It is the final manifestation of song, the final dissolution of rhythm on that route by which the song was developed. Today the song alters the course of its direction. And existence demolishes.

All culture grew from songs and dances.

But songs dissipated. And artistic prose bloomed such marvelous flowers, and the philosophy from the Middle Ages' scholastics to our days sprouted such profound and whirling thoughts, and such complexity was disclosed in social attitudes. All of this is the flower of the dying song of the nation.

Music separated from song and was immersed in the soul's depths – then from somewhere a symphony materialized. But its place is in a concert hall, that is, four walls, and its symbols are electrical lights.

The word separated from song and developed toward every side. It formed a flower bed of poetic forms with the most refined of flowers – drama. But the stone roofs of the theater collapsed on the drama and crushed it.

[323] Edmund Husserl, 1859-1937, German philosopher.

The word was ignited with thousands of colors. Songs of paradise sparkled in history colorfully from the frescoes of Beato,[324] to the local posters. Soon the artist will become a signboard painter.

Architecture turned into an engineering art: to build bridges, American wheels, and towers is the task of the artist.

In short, the street marketplace provided materials for art. The spirit of artistry spread in the theory of knowledge and science. Windblown sandstones now lie where the meadow turned green.

Daily life is betrayed to the cinematography in the café and saloon. History is become a wax museum.

Under the ugly scab of life, Nietzsche overheard the rhythm of life. Dionysus called the spirit – the heartbeat of life. Apollon[325] called the spirit – the life of creative imagery. Both principles manifested outside of life, because life stopped being life. As a result we can define music only as the heaven of the soul, while prose is the cloud of this heaven. Clouds descend from heaven. The body evolves from rhythm, the union of rhythm with imagery. The symbol of the radiance of body and soul: the planned route is here turned toward heroism, that is, the salvation of humanity. The protective barricade from chaos derived from lifeless images, thoughts and knowledge is removed. Culture collapses. The bear or evil spirit attacks us. But the image and ugliness, light and darkness, symbols of psychological division, they are the branches of the tree of knowledge of good and evil. The struggle of a person against fate is the struggle of the hero against his personal dream. The tree of knowledge of good and evil contains one common trunk of life. The return to the basic trunk of this tree is the motto of the future. The channel bed of life deepens. The earlier channel bed appears as just an imagination, and a culture with its towers of steel, knowledge and philosophy appears as a hallucination. Its towers are towers of clouds. They dissipate and dissolve into darkness. Already the primordial roughness and beauty of

[324] Fra Angelico, 1395-1455, Italian Renaissance painter.

[325] Apollon Aleksandrovich Grigoryev, 1822-1864, Russian poet, literary critic, songwriter, and translator of English drama into Russian.

heroism exuded its odor upon us from the *Ring of the Nibelung*.[326] There is a song regarding our future when Siegfried will again struggle against Wotan the bear. Wotan is to wander about the land in the disguise of a pilgrim. Again heaven is to unite with the land, and gods and people will freely wander.

The tree of life turns history into the tree of knowledge of good and evil, and the hero divides into a contemplator and worker. The worker manufactures goods, the contemplator slides over him in a cloud of thoughts. The former is a slave; the latter is god and king. The slave is in the image of deity, and here is our assignment in the historical culture. God in us manifests as the slave of our personal dream.

A cloud of thoughts is goodness; the goods of life is evil. Denial of the world announces morality, and by way of this is the person as abandoned a sacrifice to objects.

* * *

Song is a symbol. The image here is discarded by rhythm. The symbol is always a reality because the symbol is always musical, while music is the life-providing element of creativity. Prose developed from song, and music as a form of art. Subsequently song is the evolution of every later arrangement of imageries and rhythms. In its history is the history of the derivation of images. [History] is the musical bond. In the basis of religion it is like a prayer. In the basis of prose it is like a lyric. In the basis of music it is the point of departure of immaculate rhythm. Here the word summons an imagery, the word itself become the image. The word here seeks embodiment in order to become [the body]. The word here creates the body of a harmonic life. The word is here rhythm, since the image is discarded from the eternal elements of the soul.

Rhythm is just like the wind that penetrates the heaven of the soul, it is like the wind that is born in the sky, because the soul is the eternal foremother of the body and the sky is the eternal foremother of the land. From the abyss of outer space, nebulae

[326] German epic music dramas composed by Richard Wagner.

with their suns and their planets are born. The spirit of music rested over the chaos. And there was light, the first day of creation, and Earth was generated from heaven.

This first day of creation is drawing near, when we speak of the new life-providing rhythm. A flood of music, presently breaking apart all forms of art, will be the day. It will wash the old world, and the song is now the ark holding us over the waves of chaos toward a new creative life. The word in the song possesses the character of an oath. We have forgotten that song is magic, and we will soon understand that we need to barricade ourselves with a magical circle of song, so it is not just music that floods us. Music spreading through all of culture is like a flood and the storm clouds of our future are on the horizon. The old chaos thunders there and shines there like lightnings. The old carries threatening stormy weather. The flood approaches.

Song is the first day of creativity, the first day of the world of art. The musical elements of the soul, is illuminated by light in song, where all is filled, as Thales said, "with gods, demons and souls."[327] Forms of art then emanate from song. Here the land of art descends from the sky.

Rhythm is the first manifestation of music. This is the wind, its turbulence causing foam ripples upon the blue ocean. Clouds are born from the altercation of winds, the smoky clouds of prose are derived from the arrangement of musical rhythms of the soul.

Just as all clouds have a lining, we also grasp the outlines of familiar images. Creative forms are born of a musical fog[328] where the colors are tonal, and where the object is strength and highness of cords.

When we say, "This is not a cloud, this is a giant, this is the mountain crest, this is the invisible chamber of an unknown city," we draw the images of creativity to the ground. Here the images become ideal, and drawing near to the ground they are capable of being seen, they are visibly real. These images of fantasy populate

[327] Thales of Miletus, 624-546 BC, Greek philosopher, mathematician and astronomer.
[328] The Russian word here can also refer to a nebula.

our world. So in art a mythic creativity begins, so in art eternal reality is unveiled.

But it is not in visibility, not in fantasy of song that life resides. Life resides in the song of music, its ethereal heaven, which created our old world also, and will the new world based on our desires.

Song unites rhythm – time, and imagery – space. in word – causality. In the series of causes and results, creativity begins a new series of causes and results. In the world of existence, a world of values is created.

Song was the beginning of creativity in art. And now when creativity in art all the more and more is becoming a lifeless creative form, song is the first summons to creativity of life-providing form. It is a summons to the person for him to become an artist of life.

Song summons. Song lives. Let the historian learn the laws of increase and dissemination of song. Let them teach us how French singing migrated into Italy and Spain, how sonnets and ballads crystallized from singing. How the poet Dante evolved from being just a troubadour, how in Greece the seven-string lyre of Terpander[329] birthed melody, and melody – verses, and verses – the great lyrics of antiquity. We are not composing smooth theories here; we are arranging vitality of life in song.

Let us be worthless, let us be forerunners of the future. We know one thing: by singing we live, by songs we live. We experience them. We experience them as did Orpheus, whose memory summons singing. The shadow of Eurydice. No, the very Eurydice now resurrected. When Orpheus played music the rocks dance.

Mythology in the example of Orpheus assigned strength to music, bringing movement to the stagnancy of matter. Song is the activity of the world transformed by music and the imagined world. Song is the world as an island washed by the waves of music. Song is the residence of children washed by the ether of the

[329] Terpander of Antissa, first half of 7th century BC, poet, and traditionally the father of Greek music and lyric poetry.

sea. This is the island to which Zarathustra invited us. He invites us to leave those faithful to the world.

Song is the single item that is disclosed in diversity. It alone can transform all songs into one song. The *Song of Songs* is love, because creativity resides in love, creativity resides in life. It is not in vain that the *Song of Songs* starts with one personage – the Beloved. This is the beloved of eternity who is loved by the prophet of the land. Revelation directs us to that same personage in heaven: we call this personage – the bride. Earthly songs, heavenly songs, are the veil of the bride of eternity, the eternal return of eternity. Is not the circle of return the wedding ring?

We know that when we sing, then in heaven we remain faithful on Earth, and remaining faithful on Earth we love heaven.

Now we know that the soul and body are a single entity, just as we know that earth and sky are a single entity. But now we also know that the land of our soul and the sky of our body is only creativity. And we also know that the province of creativity is not the distant island of Kythira,[330] but life itself. We also know that not all life is life, and not all art is creativity. But the contemporary era has made the innovators of art wise due to experience of boldness, having found a form of artistic creativity illuminating the depths of life's aspirations. It was not just in the union of poetry with music, but the unity of all art.

The supreme pinnacle of music, its most complex form, is the symphony. The supreme pinnacle of poetry, its most complex form, is tragedy. It is impossible to unite symphony and tragedy vitally, just as we cannot consider life as being a stage united with the concert hall.

We need a union of poetry and music in us, and not outside of us. We want to live actively in solely word and music, and not just to be a reflection of them. We do not want a lifeless form of a dome to crown the temple of art, but a person, a living form. And song is the news of humanity's transformation. This transformation occurring in our experiences unfolds the sole route that is the goal

[330] Island in the southern tip of Greece.

in itself. On this route during the transformation of what is visible we attain our transformation.

Here in our actions, in our words, in the sensations of a person, our personal life is that of a troubadour, and life is song. But in a troubadour we will recognize the person who has transformed his life. And his song is the news of transformation. And if humanity approaches this frontier of culture, beyond which is death, rather than new forms of life, in song and only in song can its personal fate be overheard. Then we start the song of our life.

We have forgotten how to fly, it is difficult for us to think, it is difficult for us to walk, we have no accomplishments, and our life's rhythm decays. The easiness of divine simplicity and health is what we need. Then we will find the boldness to sing of this life. Because if the living song is not life, then life is not life at all.

We need a musical program of life divided into song – accomplishment. But we have no single personal song. This signifies that our soul has no personal current in its stream. And we are not all that we are to be, but just a shadow. And our souls are not a resurrected Eurydice, quietly sleeping under the Lethe[331] of oblivion. But the Lethe overflows its banks. It will flood us if we do not listen to the songs of Orpheus summoning us.

Orpheus is calling for his Eurydice.

1908

---

[331] One of the 5 rivers of the underworld according to Greek mythology. The word also means oblivion.

# THE BOOK OF REVELATION IN RUSSIAN POETRY

## I

There is no division of any type. Life is a single entity. The appearance of many is only an illusion. No matter what kind of barricades we may erect between manifestations of the world, these barricades are directly intangible and inconceivable. They create various views of an attitude of some single item toward itself. Many of them appear as being only indirect in relation to the one, just like the diversity of folds in a fabric. The veil is torn from the world and these fabrics, people, growths, will vanish. The world like a sleeping beauty will awaken to completeness, she will shake its pearl-filled kokoshnik.[332] Her face will flare like the dust, eyes will become azure, cheeks like snow-filled clouds, lips like fire. She will arise, the beauty will start to laugh. Black storm clouds hovering over her will be dissipated by her rays. They will flare with fire and blood. The depiction of a dragon will be inscribed on them. Now the defeated red dragon will be scattered all over the clean sky.

## II

It was spring of the year 1900. A dark wing of the future cast a shadow on the day and turbulent visions in my sleep arose in my

[332] A traditional Russian headdress.

soul. A single route for humanity opened. The contour of the religion of the future surfaced. The respiration of the Eternal Wife could be heard.

Solovyov's lecture, *Regarding the End of Worldwide History*, struck like thunder.[333] But the great mystic was right. I remember him having abysmally focused eyes, with hair piled on his shoulders, appearing ironically calm, contemplative, enveloped by storm clouds of fire. His words were acutely and perceptibly expressed like jolts of lightning, and the lightnings penetrated the future. And our heart was captivated by a secret sweetness when he reverently bent his face over his manuscript like a prophet of Bible times. Picture after picture arose in the midst of the fog that hung over the future. A series of the peaks of icebergs could be identified, steep mountains glistening with snow through which we must traverse so not to fall into an abyss. And from the black canyons the smoke of dark clouds rose. The rays of the sun, reflecting the color of blood on the clouds, caused the future face of a flaming and enraged dragon to appear in the smoke.[334]

But from the immortal heights of the philosophies of Plato and Schelling, Solovyov spoke of the rose-color smile of the World Soul.[335] He understood the sweetness of the *Song of Songs* and the apparition of the Woman clothed in the Sun. And so from the philosophic heights [he] descended into this world in order to direct people to this danger that is threatening them, although exciting, but unknown to them. And in this comfortable room his roaring voice blared, and his long hands convulsively turned page after page. He struggled with a fear that was strong and imposing. It seemed that he was not precisely turning the pages, but he was removing masks from a clandestine enemy of truth. And mask after mask flew off, and mask after mask dissolved into a fog of dust. And the dust ignited. And the evil flame of the corporeal fire

---

[333] Vladimir Sergeevich Solovyov, 1853-1900, Russian religious thinker and philosopher. This lecture is part of his book, *Three Conversations*.

[334] Andrei Bely visited Vladimir Solovyov a few months before his death on July 31, 1900, and had some extensive conversations with him. These are his reflections.

[335] Friedrich Wilhelm Schelling, 1775-1854, German philosopher who was highly regarded in Russian philosophic circles. Solovyov's lecture was delivered in March 1900, in Petersburg.

ignited. And all of it whirling vanished into thick darkness. So we sat at a table drinking tea, and he, after finishing reading the text, shouted at the walls in an insanely infantile laugh as though responding to a joke. But the visions he summoned were formidable, a reflection of the spring, golden evening dusk in the window.

It was not so much that *Narrative of the Antichrist* stuck me, as much as the words of one of the characters, "And I now since last year started to also notice, and not only in the air, but in the soul. But there is no complete clarity here. It is all of some kind of alarm and as though some kind of ominous premonition."[336] In these words I deciphered all that was unclear to that point in my personal experiences. I turned to Vladimir Sergeevich with a question, whether he is deliberately underscoring the words regarding alarm, similar to the smoke enveloping the world. And Vladimir Sergeevich said that such an underscore from his side was deliberate. The subsequent words about the smoke was confirmed to be literal when the throat of the volcano and the black soot erupted, expanding over the entire world like a net, summoning a purple glaring evening dusk. In addition I understood that the causes for the appearance, in front of our eyes, of this net tossed over the world are found in the depths of individual cognizance. But the depths of cognizance rest united in a universal, ecumenical single entity. I also then understood that the hovering smoke– in its spiritual application – will fall on Russia releasing outside all the horrors of wars and internecine struggles. I waited for signs from the outside, hinting at what is occurring inside. I knew: a chimera of fireworks will be discharged over humanity.[337]

And reality did not hesitate to confirm these expectations. The words of Merezhkovsky about the apocalyptic lifelessness of European life was distributed, gathering to unveil the Coming despot. A new type appeared incarnating chaos in himself arising from these depths, a kind of hooligan. The ghost of the Mongolian

---

[336] From *Three Conversations.*

[337] Bely makes an indirect reference to the eruption of the volcano Mt Pelee on the island Martinique, on May 8, 1902.

invasion grew formidably. A whirlwind swept over European humanity, stirring storm clouds of dust. And the light turned red as a result of the dust suspended in it, so did the worldwide fire begin.

A worldwide grimace as a mask put on the world terrified Vl. Solovyov. Merezhkovsky pointed at the world's insanity, undermining humanity. The chaos from within is manifested to us as insanity, while from the outside it is a life fragmented into an innumerable quantity of distinct courses. So it is in science. Inept specialization generates a number of engineers and technicians wearing a mask of intelligence on their face, while maintaining an unprincipled and chaotic insanity in their heart. The supplement of unethical science creates the terror of the contemporary war with Japan, a war where the symbol of eminent chaos is seen to be rising.[338]

All that needs to be done is to review the brochure by Louis Nodo, *They did not know*,[339] and we will realize that all of our military operations were a slick optimistic deception. Japan was a mask we could not see through.

Solovyov profoundly foresaw this worldwide masquerade, of which we surface as participants. The smoke carried in the air, after Solovyov's death, truly, settled, as though beaten to the ground by rain. The sky was cleansed. Now on our behalf some kind of eternal azure-colored rested eyes started to sparkle, but this is the reason the dust carried through the sky settled on all these objects, falling on faces turning them sharply black, almost distorting their natural features, creating an involuntary masquerade.

The whirlwind now risen in contemporary Russia has unsettled the dust and must inevitably create a ghost of the red terror, clouds of smoke and fire, because the light penetrating the dust ignites it. Subsequently we need to remember that the red dragon, being brought to us from the east, is translucent. It is a foggy cloud, and not something concrete. And war cannot be. It is

[338] Russo-Japanese War, 1904-1905.

[339] French journalist and correspondent. Published Petersburg, 1905.

something derived from our sick imagination, it is an ostensive symbol in the struggle of the ecumenical soul against world terror, the symbol of the struggle of our souls against the chimeras and hydras of chaos. The battle against the terrifying hydra is futile: no matter how many heads of the snake we may decapitate, new will grow, until we finally realize that the hydra itself is just an illusion. It is a mask thrown on reality, behind which the Unseen is hiding. Until we realize that the mask is translucent, it will grow imposing on itself bloody worldwide-historical pictures. Ostensively the flying dragon will unite with the red rooster spreading its wings over the ancient estates in the deepest recesses of Russia. All will drown in the sea of fire. The illusion will laugh and his red laugh will consume the world in fire. It will serve as a light to illuminate those blinded due to horror [of war].[340]

L. Andreev is discredited for his subjectivity. In place of describing the massive movement of armies or the genuine portrayal of war, he as though daydreams. But this is his manner of projecting into the contemporary situation.

These are the words of Nodo, a witness to this war:

> In contemporary war, all is secretive, scattered, distant, unseen, abstract. This is a struggle of movements, signalization from the air, and electrical or heliographic communications. Get near to the front line of fighting and you will see nothing in front of you. If this is a battery, then it is hidden behind some kind of mount in a field. It seems it has no purpose or meaning and just being scorched in the open. You are constantly being deceived by a phantasmagoria. This must be war: unseen, unorganized, clandestine. Who captured Liaoyang?[341] The Japanese army? Yes of course the Japanese army, but with the help of nightmares. The demand for

[340] The reference here is to an article title *Red Laugh*, written by Leonid Andreev and published in 1904. It deals with the horror of war and which causes society to devolve into chaos, based on the events of the Russo-Japanese war.

[341] On August 25, 1904, the Battle of Liaoyang took place. This was a major battle of the Russo-Japanese war. Even though Russia retreated from the city after the battle, they claimed a victory.

> clothes, an illusion, apathy, a fantasy, daydreams, the ignorance of reality – this is of what the first campaign consisted.[342]

To grasp the reality means to tear the mask off of the Unseen, crawling to us while possessing many caricatures. Solovyov attempted to point us toward a pleasantly appearing caricature of lies thrown by the enemy on the face to the One who can unite the divided sky and land of our souls into a single and unheard-of entity. Only the glistening pedals of eternal roses can calm the raging infernal flame presently licking the world. The Eternal Wife will deliver it from this fatal danger in a minute's time. Not in vain is the eternally-feminine image of Brunhild engirdled with a fiery river. Not in vain does Fafnir stand guard over the monstrous dragon.[343]

Solovyov pointed at the caricature of insanity entering the world and invited all those overwhelmed by the apparition to dig deep so not to lose their mind. But to dig deep into the eternally-feminine sources of the soul means to unveil her face in the presence of many. Here begins the theurgic power of his poetry where the pantheism of Fet, and the individualism of Lermontov, along with the brilliant foresights of Christian Gnostics, approach and join each other.

I did not see Solovyov after the unforgettable meeting, and much was opened to me since that time. I did not understand what was in Solovyov when he discussed the eternal approaches to the Radiant Female Friend, but the twilight that girdled the horizon calmed the alarm. I understood that these alarms did not personally pertain to me, but threatened everyone. During these days I grasped the concept of the worldwide smile of the dusk and the azure of heaven's eyes. I started to understand that just as in contemporary war all is clandestine, scattered, distant, unseen and abstract, so it is in mystic waves sweeping against each other in the world, they terminate in an altercation. This struggle

---

[342] Quotes from Louis Nodo's article.

[343] It is difficult to ascertain whether Bely is referring to 2 of the characters in Richard Wagner's *Siegfried*, or to the personages of the same names in Norse mythology.

begins not with conduct made a realization by what is seen, but with a struggle against motions and air signals. All begins with a momentary and silent distant lighting. But the distant lightings increase. Its silence is echoed by thunders. Then the realization of the flashing symbols begins. Objects surrounding us become symbols, they cause people to appear as being masks. Finally the masks fall off and in front of us walking are these faces sealed by the dawn. [The dawn] is incarnated in the world. Fetters of darkness made of ice melt. The heart hears the flight of spring.

## III

The goal of the poet is to find the face of inspiration, having expressed in this face the worldwide unity of ecumenical truth. The goal of religion is to incarnate this unity. The image of the inspiration of religion in transformed into the integral face of Humanity, the face of the Woman clothed in the Sun. For this reason, art is the shortest route to religion. Here humanity, having comprehended its essence, unites into a single entity as the Eternal Wife. Creativity, brought to its consummating end, directly transfers into religious creativity – theurgy. Art with the help of marble, paint and words creates the life of the Eternal Wife. Religion removes this cover. It is possible to state that Her smile rests on every statue sculptured from marble. Also the opposite. She is the Madonna sculptured over the ages.

The primordial chaos, arranged based on the laws of arbitrary necessity, is idolized, becoming Her body. If Humanity is the most realistic of any corporate body, then nationalism appears as the first limited Humanity. Here in front of us is the access to unity during unhindered and independently active development of national strengths. The image of the inspiration must crown the development of national poetry.

The development of Russian poetry from Pushkin to our days is accompanied by three changes of its initial feature. Three covers are torn from the face of Russian inspiration, three dangers threaten its appearance. The first cover is torn from Pushkin-type inspiration; the second – from Lermontov-type inspiration;

removing the third cover causes the subsequent unveiling of the Eternal Woman. There are two courses definitely noticeable in Russian poetry. One acquires it beginning from Pushkin. The other from Lermontov. The attitude toward one or the other course defines the character of the poetry of Nekrasov, Tutchev, Fet, Vl. Solovyov, Brusov and finally Blok. These names are immersed deep into our soul. The talent of these named poets is simultaneous with their providential position in the general system of the development of national creativity. The poet, not occupied with the decipher of Pushkin's or Lermontov's secrets cannot motivate us to any depth.

Pushkin is complete, lacking nothing. In its entirety, he grasps the national unity from the outside. Under the sounds of his lyre Russia with its fields, cities and histories grows in front of us. He totally transmits an ideal applicable to all of humanity and installed in the depths of the national spirit. His capacity as an inspiration from here forward is to be reincarnated in some benefiting form. Unconsciously the deep roots of the Russian soul, expanding to the world's chaos, are specified. But the completeness of the Pushkin-type inspiration is still not yet the ideal completeness. The face of his inspiration is still not yet the unveiled image of Russian poetry. It cannot be seen behind the blizzard. The chaos of snowstorms still forms a cover around it. It still sleeps in a coffin made of ice, in an enchanted sleep. The vast amount of depth available does not suffice for Pushkin's completeness. This completeness must be fragmented, finding the road to the enchanted princess. Its elements, composing a picture for us of national completeness, are supposed to be regrouped in a new single unity. The route for further successors of the Pushkin school is fully indicated by this need. The imperishable body of the worldwide soul is to be prepared in the depths of nationalism. The unorganized chaos is solely the body of the organizing principle. As a result the Pushkin school must approach the chaos, tear the cover from it, and possess it.

The continuers of Pushkin – Nekrasov and Tutchev – hew the complete core of Pushkin's creativity, penetrating deep into the fragmented united entity.

The sky, penetrated by the Russian nature as inscribed by Pushkin, is covered by Nekrasov's melancholy and grey clouds. The deep roots that connect Pushkin's nature with the chaotic surroundings vanish. In Nekrasov's grey sky there are no terrors, no ecstasies, no abysses; only a melancholy sorrow. But this is why the chaos of Russian realism, although hidden by Pushkin under some modest humorous outer shell, is disclosed distinctly by Nekrasov.

On the other hand, Tutchev makes Pushkin's nature somewhat transparent. Tutchev directs us to knowing that the deep roots of Pushkin's poetry involuntarily grew in the worldwide chaos. This chaos so horribly gazed yet from the empty eyes of the mask of the tragedies of ancient Greece, penetrating the outspread flight of the creation of mythology. In descriptions of Russian nature the creativity of Tutchev involuntarily echoes the creativity of Hellenism. The mythological repetitions of Tutchev so strangely coincide with the description of Russian nature.

Pushkin's vein of influence in Tutchev is uniformly fragmented. From this point forward it has [2] directions:

1. Toward the incarnation of chaos in the forms of contemporary realism.
2. Toward the incarnation of chaos in the forms of ancient Greece.

The representative of the first vein surfaces as Valerie Brusov. The representative of the second is Vyacheslav Ivanov, whose poetry echoes the ancient schools for us.

That the route from the superficial depiction of national wholeness to the search for the ideal imperishable body of the Russian inspiration lies in individualism is here disclosed. Here occur encounters and struggles in the depths of the spirit, as Brusov states. But Nekrasov in his own way points at the chaos of the outer conditions of the Russian life. The fragmentation of Pushkin's united entity is expressed by Nekrasov and Tutchev in a manner that both of them thirst and cannot approach and join with the superficiality of the vein of Russian realism. Both strive to shove their poetry into narrow frames of inclinations: Nekrasov into nationalism; Tutchev into slavophilism.[344] Other than this Nekrasov is the citizen, while Tutchev is the poet-politician and aristocrat. In Nekrasov's civil pursuits however we find an original fractured Byron[345] and Pechorin[346] character. Here his connection with Lermontov is made apparent (of this we will further speak later). From another side, Tutchev's cord or aristocratism cuts deeply across the nationalistic cords. Tutchev likewise feared chaos. His chaos echoes from a distant as an approaching nighttime storm. His chaos is the chaos of elements, not materialized in the trivialities of mundane life. From another side, the chaotic picture of Russian life on its surface is depicted by Nekrasov.

Grateful for Brusov we now have the capacity to look at Pushkin's poetry through a prism of sufficient depth. This new point of view opens a number of perspectives. The circle of development of Pushkin's school becomes isolated, while the providence of Russian poetry opens.

The indivisible completeness of Brusov's form, depicting the land, body, is deprived however of the fire of religious heights. The beautiful body of its inspiration is not yet enlivened. It is mechanized by chaos. This is a robot, moved by steam and electricity. If the creation of Brusov's muse is understood in the meaning of a created entity, then the moon and stars can appear at her feet as with the Woman clothed in the sun. If this creation clearly inclines toward the side of the beast, there is a scarlet beast under its feet: this will be the great whore. And the image of the Radiant Woman is contradistinctive to the beast born in the depths of another tread of Russian poetry, acquiring its beginning from Lermontov.

Russian poetry is tied to Western European. This is culminated with world symbols: such a symbol of eternal

---

[344] Intellectual movement in Russia of the 19th century to concentrate on Russian being more Slavic, and distancing itself from European concepts and influence.

[345] Referring to the Byronic hero, the type based on English romantic poet Lord George Gordon Byron, the solitary figure unable to achieve his goals and so doomed to self-imposed suffering.

[346] Grigori Pechorin, main character in Lermontov's set of stories comprising *Hero of Our Time*.

womanhood is presented by the images of Beatrice,[347] Margarita,[348] and etc. Such a symbol is Prometheus, Manfred.[349] These symbols are produced under the cover of aestheticism.

Initially we said that the 3 personages must be torn from the face of the Russian muse. The first that flies off is the godlike face of Pushkin's muse, behind which hides chaos. The second is a partial mask that hides the face of the Heavenly Vision. The third face is worldwide; his is the Face of the Red Death, with the worldwide struggle between the Beast and Woman providing the conditions. The content of every tragedy is contained in this struggle. The poetry of western Europe tells us of this struggle from the outside: tragedy is the formal definition of the struggle in the Book of Revelation. Russian poetry installs a bridge to access religion, it appears as the unifying link between the tragic ideology of European humanity and the final church of the believers that is amassed for this struggle against the Beast.

Russian poetry with both of its oars is profoundly deep in the life of the world. The question of its ascent is decided only by the transformation of Heaven and Earth at the descent of the city New Jerusalem. Only here will be find the resolution to Pushkin's and Lermontov's secret.

## IV

We believe that You will disclose this to us, let us know that will there be no more October fogs and February yellow thaws. Let them think that You are still sleeping in your casket made of ice.

No, You have resurrected.

You have promised to appear in the color of a pink rose, and the soul prayerfully reclines in front of You, and in the dusks – the crimson lamps –your prayerful respiration is overheard.

Appear!

---

[347] Probably the guide in Dante's *Divine Comedy*.

[348] Margarita was the name of the reincarnation of the feminine aspect of God, or Sophia Divine Wisdom, in Anna Schmidt's *The Third Testament*.

[349] Not identifiable.

It is time. The world is ripe as gold fruit overflowing with sweetness. The world is turbulent without You.

Appear!

1905

# THE EMBLEMATIC OF MEANING

## AN INTRODUCTION TO THE THEORY OF SYMBOLISM[350]

( Selections )

### 1

What is the meaning of aesthetics of symbolism? What is its ideological justification?

Symbolic art of the recent decades is derived from the side of form, and in essence is in no way distinct from techniques of eternal art. In one situation, we encounter in the new trends the return to forgotten forms of German romanticism. In another situation the orient appears in front of us. In a third situation, in front of us is a visible emergence of new techniques. These techniques, with a more intensive review, appear as nothing more than newly-conceived unions of old techniques or their greater detailing.

Symbolic art, taken from the side of conceptual content does not appear for us in the majority of situations as new. So for example, the newly-conceived ideology of Maeterlinck dramas,[351] its elusive trend, appears as the result of an education of the old

[350] This treatise is probably typical of the type of lecture that Bely would delivery.

[351] Maurice Polydore Maeterlinck, 1862-1949, a Belgian poet and essayist. He wrote symbolist plays such as *Unforgiven*, *The Blind*, *There Within*, *Pelleas and Melisande*, and *The Death of Tintagiles*. Three of his dramas were performed in 1904 at the Moscow Art Theater under Constantine Stanislavsky.

mystics. Let us recollect the influence of Ruusbroec[352] on Maeterlinck, or the newly-conceived passion of Hamsun pantheism,[353] as being in essence a transmission of certain characteristics of Taoism into realistic ideology.

Where the preaching of new forms of humanity's relationships begin in contemporary art, religious principles approach and join them, but hardly something new, or as with Nietzsche these attempts to apply in a practical manner ancient wisdom to the trending historical period encounter us. The teaching of the new person, of the impending destiny of Arian culture, a summons to creating individualism, and a rejection of compromised forms of morality – all of this we already encountered in the philosophical and religious currents of India, as old as the world.

All strength, the entire future of what is called the new art, resides in this unrelenting aspiration to unify art techniques of diverse cultures, in this outburst to create a new attitude toward realism through a route of the review of a series of forgotten ecumenical ideologies. This is where the newly-conceived eclecticism of our epoch starts. I do not know whether Nietzsche was right, who eventually condemned the Alexandrian period of ancient culture.[354] Know that this period, crisscrossing the various routes of thought and contemplation, is presented to us and up to now as a foundational base when we, aspiring into the depths of time, mix the Alexandrian school with the Socratic school into one illness, into one degeneration. Nietzsche doomed his individual route of development to a ruthless nietzschean judgment. What caused Nietzsche to be this way, and for which we love him, is nothing else than Alexandrian. If he was not Alexandrian deep in his soul, he would not have said such things about Heraclitus,[355] the mysterials, Wagner, and especially he would not have

[352] John van Ruusbroec or Ruyssbroech, 1293/1294 – 1381, Dutch mystic and Augustinian monk whose works has traits of pantheism. Maeterlinck translated some of his works into French, and included parts of others in his own works.

[353] The compositions of Knut Hamsun, 1859-1952, Norwegian writer. Some of his writings were published by *Scorpion*, in Russian translation in 1900,

[354] meaning the philosophy of later Hellenism, from the 1st century BC to the 4th century AD, including neo-Pythagorism and neo-Platonism, both of which had a mystic trend.

[355] Heraclitus of Ephesus, 535 BC – 475 BC, pre-Socratic Greek philosopher.

composed *Zarathustra*. In creating the new he needs to turn to the old.

What is genuinely new, what captivates us in symbolism, is the attempt to illuminate the deepest contradictions of contemporary culture through colorful rays of diverse cultures. We at present reside as though we are reliving all of the past: India, Persia, Egypt; as with Greece so with the Middle Ages. They revive and the epochs migrate past us, whichever are closed to us individually. I heard said that during the important hours of a person's life his entire life flies in front of his spiritual gaze. At present the entirety of humanity's life is flying in front of us. So we conclude that the important hour of its life has already struck for all of humanity. We genuinely touch something that is new, but touch it in its old form. In this pressuring abundance of the old the innovative has the appellation of symbolism.

And this is why the literary platform of symbolism attempts to at least summarize the individual pronouncements of artists regarding their creativity. And this is why the ideology of symbolism needs to be a wide ideology. The principles of symbolism must depict for as a solid philosophic system. Symbolism as only an ideology is impossible.

So what are the prolegomena[356] to such an ideology? What is its creative meaning?

## 2

We count exact science[357] as the basis of our positive knowledge of realism. In the process of genetic development exact science develops from the inexact. Philosophy generated the natural sciences, cabbalism and magic [generated] mathematics, out of astrology grew astronomy, chemistry evolved from alchemy. If we are to count knowledge as only exact knowledge, then the genesis

[356] Here as the explanatory introduction to some kind of system of ideas.

[357] Exact science Bely considers mathematics, chemistry and physics, as opposed to special sciences such as biology, medicine and physiology. Imprecise or inexact science Bely considers astrology, philosophy, psychology, and the such. Natural sciences Bely considers the plant and animal studies.

of this knowledge discloses to us the picture of its birth from non-knowledge: so non-knowledge birthed knowledge.

So how did knowledge evolve from non-knowledge?

It evolved through the route of limiting the object of knowledge. Earlier such an object was the universe; then we learned about the universe form some kind of defined point of view. This point of view generated science, the point of view developed into methods.

Subsequently with the fragmentation of science each distinct branch grew into its self-supporting science. The precise method of research transformed into many methods. The principles of a special science subsequently developed into a self-supporting sphere. They started to guide the development of special sciences and so methodology appeared, and so did the individual branches of the logic of science.

Just recently we knew what a scientific view of the world actually is. This scientific view of the world appeared as a synthesis of many positive branches of knowledge. At one time it seemed that such a concept of the world was materialistic. But then we realized that material of this type did not exist.[358] The special science of physics overthrew the scientific view of the world of its era. For some interval a system of sciences was counted as a scientific view of the world. O.Comte proposed one of such systems.[359] But special sciences developed independently from scientific systems and views of the world, and one system failed after another. In later eras they attempted to place conclusions of any one of any of the exact sciences – chemistry, physics, mechanics – at the center of the scientific view of the world. But then at some time it turned out that the conclusions of any science did not pertain to the entirety of this universal outlook.

So for example we spoke about as though energy or work appearing as the essence of all living processes. We have to this point assured energetical philosophers that philosophy from their

---

[358] Bely could be referring to ether, that some say exists although it is yet to be proven. A 5th elemental in addition to earth, air, fire and water, but intangible.

[359] Auguste Comte, 1798-1857, French philosopher.

perspective is energetics. But his type of attempt to scientifically substantiate our view of the world is subject to a fiasco. The understanding of energy is defined just in this sphere where the understanding of mechanical work is tied with this understanding. In thermodynamics we cannot proceed without a defined understanding of energy. But this understanding is provided beyond the limit of exact science, it becomes a definition having many meanings and is completely unclear. Thermodynamics builds an understanding about energy with the help of a series of formulas and mechanical equations, moving the horizon of one of the sciences, but it is far from completely explaining to us the problems of our cognizance. Yes and even energetical principles are defined only with the formula K+P= some constant, meaning, with the increase of K, then P needs to decrease to keep the constant in a closed-loop system of energy. Even if we were to recognize the role of substance as energy, we could identify the world as a closed-loop system of energy, except that now the understanding of substance would replace the understanding of energy, but this would not completely explain the situation of the world as a closed-loop system of energy. This would not explain either world or power. But by accepting substance in place of energy, we essentially allocate a dynamic principle using all the attributes of scholastic philosophy.

A scientific view of the world in the sense of a view of the world that is derived from a system of exact sciences cannot exist in our days. The development of any science leads to its centralization in a defined method. The principles of methods form a specific logic of any science, the language of this language is such that it is capable of interpreting all apparitions of realism in the language of that special science, but there are many special sciences. There are as many interpretations of realism as there are methods for this. The scientific view of the world in essence is the view of the world where the world is interpreted as a special figure. So they changed philosophy as a specialized science at some arbitrary time into a history of philosophy, sociology, psychology and even thermodynamics. This occurred because at this arbitrary time the various methods of the special sciences provided answers to the questions relating to life's meaning. And of course the answers were contradictory. Some said, "There is no thought without phosphorus." And there were right in their own respect, just as those were right in their respect who said the opposite, "There is no phosphorous without thought."[360] These were conditional, emblematic answers where even life was exchanged by some emblem, by some "understanding of life." Meanwhile the very answers were accepted as life-providing. It is not amazing that all of this led from crisis to crisis of the view of the world. In front of us were erected fantastic chambers of scientific views of the world and they all collapsed. From the fragments of materialism a block of ice was formed, the synthetic philosophy of Herbert Spencer, and it also dispersed.

The matter is that science and ideology are incompatible. Ideology cannot from here on lie either as the basis of a special science or as its conclusions. Ideology cannot likewise lie as the basis of a system of exact sciences. An ideology of such a type at present can only be built on a compilation of errors.

Uniting the conclusions of scientific knowledge, I do not entirely ascertain the methods of research that led me to these conclusion. Each scientific discipline is guided by its individual methods. For me to utilize for example physiological methods in psychology I cannot come to any conclusion of the composition of the soul any more than I can that whether the soul even exists. And because in the principles of physiological research the very terms of psychological processes are redefined by the terms of physical processes. Energy in a dynamic understanding likewise manifests as a substance, as does the soul in the animistic understanding. Subsequently the question migrates to a question of substance. Next is to investigate the genetic evolution of the basic understanding of one or another special science, and further on to critically study the very essence of genetic methods as

[360] In 1715, the element phosphorous was discovered in the brain. The presence of phosphorous was so significant that someone created the statement as confirmation, "There is no thought without phosphorous." But this was used later by Friedrich Engels, the German socialist political philosopher, against those who were trying to over simplify materialism, and which he called vulgar materialism.

unifying a group of popular sciences. And only then will the energetic and animistic interpretations of processes of psychological activity be presented in a more correct light.

Special logic demands a basis that is generally logic in basis. But this type of basis subjects us to the sphere of the theory of knowledge. A theory of knowledge is an introduction into each type of ideology.

But it is too often that the tasks of the theory of knowledge are understood in just the light of special logics of science: psychology, sociology, natural science, have installed the theory of knowledge in a subjective position relative to their individual logic. The logic of one of the sciences not just once in the history of philosophy has aspired to take the place of the logic of a specific science. The logic of science cannot be identified with distinct logics.

Subjecting the logic of science to one of such methods we inevitably receive a one-sided view of any subject of science. Uniting the results of many methodological routes and calling this union – a scientific view of the world, we acquire a deeply thought-out and correctly reasoning vinaigrette of understanding. As the basis of a genuine view of the world a classification of science based on plausible methods must be instituted, and not based on the results of such methods. But the very principle of these methods as methods that are indispensable and generally mandatory must serve as the foundational classification.

So the question of the scientific view of the world boils down to the deduction of science about sciences. Such an independent science can be gnoseology. But to the extent its task is in the search of common and indispensable rational forms, to that extent the view of the world based on its concepts and connections does not enter into its closest task.

It seems this view of the world would be a general and indispensable metaphysics. At the present time such a metaphysic has not developed a theory of knowledge at all, and so the view of the world as a single object is outside the limits of its competency. Later we will strive to prove that the very view of the world acquires during our days an unexpected form.

And if the theory of knowledge is incapable to give us a view of the world as a single object, then of course it is not in science or in a system of sciences that we acquire this view of the world. And so the dogmas of scientific views of the world in the best state are utopian fantasies in the style of the novels of Wells[361] and Flammarion.[362] They imply or say their feelings, but they never speak in a clear language. The precision of science is tied in groups, and each group can continue unto infinity, but between it and adjacent groups is the abyss. All the groups are stretched in one direction, depicting as though a series of parallel lines that are not crossing. But all the lines lie on one plain. This plain is causality. And so the scientific-dogmatic resolutions of problems of causality are mixed along the route of situating them under the reasons for understanding energy, power, the atom, volition, and such similar understandings. Know that here we have a matter dealing with the explanation of the common entirety of this or one of its parts. To say that cause is power is to say that as though the single item is the same as a third of it.

This vinaigrette from the limited methodological understanding called the scientific view of the world leads to the heteronomy of each of these distinct understandings. Investigating these very limited understandings in the process of their historical formation, we from the one side constantly affix to them new and newer understandings. Yesterday's limit ceases to be a limit. The region beyond the limits in science and metaphysics becomes a limited knowledge. For example: molecule – atom – ion; force – power – work; the object – I – single entity – volition; and etc. Investigating these understandings as understandings derived from rational conclusions we subject the theory of knowledge to a exact science.

From another respect this same inescapability encounters us. The very plane of the scientific formation of understanding does intersect at least once the question of the meaning of this formation. The meaning of life constantly motivates us to the

---

361 H.G. Wells

362 Camille Flammarion, 1842-1925, French astronomer and author of science books and science fiction novels.

creation of literature. The very formation of scientific terms distances our aspiration toward this further and further, so that the understanding of this serves for our consolation and to explain to us the riddles of our existence.

And particularly herein is the goal of all of life's view of the world.

This is why science and ideology do not intersect one another anywhere. A compulsive unification to science of any type of ideology that exists only insults science. But also the opposite occurs. It insults our most clandestine aspiration to possess an ideology, one that would be valuable and precious to us.

Is there a knowledge of mathematical, dynamic and other emblems? It is just confined in the ability to apply them in action?

I do not know whether I should call science – knowledge in general. The historical meaning of knowledge changes. The character of this change consists in that the meaning of knowledge had led to the ability to install and utilize functional dependence. But is it possible to speak of meaning as being dependant? It would be strange to now deliberate on the meaning of function, differentiation and integrals. Differential is differential – here science responds for the most part. Science banishes the question of the life-long meaning of appearance. It weighs and binds. They say that as if science is a premonition of appearance, but the meaning of life is not retained in an apparition.

If there is knowledge there is also the knowledge of the meaning of life, but science is still not knowledge. Science proceeds from nonknowledge to more nonknowledge, science is a systematic of every type of nonknowledge.[363]

## 3

Critical philosophy deals with the basic problems of comprehension. It defines the basic comprehensive forms, without which it is impossible to think. But the task of critical philosophy is here still not exhausted. A tie between the distinct

---

363 This is funny, but it is what Bely wrote.

comprehensive forms needs to be installed, to install their theoretical place where one is in proper relation to the other. The systematic description of these forms depend on the norm of comprehension. Some gnoseologies, for example, Simmel,[364] enjoys describing comprehension. Others for example, Rickert,[365] sees in the theory of knowledge a teleological time in the organization of comprehensive forms. The norm of knowledge systematizes the category of contemplative thought. The tie of comprehensive forms, viewed as the product of partitioning, supposes a theory of partitioning, and such a theory surfaces as a theory of knowledge. Defining ourselves as a theory of knowledge, critical philosophy occupies an independent place in the series of other sciences. Not suppressing the freedom of development of any science, it directs the mind to what we can await from any of these sciences. It places solid boundaries for one or another scientific method. Every other type of science, infinitely approaching these boundaries, will never cross them. The relationship of the series of the magnitude of changes to their constant is located here. The theory of comprehension is the constant of all knowledge. Any science is defined as a systematic exposition of knowledge regarding any knowledge. For a theory of knowledge, knowledge itself becomes the subject.

Comprehension is not simple knowledge. It is, to say it best, knowledge about knowledge. Knowledge belongs to science in the primordial meaning of the word. The sting of critical philosophy is not directed against the precise meaning of scientific knowledge. It is directed against other methods of the expansion of knowledge. Just as knowledge is about knowledge, comprehension appears relatively as a knowledge that is somehow beyond our frontiers. Comprehension in this sense is after-knowledge. One of the inherent tasks of knowledge is the installation of terminal borders for knowledge. The theory of knowledge in this sense as though concludes groups of sciences in the regions of one circumference. The relationship between it and science is the

---

[364] Georg Simmel, 1858-1918. German sociologist and philosopher.
[365] Heinrich John Rickert, 1863-1936. German neo-Kantian philosopher.

relationship of the eccentric sphere to the concentric. They forgive us for the paradox: the eccentric conclusions of critical philosophy for the healthy mind are eccentric in the literal and transmittable sense. The sphere of this meaning falls between the concentric circle of science and the eccentric circumference of comprehension. The ordinary healthy mind becomes circular in science and becomes eccentric in theoretical philosophy. The healthy mind does not contain its *Standpunct.*[366] The theory of knowledge is a hammer striking the healthy mind. In vain is the healthy mind concentrated on science. Science manifests itself as an anvil. The hammer of comprehension strikes according to knowledge, and the healthy mind is not apparent in all of this.

## 6

The artist and philosopher encountering each other on a progressing route of their development will not leave each other tomorrow. Both know that they cannot go backward. Where will they return? To the world of empirical reality? But such a world does not presently exist. What exists are many methods of knowledge that evolved the world from its indivisible particles, powers, ions, and etc. But all of these particles, powers and ions are presented to us out of necessity as the product of comprehensive activity. The activity itself is the product of values. And of what does value consist? It is not in the subject, and it is not in the object. It is in life's creativity. But along with this the single symbolic life – the world of value – is disclosed, although not deciphered in its entirety, and appearing to us in all simplicity, enticement and diversity, being the Alpha and Omega of all theory. It is the symbol of a certain mystery. The approach to this mystery is an increasingly growing boil of creative aspiration that carries us, as though a phoenix arising from ashes, over the cosmic dust of time and space. All theories terminate under our feet. All reality flies away like a dream, and it is only in creativity that reality, value and life's meaning remain.

---

[366] German: point of view, position.

Here we return to reality, to this symbolic wholeness that is not disclosed by comprehension. Through the objective existence provided us we fly upon the logs of comprehension where existence – as least as comprehension – dreams and from there again we soar to the symbolic wholeness. Then we begin to understand that comprehension is the dream of this wholeness. In a dream we fall asleep to dream. Dream after dream moves across our eyes. Meaning is replaced by some other meaning. And nonetheless we are dreaming and we are not aware of vigilance until we realize that the very process of wakening from one sleep to another sleep is the reality, but it is a creative reality. All that is in us creates its dreams and then overcomes them. We call valuable what our dreams create. But this valuable object is a symbol. We call what is created in dreams – realities. All of these realities are colorful and wealthy. But there is one category of the laws of reality: the realities perceived in laws appear to us as an image of objective reality. But it is this way as long as we are outside of reality. Reality understood as creativity is provided in the world to move the ladder of reality, and so we proceed climbing this ladder. Every new step is a symbolic valuable. If we are standing below this step it is a summons and aspiration to go further. If we have reached it, it is reality. If we have passed it, it now seems as a lifeless part of our nature.

Returning to reality we will acknowledge that very reality from which we floated away at some time along the sea of comprehension. Now we again have returned to it – returned to our homeland. From now on we will reside at our homeland forever, because all the steps of reality are solely the inexhaustible wealth of our homeland: flowers and the fruits of the tree of life. Our homeland was a lost at some time, and is now a returned, paradise. The sky of comprehension, just as the land of life, from here on is the firmament where land and sky merge into one. The land here is the symbolic land of Adam Kadmon.[367] The wisdom of the hermits defines – and with good reason – the symbolic composition of this land. Into it enter the moon, sun, Venus,

[367] The original or primordial man in Kabbalist religious philosophy.

Jupiter. It composes the Zodiac, and the human himself surfaces as Adam Kadmon. Now without good reason does activity force us to see the mysterial in life where journeying for the search of meaning is similar to the trials of the novitiate subject to the dangers of death in land, water and fire. Meaning is maintained in activity. Activity is unbreakable, whole, free and omnipotent. Immaculate comprehension, approaching reality, allots terminological significance to it. The terms of undefiled knowledge and comprehension are only symbols of reality, but when we reach reality using these terms, we can speak of it just in symbolic figures. It is itself a living image, unexplainable in terms. But we think in terms, and so our words regarding reality are only symbols.

## 8

The supreme historical religions, rising to the summit of the location of theosophy, accept some form of gnosticism migrating into mystical criticism, or else a form of theurgy at the frontier of magic. In the first case they possess courage, denying the primacy of creativity, expounding it as an instrument they use to deny comprehension. In the second case they permeate comprehension using religious creativity or attempt to destroy it with the help of secret sacraments. Characteristically, Buddhism often excessively accepted a shade of mystical criticism, while Christianity took a theurgic form of mystery in its teachings of the sacraments.

Theosophy is the systematization of systematizations. It is as though a view of the world and human nature from outside the world. It does not transform anything, does not defeat anything, its meaning consists in the process of perfection. It perfects meaninglessness. It systematizes the sum of meaninglessly appearing images, forms and norms. Existent theosophy appears to us either in the visible form of Gnostic synthesis, or in the visible form of shoots of former and long passed magical, theurgic and religious systems. The reality of this is just that it has still not risen to the task of true theosophy. During the present epoch theosophy is at least the threshold to a series of resurrected trends

– some new, some old, and some not yet established in our contemporary era. As a result its awesome meaning, although chilling to the soul, is hid from us. To place the drama of our understandings at the top is without value and a suffering without purpose. It is yet traveling to its own realm, there, where eyes close, where hands drop, and the heart stops.

Having climbed to the top of the ladder of comprehension we notice that this ladder is filled with the most profound of valuables, although they are already there because it is defined for the search of such valuables in another aspect. But establishing a basis for value in this other aspect we see nothing other than creativity, while establishing a basis at the pinnacles of this creativity we speedily slide down along the ladder of creativity.

Here on the summits, where both comprehension and creativity appear below us, we remain in complete isolation and abandonment. It depends on us to accept this final meaninglessness as death or as the final temptation. But remembering the series of words that fell from us while we were climbing to the heights in the reality of comprehension and creativity, we cannot but think that here is the temptation.

The magic of ecstasy must unite with the ice of gnosticism so the postulated wholeness can be transformed into the condition of comprehension and creativity through a free establishment. We must accept the symbol as an incarnation. If our comprehension has not frozen like ice and the creative ecstasy has not turned us into a flame, but we have already climbed to the summits of the final temptation, the living water of comprehension will drown the smoldering coal of creativity within us, and this coal will turn the water into steam. The meaning of existence will collapse in the steam and ashes, and the sole response that we will here receive is the following, "Woe, woe to those living on earth."[368] Here in the terminating deserts of meaninglessness the horrible judgment will be executed on the world and us and in us truly.

[368] Rev 12:12

## 12

Symbolic wholeness is the wholeness of a series of comprehensions in a series of creativities. But we split the wholes with a metaphysical definition of this series.

All of this wholeness crowns the ladder of creativity, appearing to us in images and forms similar to a human. This is why the ladder of humanity's creativity terminates with the fixing of the similarity of a human with this wholeness. Speaking in the language of religion creativity leads us to the manifestation of God. The worldwide Logos accepts the Personage of humanity. The pinnacle of creativity is indicated by the words of the Book of Revelation:

> To the conqueror will I give to sit with Me on My throne as I conquered and sat with the Father on His throne.[369]

And defining theurgy from the aspect of metaphysics this is why we can say that its task – the metaphysical wholeness to manifest in the form of a personage of humanity – is to transform the word (principle) into flesh, into a content of our reality. In figurative language this means, "The Word is recreated as Flesh." As the apostle writes says:

> In the beginning was the Word, and the Word was with God and the Word was God.[370] What was from the beginning, what we heard, what we saw with our eyes, what we watched, and what our hands touched – about the Word of Life.[371]

The ladder of creativity, the Symbol manifesting in the Flesh, the very metaphysical definitions, all are subject to theurgic practice.

As soon as we attempt to emblematically represent wholeness in a series of comprehensions and in a series of creativities, it now manifests in a dual manner. The very expression, "Word becoming

---

[369] Rev 3:21
[370] John 1:1
[371] 1 John 1:1

Flesh," dooms us to a duality. Any assertion in general of wholeness is impossible as every assertion consists of a subject and predicate. In the assertion – Word is Flesh, the verb – is, is used as a connector. The duality is dependant on it being a wholeness, and so this wholeness divides into a duality and manifests the first triad of wholeness. This tripartite stage is the first definition of wholeness. It is the symbol of this wholeness, because we call the symbolic wholeness – a symbol and depict it as a triad.

16

Our searches for meaning and value in life will materialize as futile at every occasion, until we finally guess that they cannot be crowned with success in one or the other comprehensive spheres. Then we will take the action to seek meaning in the subsequent sphere. And it will be just as futile. The ladder of our ascents grow. All that seemed to be behind us now appears to be lifeless. Rising to the summit of our graphic pyramid we are convinced that the entire pyramid of knowledge is dead. And only at the top is comprehension disclosed: that the meaning and value of our activity is retained in the creativity of life. But when we want to relive the life we postponed in the past we encounter chaos, a chaos that spreads under all creativity. Wanting to depend on the image of the incarnated cosmos as on a Personage we see that the beauty of this Personage is foam on the peaks of religious creativity.

Turning to religion we see that it births out of aesthetical necessity. Religion is that foam on the peak of aesthetic waves. Turing to the elements of beauty we, in an orderly fashion, see that this beauty is the foam on the peak of waves of primordial creativity. Primordial creativity is the foam on the peak of chaos. Standing at the precipice of comprehension, and defining creativity using comprehension as something that we must relive, we see that the Personage of this creativity are the sun's rays playing on the ocean of future chaos. We find ourselves inescapably in this state of wanting to throw ourselves into the chaos of life if we do not want to freeze on the frozen precipices of comprehension. Value now manifests its chaotic personage to us. Such is our first trial. If we overcome it, if we fearlessly throw ourselves into the vortex of the swirling maelstrom, we will see that some type of strength will suddenly rise. We will see that the chaos of re-experience is not a chaos at all. It is the cosmos. The musical elements of the world echo in the roar of chaotic waves of life. It is the containment of some kind of power that forces us to create beautiful images. Then it will begin to seem to us that as though some kind of image is visiting us in the depths of life's rotations and is calling us to itself. If we follow after the summoning image we are outside of danger. The trial is passed, the first step of sanctification is ended.

So begins our ascent into the series of creativities. The image summoning us upward, all the higher, slips away from us each time we approach it. We will conquer the creative series when we sense ourselves at the summit of theurgic creativity. But the image there, the one summoning us to itself, seems at least to be normative. The star-filled sky appears as a ceiling. We die a second time in creativity just as in the past others died in comprehension, and creativity manifests just as dead. Here we are at the threshold of the second sanctification.

Descending into the province of metaphysics we sanctify all visible forms of metaphysical wholeness. We require just one thing: metaphysical wholeness must correctly lead the norm of comprehension and the norm of ethics, because it is a bridge, allegorically unifying the norm of theoretical comprehension with the norm of ethical comprehension. We orient metaphysics around these norms and this wholeness. So assurance is born in us and which solely metaphysics is capable of doing, predefining for us our comprehension as well as our conduct.

Descending further into the province of exact science we see that the symbolic wholeness – having provided emblems of this wholeness for metaphysics, gnoseology and psychology – deducts a new emblem for mechanics. The emblem of value in the province of exact sciences is the principle of physical interpretation of nature, uniting a number – as a scheme of measurement of time –

with the physiological process of life. And so the scheme of exact science manifests as the investigation of the processes of life by means of their measurement in time in physical or mechanical terms. All visible forms of exact sciences – botany, zoology, physiology – are defined by their dependence on physical and mathematical constants.

In exactly the same manner we descend the ladder of creativity and see that the symbolic wholeness in theurgic creativity manifests as the Personage of the very Deity. The symbol provides its emblem to the Personage and Name of the Living God. In theurgy this Personage is the emblem of value. In conformity with the triunity of every scheme the Personage appears as the wholeness, predefining the norm of conduct and the feminine element of religious creativity. This element is symbolized in the image of Eternal Womanhood, Sophia, or the heavenly Church. All visible forms of theurgic creativity must be oriented by a comprehension of the theurgic scheme and investigated in their relationship to the symbols of Sophia and Logos. So we see that from the side of comprehension there is a possibility to speak about the norms of theurgic creativity. We must not however forget that here we speak in the language of emblems.

Descending further into the province of religion we see that symbolic wholeness – having provided a wholeness of theurgy to this emblem– deducts a new emblem, and this time the emblem is religious. This emblem manifests as the image of Sophia Wisdom as a principle uniting the human to the wholeness. The value of the emblem in religion is the church, as the binding force of believers, the Church being a type of Sophia Wisdom.

## 19

We do not use an arbitrary term to identify a symbol. Unconditional terms of understanding symbol can be changed with any type of existence and any type of comprehension. The conditions of creativity are emblems. Further, to call a symbol –

unconditional, we easily identify the unconditional with the divine. To understand a symbol we provide conditions:

1. The Symbol is wholeness.
2. The Symbol is the wholeness of the emblem.
3. The Symbol is the wholeness of the emblem of creativity and comprehension.
4. The Symbol is the wholeness of the creativity maintaining experiences.
5. The Symbol is the wholeness of the creativity maintaining comprehension.
6. The Symbol is the wholeness of comprehension maintaining experiences.
7. The Symbol is the wholeness of the comprehension in the creativity maintaining this comprehension.
8. The Symbol is the wholeness of comprehension in the forms of experiences.
9. The Symbol is the wholeness of comprehension in the forms of comprehension.
10. The Symbol is the wholeness of creativity in the forms of experience.
11. The Symbol is the wholeness of creativity in the forms of comprehension.
12. The Symbol is the wholeness of forms and content.
13. The Symbol discloses comprehensions and creativities in emblematic series.
14. These series are emblems.
15. Symbols are perceived in emblems and forms of symbols.
16. Reality approaches the Symbol in the process of comprehensive or creative symbolism.
17. The Symbol stands as reality in this process.
18. The meaning of comprehension and creativity is maintained in the Symbol.
19. Approaching the comprehension of every type of meaning we share every form and every content through symbolic existence.

20. The meaning of our existence is unfolded in the hierarchy of symbolic disciplines of comprehension and creativity.
21. The system of symbolism is the emblematic of pure meaning.
22. Such a system is the classification of comprehension and creativity as subjected to the hierarchy of symbolism.
23. The Symbol is disclosed in symbolism. There it is created and recognized.

These are the premises of every theory of creativity. The Symbol is the criteria of determining the value of all metaphysical, theosophical, and theurgic symbolism.

## 23

Every art is symbolically the present, past and future. So of what does the meaning of our contemporary symbolism consist? What new has it provided us?

Nothing.

The school of symbolism just leads us to the union of all the announcements of artists and poets regarding the meaning of beauty in an artistic sense, and not just in emotion that awakens the image it represents within us, and it is not entirely in the rational interpretation of this image. The symbol is not divisible, not in emotion or discussions or debates. It is what it is.

The school of symbolism moved the frame of our representations regarding artistic creativity. It has shown that the canon of beauty is not only an academic canon. Using such a canon there cannot be a canon of only romanticism or only classicalism or only realism. But it has justified this, the other and the third current as various visible forms of a single creativity. Further symbolism has broken the frames of aesthetical creativity, underscoring that the province of religious creativity closely touches the artistic. The innovations of contemporary art exist at the present in a few oppressed items of the past, which has more than once flared. We today experience the life of the art of all the centuries and all nations. The earlier life proceeds past us.

This is because we stand in front of a great future.

1909

# WHY I BECAME A SYMBOLIST AND WHY I DID NOT CEASE TO BE ONE DURING ALL THE PHASES OF MY IDEALIST AND ARTISTIC DEVELOPMENT

(selections)

## 1

Why I became a symbolist. To answer this question the following is my explanation.

But first of all the basic theme of symbolism in me must be noted. Regarding this theme I distinctly separate myself as dual or even triune. I sense within myself the installation of the theme of symbolism in the manner that it sang in my soul from early childhood. And I perceive this theme even more in my efforts to later limit it: during encounters with people. An ideological moment and a social moment would occur. It was the *we* to appear as a collective. And from this second moment I distinguish 2 sub-moments. A combined nurture of symbolism in its whole intimate ideal existence and its ideological fixation as a cultural trend of Russian realism. Within this fixation I distinguish first what I have brought, and second into what we – the symbolists – agreeably splintered.

In regard to the question as to how I became a symbolist and when, I answer with a clean conscience: I did not *become* one, at no *time* did this occur, but I was *always* a symbolist, and then later I encountered the specific terms: symbol and symbolist. I go back to the age of 4 years, reflecting on colors of toys, that the colors have a symbolic representation. First is the toy itself, second is the color, and the third is its representation. The first 2 worlds are null, and there is a third world, and I reached toward the comprehension of this third world that was not provided at the time to my soul.

2

Here I must make stipulations for a correct understanding of all the later encounters of my religious problems. This problem for the most part did not flourish in our home life. My father, a professor of mathematics, possessing his own complex philosophical system, allowed for a higher power and presented his version of all the Testaments in front of me with all of its allegorical interpretations. What more interested him were the problems of the moral evolution of humanity as indicated in religious emblems. He categorically denied the validity of the church,[372] dogmas, and traditions, and he hated mysticism. He did not forbid ceremony, that is, he accepted the presence of priests with their crucifixes but out of civil respect, as he would any other person. But on the contrary, the fundamentals of natural-scientific ideology through my father ignited the atmosphere of our apartment. Based on the discussions of my father and his friends – professors of mathematics, physics, chemistry and biology – catchphrases of Darwinism, a mechanical concept of the universe, and geology and paleontology, poured into my ears. As much as I remember at the time, thunder was an accumulation of electricity, that the Art of the Covenant electrocuted the priests, that the

[372] Specifically the Russian Orthodox Church.

Earth was a globe, that the human evolved from a monkey, and that the world was not created 7,000 years ago, but had no beginning.

So this is what happened: my lively perception of the contents of the Old and New Testaments were my soul's perception of symbolism. At home they ridiculed tradition. The sole traditionally believing person was my grandmother, and who was eternally offended by my mother and father. Mother at least toward the end of her life could be considered religious, and she still sought symbols in religious images, rather than some naive reality. As a young woman she dedicated herself to the elements of music and secular amusements. My uncles and aunts from my father's side were all openly atheists or at least indifferent. This indifference characterized my mother's brothers and sisters and my governesses. They taught me to recite some prayers in a mechanical fashion and did not require of me any ostensive display of religiosity. I hid my perusals of the New Testament, while my father tried to have concepts of natural sciences grafted into me from early years. Although not yet able to read, I still memorized almost everything I saw in Paul Bert's book on zoology.[373]

During the period of 11 to 14 years of age, I experienced a strong inclination toward natural science and all that was accessible to me, and I dreamed of studying it at a college. My civilization was secular, although a life of religious symbols flowed deeply hid through me from all these worlds of symbols. The latter attempts of student Bugaev consisted in his own way of investigating and in his own way resolving questions of ecclesiasticism, tradition and orthodoxy, and this being under the influence of the Solovyovs. I experienced this as a mutiny and independent rupture from the traditions of our apartment, which was the liberal thinking of my father the professor.

I make this stipulation so it will be clear knowing the source, and then be able to see what subsequently occurred – the period of my religiosity, meaning, mysticism, and etc. This was the period of

---

[373] Paul Bert, 1833-1886. The reference is to his book *Elements of Zoology*.

my strongest revolution against the bulwarks of the positivist sphere. Here is contained the distinction in our journeys to religious dogma with the Solovyovs. They still could not see through to the end the stage I was on during the period of my attraction to Solovyov's religiously-inclined symbolism, and not toward symbolist believers. My beliefs from the initial years of my adolescence were a mutiny of boldness nourished by the will directed toward a new culture, and it was not a contrite inclination nourished by some religion pilgrimage.

3

During the ages of 14 to 17 years I grew esoterically. My symbolism was hid from others. For a long while this sphere of the hidden was a sphere hidden against my will, because my dictionary could not explain in any manner even one of my words. I disclosed my mental games to my governess, Afima Ivanovna Lavrova, when I was 14 years of age. She seemed to understand some of it and we played together. Even from adolescence it was clear to me that *this* residing in me was a special culture of the soul, something like a special organ, and that those who possessed this organ were both refined and simple people. The refined I encountered considerable later. The first simple soul of a fellow symbolist was my governess, a person very limited in secular culture and almost illiterate.

I grew, I started to become welcoming to *this*, some of the elements of culture that would drop into the world of my silent gestures from the outside would. Over the ages of 15 to 16 years I knew that *this* was gestating and assembling in me and under the influence of music – Chopin, Schumann, Beethoven, the study of German poetry – Uhland, Heine and Goethe, and stories and conversations about the Revelation of John with the maid Annushka, and who also provided me a series of Old Believer[374] legends.

---

[374] A split from the Russian Orthodox Church of those who refused to accept the ecclesiastical improvements and modifications of Patriarch Nikon Minin.

Off to the side of all this my cultivation proceeded, that is, acquisition of information provided to me by adults. Knowledge from my cultivation I greedily appropriated, but the traditional mode of conduct that was expected of me in our apartment reminded me of badly cooked food, kind of like having to chew on tar. And I would chew the cud on their tar so my lowing would not seem alien to them.[375]

I grew alone and did not know other children, as a result I later did not know how to deal with them. They intimidated me.

Then it became clear to me that because I was intimidated by children I was considered stupid by strange adults, and that I was confined to our apartment with shackles, while at the same time having a feeling of complete ingratitude. I knew I could not live long this way. Something irreversible would occur, my facade or mask would burst and *this* would pop out, and all will be in awe because *this* will seem to them criminal or at least insanity. To postpone the moment I started to dedicate myself to self-cultivation and so in this predicament my first stylization was achieved and descended successfully: I was an honor student. This seemed to be easy to me and all praised me, and I was very proud of my successes. The second year I barely reached success, and with the third year I was fed up with it, and during the 4th year I stopped learning stupidity: Ellend-Zeifert,[376] chronicles of historical data, and Greek grammatical exceptions.

The moment came when I saw within myself my individualism. These experiences were connected to me while reading the *Upanishads*, which was in 1896. Disbelief in my strengths was replaced by the feeling of the strength of *Myself*. How strange this was, I perceived myself as having a volitional nature. I understood that I was in the process of having a head-on collision, but with a soft landing. Then I quickly perceived that this was actually from many sides. I yielded to the head-on obstinacy of people of a primitive volition. I jumped to the right

[375] Before chewing gum was invented people would chew tar.
[376] Probably *Latin Grammar* by F. Ellend and M. Zeiffert.

and left, circumvented both flanks, and all at a moment when I seemed to have no will or softness of my own.

I still had no vocation in view, none. I stood at a crossroad, but knew that whichever direction the volitional energy of *this* directed me, it would be according to my will. I had many choices and clearly saw all of them: philosopher, poet, novelist, natural scientist, music composer, circus ringleader, truck driver, actor, costume designer, movie director, or even a fortune teller or sorcerer, wherever my volition would direct me. Finally I made a selection and firmly stated, "I will be a writer."

I wrote verses, ultra-decadent fragments in prose, I had an immense critical diary (but I lost it). But I was not a decadent and not a disciple of Schopenhauer.

I was a cognitive symbolist and in my own manner I redefined Schopenhauer's system as it applied to me. I utilized Schopenhauer's aesthetics in my original manner, refining them in symbolism. My ancient *this* was my volition; *that* was my presentation. The union of *this* and *that* did not turn into a law of motivation, as with Schopenhauer, but a symbolization of rhythm assembling me into a symbolist-individual. An entrance to Hartmann[377] was closed to me. An analysis of the individualism of Nietzsche was in order. But it was already clear that Nietzsche's symbolism – with the help of the superhuman – was not self-evident to a person in my situation and so unacceptable. The superhuman is the one beyond his frontiers,[378] the ascent and discharge of a person into what is not inside him. But with me there was a higher, a third something that was outside a person but in him. The superhuman is plainly the individualistic *I* as the hyper-personality. All of us are hyperpersonal. My immanence united with thoughts of *Self*, *Spirit* and *Christ* was experienced at some time in symbolizations at my Arbat apartment while under the influence of conversations in the Solovyov apartment and during encounters with the philosopher Solovyov. Primarily it was during the attempt of my individual experiences uniting the forms

---

[377] Karl Robert Eduard von Hartmann, 1842-1906, German philosopher.

[378] This is the non-translatable Russian word: трансцензус, transcenzus, meaning the passage or penetration of a person into frontiers beyond the corporeal.

of contemporariness with the Book of Revelation and Dostoyevsky. I lived through the consummation of the world at the Trinity-Arbat Church and then on Voronyukhinaya Hill in Moscow. All of this capably predestined a future mastery of first, Schopenhauer and then second, Nietzsche, pertaining to the words symbol and theurgy. The latter word I would soon encounter and I would utilize the term for the expression of the maximum pressure of symbolism in a personage, expanded in the individuality, meaning, the super-individual, according to Nietzsche. Symbolism in a general sense is the current of volitional pressure in the process of its pressure on the external world. The resulting word theurgy is a symbolic current of high pressure transforming reality, the collective, and the *I*. For the process opposing transformation this transformation looks like the end of the world. The end of the world is the revolutionary step, like an electric jolt on someone sleeping. The second advent into the *I* and through the *I* is the same. In this aspect of positive discovery it is the process of transformation.

Theurgy is the rhythm of transformation in us.

Here is my passage into religion, insufficiently taught by Solovyov and his disciples. My entrance into the entire movement of religion was only through symbolism, catastrophically, bursting. My motto was, "Behold I make all things new." And so by way of this I create a new *I* and a new *We*. We are the collective, the community. It is religious in the sense of that it is saturated with the volitional energy of symbolism, which now for me is the effect of yoga on the *I* and the yoga of rhythm of the entire *I* reborn first through their individual center, the theurgic commune or the point of attachment of the center that steers the world as a boat.

In my presentations I wished for a religious community that would encompass the spiritual-revolutionary arrangement of all traditions, community designs, personalities, arts, mundane individualism, in the creation of a new culture. This newly-created energy of symbolism is a religion not having anything common with the world of traditional religion. Such a religion will be achieved with the effort of my symbolism, as I have designed it and while still an adolescent. What is now required is its germination from the personal-individual phase – symbolism under a specific person – into the individual-social phase.

This phase, as I wish it to be, is my smashing entrance with what is mine into society. It is *I* as a symbolist. If I do not appear as a social reformer, or actually a transformer, I am not a symbolist but an objectivist. The matter is not within the personal capacities of Boris Bugaev, but in the entire state of my individualism.

In the 8th grade these mottos of my symbolism still in full measure were mimicked as forms of alien systems and concepts that I affixed to my world. In 1899, Solovyov pointed me to the direction of my sail along the sea of life. The direction was the Book of Revelation, "Behold I create all things new." The compass and rudder depended on me. The rudder was the ability to deal with the problems of creativity. The arrow of the compass was symbolism, attracted by the magnet of the new world – in the maximum sense – or a new culture – in the minimum sense. Between the maximum and minimum was my subtle modulation in the discoveries and closures that my mottos provided. The little boat built hastily from old material, or the *Argo* sailing after the sun of life, is my worrisome repair of Schopenhauer's philosophy to match my whims. Personally I preached apocalypticism under the banner of catastrophism, but as a moderately minimal tragedy.

So was I during wishing so much while also unsure of myself while in high school. For the meanwhile I was a symbolist in my own way. My sole companion in symbolism, but who did not penetrate the concept of symbolism to its termination, was the young S.M. Solovyov. I was not acquainted with any of the symbolists of the era and I have to admit they did not interest me. They were decadents. But my close encounter and association with Vladimir Solovyov, Nietzsche, Merezhkovsky and Blok, were predestined.

So was I when I showed at the university.

Darwin, mechanics, problems of natural science, formed new vortexes of ideas for me. So where should I turn the rudder of my

*Argo*? How could I reconcile from the one side Solovyov and Nietzsche struggling over their possession of myself. From the other side, the problem of their struggle in my soul with the problem of natural science. The Solovyov disciples could not help me, natural science was foreign to them. Nevertheless, I first orient my route connected with Schopenhauer, my central station of ideological excursions. This line from the one side is voluntarism per Wundt,[379] and then appending the energetics of Ostwald to it within myself.[380] From the other side is the *Philosophy of the Unconscious* of Hartmann, which provided many resolutions to the problems of natural science.

I tracked a new circle of thinkers at the university: Hartmann, Hoffing,[381] Wundt, Ostwald, then Lange.[382] They the means by which my philosophy of natural science was formulated, and fed by subsequent special studies: Hertwig,[383] Quatrefages,[384] Delage,[385] Darwin, Haeckel,[386] and more. At a later date I studied Spencer to some extent.

The theory of knowledge of symbolism is still far from clear, but I live through the entire pathos of seeking it and confirming it. It must be. It is the golden fleece to which my *Argo* aspires.

The Solovyovs do not understand why I am refraining from natural science. My father, who values me particularly due to my channel of thinking in terms of natural science, does not understand what aesthetics are, or Schopenhauer or Solovyov. My friend in my art class, Vladimirov, does not understand my philosophy, he is taking classes in natural science and aesthetics. Who more understands me in my problem of my scissors[387] is A.S.

---

[379] Wilhelm Maximillian Wundt, 1832-1920. German physician and philosopher, a founding father of modern psychology.
[380] Friedrich Wilhelm Ostwald, 1853-1932. German chemist and Nobel Prize winner in Chemistry.
[381] Harald Hoffing, 1843-1931, Danish philosopher and theologian.
[382] Carl Georg Lange, 1834-1900, Danish physician and psychologist.
[383] Oscar Hertwig, 1849-1922, German zoologist who wrote about the theory of evolution.
[384] Jean Louis Arman de Quatrefages, 1810-1892, French biologist and anthropologist.
[385] Yves Delage,1854-1920, French zoologist.
[386] Ernst Heinrich Haeckel, 1834-1919. philosopher, physician, biologist and artist.

Petrovsky, also a friend in my classes. Since 1899, we have had a series of lively conversations on our views of the universe.

It is already clear to me that the route for a new union, for the purpose of a new culture, is something that will take generations, and it is not a codified system. None of those with whom I associate understand this. They each see in me an orientation toward just one of the many channels of which I am aware. For Vladimirov, he is happy with my aesthetics; with the Solovyovs it is religion, for my father it is natural science (he is very proud that Professor Yumov valued my term paper, *About the Tasks and Methods of Physics*). But not one of them is happy for me regarding the fact that I am not satisfied with aesthetics, religion and science, but that I am moving forward dealing with the problem of the entirety of symbolism.

4

I lived through the spiritual world nebulously in imaginations that were provided me by actual reality and in subjective artistic daydreams. The originality of my artistic attempts of this time consists of this. Decadents live out their daydreams, and which are often deformed into stupidity. We the symbolists possess a root of imagination, in the symbols of time which teach us to read one way or another. As far as reading in the manner we choose, as far as knowledge being the source, all of his is the esoterism of certain of my contemporaries and who will accompany me in symbolism. The epoch of encountering people and astonishing intelligence is beginning, our subjectivism is community applied.

We have nationalized our jargon, consisting in mimicking words with a new application. With words do we motion to each other, our facades and personalities change from one individualism to another individualism. Common words are vacant, but nonetheless there are other subjective forms nationalized in an uncommon meaning, as applying to our commune.

---

[387] Bely refers to cutting himself from the tangible and corporeal.

Yet they still did not understand me.

Three spheres of symbolism are denoted for me: the Sphere of Symbols, meaning symbolism as a theory and symbolization as a subject; the Sphere of the Symbol as the underlying reason for the esoterism of symbolism – the teaching of the union of all unifications. And the center of this for me is Christ. And esoteric Symbolism as the discovery of Christ and Sophia in a person in a new manner. The sphere of theory is the sphere of the concrete perception of the universe, possessing the principle of the building of meaningful emblems of comprehension and knowledge; the sphere of symbolization is the sphere possessing the styles of creativity in art. In the subjection of this sphere of symbolism and in the subjection of symbolism the sphere of the Symbol causes the principle of tri-unity – which was lying at the based of the route of symbolism – to become obsolete.

6

And I, seeing the altercation of the symbolists, I hurried as soon as I could to carry into my temporary citadel, what did not already decay. The citadel, or the polemical protection of armor, being the intimate depths of symbolism, was its service to the literary school.

Here are the perspectives of these dictums:

1. Symbolism is dependant on the entirety of historical criticism. It is an outburst of criticism is in best perspective of the future.
2. It is the construction of an ideology of a new culture.
3. Present attempts to precisely draw the contours of this culture are the temporal hypotheses of workers.
4. It is not the future school of art or the tendencies of culture, symbolism and the present epoch – to the extent it absorbs the content of this culture – that more than all becomes concrete in art. And there it is a school.

5. School is conditional. It is proletariat and has social classes, a kernel that transcends future life.
6. Every art symbolically at its supreme and profound recognition is expressed by the artists of its creativity. The school of symbolism causes these individual slogans lost in epochs and schools to become social, and they condense on the podium. The self-realization of creativity is unfolded in symbolism. Prior to symbolism it was blind; with symbolism it is recognized.
7. The task of educational theorists of symbolism is the popularization and recognition of the symbolic nerve of art. It consists of the disclosure of new creative horizons.
8. The guarantee of growth of new forms of verbal graphics is maintained in the growth of these horizons. The compositions of the symbolists have the capacity to belong to this type of school.
9. Symbolism does not supersede any truths that are located in other schools, because it is a school of its own. But it does promote its supersession as a school where other schools violate the fundamental school motto of symbolism: unity of form and content.
10. This unity must not be taken as either a dependence of form due to content (romanticism), or a dependence on content due to form (restorative classicism). The unity is the whole, and the whole is the Symbol-triad.
11. The meaning of symbolism is maintained in the disclosure of the whole as [both the] individuality and a complex, meaning a social base. Such is the transplantation of a school slogan into a project of a new philosophic culture, and here is the connection of the school with philosophic symbolism.
12. The symbol recited is a metaphor.
13. The investigation of philologists, to the extent they unearth the metaphors of language, is the linguistic base of the school of symbolism.
14. The school of symbolism sees the genesis of our language in the teaching of Wilhelm von Humbolt[388] and Potebnja.[389]

15. But the school of symbolism does not just stop at the works of Potebnja, it seeks beyond his contributions.
16. One of such searches discloses to us the wholeness of the rise of the language of metaphors and myths, where the myth is the religious content of the form of language, and this is the realization of the myth in language.
17. The disclosure of the slogans of the school of symbolism on every side regarding their form and content provides new criteria in the analysis of linguistic forms, the theory of words, the theory of styles, the theory of myths, psychology, criticism, and etc.
18. Here the school of symbolism places itself under the banner of the theory of symbolism as a justification of a new cultural creativity whose source is the new person in us.
19. The route of this new culture arises from our sociability.
20. The stabilization of symbolism is the creation of a new life.

Here are the perspectives of my school program and it is very diverse and divided into 65 articles, separated into several dozens of reports, lectures and announcements.[390] My friends did not understand me. I heard bells, a summons to depart from the hollering, dirty and purposeless involvement with others, and especially those who did not understand my altruism. But I did not depart, instead I fought to leave a better memory of symbolism and the symbolists than the one that was left by the history of recent innovative literature. Nonetheless I was eternally consoled by the warm and friendly support that I unexpectedly encountered by M.O. Gershenzon.

---

[388] Friedrich Wilhelm Christian Karl Fredinand von Humboldt, 1767-1835. Prussian philosopher and politician, and linguist who made contributions to language and education. He founded the Humboldt University of Berlin, Germany.
[389] Aleksandr Potebnja, 1835-1891. Ukrainian-Russian philosopher and linguist.
[390] These documents are either long lost or never published and not accessible.

## 9

In April and May 1912, events of my inner life unexpectedly led me to a personal encounter with R.Steiner. This encounter led to me joining Steiner's movement and which explained to me the subsequent stage of my journey. After *Emblematic*,[391] an incomplete piece of some obvious concept attached itself to me and it was rather analytical and which interested me in the questions of dialectics. Dialectics evolves from analysis and which is a statistical scheme and which is necessary in dynamics. And anthroposophy manifested itself to me in this dynamic dialecticism, and it struck at the problem of the culture of the mind in self-realization.

After the crash with Mintzlova the search for guidance in the spheres indicated by Mintzlova terminated, while the obstacles that stood between my approach to Steiner fell. These [obstacles] consisted in the one-sided and prejudiced disbelief in Steiner's Christology. Attending the courses on his application of Christianity and the lectures, *Christ and the Twentieth Century*, removed the misunderstanding I had of Steiner's Christian views and which I acquired due to seeing it through Mintzlova's prism.

The route from symbolism to anthroposophy seemed to me a continuation of the route that I already realized and which I explained in *Emblematic*. Steiner's amazing instructions to me regarding this matter, as the installation of methods of inner development and the continuous possibility of education in the field of this work, naturally led me into the enclave of Steiner's personal disciples. My joining the Anthroposophical Society was nothing less than an external implementation of a long matured inner fact. Even from back in 1907, when I finished reading Besant's tract on higher consciousness,[392] and over the course of the next 5 years, reading and contemplating literature on this topic, this just had to occur in 1912, among a series of people who

---

391 Written in 1909.

392 This could have been any one of Anne Besant's works translated into Russian.

were assembling around Steiner. There were no zigzags that occurred along this route.

10

It is difficult for me to approach the final concrete stage of what it is I did not understand and which evolved into this social severance. The tragedy with the anthroposophical environment, my final refuge, prolonged for 15 years.[393] And it surpassed other tragedies in length and sharpness. It is all clear to me now. The emotions still stir violently the surface of the water of life where my *I* was reflected.

I consider the beginning of my association with the Anthroposophical Society as July 1912, when I arrived in Munich, Germany.

Now I will say this: the conglomeration of this immense experience that was inculcated into me as a result of listening to 400 of Steiner's lectures, esoteric lessons, and meetings with Steiner in the Nicodimus style[394] while sitting in a barrel,[395] the conscious and unconscious spite of myself that I heard emanating from Russia, and the later discredit from the A.S,[396] all of this plus the difficult tragedy of my personal life – was inserted into my *I,* likewise learning from Diogenes.[397] From this barrel and over the barrel I saw my *I* high over myself. As a result I took a lamp and for several years spoke of the human and seeking the higher principle residing in him.[398] The sign of this Principle for a moment flared also over my forehead, in Dornach, when this forehead was crowned with thorns.

---

[393] This would have been from 1907, mentioned above, to 1922, the time of Bely's rupture in his relationship with Steiner.

[394] Referring to John 3:1-2.

[395] The barrel is a reference to Diogenes living in a large ceramic jar in the marketplace.

[396] Anthroposophical Society, referring to how they discredited Bely after his rupture with Steiner and then returning to Russia.

[397] Greek philosopher of the 4th Century BC. He walked about the city carrying a lamp in daytime seeking an honest person.

[398] This is a rough translation of the term Forehead of Eternity: *Челе Века,* based on commentaries.

Steiner's ability to have continual control over my inner faculties started for the most part when he accepted me into the circle of those who attended his esoteric lessons in spring 1913, which was eventually closed. And then he accepted me into a more intimate circle, the second initiation in 1914, in Sweden. This inclusion into the intimate circle and dependence on personal communication with Steiner applied my old style of thinking toward a commune of esotericists in a new style: it was the concept of brotherhood. But I constantly looked around myself when in the presence of the association, consisting of thousands of members. I concluded this was an improper transfer of the Symbolist community into the establishment of the [Anthroposophical] Society, a counterfeit, false and painful representation of some kind of esoteric fraternity, which purpose was to distinguish the Anthroposophical Society from so-called secular societies.

## 11

From 1912 to 1921, I traversed all the stages of first immersing myself deeply into the fiction of this esoteric fraternity, and then into removing myself from it. In 1913, I experience an apparition of the construction of a temple of souls. I saw the cornerstone of John's building (the building of love): a new stone of the soul upon which was inscribed a new name – watch the Book of Revelation. And as a result I was saturated by this premature symbolism, and I showed at Dornach to work on the erection of the temple of souls. For a while I was a lower level supervisor and then a woodcarver and carpenter. After a while I became a master woodcarver. I actually thought I was guarding the foundation stone of a new culture, but in reality, I exchanged John's building for the heavy labor of the Goetheanum. The stone of the soul was carved into a simple stone and this stone I carried on my shoulders until it almost buried me.[399]

The stage of my rebirth from being a [Knight] Templar – as I thought I was – into an ordinary watchman, ended with my rejection of the work. This occurred in Dornach during the heavy winter of 1914-1915. Relative to my elegant entrance into the service of the culture of the Goetheanum was my decline into a mundane duty of a watchman, and to guard over something that was to eventually be destroyed. My attitude toward some of my anthroposophical friends naturally changed. The super-idiot vanished and so did his shadow. The calloused watchman Bugaev was lauded by other watchmen, his working crew and honest adolescents, they were people I would find at the local union hall, no different. So was I isolated at Dornach.

13

Having returned to Russia in September 1916, I sensed the preceding 4 years as being an immense experience and along with it the impossibility to transfer it, not in any aspirations, not in collapses, not in a vigilantly critical view of the mutual association between anthroposophy and anthroposophists in their efforts to combine school, experience, commune and community in some kind of agreeable whole.

All of this I could not explain. Naturally my explanation carried with it a criticism of the community.

Very few devoted themselves to the work within the Moscow group of anthroposophists. I was soon tightly drawn to it with all my soul. It became natal to me. I saw life within this group, and fermentation in their moral vision, and seriousness in their deliberation, and rectitude in its aspiration. There were also some defects in the community life that evolved from the law that people, when dealt with individually, are more interesting and more profound than when considered as a group. The oppositions of the group as a whole consisted in what they opposed: social rhythm, dealing with problems of harmonic collectivism, struggle against prejudices, ignorance of symbolism, and versatility of application.

---

[399] Bely's vision was actually symbolic, meaning, an allegorical temple, while he interpreted it as a material temple.

All of this was obviously known to me and an understandable situation. But nonetheless it felt joyful for me when I was among a group of honest and healthy and unprejudiced – for the most part – people, and which was not just a group of yes-men and not a disconnected gangrenous society of esotericists. Moscow became a living Dornach all natal to me and the place felt like home to me. The other Dornach was filled with corpses, and Moscow was able to eliminate the lifeless corpses of Dornach who migrated here.

The Petersburg group did not leave me with this impression. All that was natal to me in Moscow, did not exist there. Such a group did not exist and there was no genuine connection with the west. Petersburg, having lost this living connection, turned into a cult, just as did Dornach. The fruits of the Petersburg esoteric society caused it to suffer one defeat after another over the years.

My situation in Russia was difficult. I had to somehow find an external social platform from which to work. The political life of Russia reached an extreme pressure and I had to find my political niche here.

## 14

The Leningrad Liberal Philosophical Association became at this time my personal and my individual (that is, my individualistic social) matter. I became interwoven with its activists, with its mottos, with its expansion, and the organization of it diverse audiences, and the tempo of its work. During the propagation of my anthroposophical concepts I encountered obstacles and evil suspicious eyes from the side of other anthroposophists. On the other hand some of those who were not anthroposophists here showed me unforgettable and fervent brotherly support. I will not forget the truly bad and mean attitude toward me of the anthroposophist Voloshin, who lowered himself down to the level of spreading rumors about me having no truth at all. But I will not forget the fraternal attitude toward me of Ivanov-Razumnik, who became as though a natal brother to me.

The LPA[400] in Petersburg, in the years of 1920-1921, deployed a large cultural expansion throughout Russia. The work was driving, productive and diverse. We had 300 public presentations over the course of 3 years. However by 1922, it was being suppressed, and by 1924, it was forced to close.

The innovations of the rhythm of the work attracted me, and it seems, my soul.

16

So what does this symbolize?

Anthroposophy in Russia? Or the new culture of life? Or nothing? Or is it good that in Russia there should be no members and no Society? A little remains to be said. I will note several facts, and especially those during this epoch of my life among friends consuming the years 1923-1925.

Some of my moderate friends displayed an alien attitude and which weighed heavily on me. They looked at Boris Nikolaievich as a kind of machine that spits out words, books, lectures, courses, while silent and vacant in between. But the real Boris Nikolaievich, approaching people, did not seek an auditorium, but a heartfelt, solid and social bond, and he would disregard a response of a no heartbeat to his heartbeat. With any rejection he would mechanically devolve into agitation, moving the air around him, and out of despair. Then he would saturate the emptiness growing around him with his continuously aggravating, "Maybe, Yes, maybe, No." So was his response in providing thoughts, feelings and motivations.

[400] Liberal Philosophical Association

## 21

The time for me to finish writing is past. Now the time has arrived to read into your heart what I have written. There is nothing hidden that will not become open.

Who does not have letters in his heart and rejects understanding the Apostle's words, "You are our letter inscribed on our hearts," will not understand me.[401]

I know this well.

And as a result I have finished. I have concluded myself in this regard, in explaining symbolism.

Kuchino, April 7, 1928

[401] 2 Cor 3:2-3

# RUSSIAN BIBLIOGRAPHY

Белый, Андрей, *Душа Самопознающая*

Белый, Андрей, *Между двух революций*

Белый, Андрей, *На рубеже двух столетий*

Белый, Андрей, *Начало века*

Белый, Андрей, *Сочинения в двух томов*

Белый, Андрей, *Симболизм как Миропонимание*

Глухова, Е.В., *Письма А.Р. Минцловой к Андрею Белому*

Демин, Валерий, *Андрей Белый*

Кривеллер, Клаудия, и Спивак, Моника, *Андрей Белый, Автобиографизм и Биографические Практики*

Лавров, Александр Васильевич, *Андрей Белый, Разыскания и Этюды*

Пискунова, В.М., *Воспоминания об Андрее Белом*

Спивак, Моника, *Смерть Андрея Белого*

Made in the USA
Middletown, DE
26 October 2023

41438472R00272